# A GLOSSED WYCLIFFITE PSALTER: OXFORD, BODLEIAN LIBRARY MS BODLEY 554

EARLY ENGLISH TEXT SOCIETY

O.S. 352

2019 for 2018

Bodleian Library, Oxford MS Bodl. 554, f. 26ᵛ, Psalm 51 (*Quid gloriaris*) and the beginning of Psalm 52 (*Dixit insipiens*), with marginal glosses. By permission of The Bodleian Libraries, University of Oxford

# A GLOSSED WYCLIFFITE PSALTER: OXFORD, BODLEIAN LIBRARY MS BODLEY 554

## VOLUME I

EDITED BY

MICHAEL P. KUCZYNSKI

*Published for*
THE EARLY ENGLISH TEXT SOCIETY
*by the*
OXFORD UNIVERSITY PRESS
2019 for 2018

# OXFORD

UNIVERSITY PRESS

Great Clarendon Street, Oxford, OX2 6DP,
United Kingdom

Oxford University Press is a department of the University of Oxford.
It furthers the University's objective of excellence in research, scholarship,
and education by publishing worldwide. Oxford is a registered trade mark of
Oxford University Press in the UK and in certain other countries

British Library Cataloguing in Publication Data
Data available

ISBN 9780198835202

Typeset by Alan Bennett, Oxford
Printed in Great Britain
on acid-free paper by
TJ International Ltd, Padstow, Cornwall

# PREFACE AND ACKNOWLEDGEMENTS

Oxford, Bodleian Library MS Bodley 554 (B 554) contains an extensive Middle English commentary on the Psalms and Canticles in the later version of the Wycliffite Bible. The commentary, which takes the form of *catenae* or chain-like series of marginal glosses, is unique to this manuscript, although fragments of it survive in several other copies of the Wycliffite Bible. B 554 was assembled in the early fifteenth century by a compiler sympathetic to Wycliffite ideas. It has been described accurately by Mary Dove, in her critical study *The First English Bible* (2007), as preserving the Wycliffite Psalter glosses better than any other manuscript.

This edition brings the B 554 commentary into print for the first time, within a critical and contextual framework. Volume 1 comprises an Introduction, Bibliography, and the edited texts of Psalms 1 through 119 and their glosses on facing pages, with full critical apparatus for each set of texts. Volume 2 will comprise the edited texts of Psalms 120 through Canticles and their glosses with full critical apparatus for each, followed by Latin Sources and Explanatory Notes to the glosses, a comprehensive Glossary, an Appendix of Hebrew Words in B 554, and indexes of Scriptural References and Allusions, Proper Names, and Key Subjects.

Many but not all copies of the Wycliffite Bible contain marginal glosses. Most of these are manuscripts of the later version of the Wycliffite Bible, a more readable, idiomatic reworking of the early Latinate translation. I have traced some of the glosses that comprise the B 554 commentary in twenty-two other manuscripts containing the Wycliffite Bible translation of the Psalms, all but one of these the later version.

The contents of B 554 deserve to be better known, given renewed scholarly interest in the Middle English Psalms, the history of the Wycliffite movement, and the Wycliffite Bible translation project specifically. In their monumental four-volume edition of Wycliffite Bible, Josiah Forshall and Sir Frederic Madden print numerous marginal glosses that survive in several manuscript copies of the Wycliffite Old and New Testaments. B 554, however, with its extensive glossing of the Psalter, while it did not escape their notice entirely, came to them too late for its important and

distinctive glosses to be incorporated in their edition. Had Forshall
and Madden printed B 554's glossarial corpus, it would be clear from
their edition that the Psalms was that book of the Bible most heavily
glossed by the Wycliffites, the nearest competitors being other Old
Testament books—Ecclesiasticus with approximately 415 marginal
glosses, Proverbs with approximately 300, and Job with approximately 210. Acts, the most heavily glossed New Testament book, has
by comparison only about 95 marginal glosses. The present edition,
then, fills a significant and long-standing lacuna in Forshall and
Madden's work and could be used conveniently as a supplement to
their edition. The additional circumstance that B 554, due to its tight
sewing and torn medieval binding, has never been microfilmed or
entirely digitized, means that its place in the history of WB and its
importance to the reception of the Psalms in late medieval England
has been underappreciated by scholars and students alike, most of
whom are unable to travel to Oxford to examine the manuscript.
This edition, it is hoped, will generate a new level of attention to this
invaluable manuscript witness to early fifteenth-century scholarly
and homiletic interest in the Middle English Psalms.

*

Many institutions and individuals have supported my work on the
glossed Wycliffite Psalter in MS Bodley 554. It is my great pleasure
to thank them.

First, I must thank the several libraries in Cambridge, London,
Oxford, and (much less extensively) in Chicago, Dublin, and
Philadelphia, on whose manuscripts my research is based. Foremost
among these is the Bodleian Library, Oxford. The manuscript edited
here, important as it is, has never been microfilmed or digitized due
to concerns about its conservation. Bodley and its staff, first in Duke
Humfrey and now in the Weston Library, have been unfailingly
generous in making Bodley 554 available for my use during long
periods and facilitating my access to a wide range of other manuscripts and early printed books related to this project. Without their
support, my research would not have been possible. The Bodleian
has also been kind enough to grant permission for the reproduction
in this edition of three plates from Bodley 554. I am grateful for that
courtesy as well.

All the librarians of my home institution, Tulane University, have
provided over a long period a wide range of assistance. I should like

to single out for thanks, in our Interlibrary Loan Department, Annie Kemp and Cortney Cheri Labadie for their efficient and tireless help. In Special Collections, Kathleen McCallister (now of the College of William and Mary) and Jane Pinzino have likewise been helpful. David Banush, our Dean of Libraries and Academic Information Resources, has also provided ad hoc support.

Because I had to deal with Bodley 554 largely on site, I wish to acknowledge the generous support of the American Council of Learned Societies, the American Philosophical Society, the Bibliographical Society of America, and the Committee on Research of Tulane University, for grants in aid of international travel. A grant from the Georges Lurcy Charitable and Educational Trust, given through the School of Liberal Arts at Tulane, allowed me to purchase microfilms and digital photographs of several manuscripts involved in my work. Finally, the Newberry Library awarded me, in 2007, the Lester J. Cappon Fellowship in Documentary Editing. The fellowship supported a month's work on several early printed editions of Nicholas of Lyra's commentary on the Psalms. For this manifold financial support, I am most grateful.

My chief professional debt is to Professor Anne Hudson, who has been the tutelary spirit of this edition. Her career-long, innovative work on Wycliffite manuscripts and texts first attracted my interest to the importance of the Middle English glosses that survive in the margins of some copies of the Wycliffite Bible. Anne's encouragement of my research and detailed review of my typescript are a model of scholarly generosity. They have improved this edition at every stage. For all her help, I am deeply grateful.

While my research is not part of a new electronic edition now under way of the entire Wycliffite Bible, it is adjunct to that work. I am indebted to the head of the project, Dr Elizabeth Solopova, for her interest in my research on Bodley 554. At a key moment midway through that research, Elizabeth asked me to write a comprehensive essay on glosses and glossing in Wycliffite Bible manuscripts for a collection on new approaches to the Wycliffite Bible that appeared in 2017 and is cited frequently in this edition. Writing that essay enhanced my investigations of Bodley 554. I am grateful for Elizabeth's invitation and indeed for her enthusiasm about the Wycliffite Bible generally. Since Forshall and Madden's monumental nineteenth-century edition, the Wycliffite Bible has fallen into unfair scholarly neglect, both as a major document in English church history and as a superb example of the art of Middle English translation. Elizabeth's ground-breaking work is changing all that.

Dr Helen Spencer, the Editorial Secretary of the Early English Text Society, has shown in her dealings with me persistence and forbearance, a difficult balancing act. She has my sincere gratitude. So many individuals have discussed Bodley 554 and this edition with me that I am likely to produce a list with some lacunae. I should like nevertheless to thank by name Richard Beadle, Mishtooni Bose, Margaret Connolly, the late Mary Dove, Tony Edwards, Paul Gehl, Kantik Ghosh, Vincent Gillespie, the late George Kane, Andy Kelly, Francis Leneghan, the late Malcolm Parkes, Niamh Pattwell, Derek Pearsall, Eyal Poleg, Paul Saenger, Daniel Sawyer, Fiona Somerset, Annie Sutherland, Christina Von Nolcken, Dan Wakelin, and Nicholas Watson. When I required sudden help with a manuscript in the collection of Trinity College, Dublin and could not get there myself, I had only to say the word, and V. J. Scattergood produced in short order comprehensive transcriptions for my use. I am especially grateful to John for that collegial effort. I have also received particular help with checking manuscripts from Mary Wellesley at the British Library and James Freeman at the Cambridge University Library. Kind thanks to them both.

Several individuals have given help both professional and personal in nature. Without it, I could not have completed this project. For words spoken, deeds done, I am indebted to Michael Bernstein, Peter Cooley, Edwin and Marlys Craun, Martha Driver, Tom Frazel, Ralph Hanna, Dennis Kehoe, Jim Kilroy, Joseph Lombardi, SJ, James H. O'Neill, Barb Ryan, Jerry Singerman, and Bob Yeager. Eric Stanley's passing shortly before this edition reached EETS was a particular blow. I met him in 1980 and we had been friends ever since. One of our last conversations was about King Alfred and the Psalms. *Eadig byð se mer þe his tohopa byð to smylcum Drihtne!*

Professor Kehoe kindly answered all my questions about the Greek that appears in the explanatory notes. My erstwhile neighbor, Rabbi Yochanan Rivkin, and Dr Poleg did the same for my questions about the Hebrew. Peter Albers helped with some last-minute technical difficulties. Bonnie Blackburn has been the most attentive of copy-editors. Her insights have improved in several ways the clarity of presentation in both these volumes and have saved me from numerous errors. Alan Bennett has typeset with great art and precision a uniquely challenging text. Of course, any errors that remain in these pages are my own.

My most profound debt is to my family—my wife, Christina, and my children, Sarah and Henry. Their love and support have made not only this edition but all things possible.

M.P.K.

Tulane University

# CONTENTS

VOLUME I

# LIST OF ILLUSTRATIONS

# MANUSCRIPT SIGLA

| | |
|---|---|
| A | London, British Library MS Royal 1.C.viii |
| B 554 | Oxford, Bodleian Library MS Bodl. 554 |
| b | London, British Library MS Harley 2249 |
| C | London, British Library MS Cotton Claudius E.ii |
| C_J_E.14 | Cambridge, St John's College MS E.14 |
| D_70 | Dublin, Trinity College MS 70 |
| G | Oxford, Lincoln College MS Lat. 119 |
| I | Oxford, Bodleian Library MS Bodl. 277 |
| i | London, British Library MS Addit. 10046 |
| K | Oxford, Bodleian Library MS Fairfax 2 |
| k | London, British Library MS Addit. 10047 |
| k2 | London, British Library MS Addit. 31044 |
| L | Oxford, Bodleian Library MS Bodl. 296 |
| L2 | Oxford, Bodleian Library MS Laud misc. 182 |
| M | Oxford, Queen's College MS 388 |
| O | Oxford, New College MS 66 |
| P | Cambridge, Emmanuel College MS 21 |
| Q | Cambridge, Cambridge University Library Mm.2.15 |
| R | Cambridge, Cambridge University Library Dd.1.27 |
| S | Cambridge, Corpus Christi College, Parker MS 147 |
| U | London, Lambeth Palace Library MS 25 |
| V | London, Lambeth Palace Library MS 1033 |
| X | Oxford, Christ Church MS 145 |

# ABBREVIATIONS

| | |
|---|---|
| Addit. | Additional (in manuscript shelfmark references) |
| AU | Augustine, *Enarrationes in Psalmos*, PL 36 and 37 (1861) |
| AV | Authorized Version of the Bible |
| BLR | *Bodleian Library Record* |
| Breviarium | Pseudo-Jerome, *Breviarium in Psalmos*, PL 26, cols. 821–1328 (1845) |
| canc. | cancelled |
| Cassiodorus | Cassiodorus, *Expositio Psalmorum*, PL 70 (1865) |
| CMS | Central Midland Standard |
| Dove | M. Dove, *The First English Bible: The Text and Contexts of the Wycliffite Versions* (Cambridge, 2007) |
| DR | *The Holy Bible, Translated from the Latin Vulgate* (Baltimore, 1914) |
| EAEB | *The Earliest Advocates of the English Bible: The Texts of the Medieval Debate*, ed. M. Dove (Exeter, 2010) |
| EETS | Early English Text Society |
| EPP | *The Earliest Complete English Prose Psalter*, ed. K. D. Bülbring, EETS os 97 (1891; repr. 1987) |
| EV | Early Version of the Wycliffite Bible |
| EWS | *English Wycliffite Sermons*, ed. P. Gradon and A. Hudson, 5 vols. (Oxford, 1983–96) |
| FM | *The Holy Bible . . . Made from the Latin Vulgate by John Wycliffe and his Followers*, ed. J. Forshall and F. Madden, 4 vols. (Oxford, 1850) |
| Forshall | *Remonstrance against Romish Corruptions in the Church*, ed. J. Forshall (London, 1851) |
| Gall. | Gallicanum, Jerome's second translation of the Psalms, from the Greek Septuagint and the basis for the Vulgate text |

| | |
|---|---|
| *GG* | *Glossed Gospels* (see Hudson, *Doctors in English*) |
| GO | Glossa Ordinaria, cited after *Bibliorum Sacrorum cum Glossa Ordinaria*, 6 vols. (Venice, 1603) |
| Gratian | *Decretum Gratiani*, PL 187 (1865) |
| Gruber | *Rashi's Commentary on the Psalms*, ed. and trans. Mayer I. Gruber (Philadelphia, 2007) |
| Hebr. | Hebraicum, Jerome's third translation of the Psalms, corrected against the Hebrew text; identified in the B 554 glosses as 'Ieroms translacioun' |
| Hebrew | Hebrew text of the Psalms; identified in the B 554 glosses as 'Ebreu' |
| Isidore | The *Etymologies* of Isidore of Seville, trans. Stephen A. Barney, W. J. Lewis, J. A. Beach, and Oliver Berghof (Cambridge, 2006) |
| *JBL* | *Journal of Biblical Literature* |
| *JEGP* | *Journal of English and Germanic Philology* |
| *LALME* | A. McIntosh, M. L. Samuels, and M. Benskin, *Linguistic Atlas of Late Medieval English*, rev. M. Benskin and M. Lang (Aberdeen, 1986), http://www.lel.ed.ac.uk/ihd/elalme/elalme.html |
| *LL* | *The Lanterne of Liȝt, Edited from MS. Harley 2324*, ed. L. M. Swinburn, EETS os 151 (1917) |
| Lombard | Peter Lombard, *Commentarium in Psalmos*, PL 191 (1854), cols. 55–1296 |
| LV | Later Version of the Wycliffite Bible |
| LXX | *Septuaginta*, ed. A. Rahlfs and R. Hanhart (Stuttgart, 2007) |
| LY | Nicholas of Lyra, *Postilla super librum Psalmorum*, as printed in *Bibliorum Sacrorum cum Glossa Ordinaria*, 6 vols. (Venice, 1603) |
| *MA* | *Medium Aevum* |
| ME | Middle English |
| *MED* | *Middle English Dictionary*, ed. H. Kurath, S. M. Kuhn et al. (Ann Arbor, 1952–99) |

| | |
|---|---|
| *Nominibus* | Jerome, *Liber de Nominibus Hebraicis*, PL 23: 815–904 (1845) |
| NT | New Testament |
| *ODCC* | *The Oxford Dictionary of the Christian Church*, ed. F. L. Cross, 3rd edn. rev., ed. E. A. Livingstone (Oxford, 2005) |
| om. | omitted |
| ONT | Old and New Testaments |
| os | original series |
| OT | Old Testament |
| PG | Patrologia Graeca |
| PL | Patrologia Latina |
| *PR* | A. Hudson, *The Premature Reformation: Wycliffite Texts and Lollard History* (Oxford, 1988) |
| Ps(s). | Psalm(s) |
| Rolle Lat. | *D. Richardi Pampolitani . . . in Psalterium Dauidicum* (Cologne, 1536) |
| *Rosarium* | *The Middle English Translation of the Rosarium Theologie: A selection, ed. from Cbr., Gonville and Caius Coll. MS 354/581*, ed. Christina von Nolcken (Heidelberg, 1979) |
| *Rosarium* MS | Cambridge, Gonville and Caius College MS 354/581 |
| *SC* | *A Summary Catalogue of Western Manuscripts in the Bodleian Library at Oxford* (Oxford, 1895–1953) |
| SJO 171 | Wyclif, *Postilla super totam Bibliam*, Oxford, St John's College MS 171 |
| *STh* | Thomas Aquinas, *Summa Theologica*, 2nd rev. edn., trans. Fathers of the English Dominican Province, 5 vols. (repr. Westminster, 1981) |
| TCO 93 | Middle English summary of the Bible, Oxford, Trinity College MS 93 |
| Vulg. | *Biblia Sacra Vulgata*, 5th edn., ed. R. Weber, rev. R. Gryson (Stuttgart, 2007) |
| WB | Wycliffite Bible |

# INTRODUCTION

## I. THE GLOSSES

The Psalms and their related biblical Canticles—collectively the Psalter—were central to medieval life. They were the most important liturgical text of the Middle Ages and were also regarded, by scholars and lay people alike, as a digest of the wisdom of all Scripture. As a result, these ancient poems were performed regularly by medieval clerics, invoked by preachers, and commented upon by academics. Oxford, Bodleian Library MS Bodl. 554 (B 554) witnesses to all three of these cultural uses of the medieval Psalter. Pre-eminently, B 554 indicates, by way of the ample glosses that fill its margins, the necessary interrelationship between the Psalter and learned expositions of its texts during the Middle Ages. In particular, the contents and layout of the manuscript reflect the special significance of the Psalter to the Wycliffites, fifteenth-century church reformers who were inspired by the teachings of the Oxford theologian John Wyclif (d. 1384).

The person or persons who planned B 554 extracted and translated, or had someone else extract and translate for them, the glosses that fill its margins from respected Latin sources: primarily from the continuous literal gloss on the Psalms in the *Postilla super totam Bibliam* of Nicholas of Lyra, OFM (1270–1349), arguably the most comprehensive and authoritative commentary on Scripture of the high Middle Ages (hereafter LY); and secondarily from the massive *Enarrationes in Psalmos* of Augustine (354–430), one of that foundational author's most popular works (hereafter AU). B 554 also contains a handful of glosses from the twelfth-century Glossa Ordinaria (hereafter GO), usually cited in B 554 simply as 'the common gloss' but in a few cases more particularly by naming Cassiodorus, whose *Expositio Psalmorum* the B 554 compiler seems to have accessed by way of GO. The compiler occasionally coordinates GO material in the margins of B 554 with the material he draws from LY.

I describe the glosses, which number 1,363 in this edition, collectively as a commentary because they are not only individuated in B 554 but also in many cases interrelated.[1] Sometimes brief and at

---

[1] On this number, see Editorial Method.

other times expansive, the glosses are always linked by red *signes-de-renvoi* or tie-marks to the titles, words, and phrases of the psalms and canticles that the glosses explain (see the Frontispiece). They also, however, fall into self-defining groups across the length of the book, according to certain preferred topics and themes that may have guided their collection before the manuscript was copied.[2] The title glosses, which represent the bulk of glossarial material shared with other LV manuscripts, introduce nearly all the psalms in B 554. These consistently emphasize historical, christological, and moral interpretations of the Psalter as well as the relationships medieval commentators such as Lyra and Augustine perceived between these levels of exegetical meaning. With only a few exceptions, the compiler assembles this subgroup of title glosses from LY, where expositions are normally based on the Hebrew texts of the psalm titles themselves.[3] Both the LY and AU glosses in B 554 concentrate on individual words, phrases, and entire verses and groups of verses in the psalms under discussion and often touch on ideas and concerns that are characteristic of later Wycliffism. Some of these glosses can have a cumulative, mildly polemical impact across the length of the book.[4] The compiler's primary purpose, however, is to establish, particularly by way of his LY glosses, a text of the Psalms that accords better than the Vulgate and WB LV do with the original Hebrew version, on which Lyra was for the high Middle Ages the undisputed exegetical authority.

Other self-defining groups of glosses distributed across B 554 reflect persistent interest in the identity of the church as an assembly of believers and mystical communion as well as its status as an institution defined by its clerical hierarchy (deacons, priests, and bishops); the conflict between true and false teachers and doctrine; the essential role of preaching and of virtuous preachers to the

[2] See Index of Key Subjects.

[3] There was a tradition of explicitly Christian titles to the Psalms in the Middle Ages. These were more aggressively allegorical and survive in six series. For editions and commentary, see *Les 'tituli Psalmorum' des manuscrits latins*, ed. P. Salmon, Collectanea Biblica Latina, 12 (Rome, 1959). Even when they are glossed christologically, the titles in B 554 nearly always restore the Hebrew originals and Jerome's versions of them.

[4] This concatenating impulse was a feature of Wycliffite exegetical practice adapted from such Scholastic practitioners as Peter Lombard (1100–60) and Thomas Aquinas (1225–74). See A. Hudson, *Doctors in English: A Study of the Wycliffite Gospel Commentaries* (Liverpool, 2015), pp. liii–xcv and, on the Psalms specifically, M. P. Kuczynski, 'An Unpublished Lollard Psalms *Catena* in Huntington Library MS 501', *Journal of the Early Book Society*, 13 (2010), 95–138.

church's evangelical effort to spread divine truth; the priority of
mental over verbal prayer; disapproval of overly elaborate song
during church services; and the need for both faith and perseverance
in the face of life's everyday tribulations, especially the sufferings
brought on by the persecutions of Antichrist and his followers. The
B 554 glosses, in short, are not simply sporadic local attempts to
make sense out of difficult passages in the Psalms, although they
often have and achieve that aim. They are also a more-or-less
cohesive effort to comment, across the length of the Middle
English prose psalter in WB LV, on both the textual accuracy of
its translation and that translation's immediate relevance to the
individual and social concerns of Christians in early fifteenth-
century England. An entirely orthodox clerical or lay reader could
profit devotionally and morally from the materials assembled in B
554 without fear of heresy. At the same time, it seems necessary to
observe that, even if B 554's materials were not assembled and copied
out in the manuscript at hand by someone with a specifically
Wycliffite agenda, they could be appreciated, taken up, and used
from that ideological perspective.

II. DESCRIPTION OF THE BASE MANUSCRIPT

**B 554: Oxford, Bodleian Library MS Bodl. 554**          s. xv[I]

SC 2326; FM no description; Solopova, *Manuscripts of the Wycliffite
Bible*, no. 6.[5] Written in England.

B 554 is an unprepossessing quarto of ninety parchment leaves,
thin and relatively low-grade, some of these damaged in ruling
through with a sharp point and by staining and rubbing. They are
approximately 235 × 165 mm in size, trimmed slightly in rebinding
with an occasional loss of text. The manuscript is ruled in ink for a
single column, averaging 31 lines of biblical text per side, with single
vertical and horizontal bounding lines, the written space measuring
approximately 115 × 93 mm and containing the WB LV Psalms and

[5] See also the recent description of the manuscript in R. Hanna, *The English Manuscripts
of Richard Rolle: A Descriptive Catalogue* (Exeter, 2010), 139–40. I use throughout the
manuscript sigla introduced by Forshall and Madden and supplemented since by C.
Lindberg, 'The Manuscripts and Versions of the Wycliffite Bible—A Preliminary Survey',
*Studia Neophilologica*, 42 (1970), 333–47 and Dove, 281–306.

Canticles copied out as prose. The book's margins are not ruled, although a further set of bounding lines also defines that space, which contains the glosses. The number of lines of glossarial text per side in the margins is highly variable.

Quire signatures are in the hand of the text scribe, *a* through *l*, sometimes trimmed, in the lower right-hand corners of leaves, a second set appearing in some lower margins (e.g. f. 43$^r$, *fiij*) in another medieval hand. A third set is in the upper right-hand corners of quire *f* only (e.g. f. 48$^v$), made crudely with a stylus or crayon, perhaps by the parchment-maker. Foliation is in modern ink, ff. i + 1–89.

COLLATION: F. i is a largely blank parchment flyleaf with bits of writing now illegible; ff. 1–88 are in gatherings, 1–11$^8$; f. 89 is another flyleaf. The front flyleaf is the last leaf of a gathering of four: the stub of the first leaf is glued to the top board of the book, its second leaf is glued over this as the book's upper pastedown, and its third leaf is cut out. The back flyleaf, f. 89, is the first leaf of a single folded sheet, the second of which is B 554's lower pastedown. Catchwords and catchphrases by the text scribe contain punctuation but are undecorated.

BINDING: This is late fifteenth-century, bevelled wooden boards covered with red leather, and is heavily worn. The spine is torn badly, exposing the book's sewing on five cords. A chain-staple mark survives on the lower edge of the upper board.

CONTENTS: 1. Ff. 1$^r$–87$^v$: the Psalms and Canticles in WB LV in the ruled space at the centre of each page, with the glosses arranged around and linked to the biblical text by tie-marks in the margins. The Psalms and Canticles text begins: '*Beatus uir* (Latin cue in the margin). Blessid is þe man þat ȝede not in þe councel of wickid men . . .'; and ends: 'Liȝt to þe schewyng of heþene men; and glorie of þi puple Israel'. '[*T*]*e Deum laudamus* . . .', the text of this canticle never copied. Ff. 1$^r$–85$^r$: the marginal glosses begin: 'þat is, in þe false doctryn of vnfeiþful men. *Lire here*. . . .'; and end in Canticle 6, *Audite celi que loquar* [Deut. 32: 22]: 'þat is, peyne'.

2. F. 81$^{r-v}$: the Prayer of Manasseh: *Here bigynneþ þe preier of Manasses kyng of Iuda* [2 Chron. 37]. The prayer is apocryphal. It often appears, however, in copies of the Wycliffite Bible at the end of 2 Chronicles. The practice of including it among the biblical canticles derives from its appearance there in some early Greek Bibles.[6] The Wycliffites had a special interest in the prayer because

6 See *ODCC*, 'Manasses, Prayer of'.

of King Manasseh's notoriety as an idolater (see 4 Kgs. 21: 1–18) who repented.[7]

3. Ff. 81ᵛ–86ʳ: Weekly canticles: i. *Confitebor tibi Domino quoniam ira* (Isa. 12); ii. *Ego dixi* (Isa. 38: 10–21); iii. *Exultauit cor meum in Domino* (1 Kgs. 2: 1–11); iv. *Cantemus Domino* (Exod. 15: 1–20); v. *Domine audiui* (Hab. 3); vi. *Audite celi que loquar* (Deut. 32: 1–44).

4. Ff. 86ʳ–87ᵛ: Daily canticles: i. *Benedicite omnia opera Domini Domino* (Dan. 57–88); ii. *Benedictus Dominus Deus Israel* (Luke 1: 68–79); iii. *Magnificat anima mea* (Luke 1: 46–55); iv. *Nunc dimittis* (Luke 2: 29–32); v. The rubric to [*T*]*e deum laudamus*, the text of this canticle not copied.

5. F. 88ʳ: An extract from the writings of the medieval French liturgist John Beleth (d. 1185), on the major and minor litanies: F. 88ʳ begins: 'Due sunt letanie, maior et minor, maior fit in festo beati Marci . . .'; ends: 'et ibi habuit ciuitas pro ut nos de sanctis noui testamenti'. This text is written in a late fifteenth-century Secretary hand.[8]

6. Ff. 88ᵛ–89ʳ: A list of the sins of thought, word, deed, and omission adapted from Richard Rolle's *Form of Living* (*c*.1349): Ff. 88ᵛ–89ʳ begins: 'Here biþ þe synnes of þouȝt: Ivel þouȝt, wickyt will, wel suposing . . .; ends: 'þeis and mony oþere þat men may fynd hymsilf defoules þe soule.' The Rolle text is also in a late fifteenth-century Secretary hand contemporary with but probably not the same as that of the Beleth extract.[9]

7. Lower pastedown: A medical recipe 'To provoke vryne', written in a sixteenth-century hand.

HANDWRITING AND SCRIBAL PRACTICE: A single scribe has written the Psalms and Canticles throughout B 554, in a uniform and handsome English Textura that bears some resemblance to the textura scripts in other WB manuscripts, such as the hand of ff. 1ʳ–64ʳ of Cambridge University Library MS Ll.1.13, a lectionary and New Testament in LV. One of the distinguishing features of the scribe's alphabet is an otiose hairline loop added sometimes as he

---

[7] See *EAEB* 48/1628 ff. for the use of Manasseh as an exemplar against idolatry in WB GP. On its apocryphal status, signalled in WB, see the gloss at FM ii. 475 in EV: 'This preyere of Manasses is not in Ebrue'; and in LV: 'This is the preyere of Manasses, but it is not in Ebreu, nether it is of the text. *Lire here.*'

[8] Published in E. Solopova, 'A Previously Unidentified Extract about the Litany in a Wycliffite Psalter (Oxford, Bodleian Library, MS. Bodl. 554)', *BLR* 24 (2011), 217–23.

[9] Published in M. P. Kuczynski, 'A Fragment of Richard Rolle's *Form of Living* in MS Bodley 554', *BLR* 15 (1994), 20–32.

xxiiII. DESCRIPTION OF THE BASE MANUSCRIPT

finishes the last stroke of *w*. Throughout the text of Psalms and
Canticles, the scribe regularly underlines lightly, and in a few places
more heavily in black or in red, words that do not occur in the Latin
biblical text or that are necessary in the English version to render the
text grammatical: for example, 'Not so wickid men, not so; but þei
ben as dust' (Ps. 4: 1). Also, some of these underlined words are
intertextual glosses that offer roughly synonymous alternatives for
words that they follow: for instance: 'And I shal þenke in alle þi
werkis; and I shal be excercisid, eþer occupied, in þi fyndingis' (Ps.
76: 13).[10] Underlining this kind of material became standard practice
in the production of copies of WB LV.

The B 554 text scribe also copied the book's rubrics—psalm cues,
titles, and the authorial attributions that conclude most glosses—and
probably, although this is impossible to determine with certainty, the
tie-marks that link the glosses to their lemmata in the biblical text,
the red underlining of lemmata throughout the marginal glosses, and
a small amount of underlining and cancellation done in red throughout the Psalms text and glosses. To prepare for the later insertion of
tie-marks, the scribe, or someone else working through the Psalms
and Canticles systematically after he copied them, pointed the
biblical text deliberately and almost always accurately, placing a
black dot above words and phrases to be glossed. These remain
visible in some cases beneath the red ink of the tie-marks.[11] The tie-
marks themselves resemble some of the distinctive indexing symbols
designed by Robert Grosseteste, a valued authority for the Wycliffites. The resemblance is probably coincidental, however, since in B
554 they serve merely a linking rather than an indexing function: that
is, their various forms do not seem to have been used by the glossator
to indicate interrelationships in terms of topic and theme in certain
groups of glosses to the reader.[12] One recent scholar has also
compared these marks in their shape and function to keys, designed

[10] On intertextual as compared with marginal glossing, see M. P. Kuczynski, 'Glossing
and Glosses', in E. Solopova (ed.), *The Wycliffite Bible: Origin, History, and Interpretation*
(Leiden, 2017), 346–67 at 348–9.

[11] The same type of pointing occurs in the margins of MS Bodley 143, a copy of *GG*
(short Luke), to signal placement of authorial attributions.

[12] See R. W. Hunt, 'Manuscripts Containing the Indexing Symbols of Robert
Grosseteste', *BLR* 4 (1953), 241–54 and S. Harrison Thomson, 'Grosseteste's Concordantial Signs', *Medievalia et Humanistica*, 9 (1955), 39–53. One frequent tie-mark in B 554,
the dumb-bell shape bisected by a single cross-stroke, identifies passages in some
Grosseteste manuscripts on the themes 'De discordia' and 'De auribus', suggesting how
accidental is the relationship between tie-mark shape and lemma in B 554.

to open the sense of the text of the Psalms by way of the exegetical matter in B 554.[13] While the graphic similarity is accidental, it does suggest the importance of efficient use of the glosses to the B 554 compiler and whoever helped him to realize the format of his volume: without guided access to the book's marginal material, the meaning of the Psalms and Canticles in B 554—their complex and interrelated philological, historical, christological, and moral senses— would have remained for most readers more or less obscure.[14]

The most basic form of these tie-marks, a small circle with a pen-stroke to the right, actually pre-dates Grosseteste, appearing for example throughout Chicago, Newberry Library MS 13, a copy of the first third of Augustine's *Enarrationes in Psalmos* that was written in England at Ford Abbey in 1150, as a device that links additional text to the main commentary columns.[15] This symbol, once one is in the habit of looking for it, can be found in many twelfth- through fifteenth-century Latin manuscripts, most of these of a biblical, exegetical, or homiletic complexion. Its use and possible further development in B 554 points to a context of Latin learning that informed the conception and use of this vernacular psalter, presumably the same context that gave rise to the Wycliffite Bible project itself. A variety of tie-marks in B 554 is developed from this simplest form: for example, with the right-hand stroke bisected by one or two hairlines (see the Frontispiece) or finished with a hook-like down-stroke or another circle, this dumbbell-shape often bisected by one or two hairlines. This 'set of subtly differentiated symbols', as Dan Wakelin has aptly described it, is the anonymous glossator's way of managing for his reader margins that are sometimes dense with annotation. The system enables orderly access to the sacred page in B 554.[16]

Furthermore, as Pl. 1 and the diagram in Fig. 1 of f. 69[r] suggest, the tie-marks facilitate continuous reading—mental interlineation really—of text and marginal gloss in B 554, even on pages crowded with tightly written marginal notation. Continuous reading of Ps. 118: 137–53 and its commentary in the example

---

[13] In the labelling for B 554 at the exhibit 'Designing English: Early Literature on the Page', ST Lee Gallery, Weston Library, Bodleian Library, Oxford, 1 Dec. 2017–22 Apr. 2018.

[14] See D. Wakelin, *Designing English: Early English Literature on the Page* (Oxford, 2018), 90–2.

[15] P. Saenger, *A Catalogue of the Pre-1500 Western Manuscript Books at the Newberry Library* (Chicago, 1989), 28, no. 13 (344984).

[16] Wakelin, *Designing English*, 90.

shown here requires that the reader begin his ocular journey in the upper right-hand margin of the page, with gloss (1) in the diagram (glosses 1094 and 1095 in this edition); that his eye then migrate across the text-block to the left-hand margin and gloss (2); then back across the block to the right-hand margin again and glosses (3) and (4); again to the left for gloss (5) and after that down to the roomier bottom margin for the long comment, gloss (6), on 'I criede'; back up to the right-hand margin once more for glosses (7) and (8); across again to the left-hand margin and gloss (9); and finally back to the right-hand margin to read the final annotations on this page, glosses (10) and (11)—all the while maintaining the correct links between each gloss and its lemma. The variety of the tie-marks directs this kind of eye movement. On pages in B 554 especially congested with glosses—and some are even more crowded than the example explored here—no tie-mark shape ever repeats itself in the sequence. The scribe does not assign particular shapes to particular types of glosses: for example, AU as opposed to LY or spiritual as opposed to literal ones. The variety of shapes itself is the chief feature of the scribe's organizational use of this essential linking device in the manuscript.

The tie-marks are necessary because of the manuscript's complex design. Why did the compiler not follow a simpler method in laying out his glosses, so that they would appear in regular sequence with the verses down one or the other margin, with longer title glosses regularly rather than irregularly (although consistently) in the roomier bottom margins of the leaf? The simplest explanation is that the relationship between text and gloss was not worked out before the glosses were assembled and copied but on an ad hoc basis, after the copying of the biblical text itself. The compiler may have originally envisaged a book in which only certain psalms would receive glosses. He might have decided, however, during the process of culling materials from the Latin commentators, that he wished to attend to all the psalms, at least in some degree. None of the 150 psalms appears without glosses in B 554.

The complex *mise en page* of B 554 could also have resulted simply from the wide disparity of the numbers of glosses attached to particular psalms in the manuscript. Both because individual psalms vary in length and because the interpretative problems posed by certain psalms are more complex than those posed by others, the scribe would have been faced with difficulties of marginal arrangement that changed from leaf to leaf or even side to side. Had the links between text and gloss been worked out carefully before either was copied, the kind of complexities of text–gloss reading I describe in Fig. 1 might have been avoided. This type of planning, which was habitual if not invariable in the copying of manuscripts of the Wycliffite *Glossed Gospels* (see my discussion below) does not seem to have occurred in the case of B 554. Certainly folio rather than quarto format would have permitted a regular verse-by-verse arrangement of glosses. From the start, however, B 554 was envisaged as a portable book. It is quite possible that the person who used B 554 would know in advance of accessing the marginal glosses which verse or verses of the Psalter he was going to explicate, and to what end.

Symbols similar to B 554's tie-marks, made more cursorily and not rubricated, appear as a mechanism for linking text and gloss in another Wycliffite psalter that shares Augustinian commentary with B 554, Trinity College, Dublin MS 70 (Pl. 3). They also appear with the same linking function in the margins of New College MS 67, a heavily glossed WB NT in an idiosyncratic version of EV, the revised text of which may have been influenced by LV. They can be found in other more deluxe folio copies of WB as well, such as London, British Library MS Cotton Claudius E.ii, an LV ONT, which also contains glosses on the Psalms. Among the surviving copies of WB, however, New College MS 67 is the closest codicological analogue to B 554—a small-format, portable volume written on low-grade parchment with extensive marginal glossing keyed systematically to the main biblical text, on some leaves nearly filling the marginal space.[17]

The glosses in B 554 are written in a readable if occasionally crabbed Anglicana script, also probably by the text scribe: the graphs of two-compartment *a*, *k*, *þ*, and *w*, for example, recall those more formally treated letterforms in the biblical text. The use of Anglicana for the glosses establishes in this vernacular psalter a hierarchy of scripts that was traditional in medieval glossed Latin Bibles: the use of a more formal hand for the copying of the sacred text, God's

---

[17] See E. Solopova, *Manuscripts of the Wycliffite Bible in the Bodleian and Oxford College Libraries* (Liverpool, 2016), 21–2, Plate 16, and no. 57. A similar type of symbol appears in Philadelphia, University of Pennsylvania, Van Pelt Library MS 77, a copy of Seneca's tragedies with commentary attributed to Nicholas Trevet, made in England *c*.1360–70 (see e.g. f. 23$^{r-v}$), where it is used in the margins to link corrections, omitted passages, and explanatory glosses to the text.

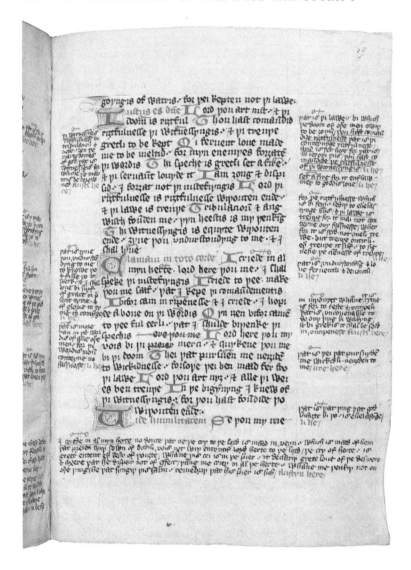

PL. 1. Bodleian Library, Oxford MS Bodl. 554, f. 69<sup>r</sup>, Psalm 118: 137–53 (*Iustus es Domine*, etc.). By permission of The Bodleian Libraries, University of Oxford

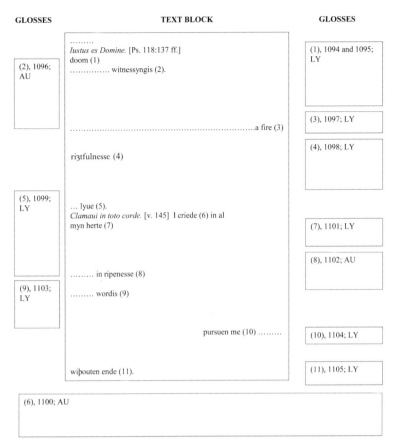

GLOSSES                    TEXT BLOCK                    GLOSSES

(2), 1096;
AU

*Iustus es Domine.* [Ps. 118:137 ff.]
doom (1)
............... witnessyngis (2).

(1), 1094 and 1095;
LY

.............................................................................a fire (3)

(3), 1097; LY

ri3tfulnesse (4)

(4), 1098; LY

(5), 1099;
LY

... lyue (5).
*Clamaui in toto corde.* [v. 145] I criede (6) in al
myn herte (7)

(7), 1101; LY

(8), 1102; AU

......... in ripenesse (8)

(9), 1103;
LY

......... wordis (9)

pursuen me (10) .........

(10), 1104; LY

wiþouten ende (11).

(11), 1105; LY

(6), 1100; AU

LONGER GLOSS

FIG. 1. Diagram of Bodleian Library, Oxford MS Bodl. 554, f. 69ʳ,
Psalm 118: 137–53 (*Iustus es Domine*, etc.)

word, and of a less formal script (sometimes a variant of the formal text hand) for the surrounding commentary, man's interpretation.

Despite the admittedly modest, informal appearance of B 554 when compared to other deluxe folio copies of WB, its scribe is careful to punctuate his biblical and gloss texts carefully. He marks the ends of psalm verses and minor pauses with the *punctus*, notes *metrum* with the *punctus elevatus*, and occasionally indicates questions in the Psalms with the *punctus interrogativus*. In the glosses he uses the *punctus elevatus* regularly to indicate pauses in the sense of the text and slash marks variously to set off lemmata, individual glosses that are joined together in long marginal sequences (separated by semicolons in this edition), and the authorial attributions that conclude most glosses. He corrects the marginal glosses as sedulously as he does the biblical text, cancelling errors both by sub-pointing and by lining through in black and, less often, in red. There are frequent insertions of bits of missing text, by the main scribe and two other subsequent scribes or readers, in the margins, between the lines, and in the gaps between letters and words. All of these corrections are recorded in the apparatus to this edition. A fifteenth-century owner, perhaps influenced by an observation in 6: 27 (Ps. 6, gloss 27) concerning this favourite devotional subgroup, has numbered the seven penitential psalms in the margins of B 554 with Roman numerals.[18] However else B 554 was used, it served at some point during the late fifteenth century, for at least one reader, a private devotional purpose.

DECORATION: B 554 is modestly decorated and with a practical rather than aesthetic aim. Three- and four-line blue initials with red pen-work identify the standard liturgical divisions of the Psalter at Psalms 26, 38, 52, 68, 80, 97, and 109.[19] Similarly treated two-line initials identify the beginnings of psalms and canticles, with one-line red initials marking the beginnings of verses. Each psalm commences with a rubricated title and its Latin cue. The cues appear in the margins through f. 15ʳ, but then move into the text block itself, where instead of the first verses of psalms they themselves are introduced with large blue initials for the rest of the book. This change in format, like the sporadic use of a red paraph mark in some

[18] On the 6th-c. development of the devotion and its popularity in the Middle Ages, see M. S. Driscoll, 'The Seven Penitential Psalms: Their Designation and Usages from the Middle Ages Onwards', *Ecclesia Orans*, 17 (2000), 153–201.
[19] Solopova, *Manuscripts of the Wycliffite Bible*, 72.

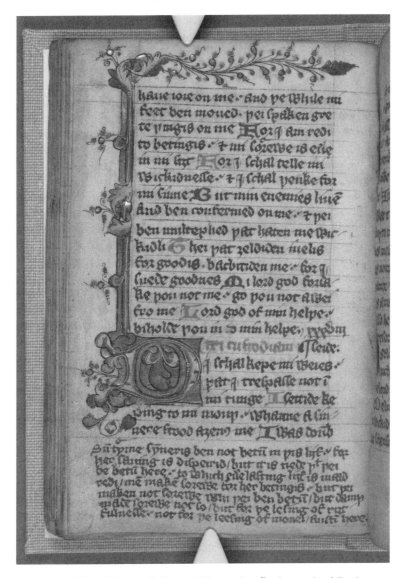

Pl. 2. Dublin, Trinity College MS 70, f. 37ᵛ, the end of Psalm 37 (*Domine ne in furore*), with an Augustinian gloss on v. 18. By permission of The Board of Trinity College Dublin

of the later title glosses to distinguish the beginning of the secondary 'gostli' (spiritual) interpretations of many psalms from their primary historical explanations, suggests that the layout and design of B 554 was not firmly established when copying of the manuscript began. The fact, important to the Wycliffites, that these spiritual interpretations depend upon and are foundationless without the historical explanations, is suggested clearly on f. 30ᵛ of the manuscript: here the rubricator draws a line connecting the end of the historical title gloss of Psalm 61 (*Nonne Deo subiecta erit*) in the inner margin of the page to the beginning of the spiritual gloss in the bottom margin.

DIALECT, PHRASING, AND VOCABULARY: Although the idea of Central Midland Standard (CMS) as a set or pre-determined dialect for the copying of WB has recently been challenged, B 554 remains one of a group of fifteen LV copies written in what has been defined as Type I of that dialect. Its language, according to Ralph Hanna, may be localizable to north Bedfordshire. This suggestion, however, apparently depends on information in *LALME* that, as Anne Hudson has shown, is seriously problematic.[20] It is worth noting in this regard that Dublin, Trinity College MS 70, one of the other manuscripts examined for this edition and one that contains some B 554 glosses, has been localized by *LALME* to Bedfordshire. The atlas analysis, however, is based on the texts of the primer-associated religious prose tracts copied with the Psalms and Canticles in that manuscript, on ff. 30ʳ–195ʳ, not the Psalms and Canticles text itself.[21]

Both the biblical text and glosses in B 554 display consistently the following Type I CMS forms: *lijf/liyf* (the first spelling more common in the text and the second in the glosses, but with overlap), *hiȝ*, *siȝ*, *chirche*, *silf*, *ony*, *fier* (very frequently throughout both text and gloss), and *ȝoue*. In general there is strong congruity between the language of text and gloss in B 554, as is suggested by those instances in which the glosses themselves—in addition to their

---

[20] See Hanna, *English Manuscripts of Richard Rolle*, 139, who takes up B 554 regarding its *Form of Living* fragment and M. Peikola, 'The Wycliffite Bible and Central Midland Standard: Assessing the Manuscript Evidence', *Nordic Journal of English Studies*, 2 (2003), 29–51. On the problematic assertion of a localizable and standard orthography of Wycliffite texts, the analyses of *LALME* notwithstanding, see A. Hudson, 'Observations on the "Wycliffite Orthography"', in Simon Horobin and Aditi Nafde (eds.), *Pursuing Middle English Manuscripts and their Texts: Essays in Honour of Ralph Hanna* (Turnhout, 2017), 77–98, and 92–3 on Bedfordshire localization in particular.

[21] See *LALME*, LP 9480, Grid 510258, Bedfordshire.

citation of lemmata, which almost always agree with the Psalms text—quote or paraphrase psalm verses:

Ps. 1: 4

Text: Not so wickid men, not so; but þei ben as dust.
Gloss: Wickid men ben chaf. (61: 460)

Ps. 61: 5

Text: Wiþ her mouþ þei blessiden, and in her herte þei cursiden
Gloss: þou blessist wiþ þe mouþ and cursist wiþ þe herte. (132: 1182)

Ps. 73: 9

Text: We han not seyn oure signes.
Gloss: We siȝen not oure signes. (73: 591)

Ps. 78: 10

Text: be he knowun among naciouns
Gloss: Be knowun among naciouns. (78: 654)

Ps. 142: 2

Text: And entre þou not into doom wiþ þi seruaunt; for ech man lyuynge shal not be maad iust in þi siȝt.
Gloss: Lord entre þou not into doom wiþ þi seruaunt, for ech man lyuyng shal not be maad iust in þi siȝt. (42: 299)

The only persistent orthographic variation between text and gloss throughout B 554 is the use of 'I' in the text and 'Y' in the glosses for the first personal pronoun. There is, nevertheless, occasional variation as follows:

twice in the biblical text the preposition 'þoru' occurs, at Ps. 135: 14 and 16, where 'þorouȝ' occurs in the glosses, for instance, at 28: 176;

once in the biblical text the pronoun 'self' occurs, at C8: 73, where 'silf' is the common form in both text and glosses;

once in the biblical text the verb 'sai' occurs, at C5: 7, for the past tense singular of 'to see' and once 'saien' occurs for the past tense plural, at C5: 10, where 'siȝ' and 'siȝen', one time at 73: 591, are the more common forms in the glosses;

once in the glosses the pronoun 'eche' occurs, at 25: 164, where 'ech' appears otherwise throughout text and gloss;

once in the glosses the pronoun 'eny' occurs, at 100: 830, where 'ony' appears otherwise throughout text and gloss;

twice in the glosses, both times at 2: 11, the adjective 'Hebreu', is spelled with an initial 'H', although without the 'H' several times elsewhere in the glosses;

two spellings of the adjective 'little' occur in B 554: 'litle' predominating in the biblical text and 'litil' in the glosses, although both text and gloss at times share each form; and finally,

the plural noun 'subjects' is spelled 'soietis' twice in the glosses at 44: 319 and 'sugetis' once at 71: 553 and the past participle 'subject' is spelled 'soiet' once at 108: 957 and 'suget' six times in the Psalms text, at 8: 8, 17: 48, 36: 7, 61: 2, 6, 143: 2, and six times in the glosses as well, 35: 240, 59: 446, 451 (twice), 130: 1163, 143: 1264.

Although none of these cases represents a wide range of variation between the biblical texts and glosses in B 554, the orthography in the manuscript is fluctuating. It seems best to avoid, therefore, *LALME* evidence notwithstanding, any narrow effort at geographical localization of the language of B 554.

Some specifics of phrasing and vocabulary in the B 554 glosses are especially interesting in relation to the language of other Wycliffite biblical and polemical texts.

Phrasing: At 88: 735, the B 554 glossator translates Augustine's 'De coelis ergo nulla dubitatio est, quoniam intelligantur praedicatores verbi veritatis' ('therefore, there is no doubt about the heavens, since they are understood as preachers of the word of truth') using an epistemic adverbial construction: 'No doute, heuenys ben seid þe prechouris of Goddis word'.[22] At 118: 1100, the glossator uses the same construction to translate Augustine's 'Clamor ad Dominum, qui fit ab orantibus, si sonitu corporalis vocis fiat, non intento in Deum corde; quis dubitet inaniter fieri?' ('a cry to the Lord that comes from those praying, if it should be made with the sound of the body's voice, but without the heart intent on God, who would not

---

[22] On epistemic adverbs, which are used to indicate probability or certainty, see A. Simon-Vandenbergen, 'No Doubt and Related Expressions', in M. Hannay and G. J. Steen (eds.), *Structural-Functional Studies in English Grammar: In Honour of Lachlan Mackenzie* (Amsterdam, 2007), 9–34.

doubt that it is made in vain?'): 'No doute þat ne þe cry to þe Lord is maad in veyn, which is maad of hem þat preien wiþ sown of bodili vois, not wiþ ententif herte to þe Lord.' The earliest use of this epistemic adverb in English has been identified by one scholar as occurring in the WB General Prologue (GP), where it occurs twice: 'no doute he shal fynde many biblis in Latyn ful false if he loke many, nameli newe'; 'no doute a symple man wiþ Goddis grace and greet trauele myete expowne myche openliere and shortliere þe Bible in English þan þe elde grete doctours han expowned it in Latyn'.[23] Additionally, *MED doute*, n., 1.d., indicates use of the construction in the Wycliffite treatise against clergy holding property: 'And no dowte þou3 Siluestre . . .' (Matthew, 378).

Vocabulary: At 108: 964, the B 554 glossator translates Lyra's Latin phrase 'condimento carentis' as Middle English 'wantynge souful', that is, lacking in seasoning or flavour. 'Souful' is an infrequent word in ME, derived from OE *sufel*. Several of the instances given at *MED souel*, n. 2. are from the WB EV OT in Bodley 959 (FM siglum *k*) and from the Wycliffite sermons in Bodley 788.

Twice in B 554, at 118: 1065 and 118: 1083, the glosses use the noun 'vilete', moral abasement or outrage, to translate respectively Lat. 'vilitate' and 'enormitatem' from LY. The word is rare in Middle English, occurring as well in WB LV at Deut. 24: 1 for Lat. 'foeditatem'.

On another point of vocabulary: At 118: 1026, Augustine quotes from an old Latin version of the Psalms, probably a Romanum psalter of the Ambrosian rite: 'Et viam justificationum tuarum insinua mihi.' He goes on to note that 'some Latin Bibles' ('nonnulli codices') read 'instrue me' instead, as does the Vulgate, which Augustine says more accurately ('expressius') captures the sense of the Greek Septuagint: 'synetison me' ('make me understand').[24] The B 554 gloss reads: 'In Greek it is seid openliere: Make þou me to vndurstonde þi iustefiyngis. *Austin here.*' The comparative adverb 'openliere' occurs also in WB GP, where it refers to the exposition rather than translation of Scripture: 'a symple man wiþ Goddis grace and greet trauele my3te expowne myche openliere and shortliere þe Bible in English þan þe elde grete doctours han expowned it in

[23] *EAEB*, 81/2849 and 82/2868.
[24] For Augustine's old Latin version, see Sabatier, ii. 234, note to v. 27.

Latyn'.[25] But for the Wycliffites these two processes were intertwined, since they acknowledged the practice of translation itself to be inherently glossarial because it was necessarily interpretative.

PROVENANCE: A late medieval Oxford provenance is possible for B 554. On the lower pastedown, just above the medical recipe, the following note appears in a late fifteenth-century hand: 'Thes bent þe personell owyng eu [of?] John Boket [Beket?]'. 'Thes' could refer either to the contents of B 554 or to an itemized list of Boket's possessions that was intended for but never copied after this note on the pastedown. 'Boket' is a common name. Emden however, it should be noted, lists a John Boket, MA who, according to the cartulary of Oseney Abbey, lived in 1453 in Schools Street, an area that in the eighteenth century was incorporated into Radcliffe Square.[26] The Beleth and Rolle texts added to B 554 have led Elizabeth Solopova to propose a possible fifteenth-century clerical ownership of the volume.[27]

By the early seventeenth century, B 554 was in lay hands. In 1607, it was a gift to Bodley from Sir Richard Wolseley (c.1589–1621), 1st baronet, landowner, and later a member of the House of Commons, who matriculated at Magdalen College, Oxford in 1605 at age 16.[28] This Wolseley may be the same person as a Richard Worseley, who also in 1607 gave Bodley another of its medieval religious manuscripts. This is now MS Bodley 90, a thirteenth-century devotional miscellany in French and Latin that contains sermons on the Seven Deadly Sins, a treatise on confession, selections from the Gospel of Nicodemus, theological notes, and some short apocryphal pieces

---

[25] *EAEB* 82/2868. Paul Schaffner of the ongoing *MED* Project points out to me that the formation of comparative adverbs occurs elsewhere in Wycliffite texts with a scholastic bent. He also notes, however, that the practice is not exclusive to Wycliffite translators. It can be found in Pecock, as a mark of his Latinate style, some Middle English medical texts, and indeed in Malory (personal correspondence).

[26] A. B. Emden, *A Biographical Register of the University of Oxford to A.D. 1500*, 3 vols. (Oxford, 1957–9), i. 210. Note also John Beket of Pattiswick, Essex, a teacher accused *c.*1400 of ascribing to and circulating Lollard beliefs, although there is nothing other than the relatively common name to bring such a person within the orbit of ownership and influence of B 554. A. Hudson, *The Premature Revolution: Wycliffite Texts and Lollard History* (Oxford, 1988), 275, 361, and 385, citing Archbishop Arundel's *Register*, f. 408ʳ.

[27] E. Solopova, 'Manuscript Evidence for the Patronage, Ownership, and Use of the Wycliffite Bible', in E. Poleg and L. Light (eds.), *Form and Function in the Late Medieval Bible* (Leiden, 2013), 333–49 at 342–3.

[28] 'Liber continens expositionem vel glossam in Psalmos Anglice. 4°. MS' (*SC* II, part I, no. 2326).

about Christ.[29] Other, obscure evidence of provenance survives on the cover and first leaf of B 554 in the form of two earlier shelfmarks: 'Th. P 914' and 'NE E.6.7'. The precise significance of these I have not been able to trace. 'Th' in the first shelfmark might indicate the theological complexion of B 554 and 'P', also in the first, the fact that the manuscript is a psalter.

### III. OTHER MANUSCRIPTS CONTAINING B 554 GLOSSES

In most of the manuscripts described summarily below, the occurrence of B 554 glossarial material consists of the title glosses alone, and usually not all of them. A subgroup of these manuscripts, no doubt related to a common ancestor, contains title glosses only through Psalm 72. One of these, London, British Library MS Addit. 10047, contains only the texts of Psalms 1–72 with their title glosses, but it can hardly have been the source of this subgroup, since its treatment of the title glosses (see below) is distinctive in ways that the content and presentation of this material in other copies containing only the title glosses to Psalms 1–72 are not.

Regarding other possible relationships between the manuscripts: The B 554 glosses are likely to have been culled from their voluminous Latin sources and to have circulated in greater or lesser numbers, more or less unsystematically, among those who produced and owned copies of WB in the early fifteenth century. The title glosses themselves, for example, could have been copied comfortably within a single quire and circulated in that form, independently from the other B 554 glosses. B 554, although it represents the fullest account of the Wycliffite glosses on the Psalms to have been identified, should not be understood as a direct source, in any sense, for the gloss texts in any of the other WB copies described below.

Eleven manuscripts contain title glosses and other glosses. Five of these, sigla CGPSX, have in addition to title glosses only one other gloss, placed in the margins. In four of these, sigla CGSX, this is the B 554 gloss at Ps. 101: 4: 'My boonys han dried up as critouns: þat is, þat

[29] SC II, part 1, no. 1887. On Worseley, see J. Foster, *Alumni Oxoniensis: The Members of the University of Oxford, 1500–1714*, 4 vols. (London, 1891–2), iv. 1681.

þat dwelliþ in þe panne of þe friyng. *Lire here*' (see my note to 101: 836). This gloss may have attracted special attention because the word 'critouns' is odd. Some of the manuscripts described below, most notably sigla I and M, contain intertextual glosses related to certain of the shorter marginal glosses in B 554. One of the concerns of the Wycliffite translators and their copyists was the segregation of text and gloss in Scripture, to ensure as unadulterated a text of the Bible as possible. In London, Lambeth Palace MS 1033, an LV copy that shares glosses with B 554, the scribe therefore has written the following cautionary rubric at the start of Isaiah: *Here endiþ þe prolog on Isaye, and here bigynneþ þe text of Isaye, wiþ a shorte glose on þe derke* [obscure] *wordis. And loke ech man þat he write þe text hool bi it silf and þe glose in þe margyn eþer leue it alone* (f. 137ᵛ). Complicating matters further, someone has then lined through the cautionary part of the rubric entirely (*wiþ a shorte . . . leue it alone*). Translation and glossing, as I have said, were inextricably interrelated processes for the Wycliffites. This interrelationship, however, was a source of anxiety, given how readily interpretative material could migrate across the text–gloss divide. There is likely to be more intertextual material in other WB copies that contain the Psalms that duplicates glosses placed in the margins of B 554 as well as more marginal glossing to the Psalms in other copies of WB. It merits further ferreting out and study.[30] All material of this type that I have been able to trace is recorded in the apparatus to this volume.

Dates for the manuscripts described below are those given in Dove (who usually follows FM) and Solopova *Manuscripts of the Wycliffite Bible*, in the case of Oxford copies; otherwise generally s. xv¹.

The other WB copies containing glosses that appear in B 554 can be grouped as follows:

## Manuscripts containing Only Title Glosses

### A: London, British Library Royal 1.C.VIII          *c.*1475–1500

ONT LV (FM no. 6, their base for the Psalms). Folio, double columns. Psalms on ff. 167ʳ–186ʳ, beginning a new leaf after the end of Job: *Here*

---

[30] For a series of glosses to the Psalms in MS Longleat 3, an ONT EV, extracted from a Wycliffite revision of Rolle's *English Psalter*, see M. P. Kuczynski, 'Extracts from a Revised Version of Richard Rolle's *English Psalter* in MS Longleat 3, an Early Version Wycliffite Bible', *MA* 85 (2016), 217–35.

*bigynneþ þe Sauter, which is red comynly in chirchis . . . Here endiþ þe Sauter*, in red. Title glosses in Psalms 6–55, with occasional interruptions in the sequence, are done in red by the rubricator and strictly current with the titles themselves, but usually distinguished by the phrase 'a glos' and blue paraphs. On f. 175ᵛ, the title to Psalm 66 is erroneously identified in the margin as 'A glos' by the scribe, suggesting that the division between title and title gloss might have been unclear for some WB copyists. Cf. sigla k and K below.

## C_J_E.14: Cambridge, St John's College MS E.14          s. xvᴵ

Psalms–Ecclesiasticus LV (FM no. 129). Small quarto, double columns. Psalms with Canticles and the Athanasian Creed, *Quicunque vult*, on ff. 1ʳ–76ʳ. The beginning and some subsequent parts of the first psalms are eaten away by damp at the gutter; Psalms end on f. 63ʳ: *Here endiþ þe Sauter*, in red; *Explicit* at close of the creed on f. 76ʳ. The Latin cues and titles of Psalms in the text in red, cues signalled with blue initial capitals. Title glosses in Psalms 2–71, with some interruptions, are done within the text by the scribe. A quire missing between Psalms 92 and 106 that might have contained additional glosses.

## I: Oxford, Bodleian Library MS Bodl. 277          1415–25?

ONT LV (FM no. 60, Solopova, *Manuscripts of the Wycliffite Bible*, no. 3). Folio, double columns. Psalms at ff. 167ʳ–186ᵛ, beginning: *Here endiþ Iob and bigynniþ þe Sauter . . . Here endiþ þe Sauter of Dauid þe prophete*, in red. Sporadic title glosses in the margins by the text scribe, beginning at Psalm 92 (f. 179ʳ). The illuminator deliberately works his elaborate floral decorations in the margins around the glosses (see Solopova, plate no. 4). Occasional attributions of glosses to 'Lyre', underlined lightly in red. Omits some intertextual glosses common to most LV copies and includes some unique intertextual glosses, which occasionally extend into the margins and may be related to some B 554 marginal glosses.[31]

## i: London, British Library MS Addit. 10046          c.1430 (FM)

Psalms LV (FM no. 36). Octavo, double columns. Psalms on ff. 5ʳ–115ᵛ, beginning: 'Beatus vir qui non abiit in consilio . . .'. Title glosses by the text scribe in the margins, through Ps. 72 (f. 61ᵛ).

---

[31] See A. Sutherland, 'The Wycliffite Psalms', in Solopova, *Manuscripts of the Wycliffite Bible*, 196.

Each of these is identified consistently as 'A glos(e)'. The manuscript begins with the preface to Rolle's *English Psalter* (f. 2ʳ) and an excerpt from chapter 12 of WB GP on the levels of meaning in Scripture (f. 4ᵛ).

### k: London, British Library MS Addit. 10047

s. xvⁱ, perhaps later

Psalms 1–72 LV (FM no. 37). Quarto, single column. Psalms on ff. 1ʳ–143ᵛ (through Ps. 72), beginning: *Here bygynnyth the psalmes of Dauith þat is clepid þe Sauter*, in red. Title glosses to Psalms 2–72, conflated often with the text of the rubricated psalm titles themselves at the head of each psalm, written throughout by the rubricator.

### L: Oxford, Bodleian Library MS Bodl. 296

end 14th c.–early 15th c.

Genesis–Psalms LV (*SC* 2467, FM no. 61, Solopova, *Manuscripts of the Wycliffite Bible*, no. 4). Folio, double columns. A rare WB in cursive, written in Anglicana Formata. Psalms on ff. 177ʳ–197ʳ (ending imperfectly in Ps. 148), beginning: *[H]ere bigynneþ þe Sauter, which is red comynly in chirchis*, in red. Title glosses in Psalms 4–72, in the margins by the text scribe, in a smaller version of his cursive text hand.

### Manuscripts containing Title Glosses and Other Glosses

### b: London, British Library MS Harley 2249      c.1410–20

OT LV (FM no. 17). Folio, double columns. Psalms on ff. 145ʳ–173ᵛ (ending imperfectly in Ps. 144), beginning: *Here endeþ Ioob; and here bigynneþ þe Sauter, which is red comounli in þe chirche* [MS *chirle*], in red. Title glosses to Psalms 4–72 situated very neatly in the margins and written by the text scribe, introduced regularly with 'A glos' in a red box. Two additional short marginal glosses that are also in B 554: at Ps. 58: 5, 'Lord I ran wiþout wickidnesse and dresside': "my werkis" Li. here' (f. 156ʳ), usually intertextual in other WB LV copies; and at Ps. 101: 4, the 'critouns' gloss.

### C: London, British Library MS Cotton Claudius E.ii      c.1410

ONT LV (FM no. 9). Folio, double columns. Psalms on ff. 152ʳ–170ʳ, beginning: *Here endiþ þe book of Ioob; and here bigynneþ þe Sauter which is red comynli in chirchis*, in red. Title and other glosses

throughout, in the margins done by the text scribe, keyed to their
lemmata in the text by tie-marks like those used in B 554. The most
heavily glossed WB LV OT, with systematic glosses also in 1–4
Kings, Job, and Proverbs–Isaiah 8: 4. Dove suggests, although her
evidence is not clear, that the glosses, shared with British Library
MS Royal 1.C.ix, an LV OT through Job, are 'very likely to be the
work of the translators' and 'that both sets of glosses undoubtedly
derive from the same original'.[32]

### G: Oxford, Lincoln College MS Lat. 119            s. xv[1]

ONT LV (FM no. 101, Solopova, *Manuscripts of the Wycliffite Bible*,
no. 55). Folio, double columns. Psalms at ff. 152[r]–168[r], beginning
imperfectly in Psalm 17: 'and I shal not turne til þei faylen. I shal
alto breke hem and þei shulen not mowe stonden, þei shulen falle
vndir my feet.' Title glosses to Psalms 19–72, in the margins by the
text scribe, in a smaller version of his text hand. Also at Ps. 101: 4,
the 'critouns' gloss. A later fifteenth-century cursive hand adds in
the margins paraphrases of psalm verses and moralizing comments
perhaps related to B 554 glosses: for example, to Psalm 29: 'þe
seyntis of þe Lord synge to þe Lord'; to Psalm 31: 'for diliueraunce
oute of trybulacion'; to Psalm 31 again: 'for synners' (f. 153[r–v]).

### K: Oxford, Bodleian Library MS Fairfax 2
#### 1408 (internal evidence)

ONT LV (FM no. 71, Solopova, *Manuscripts of the Wycliffite Bible*,
no. 21). Folio, double columns. Psalter at ff. 166[r]–187[v], with a
prologue (FM ii. 736–8) beginning on f. 165[v] and running onto
f. 166[r], where the Psalms begin: *Here endeþ þe prolog of þe Sauter. Se
now þe booc* [*wich is rad comynli in chirchis*, in red, the last part of the
rubric added in the margin by a second hand. Title glosses at Psalms
1–150 and other glosses, intertextual and marginal, by two scribes,
the second sometimes correcting the first by erasure, overwriting, or
completing the first scribe's work: for example, at the title of Psalm
93: 'In þis salm, Moises aȝenclepeþ þe puple fro errour [aboute
Goddis purueaunce and schewiþ þat Goddis purueaunce strecchiþ
forþ to alle þingis, and punyschiþ iustli synneris. *Lire here.*' As the
copying proceeded, glosses were increasingly signalled by 'A glos'
(underlined) and attributed to 'Lire'.

---

[32] Dove, 164 and 167 respectively.

## O: Oxford, New College MS 66                    1415–25?

Genesis–Psalms LV (FM no. 97, Solopova, *Manuscripts of the Wycliffite Bible*, no. 56). Folio, double columns. Psalms on ff. 211ʳ–234ᵛ, beginning: *Here bygynnyþ þe Sauter þe which is reed comynly in chirchis*, in red. Only a few glosses: title glosses to Psalms 4 and 5, signalled by the word 'Glos' in red and in a red box; at Psalms 25–59, five short glosses, two of these intertextual and the others in the margins, like the title glosses in the text scribe's hand. The manuscript also contains prologues to some biblical books, including two prologues to the Psalter, at f. 210ʳ⁻ᵛ: 'Whanne it is knowun' (FM ii. 736–8) and 'Dauiþ þe sone of Gesse' (FM ii. 738).

## P: Cambridge, Emmanuel College MS 21                    *c.*1420

ONT LV (FM no. 118). Folio, double columns. Psalms ff. 159ʳ–176ᵛ, beginning: *Here biginniþ þe Sauter, which is redd comynli in chirchis*, in red. No explicit, but at the bottom of f. 176ᵛ, after the text of Psalms, *Here biginniþ þe Prouerbis of Salomon*, in red. Title glosses in Psalms 2–72, in the margins done by the text scribe, those in the outside margins of the book sometimes severely cropped. One additional gloss, intertextual in most copies, here marginal as in B 554 (25: 12/163): 'Mi <u>foot</u> stood in riȝtfulnesse': 'þat is, affeccioun' (f. 19ʳ, Pl. 3).

## Q: Cambridge, Cambridge University Library Mm.2.15
*c.*1410–20

ONT LV (FM no. 112). Folio, double columns. Psalms on ff. 147ᵛ–164ʳ, beginning: *Here endiþ Iob and here bigynniþ þe Sauteer, which is red comounli in chirchis*, in red. Title glosses at Psalms 2–72, in the margins done by the text scribe. Through Psalm 6, but no farther, the title glosses are headed 'A glos' or 'A glose' (underlined). Four short glosses to Psalms 25, 58, 59, and 101, this last the 'critouns' gloss. Next to Ps. 108: 18: 'And he louyde cursyng, etc.', in the margin: 'Of curseris' (f. 160ʳ).

## S: Cambridge, Corpus Christi College, Parker MS 147
*c.*1410–30

ONT LV (FM no. 116). Folio, double columns. Psalms at ff. 147ᵛ–164ʳ, beginning: *Here endiþ Iob, and here bigynniþ þe Sauteer, which is red comounli in chirchis*, in red. Title glosses at Psalms 2–72, in the margins by the text scribe, in a smaller version of his text hand.

These are signalled by 'A gloos', sometimes in an open-top red box, the glosses themselves regularly surrounded by a scroll motif in red. Two additional marginal glosses, at Psalm 25 the 'foot . . . affeccioun' gloss; at Psalm 101 the 'critouns' gloss. In a later fifteenth-century hand, next to Ps. 103: 17, 'The hous of þe gerfaukun, etc.', a Latin note expressing the opinion of the writer that Wyclif was ignorant of pure Latin style ('ignarus Latinitatis') because he accepted 'griffal-cus' (a large falcon used for hawking) as an equivalent of Vulgate 'erodii' (heron).

## U: London, Lambeth Palace Library MS 25     *c*.1390–1400

Genesis–Deuteronomy EV, Joshua–Apocalypse LV (FM no. 46). Folio, double columns. Psalms on ff. 178$^r$–197$^r$, beginning without a title: 'Blessed is þe man, etc.', but with a decorated initial capital. Title glosses in Psalms 2–47, in the margins done by the text scribe and sometimes marked with a blue paraph. Some brief glosses that are marginal in B 554 are intertextual here and attributed, within the lines of the text, to Lyra: for example, at Ps. 58: 5, 'dresside <u>my werkis</u>, li. he.' (f. 185$^r$).

## V: London, Lambeth Palace Library MS 1033     *c*.1410–20

OT LV (FM no. 50). Folio, double columns. Psalms on ff. 65$^r$–98$^v$, beginning: *Here endiþ Ioob and bigynneþ þe Sauter*, in red. Only a few title glosses, done by the text scribe, but several other marginal glosses throughout that sometimes display significant variants from those in B 554 as recorded in the textual notes to this edition. The marginal glosses, possibly in a second hand, are linked to their lemmata in the text with tie-marks like those in B 554.

## X: Oxford, Christ Church MS 145     end 14th c.

ONT EV (FM no. 91, Solopova, *Manuscripts of the Wycliffite Bible*, no. 48). Folio, double columns. Psalms at ff. 174$^v$–192$^v$, beginning: *þe book bygynneth of ympnes and solitarie speches of þe profete Dauyd*, in red. No explicit, but a blank line after the end of Psalm 150, perhaps intended for one that was not copied. An anomaly among the copies described here, being an ONT in EV but with the title glosses common to many LV copies, added by a second, probably early fifteenth-century, hand. These are marked consistently 'A glos', just above or beside their positions in the margins. When in the bottom margins, the title glosses are sometimes written within the lines ruled

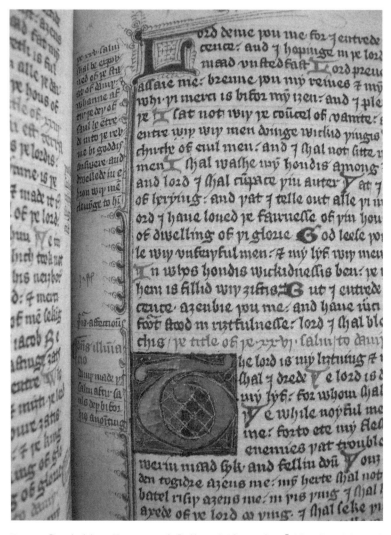

PL. 3. Cambridge, Emmanuel College MS 21, f. 19ʳ (detail), title and shorter marginal gloss to Psalm 25 (*Iudica me Domine*). By permission of The Master and Fellows of Emmanuel College, Cambridge

for the double columns of biblical text. The 'critouns' gloss at f. 186ᵛ, in the margin.

## Manuscripts containing Other Glosses but No Title Glosses

### D_70: Dublin, Trinity College MS 70                s. xv¹

Psalms LV (unknown to FM).³³ Octavo, single column. Also contains Canticles and primer. Psalms at ff. 1ʳ–157ʳ, beginning imperfectly at Psalm 2: 'heþene men; and puplis, etc.'. In Psalms 30–7, several of B 554's Augustinian glosses, on moral rather than philological points, keyed to their lemmata in the text with tie-marks like those in B 554, but no Lyran glosses, to the titles or otherwise.

### L2: Oxford, Bodleian Library MS Laud misc. 182      s. xv¹

ONT extracts LV (FM no. 182, Solopova, *Manuscripts of the Wycliffite Bible*, no. 32). Octavo, single column. Nine complete psalms from WB LV, Psalms 1, 2, 4, 5, 6, 36, 50, 70, and 98 on ff. 91ʳ–99ʳ, beginning: *Here enden two chapitres of Ioob; and here bigynneþ þe firste salme of þe Sauter*, in red. Psalm 36 only contains three marginal glosses also in B 554, one Augustinian and two Lyran, linked to the text with B 554-style tie-marks, although here cruder and not rubricated. Other short glosses in full chapters and extracts from Genesis, Exodus, Deuteronomy, and 1 Kings, but after those in the Psalter, none in the Daniel through the NT extracts. On ff. 311ʳ– 312ʳ, another brief catena on the Psalms containing extracts from Psalms 5, 6, 50, 71, 83, 95, 115, 118, and 138. For text and discussion, see Kuczynski, 'An Unpublished Lollard Psalms *Catena*'.

### M: Oxford, Queen's College MS 388                    s. xv¹

ONT LV (FM no. 101, Solopova, *Manuscripts of the Wycliffite Bible*, no. 61). Folio, double columns. Psalms at ff. 197ʳ–220ʳ, beginning: *This book Sauter is clepid, þat is to seie þe book of songis*, in red. The Psalms also have a unique colophon: *Here endiþ þe Sauter, but more salmes sumen þat ben writen in þe Sauter whiche ben writen in diuerse capitles* [sic] *of þe Bible, bifore and after whiche it is no nede to writen hem twies þer, for we enden here and here bigynneþ a prologe vpon*

---

³³ Discussed in detail in M. P. Kuczynski, 'An Important Lollard Psalter in Trinity College, Dublin', *Studies: An Irish Quarterly Review*, 99 (2010), 181–7.

*prouerbis of Salomon*, also in red. This comment presumably refers to the various canticles frequently copied with the Psalter. Queens 388 is distinctive also in having several B 554 marginal glosses inter-textually and underlined; and conversely in having some of B 554's intertextual glosses copied in its margins. Cf. siglum I above.

## Miscellaneous Manuscripts

Two manuscripts examined for this edition contain only a single gloss each shared with B 554:

### k2: London, British Library MS Addit. 31044    *c.*1400 (Dove)

Psalms–Ecclesiasticus LV (FM no. 184). A folio ruled for two columns; begins with a copy of Rolle's prologue to his *English Psalter* and an expansive rubric derived from Rolle: *Here biginneþ þe Sauter, þe which is comynli vsid to be rad in holy chirche seruyse. For it is a book of greet deuocioun and of hiȝ goostly conceyuynge, in which book holy men fynden ful myche swetnesse and parfiȝt vndirstondinge of goostly counfort. Also, þis book shewiþ þe meedis* [rewards] *of iust men and the medis of vniust men, þe reward of euery man aftir his trauele* (f. 11ʳ). The single marginal gloss appears in a black box beside Ps. 39: 16, 'Wel! wel!': 'þat is, in scorn' (f. 33ᵛ).

### R: Cambridge, Cambridge University Library Dd.1.27, vol. 1    *c.*1430 (Dove)

OT LV (FM no. 106). A folio ruled for two columns; contains only one gloss that agrees with B 554, written intertextually and under-lined at Ps. 25: 12: 'My foot, þat is affeccioun' (f. 238ʳ). In the margin next to this, another fifteenth-century hand has written: 'þe holy preour of Dauiþ'. The scribe and this second hand also make marginal notes to certain psalms on Antichrist. The first, 'Nota de Anticristo', is done by the text scribe at Ps. 9: 25: 'The synnere wraþþide þe Lord' (f. 223ʳ). This verse occurs in the middle of a series on the wicked that B 554 explains as being about 'Antecrist and hise sueris' (see 9: 23/53).

IV. THE CONTEXT OF B 554

The Psalms and Canticles glossed in B 554 agree in nearly all of their readings with the text of WB LV as edited by Forshall and Madden.

The process of glossing them in the manuscript is both traditional and in certain respects characteristically Wycliffite. Indeed, the history and significance of WB EV and LV themselves cannot be properly understood apart from the Middle English glosses that accompany the versions in most manuscript copies.[34] The B 554 marginal glosses are in the long tradition of Latin exegesis of sacred Scripture, which appears throughout the Middle Ages not only in large-scale folio Bibles prepared for professional academic use, but also in smaller-scale books, such as quarto-sized psalters that were evidently used in private liturgical and scholarly circumstances (Pl. 4). Monks, friars, and secular clergy during the Middle Ages did not understand the Scriptures as auto-exegetical. Indeed, they regarded them as replete with both small and large difficulties: for example, the names of strange creatures and people; and, as Augustine notes more than once in his treatise *De Doctrina Christiana*, episodes such as the sexual immorality of the patriarchs that seem to fly in the face of the 'law of charity'.[35] Even the four gospels themselves, texts that record the direct revelation and words of Christ, are disharmonious, reporting the same episodes from Christ's life differently.[36] The divine text could not stand on its own. It required critical study, by way of the commentators. And the Psalms, because of their verbal density and uniquely prophetic status (see below), were especially in need of authoritative exposition.

In copies of WB EV, explanatory glosses to the text are almost always intertextual: words and short phrases that provide alternate translations for difficult words, such as at Gen. 6: 17 'watris of diluuye', a close translation of the Vulgate's 'diluvii aquas', which is then immediately glossed: 'ether greet flood'.[37] Scribes regularly underline this type of intertextual gloss in LV copies, in order to distinguish such matter clearly from the primary biblical text. This practice respects the integrity of the Latin original and reminds the reader of the laborious process of interpretation the Wycliffite translators engaged to arrive at a vernacular idiom that best

---

[34] Kuczynski, 'Glossing and Glosses' gives a comprehensive overview.

[35] See for a summary of Augustine's position, *De Doctrina Christiana*, Book I, chs. xxxv–xxxvii, sections 39–41, at PL 34: 30–1.

[36] On medieval efforts to deal with the problem, see B. A. Pitts, *The Anglo-Norman Gospel Harmony: A Translation of the 'Estoire de l'Evangile' (Dublin, Christ Church C6.1.1, Liber niger)* (Tempe, 2014), 1–18.

[37] FM i. 90.

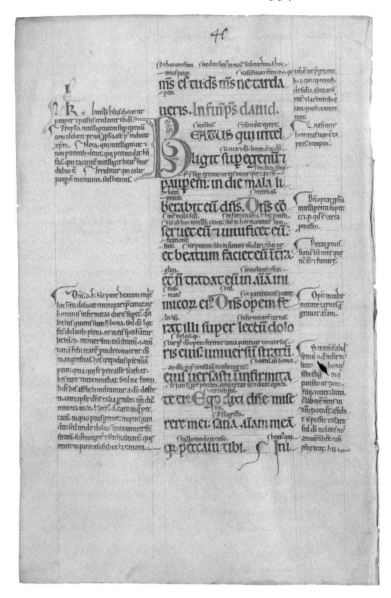

PL. 4. Tulane University, New Orleans, uncatalogued manuscript fragment, f. 39ᵛ, glossed Psalter, France, 13th c. By permission of The Howard-Tilton Memorial Library, Tulane University

represents the meaning of the Vulgate. The anonymous author of WB GP explains at one point the importance of Latin glosses to establishing a reliable exemplar for the English versions. The translators, he says, used 'many elde biblis, and oþere doctors and comyn [here perhaps meaning readily available] glosis . . . to make o Latyn Bible sumdeel trewe, and þanne to studie it of þe newe [all over again], þe text wiþ þe glose and oþere doctours'.[38] This procedure, he explains further, also involved discussions 'wiþ elde gramariens and eld dyuynes of harde wordis and harde sentensis, hou þo myȝten be vndurstonde best and translatid'.[39]

Concerning the Old Testament specifically, the Wycliffite translators, like Jerome himself, sought to recover inasmuch as possible the *Hebraica veritas* ('Hebrew verity or truth') that had become clouded by the Greek translation of the Septuagint (LXX). The GP author laments that 'þe comyne Latyn biblis han more nede to be correctid, as many as I haue seyn in my liyf, þan haþ þe Englisch Bible late translatid'.[40] He notes, therefore, that he has drawn exegeses from authorities such as Jerome and Lyra, arranging them in the margins of his translations to indicate thereby 'what þe Ebreu haþ, and hou it is vndurstonden in sum [a particular] place'.[41] Then he turns to the special problem of the Psalms:

and I dide þis moost in þe Sauter, þat of alle oure bookis discordiþ moost fro Ebrew, for þe chirche rediþ noȝt þe Sauter bi þe laste translacioun of Ierom, out of Ebreu into Latyn, but anoþere translacioun of oþere men þat hadden myche lasse kunnyng and lasse hoolynesse þan Ierom hadde.[42]

In other words, the textual history of the Psalms in Latin is very complicated.[43]

During the Middle Ages, three discrepant Latin versions of this important book were in circulation at the same time, all attributed to Jerome, along with other Latin versions that belong to what scholars call the *vetus Latina* ('old Latin') tradition, readings from which sometimes persist, for example, in the Psalms exegesis of Augustine. Jerome's Romanum, made from LXX, was widely used in the liturgy, at least until the thirteenth century; the Gallicanum, made from the multiple Greek texts of Psalms available to Jerome and his contemporaries in Origen's *Hexapla*, including LXX, was used in

---

[38] *EAEB*, 80/2803–6.  [39] *EAEB*, 80/2807–8.  [40] *EAEB*, 82/2350–2.
[41] *EAEB*, 82/2855–6.  [42] *EAEB*, 82/2856–60.
[43] See in *ODCC* the entries on 'Psalms, Book of' and 'Psalters'.

the breviary and became the basis of the Vulgate; and the Hebraicum, made from the original Hebrew, was known and used almost exclusively by scholars. Among the Wycliffite translators themselves, it is likely that there was some confusion and even ignorance concerning the nature and authorship of the three versions specifically. The author of WB GP, for example, praises Jerome's final ('laste') translation, the Hebraicum, but seems to attribute his second version of the Psalter, the Gallicanum, to 'othere men that hadden myche lasse kunnyng and lasse hoolynesse than Ierom hadde'.[44]

Jerome's sense of the difficulty of capturing the Hebrew truth of the Psalms accurately in Latin is reflected in a letter he wrote to the Gothic clergymen Sunnia and Friþila, 'concerning places in their copy of the Psalter which had been corrupted from the Septuagint'. Here, moving sequentially through the Psalms, although he does not take up each one, Jerome explains to his correspondents 'wherever there is in the Psalter a discrepancy between the Latin and Greek texts, which of the readings in question expresses the corresponding Hebrew text more faithfully'.[45] His explanations are meticulous and reflect a desire to stabilize the text of the Psalter as much as possible by providing variant readings and analyses of the relative merits of the variants. One of his examples is related directly to the substance of a LY gloss in B 554, at 103: 879. The Psalmist is praising the greatness of God's creation, which he has fashioned in his wisdom as a rich gift to men. He describes the great expanse of the sea, in Jerome's Gallican version as 'spatiosum manibus': in WB LV, translated from this, 'large to hondis'. Jerome has been questioned by his correspondents about the fact that the Greek for 'manibus' does not appear in LXX. He explains, however, that 'it has been added in the Septuagint under an asterisk'—as 'manibus' itself is today in the Stuttgart edition of the Vulgate—on the supposition that it was omitted 'through an error of the transcribers'.[46] (The ignorance of editors, scribes, and translators comes in for repeated

---

[44] *EAEB*, 82/2850–62. The text that modern scholarship knows as the Romanum was probably not Jerome's own, but one already established from various old Latin readings to which he made extensive corrections. See J. N. D. Kelly, *Jerome: His Life, Writings, and Controversies* (New York, 1975), 89.

[45] M. Metlen, 'Letter of St. Jerome to the Gothic Clergymen Sunnia and Friþila concerning Places in their Copy of the Psalter which Had Been Corrupted from the Septuagint', *JEGP* 36 (1937), 515–42 at 516.

[46] Ibid. 536.

critique in the B 554 glosses, by way of LY.). The emendation, Jerome insists, is crucial to the sense and thus he incorporates it in his Hebrew translation, since he finds it supported by the original Hebrew. Lyra explains the matter in his *Postilla*, in support of Jerome: the Hebrew word that occurs in the psalm text at this point, 'yad', can mean both 'hand' and 'place'. Thus, following the best rabbinic authorities, the text must mean (as Jerome had suggested) 'the sea is wide of hands'—that is, very spacious.

Lyra, the second exegete mentioned by the GP author, was the major fourteenth-century Christian authority on the Hebrew sense of the Old Testament, a thorough and conservative scholar whose interpretations remain as close as possible to Scripture's literal sense.[47] The medieval tradition of commenting on the Bible as a means of elucidating its meaning was accretive. It produced, by the high Middle Ages, many outlandish and even self-serving spiritual interpretations of Scripture.[48] Despite their necessary reliance on Latin exegesis, the Wycliffites were thus also rightly suspicious of biblical glossing. Ideally, exegesis illuminates Scripture's sense in service to the truth: it is handmaiden to the ultimate authority of the divine word. The author of a Wycliffite treatise on dominion, however, cautions that 'Many falce gloseris maken goddis lawe derk and letten [hinder] seculere men to susteyne it and kepen it; of siche false gloseris schulde ech man be war'.[49] Exegesis that obscures rather than reveals the truth of sacred Scripture is not only philologically suspicious but also morally corrupt. It has pernicious effects on the entire Christian community.

The phrase 'false gloseris' allows nevertheless that there may be good ones. Lyra, according to the Wycliffite view, is pre-eminent in this category. For him, the literal sense of the Psalms is admittedly capacious: it includes, as the B 554 glosses themselves make clear, the figurative, moral, and especially christological meanings of the Psalter, many of which, being messianic in character, are quoted by Christ himself and his apostles throughout the gospels. They are also invoked by Paul, who is praised as 'last of the apostles' in a B 554 gloss (67: 517), in various of his epistles, especially his letter to

[47] G. Dahan (ed.), *Nicolas de Lyre, franciscain du XIV^e siècle, exégète et théologien* (Turnhout, 2011).

[48] See, for example, B. Smalley, *The Study of the Bible in the Middle Ages*, 3rd edn. rev. (Oxford, 1983), 284–5.

[49] *The English Works of Wyclif hitherto Unprinted*, ed. F. D. Matthew, EETS OS 74 (1880), 284.

the Hebrews (see Latin Sources and Explanatory Notes). Indeed, the unusually direct Christology of the Psalms was yet another reason why understanding their precise literal sense was crucial to their correct use, in both prayer and study, by medieval Christians. The WB GP author observes, in a tradition that goes back to Augustine, that the Psalms are a digest of the wisdom of the entire Bible, being a uniquely clear and complete prophecy of the life of Christ:

þe Sauter comprehendiþ al þe elde and newe testament and techiþ pleynli [fully] þe mysteries of þe Trinite and of Cristis incarnacioun, passioun, risyng aȝen and stiyng [ascension] into heuene and sendyng doun of þe Hooli Goost and prechyng of þe gospel, and þe coming of Antecrist, and þe general doom of Crist, and þe glorie of chosun men to blisse and þe peynes of hem þat shulen be dampned to helle.[50]

Lyra was specially qualified to comment on the complexities of the Psalter's literal sense in a responsible way, since he returns throughout his exegesis on the Psalms to the Hebrew originals and to authoritative Hebrew commentary. Most important, he uses the works of the highly regarded medieval French commentator known as 'Rashi', the acronym for Rabbi Solomon Isaac (c. 1040–1105), who, by way of Lyra's *Postilla*, appears by name three times in the margins of B 554 as 'Rabi Salomon'.[51]

Over 80 per cent of the marginal glosses in B 554 derive from the Psalms portion of Lyra's *Postilla super totam Bibliam*. Nearly all the remaining 20 per cent are from Augustine's *Enarrationes in Psalmos* and only a handful from a third source, called by the B 554 glossator 'þe comyn glos', that is, GO. This was a standard collection of authorities on the Bible that developed in the early twelfth century under the influence of Anselm of Laon (1050–1117). It seems to have provided the B 554 glossator with his access to the insights of the *Expositio Psalmorum* of Cassiodorus (485–585), whose works while

---

[50] *EAEB* 58/2007–12.

[51] Many more of the B 554 glosses derived from LY advance Rashi's views, without naming him. On Rashi's medieval influence, see D. C. Klepper, *The Insight of Unbelievers: Nicholas of Lyra and Christian Reading of Jewish Text in the Later Middle Ages* (Philadelphia, 2007) and H. Hailperin, *Rashi and the Christian Scholars* (Pittsburgh, 1963). Although Nicholas often cites Rashi in support of his literal interpretations of the Psalms, he also rejects some of Rashi's views, especially when they compromise his christological emphasis. For an analysis of the underlying incompatibilities of Rashi's and medieval Christian interpretations of the Psalms, see E. Shereshevsky, 'Rashi's and Christian Interpretations', *Jewish Quarterly Review*, NS 61 (1970), 76–86.

respected would have been less readily available to a late medieval academic than either those of Lyra or Augustine.

One noteworthy feature of the B 554 commentary is the occasional interplay in it between Lyra's academic text, which itself often mentions Augustine's work and uses it critically (cf. 79: 656 and 95: 805), and Augustine's pulpit-style expositions. The *Enarrationes* are elaborately rhetorical interpretations of the Psalms that began life as a series of sermons and whose oral character has a residual presence in a few of B 554's AU glosses, where Augustine can be heard across the ages exhorting his 'Dereworþest briþeren', for instance, to manage the moral conduct of 'ȝoure housis, ȝoure sones, and ȝoure meynees' (50: 379). Augustine anticipates in his interpretations of the Psalms and is often the source of many of Lyra's christological readings, a fact registered occasionally in B 554. At the same time, he was not as self-disciplined an exegete as Lyra was. For instance, beginning his exposition of Psalm 127 (*Beati omnes*), in a passage that incidentally does not appear in B 554, Augustine explains to his congregation that the Psalmist has given them a 'wrapped-up package' ('involucrum'), designed to delight when one opens it and starts to unpack its multiple contents. The discourse that ensues is a rhetorical tour de force, such as one would never find in Lyra's scholarly comments. Like a modern literary critic (the analogy is admittedly a distant one), in preaching the Psalms, Augustine at times seems to indulge in the act of interpretation and exposition for its own sake.

For this reason, at only a few points in the margins of B 554 does the manuscript's compiler allow Augustine to take precedence over Lyra—for example, at the head of Psalm 85 (*Inclina Domine aurem tuam*). This is a brief psalm with a dense christological meaning, interpreted by Augustine as epitomizing the layered exegetical significances and variety of vocalizations of the Psalms. Alluding to Paul's analogy of Christ's Mystical Body, a theme repeated several times throughout both the AU and LY glosses in B 554, Augustine discusses the multiple speakers of the Psalms. He observes how in the Psalter Christ prays in his divine voice for us, prays in his human voice with us, and is prayed to in his transcendent godhead by us:

God myȝte ȝyue no grettir good to men, þan þat he made his kyndli sone heed to hem and shapide hem as membris of hym, þat he shulde be þe sone of God and þe sone of man, o God wiþ þe fadir and o man wiþ men. Ihesu

Crist is oure prest and preieþ for us, and he as oure heed preieþ in us, and he as oure God is preied of us. *Austin on þe title of lxxxv salm.*

B 554's combination and coordination of two very different but complementary commentaries on the Psalms, those of Lyra and Augustine, makes the manuscript's rough-but-ready design and purpose loosely akin to the more exquisite coordinating of different exegetical authorities on Scripture that one finds in the Wycliffite *Glossed Gospels* (*GG*). Anne Hudson explores in her recent study and edition of *GG*, for example, how carefully the division of the biblical text to receive glossing was carried out for these major vernacular commentaries. These divisions are directly related to manuscript format. In the frontispiece Hudson reproduces, from York Minster Library MS XVI, D.2, f. 1ʳ, blocks of biblical text are copied in a larger and more formal script than the commentary, both of them being written in double columns for ease of reference. The scribe then arranges the names of authorities ('Crisostom', 'Ierom', 'Rabanus') meticulously up and down the inner and outer margins of the folio next to the appropriate commentary blocks, which repeat the biblical lemma, underlined in red, and are subdivided with red paraph marks. This kind of elegant layout facilitates more efficient coordination of text and gloss than does that of B 554: cf. in this edition the Frontispiece, Pl. 2 above, and the frontispiece to volume 2. At the same time, Hudson also concludes that the division of the gospel texts into sections was probably 'not finalized' before the translation of the glossarial material itself and 'that it was subject to modification over some time and probably to more than one revision'.[52] She notes further, concerning the commentaries themselves, that there seems to have been 'no single "recipe" that controlled the production . . . for each of the four gospels'. On the contrary, 'each gospel's commentary reveals individual methods of production and eccentricities of citation',[53] probably occasioned by the complexities involved in producing manuscript books that have two interrelated aims: to represent biblical text and gloss accurately while also coordinating and differentiating these on the page. B 554 remains by comparison with the York manuscript of *GG* a very modest production. Its problems of formatting, however, are still usefully studied alongside Hudson's minute analysis of the planning and production challenges of *GG*.

[52] Hudson *Doctors in English*, p. xlvii.

[53] Ibid. p. liii.

## V. PLANNING AND ASSEMBLING B 554

B 554 is a carefully if not artfully planned book. The chief difficulty its compiler faced was in arranging his copious commentary within a small and often cramped textual space. His glossarial materials differ in extent from psalm to psalm, so that some leaves in the manuscript contain only a few short glosses, whereas others are crammed with several long and short ones, nearly to their edges. And it is, of course, impossible to know when he embarked on commenting on the Psalms and Canticles in the first instance, if B 554's compiler knew how expansive, given his multiple interests, his glossing might need to be.

The B 554 scribe's handwriting is relatively uniform. On heavily glossed leaves, however, he must run long sequences of glosses together, linking them with a single tie-mark to their initial lemma in the biblical text. It becomes the reader's job then (if we wish to imagine a medieval reader besides the compiler) to track subsequent lemmata throughout two or more psalm verses and along the length of a substantial marginal gloss, moving back and forth between text and gloss as he does so. This feature of the manuscript's complex layout raises the question of whether B 554 was in fact planned to receive such ample glosses. The matter cannot be resolved definitively. The margins left around the biblical text on each side, except along the book's gutter, are large enough to receive some commentary. They are not, however, lined for text. Moreover, the text block in the manuscript is never once disturbed to accommodate the glosses. Rather, and especially on heavily congested pages, some glosses have to be fitted in around the biblical text itself, which occasionally extends slightly into the right-hand margins (see the Frontispiece to vol. 2). In short, the B 554 glosses, at least in their amplitude, might have been an afterthought.

Also, treatment of both text and gloss in B 554 suggests that certain details concerning their presentation were still being deliberated while the manuscript was being written. For example, Latin psalm cues, in red, begin each psalm: this is the traditional way in which, rather than by number, the Psalms are identified in medieval psalters. Sometimes early in the manuscript, however, these Latin cues are not written on the line at the start of the Middle English verses, but adjacent to them in the margins. In two early cases, they appear at some distance from the psalm that they cue—once, for example, on the verso of the leaf where the psalm text begins. The design of the manuscript seems to stabilize after its first fifteen folios. After this point, Latin cues are always on the line within the text block of psalms texts. Moreover, the secondary 'gostli' or spiritual interpretations that follow the primary historical and christological ones in title glosses are regularly distinguished from these materials by red paraphs. The question of when B 554 was rubricated impinges on the question of whether its glosses were an afterthought. It cannot, however, be confidently resolved. On f. 38$^r$, for example, the rubricated title of Psalm 73 (*Ut quid Deus repulisti*) overlaps slightly a gloss copied down the right-hand margin. This detail suggests that text and gloss were rubricated straight through after both were written out by the scribe, and thus that the decision to include glosses may have been part of the compiler's original plan.

The process of assembling materials that led to production of B 554 will have been laborious but remains very obscure. Lyra's *Postilla* and Augustine's *Enarrationes* are both voluminous works, each of them filling multiple folio volumes. It is possible that the B 554 compiler had direct access to complete tomes and worked his way through them to isolate the relatively small percentage of materials from the whole that he needed for the margins of his psalter. More likely, however, he relied on parts of the works in question or on intermediary texts that would have made his access to particular areas of emphasis in these longer works more efficient.

Lyra on the Psalms alone circulated independent of his commentary on the entire Bible during the Middle Ages and would have been accessible in this form at an intellectual centre such as Oxford, if that in fact is where B 554 was planned and written. Bodleian Library MS e museo 5, for example, is a portable folio of 162 leaves. Its second part, comprising ff. 33$^r$–159$^r$, is a copy of Lyra *super Psalterium* written in England in the early fifteenth century.[54] In two instances, a late medieval reader has noted passages on the relationship between the contemplative and active lives (f. 138$^r$) and concerning translation of Scripture (f. 139$^r$). The first of these passages, coincidentally, is translated in B 554, at Ps. 118: 1056. This copy of

[54] *SC* no. 3501. The first part of the manuscript is Latin sermons, copied in the mid-15th c. Cf. in terms of format London, British Library MS Royal 20.E.viii, a very large 15th-c. folio of Lyra on the Psalms (the second half of a set, the first volume being Lyra on the Heptateuch) which would have had to be used on a reading stand.

Lyra *super Psalterium*, had it been written a little bit earlier (its scribe dates it 1452), would have provided a compiler with everything he needed to assemble the Lyran materials translated and copied into the margins of B 554.

Lyra was available in other codicological contexts in fifteenth-century England as well. I have examined two of these as analogues rather than sources for many of the glosses in B 554 and present the results of my investigations in the Latin Sources and Explanatory Notes section of this edition. Beryl Smalley explained many years ago that Wyclif wrote his own *postilla* on the entire Bible as a series of lectures, sometime after 1372 and completed by 1379, when he was teaching at Oxford.[55] A section of this work, including his commentary on the Psalms, is now St John's College, Oxford MS 171, written in England in the first quarter of the fifteenth century.[56] In his exegeses of the Psalms, Wyclif cites the full range of authorities invoked in B 554, including GO, AU, and most heavily of course, LY. My notes trace the high level of congruence between the B 554 glosses and Wyclif's commentary. The overlap is not entire, but it does reveal shared interests between the two commentaries, including a strong area of concern in both with disparities between Jerome's Gallican and Hebrew versions and the original Hebrew texts of the Psalms. Smalley, in analysing Wyclif's method, satirizes him somewhat for his moments of self-indulgence.[57] To be sure, he mixes at times his own Latin style and exegetical approach with Lyra's, varying his source's remarks by use of synonyms and amplifying much of its matter. Also, there are passages from LY translated in the margins of B 554 that do not figure in Wyclif's treatment. It is impossible, therefore, that his *postilla* was a standalone source for the B 554 glosses. The work certainly, however, could have inspired the B 554 compiler's work and provided him with a second-hand account of Lyra's methods and insights, sending him—possibly by way of other scholarly inter-mediaries—back to Lyra's originals.

Another fifteenth-century text that relies heavily on LY and that is analogous to the B 554 glosses in several respects is the Middle

---

[55] B. Smalley, 'John Wyclif's *Postilla super totam bibliam*', *BLR* 4 (1953)', 186–205.

[56] For a description, see R. Hanna, *A Descriptive Catalogue of the Western Medieval Manuscripts of St. John's College, Oxford* (Oxford, 2002), no. 171, pp. 235–7.

[57] B. Smalley, 'Wyclif's *Postilla* on the Old Testament and his *Principium*', in *Oxford Studies Presented to Daniel Callus* (Oxford, 1964), 253–96 at 254–5.

English biblical summary preserved uniquely in Trinity College, Oxford MS 93, which according to Elizabeth Solopova makes use of WB EV and LV.[58] In its Psalms part, this work is too brief to have served as a standalone source for B 554. It shares nevertheless some Lyran glosses with B 554 and exhibits in these some interesting variants from B 554, including some amplifications of materials found there that I record in my explanatory notes. Sometimes the TCO 93 commentator stays closer to LY stylistically than the B 554 translator. For example, in the title gloss of Psalm 29 (*Exaltabo te Domine*), B 554 observes that 'Gostli, þis salm mai be expowned of ech cristen man, þat knowiþ bi Goddis reuelacioun eþer resonable euydence þat God haþ forȝoue a greuouse synne to him'. TCO 93 translates LY more closely than this by means of cognates: 'Morali mey þis psalme be oonderstanden of ich feythful man, which by reuelacion of God or probable coniuecture [*probabili coniectura*] knowleches his syn forgifen of God' (f. 41ʳ). A broader parallel between the two works is B 554 and TCO 93's shared use of GO alongside LY as a source. Despite Lyra's pre-eminent exegetical authority, GO remained a highly convenient way for late medieval students of Scripture to access indirectly the insights of harder-to-get commentaries, such as the works of Cassiodorus. TCO 93 uses GO much more extensively than B 554 does, and differently. The TCO 93 commentator explains his method at the close of his summary of the Psalms: whereas Lyra prioritizes the literal sense, he writes, GO—'þe comyn glose', as in B 554—provides additional useful exegeses of the text. Therefore, he goes on, when Lyra's exegesis 'diuerses [diverges] noght or litel' from GO, the commentator says that he prefers to cite GO. When, however, he requires 'moral vnderstanding', the commentator says that he provides this from Lyra (f. 68ʳ). The TCO 93 commentator's method, it would seem, is the reverse of that of the B 554 compiler, who prefers Lyra on the literal over the moral sense and cites GO only when he needs an additional moral or spiritual reading.

Regarding his Augustinian material, the B 554 compiler could have accessed much but not all of that indirectly too, by way of Peter Lombard's twelfth-century *Commentarium in Psalmos*. Lombard uses Augustine's *Enarrationes* heavily. Lombard's work survives in many medieval copies and was very influential in late medieval

[58] Described by Solopova, *Manuscripts of the Wycliffite Bible*, in her catalogue of Oxford WB copies, no. 62, pp. 274–7.

INTRODUCTION

England.[59] It was, for example, the primary Latin source for Richard Rolle's *English Psalter* commentary (*c.*1349) and, as Anne Hudson has shown, was used by the Wycliffites again to check Rolle's work when they revised his commentary more than once during the early years of the fifteenth century, the same period when B 554 was probably being planned, written, and used.[60] There is a high degree of overlap (about two-thirds) between B 554's use of AU and Peter Lombard's citations from the *Enarrationes*, as I record in my Latin Sources and Explanatory Notes. The overlap is not entire, however, nor is Augustine's Latin phrasing in Lombard's commentary (that is, the version of Lombard printed by Migne[61]) always congruent with B 554's Augustinian translations, since Lombard sometimes conflates Augustine's phrasing, in the process of concatenating their insights, with that of other authorities he is extracting and assembling.

It seems likely, given the thematic cohesion of many of the B 554 glosses into subgroups such as those listed in my Index of Key Subjects, that the manuscript's compiler, or someone working for him, culled and organized the materials translated in this glossed book of Psalms from primary rather than secondary sources, perhaps keying them to a list of verses, including psalm titles, to which he wanted to give special expository attention.[62] Interestingly, Hudson discusses in her study of the York manuscript of *GG* 'a list . . . in the same hand of the main text and after a gap of only four lines', of seventeen topics that appears at the end of the sequence of commentaries on the Sunday gospels. These are sometimes used to identify passages within the commentaries that take up the topics, which involve a range of matters also addressed in many of the B 554 glosses, related for example to morality (e.g. *De confessione*), theology (e.g. *De sacramento altaris*), and ecclesiology (e.g. *De officiis prelatorum*).[63] This list, and such other Wycliffite ephemera as a

[59] See M. L. Colish, *Peter Lombard*, 2 vols. (Leiden, 1994), i. 155–88.
[60] *Two Revisions of Richard Rolle's English Psalter Commentary*, ed. A. Hudson, 3 vols., EETS os 340, 341, and 343 (2012–14), i, pp. xxxiv–xxxv.
[61] I am aware of course of the problems with using modern editions, and especially Migne, in studying medieval texts. On Migne's Lombard edition and study of RV1, see *Two Revisions*, ed. Hudson, i, p. xxxv. Regarding study of *GG*, see Hudson, *Doctors in English*, 101–5.
[62] Dove, 160–1 suggests that the Wycliffites sought to produce a complete glossed Bible, but it is not clear that they did. Not even B 554 comes close to being a 'complete' glossed psalter, however such a book might be imagined.
[63] See Hudson, *Doctors in English*, pp. xcvi–cxvi for discussion of the topics; 60–84 for edited extracts.

surviving binding strip from a WB EV that lists biblical references under such headings as 'idolatry' and 'swearing', suggest a concordantial approach to Scripture that is directly related to a glossarial impulse: that is, an analytical method of applying the Bible to the moral life that may have informed the assembly of the glosses copied in B 554.[64] This method is both reflected in and further facilitated by the strategic selection and coordination of materials from a larger exegetical corpus. Among a surviving inventory of the Lollard John Purvey's possessions are *liber vocatus Lira super epistolas Pauli* ('a book entitled *Lyra upon the Pauline Epistles'*), *Augustinus in forello* ('a softbound volume by Augustine'), and *1 paunflot Augustinus super Spalterinium* ('a pamphlet, *Augustine upon the Psalter'*), this last item possibly an anthology of extracts from the *Enarrationes*.[65] This type of softbound anthology would have been an ideal way of managing extracts from a large exegetical work as they were being assembled for translation, coordination, and copying in a volume like B 554.

Another promising area of further investigation for influences on the motives and processes, both academic and practical, behind the assembly of B 554 is the work of a relatively obscure Franciscan disciple of Lyra, William Norton (fl. 1403; *Nortonus*, sometimes called *Northonus* or *Mortonus*). Norton was based in Coventry but may have studied in Oxford. He wrote extensive and extremely handy Latin *tabulae* and *quaestiones* to Lyra's entire *Postilla*, intended to help scholars manage the exegetical bulk. This work won Norton praise among his contemporaries for being 'erudite in philosophy and theology'.[66] Norton's manuscripts survive mainly in Oxford libraries: three of them are in Bodley (MSS Bodley 42, Laud Misc. 156, and Rawlinson G.40, pt. C, this last incomplete) and one each is in the college collections of Exeter (MS 16), Lincoln (MS lat. 69), and Merton (MS 12). Two additional manuscripts are in the Cambridge University Library (MS Ff.4.38) and Eton College Library (MS 108, pt. 2). A sample of Norton's tables and the colophon to this part of his text in the Eton manuscript appears as Pl. 1 in the second volume of this edition. Following a standard Scholastic practice, Norton alphabetized his tables and questions, entitling them a *Repertorium* or

---

[64] On this binding strip, see Kuczynski, 'Extracts from a Revised Version', 230–2.

[65] See M. Jurkowski, 'New Light on John Purvey', *English Historical Review*, 110 (1995), 1180–90.

[66] Tanner, *Bibliotheca Britannico-Hibernica* (London, 1748), 550.

'inventory' of Lyra.[67] In Merton MS 12, for example, a collection of aids to biblical study that can be dated to the fifteenth century and has an early Oxford provenance, Norton's tables and questions keep company with Petrus Aureoli, OFM on the literal sense of Scripture (one of Wyclif's favourite sources in his *postilla*), an inventory of scriptural vocabulary, pseudo-Augustine on the Psalms (a treatise now attributed to Alcuin), and an anonymous treatise, *Expositio Litteralis Psalterii* (ff. 265$^v$–283$^v$), a text that may have been influenced by Lyra.[68] Norton's work, and other Franciscan works like it, could have contributed to the conception and assembly of B 554's glosses, if they were available to the presumably Wycliffite compiler of the manuscript.[69]

One final note concerning the B 554 compiler's use of LY is in order. In WB GP, its author observes that 'Lire cam late [recently] to me'.[70] Hargreaves and Dove following him argue that the WB translators used Lyra's work extensively in revising EV to LV. Hargreaves provides several examples of what he understands to be Lyra-influenced translations in the Psalms specifically; Dove adds further examples from other biblical books, implying sensibly at one point, however, that Lyra's influence might have been variable across the WB project, the translators making their version under the influence of Lyra 'as and when they could'—that is, as parts of the *Postilla*, rather than the entire thing, became available for their

---

[67] Norton's tables contain entries not only on Lyra's exegetical subjects, keyed to Scripture by chapter, but also entries that index Lyra's comments about Jerome's work as a translator of Scripture, his different versions of the Psalter, and the merits of Greek, Latin, and Hebrew as languages for the dissemination of divine truth. His questions sometimes take up matters related to materials in the B 554 glosses, such as the stories of David's pursuit by Saul and whether David's playing for Saul when he was beset by a demon proves the exorcising power of music ('Vtrum demones virtute melodie prout expelli a corporibus obsessis. *1 Regum 16'.*)

[68] See R. M. Thomson, *A Descriptive Catalogue of the Medieval Manuscripts of Merton College, Oxford* (Cambridge, 2009), 12–13. On the pseudo-Augustine text, see J. Black, 'Psalm Uses in Carolingian Prayerbooks: Alcuin and the Preface to *De psalmorum usu*', *Medieval Studies*, 64 (2002)', 1–60. He provides a new edition of the text *De Psalmodiae Bono*, previously available only at PL 101: 465–68.

[69] On possible connections between Franciscan books and WB, see A. Hudson, 'Five Problems in Wycliffite Texts and a Suggestion', *MA* 80 (2011)', 301–24. M. Deanesly, *The Lollard Bible and Other Medieval Biblical Versions* (repr. Cambridge, 1966), 176 n. 1 mentions Norton's 'alphabetical table of Lyra's glosses'. On Norton's manuscripts, see R. Sharpe, *A Handlist of the Latin Writers of Great Britain and Ireland before 1540* (Turnhout, 2001), 795, no. 2133.

[70] *EAEB*, 73/2555.

use.[71] A few of Hargreaves's examples are taken up in my explanatory notes.

Nearly 400 variant translations of psalm verses appear throughout the B 554 glosses, however. The glosses compare the WB LV text of Psalms sixty-two times to Jerome's Hebrew version, forty-six times to the original Hebrew, 118 times to the original Hebrew and Jerome's Hebrew version cited together and in agreement, and twenty-six times to the original Hebrew and Jerome's Hebrew version when these versions disagree. Additionally, five B 554 glosses compare the WB LV text with LXX. This is a nearly complete plundering of Lyra on the Psalms for philological information that could be used to adjust the Vulgate and a Middle English translation made from it. By my rough count, the B 554 compiler misses only about 140 cases of comparison by Lyra of the Gallicanum with either the original Hebrew, Jerome's Hebrew version, or both, and all but about twenty-five of these concern Lyra's long discussions of variant psalm *tituli*. Of the approximately twenty-five, about a third concern Lyra's extended analyses of different verb tenses and number between the Gallican and the original Hebrew and Jerome's Hebrew version, information that may have been less interesting to the B 554 compiler than differences in vocabulary between the various versions of the Psalms. In short, the Latin extracts for the glosses in B 554 that are textual-critical in nature would have been culled as a subgroup from Lyra *in toto* on the Psalms, perhaps at a stage in the LV translation process early enough to allow for their use in some of the revising (Hargreaves's view) or more likely later than that—then to be combined with other matter from both LY and AU as glosses for a scholarly audience of clerics. Such an audience would find their clarification of LV's sense, on this or that verse, especially helpful within a homiletic context.

For the question should be asked, Hargreaves's view notwithstanding, why extensive philological material of this type, if it was available to the Wycliffite translators as they were preparing LV, did not influence in a more widespread way the shape and character of the Psalms text they produced? Although it is possible that a revised WB LV psalter that is more congruent with Jerome's Hebrew version than with the Gallicanum may one day come to light, it is probable, I suspect, that B 554 is a radically idiosyncratic book: a one-off attempt, by a compiler whose interests involved but also

---

[71] Dove, 152–72.

extended well beyond fine points of biblical philology, to produce a
textually more accurate version of the Psalms for his personal use.

It should be observed that a text of the WB LV Psalms adjusted in
the light of the philological marginal glosses in B 554 might have
proved less rather than more transparent in its meaning than the LV
Psalms themselves. It would have been in this or that verse closer, in
theory, to the *Hebraica veritas* but perhaps less legible and pastorally
useful overall than LV: except in the sense of strictness of accuracy, a
step backwards as it were in the Wycliffite translation project. To be
sure, some of the adjustments could clarify the text and render it
more literal and historical: for example, if at Ps. 82: 8 the reading
'aliens' ('strangers') were adjusted by way of the Hebrew reading
(given at gloss 684), 'Filisteis' ('Philistines'). The same Hebraic
alternative is given for LV 'aliens' two other times in B 554 as
well, at 59: 452 and 86: 716, suggesting the compiler's interest in a
more literal and historical reading of such verses.

In other cases, however, the figurative language of the Gallicanum
could become more ambiguous if corrected against the original
Hebrew and Jerome's Hebrew version. To take only one example:
at Ps. 57: 8–9, the Psalmist says the following concerning those who
work wickedness and incur as a result the wrath of God:

[8] Thei shulen come to nouȝt, as watir rennynge awei; he bente his bouwe
til þei ben maad sijk. [9] As wex þat fletiþ awei, þei schulen be takun awei;
fier felde aboue; and þei sien not þe sunne.

The B 554 gloss (424) notes concerning v. 9:

As wexe þat fletiþ: in Ebreu þus, as a long clooþ maad rotun þei shulen be
doon awei; in Ieroms translacioun þus, as a worm maad rotun passe þei forþ.

Changing the figure of flowing wax to the true Hebrew one of rotten
clothing in the Middle English translation would be straightforward
enough. Adjusting the text according to Jerome's Hebrew version,
however, or trying to reconcile that with the original Hebrew before
making an adjustment, could produce in the vernacular a whole new
order of ambiguity. Rashi observes, for example, that rabbinic scholars
interpret the Hebrew text at this point to refer variously to a 'slug'
(Jerome's 'worm'), 'molars', or 'a flood of water'.[72] The Hebrew and
Jerome's Hebrew readings provided throughout the B 554 glosses open

[72] Gruber, 410–11.

at times a window on the bewildering varieties of the significance of the
divine word when it is considered across three languages: from Hebrew
through Greek and into Latin. This variety might well be multiplied
rather than resolved while moving the text into the Middle English
vernacular by way of the Hebrew original and Jerome's Hebrew
version, despite the best intentions of a translator attempting to
respect and to restore, using LY, the 'Hebrew truth' of the Psalms.

In reading the B 554 glosses, one often feels a sense of belatedness
concerning how much very complicated textual and interpretative
matter about the Psalms is coming into the hands of the glossator
after it might have proved helpful. For whom, one wonders, and for
what purposes was such information, as it is recorded in the margins
of B 554, intended? How was it regarded by its compiler and how
might it, in practical circumstances, have been used?

## VI. WHO USED B 554?

Just as the identity of B 554's compiler and the manuscript's process
of assembly is obscure, so too is the identity of its original owner (I
have been assuming the compiler himself) and the nature of its
subsequent medieval readership. The book clearly originated in an
academic milieu, where matters concerning variant textual readings
of the Psalter and their relevance to the historical, christological, and
moral significances of the Psalms were considered inherently
important and even pressing. The style of the Middle English
glosses, it should be said, is clear but not easy. It can be colloquial.
But it can also recall the verbal strictures of WB EV, where respect
for the Latin syntax of the translators' sources led to many problems
with readability. This is especially evident in B 554's Augustinian
glosses, when in some cases the translator tries to preserve
in Middle English the rhetoric of Augustine's originals, their
intricate parallel structures, rather than concentrating on conveying
Augustine's basic sense. Whoever translated B 554 glosses, whether
their compiler himself or someone deputized to do the work, he felt
a more-or-less praiseworthy obligation to follow his sources faithfully. This was of the highest importance in translating LY, since
Lyra's Latin renderings of the Hebrew originals of the Psalms
represent the glossator's only reliable mode of access to that ancient
source.

One of the ironies of B 554 is that, despite the manuscript's many references to the original 'Ebreu' and its appeal, by way of its glosses, to the insights of 'þe eld doctours of Ebreis' (2: cue/7), the 'Hebrew' text that actually appears in the book's margins is at two levels removed from the Hebrew Psalms themselves: the B 554 glossator got his Hebrew through Lyra's Latin translation of it and then, in turn, rendered that Latin version of the Hebrew into Middle English. While there is much Hebrew learning in B 554, some of it comes across as hopelessly cryptic and is mingled in the margins of B 554 with other materials, whose relationship with this Hebrew lore can take a scholar's ingenuity to discern. The information would have been useful primarily to someone who was also highly competent with the Latin sources behind the Middle English glosses and who could check their wider contexts in LY.

For example, almost all the psalms begin with *tituli* or titles, sometimes called by scholars 'inscriptions' or 'super-inscriptions' because they appear in ancient manuscripts, as they do in B 554, at the head of each psalm.[73] The Wycliffites followed Jerome in regarding the titles themselves as part of the divinely inspired text of the Psalms.[74] WB LV titles to the Psalms derive primarily (but not exclusively) from those in Jerome's Hebrew version. As Richard W. Pfaff points out, the LXX titles that are translated into Latin in the Gallicanum are especially problematic, since 'the Septuagintal translators . . . occasionally made rather wild stabs at Greek equivalents' for Hebrew words—most famously, perhaps, by mis-representing the common phrase in the Hebrew titles 'to the choirmaster' as 'eis to telos' ('in the end'), a phrase that became in the Gallicanum persistently 'in finem'.[75] Only at Psalms 9, 37, 38, 72, 81, 87, 130, and 137 do the Wycliffite translators provide the Gallicanum titles, although in these cases the B 554 compiler makes sure to compare them to those in Jerome's Hebrew—for instance, at 37: title/254 and at 38: title/260. Special care is taken in LV and in B 554's copy of it to avoid assigning a title to a psalm that

---

[73] See R. W. Pfaff, 'The *Tituli*' in M. Gibson, T. A. Heslop, and R. W. Pfaff (eds.), *The Eadwine Psalter: Text, Image, and Monastic Culture in Twelfth-Century Canterbury* (London, 1992), 88–93.

[74] See Jerome, 'Tractatus De Psalmo V', in *Tractatus sive Homiliae in Psalmos, in Marci evangelium, aliaque varia argumenta*, ed. G. Morin (Maredsous, 1897), 10.

[75] Pfaff, 'The *Tituli*', 88.

does not have one at all in Jerome's Hebrew version, even when one occurs in the Gallicanum (e.g. at Psalms 2 and 42).

Furthermore, Lyra spends a great deal of time in his *Postilla*, at the beginning of his exegesis of each psalm, discriminating between the Hebrew titles and Jerome's Hebrew versions of these to arrive at a definitive understanding of their texts. Much of this effort at discrimination also turns up in B 554, in the glosses to psalm titles mainly and even within the rubricated texts of the title glosses themselves occasionally—for example, in the opening rubrics to Psalms 54–9. For Jerome, Lyra, and the Wycliffites, the basic sense of the Psalms is related to their titles.

These titles describe variously the authorship, subject matter, and historical occasions of individual psalms and sometimes their poetic characteristics, musical settings, and liturgical functions. They provided for the Wycliffite translators an interpretative infrastructure that keeps the sense of the Psalter 'literal'—grounded in the established textual tradition of the Hebrew Psalms. In Hebrew, the titles frequently contain words that are equivocal or entirely obscure in meaning, about which rabbinical scholars and Lyra himself following them debate murkily. To complicate matters further, when the compiler assembled these titles and title glosses in B 554, he deliberately gave them a tropological dimension: he moves from the end of Lyra's commentaries on each psalm a summary moral gloss with which he routinely concludes, and runs this instead concurrently with the historical or christological title glosses at the beginning of each psalm in B 554. For this reason, Dove, not inappropriately, calls these long opening glosses 'mini-prologues' to the B 554 Psalms.[76] They predispose readers of the manuscript to interpret the psalm at hand and shorter verse-by-verse glosses that follow in certain ways, although it is also worth noting that they do not unduly constrain the compiler's selection of individual glosses, which can cover in this or that psalm either a major or a number of minor but related themes.

For instance, B 554, following Jerome's Hebrew version, gives the title of one of the major messianic psalms, Psalm 44 (*Eructauit cor meum*), as follows: '*þe title of xliiij salm. To þe ouercomere for þe lilies, þe moost loued song of lernyng of þe sones of Chore*'. The Sons of Korah, like Asaph and Moses, are extra-Davidic psalmists. (The Wycliffites agreed with Jerome rather than Augustine that David did not compose all the

----

[76] Dove, 156.

psalms. Some of the B 554 glosses discuss the key role that the
Levites—'dekenes'—played in singing if not actually composing
many of the psalms.) At the title gloss, 44: title/312, B 554 acknowledges by way of LY the congruence of the title in Jerome's Hebrew
version with that in the original Hebrew. B 554 mentions the Sons of
Korah several times, following LY in each case, in the titles to Psalms
41, 43, 44, 45, 46, 47, 83, 84, 86, and 87, and, most conspicuously, in
the title gloss to Psalm 86, where the glossator likens them to David in
knowing 'bi þe spirit of profesie' the mysteries of Christ and Holy
Church (86: title/712). What the phrase '*for þe lilies*' means in the title
to Psalm 44, however, is a complicated puzzle. Hebrew *sosannim*, Lyra
reports following some of his Hebrew sources, signifies not flowers but
the melody to which this psalm should be sung. Rashi proposes a
different interpretation, one that Lyra acknowledges but rejects. He
identifies 'the lilies' as a figure for Torah scholars, who are beautiful in
their understanding of the divine word and by that understanding
cause good deeds to blossom.[77]

The B 554 glossator ignores the controversy altogether, abbreviating
the gloss in LY in order to concentrate his reader's attentions on the
christological dimension of the psalm: 'þus it is in Ieroms translacioun
and þe Ebreu acordiþ. þis salm is seid of Crist and of hooli chirche,
modir and virgyn, for Poul in þe firste capitulo to Ebreis [Paul's epistle
to the Hebrews] aleggiþ þis salm seid of Crist to þe lettre' (f. 22ᵛ). This
particular christological title gloss, atypically for B 554, is not
immediately followed by a 'gostli' coda. The moral reading of the
psalm has to wait until the glossator's comment on v. 7, again following
LY, and his interpretation of God as an ideal kind who reigns in truth
and righteousness, a model for those earthly kings who unlike tyrants
'sekiþ þe comyn good of soietis' (44: 7/319). The type of learning I
have been reporting here—the exegetical disagreements that inform it
and its extended moral applications—would, I assume, seem esoteric
to the lay reader. Because it figures prominently in the B 554 glosses,
they are likely to have been assembled and intended for a learned rather
than a 'lewed' audience.

Some of the B 554 glosses address complicated theological
problems that likewise would be of interest primarily to academics.
For example, during his commentary on Psalm 15 (*Conserua me
Domine*), the glossator translates a postil from Lyra concerning

[77] Gruber, 349. Lyra interestingly accepts Rashi's gloss of the phrase on the title for Psalm
59 (Masoretic 60), which also reads '*for þe lilies*', and B 554 follows him (59: title / 445).

whether Christ's body began to decompose in the tomb before his resurrection (15: 10/84). On Psalm 109 (*Dixit Dominus Domino meo*), he translates another Scholastic remark by Lyra, on the coeternal nature of God the Father and God the Son (109: 3/970). Lyra's observations concerning the relationship between Christ's divinity ('godhed') and humanity ('manheed') accompany verses in five psalms across B 554: 18: 6/105, 21: 1/122, 21: 2/123, 40: 2/279, 98: 5/824, and 109: 3/970. The presence of such glosses is not in itself sufficient to prove that whoever compiled and used B 554 was a professional theologian. Whoever the compiler was, however, he clearly had an interest in some of the problems posed by the theology of Christ's dual nature and in the various ways in which the prophetic poetry of the Psalms addresses those problems.

The anonymous compiler's ability to coordinate different types of learned information, for example points of philology and moral theology, is likewise a mark of clerical influence on the design and use of B 554. One of the Psalter's most compelling poetic images occurs at the start of Ps. 41: 2–3. Here the Psalmist compares the soul's longing for God to the thirst of a deer for running water: 'As an hert desiriþ to þe wellis of watris; so þou, God, my soule desiriþ to þee. Mi soule þirstide to God strong quyk [Vulg. *Deum fortem viventem*].'[78] The B 554 glossator elaborates the first verse morally, by way of Augustine, and the second philologically, by way of Lyra, in the process correcting a persistent textual error:

As an hert sleeþ a serpent, and þirstiþ more, and renneþ scharpliere [more quickly] to þe welle, so sle þou þe serpent of wickidnesse, and þou shalt desire more þe welle of treuþe; as hertis swymmynge helpen hemsilf togidere, so bere we togidere oure birþuns, oon of an oþere. *Austyn here.*

Strong [*fortem*]: þus it is in Ebreu and in Ieroms translacioun, þou3 oure bookis han welle [*fontem*], bi errour of writeris eþer of vnwise amenderis. *Lire here.*

The lore in the Augustinian gloss derives from popular bestiary tradition.[79] That in the Lyran gloss is academic. Rather than

---

[78] For a discussion of the philological point concerning the relative textual merits of 'fortem' and 'fontem', an ambiguity that goes back to some of the earliest Psalms manuscripts, see Dove (2007), 182–3. See also Hargreaves, 'The Latin Text of Purvey's Psalter', *MA* 24 (1955), 73–90 at 87–9.

[79] See 'Natura cerui' in *An Old English Miscellany containing a Bestiary*, ed. R. Morris (London, 1872), 10–12. Augustine also alludes to Paul's epistle to the Gal. 6: 2: 'Bear ye one another's burdens: and so you shall fulfill the law of Christ.'

conflicting, however, the two glosses complement each other, implying that the labours of getting the sense of the Bible right and applying it to the moral life are congruent. A similar juxtaposition occurs in two glosses to Ps. 90: 5–6, /769–70, 'þou schalt not drede of ny3tis drede. Of an arowe fleynge in þe dai, of a gobelyn goynge in derknessis; of asailyng and a myddai fend':

Greuouse persecucioun – makyng siyk men in feiþ afeerd, þat knowen not 3it þat þei ben cristen men, to dispise present þingis and for to hope heuenli þingis to comynge – is a gobelyn goynge in derknessis, and takiþ hem. But he þat woot þat he is a cristen man, for to hope heuenli goodis not temporal goodis and 3yueþ stide for [welcome] greuouse persecucioun, falliþ as in þe dai. *Austyn here.*

In Ebreu it is, of deber goinge in derknessis; and of quoteb wastynge in myddai. Rabi Salomon seiþ þat 'deber' and 'quoteb' ben names of fendis. *Lire here.*

Augustine's figurative reading relates the psalm to a common Wycliffite concern at the start of the fifteenth century and a steady theme across the B 554 glosses: the need to endure persecution in a Christian spirit, even (as implied by three of the B 554 glosses) to the point of martyrdom. Lyra's literal reading involves the presentation of transliterated words from the Hebrew and derives ultimately from Rashi's interest in demonological lore.[80] Both readings present themselves as necessary. Their complementarity in B 554 suggests a coordinating intelligence at home with fine points of textual criticism and exegesis who is also pastoral-minded: perhaps a priest with university training.

In their attention to the importance of preaching and the role of 'techeris' in Holy Church, and specifically the need to distinguish between good teachers and bad ones, the B 554 glosses move into what might be called proto-polemical territory. Some of the glosses display, for example, an interest in preaching as an office undertaken in direct imitation of Christ and the apostles. For example, in Psalm 47 (*Magnus Dominus*), a gloss reports by way of LY how in Jerusalem Christ taught, performed many miracles, and died (47: title/336). Later in the same psalm, another attacks by way of AU false preachers, who 'prechen bi tunge' but 'blasfemen bi liyf' (47: 10/344), using language that recalls such polemical Wycliffite texts as

---

[80] On the presence of transliterated Hebrew words in B 554, see the Appendix.

the *Lanterne of Liʒt*.[81] Another Augustinian gloss in a later psalm connects psalmody and preaching (80: 3/666), implying thereby that prayer, study, and good behaviour inspired by reading a psalter, such as one designed like B 554, might be considered an evangelical practice. The interest in distinguishing between sound and erroneous teaching throughout many of the glosses—this is surely one element behind the compiler's desire to recover something of the 'Hebrew truth' of the Psalms—implies that B 554's compiler may have considered himself a virtuous teacher, or at least someone who had learned from one. The standard for true teaching and preaching, he points out by way of some of his glosses, was set by Christ and his apostles: we can read about this in the gospels. Unsound instruction is 'weiward' because it departs from or even actively opposes this standard, as did the teaching of the scribes and Pharisees when they rejected Jesus. The B 554 glosses follow LY in singling out these men and others like them for moral reproof, since they failed in their duty to edify—'to bilde þe puple in feiþ and vertues' (117: 22/ 1009).

In its assembly and early fifteenth-century use, B 554 might well have been a very personal book. Among the surviving copies of WB, it is a volume whose modest and portable nature belies finally its wide range of textual and exegetical authority.[82] The replete nature of its marginal commentary, so much fitted into such a short space, is surely a reflection of its compiler's enthusiasm. For scholars of the first English Bible, B 554 may recall an intriguing reference to a specific Wycliffite psalter, now lost, in the *Testimony of William Thorpe*, a purportedly autobiographical account of the Lollard priest's informal examination, during his detainment at Saltwood Castle in 1407, by Archbishop Arundel. The reference occurs after Thorpe, who has been appealing to Scripture in his defence, argues to Arundel that he would consider himself blameworthy or even deserving of damnation were he to neglect, simply because of any person's disapproval, to preach the word of God.[83] Arundel in turn comments to three of his assistants that 'þe bisinesse and þe maner'—that is, the persistent practice and method—of Thorpe and other Lollards is 'to pike out scharpe sentencis of holy writ and of doctours for to maynteyne

---

[81] See the explanatory notes for the range of parallels with *LL* in B 554.

[82] Daniel Sawyer reports to me that B 554 weighs approximately 850 grams, making it 'not only a relatively small book but also, in its current binding, seemingly quite light among small books' (personal correspondence).

[83] *Two Wycliffite Texts*, ed. A. Hudson, EETS os 301 (1993), 50/880–3.

INTRODUCTION

[defend] her sect and her loore aȝens þe ordenaunce of holi chirche'.[84]
He then angrily assures Thorpe that he will not return a psalter that he
had confiscated from him at Canterbury, since if he did so the Lollard
'woldist gadere out þereof [collect from it] and recorde scharpe verses
aȝens vs'.[85]

The exact nature of Thorpe's psalter is unclear. It could well have
been, however, a book designed like B 554. In his 1548 catalogue of
British writers, John Bale, based probably on this episode in the
*Testimony*, attributes to Thorpe *Glossulas quoque paruas in psalterium
et alia* ('Short glosses on the psalms and other [books of Scripture]'),
implying that Thorpe's psalter was glossed.[86] In her 1927 study,
*Writings Ascribed to Richard Rolle and Materials for his Biography*,
Hope Emily Allen suggests, less elliptically, that Thorpe may have
assisted in producing the fifteenth-century Wycliffite revisions to
Richard Rolle's *English Psalter* commentary (although there is no
evidence for his involvement) and that the Psalter to which Arundel
refers may therefore have been in fact a revised copy of Rolle's text.[87]
Others since have sensibly queried Allen's suggestion, observing that
many of the surviving copies of revised Rolle are in large folio format
and that the Wycliffite revisions themselves are often so expansive
that citing from them efficiently and accurately, especially in
circumstances of tense oral argument, would be cumbersome. A
volume like B 554 would have enabled rather than hindered
Thorpe's defence, however, replete as its margins are with organized
and accessible textual, homiletic, and polemical information.

A more distant but nevertheless plausible scenario would be
mendicant ownership or use of B 554. This might seem unlikely,
but the emphasis throughout the manuscript's glosses on preaching
and, to a more limited extent, confession are noteworthy in the light
of the friars' office. (Certainly one of the book's addenda, the list of
sins of thought, word, deed, and omission from Richard Rolle's *Form
of Living* would be of practical use to a confessor.) The B 554
compiler's interest in the apostolic tradition of evangelization, his
double concern with learning and with cautions against it (Christ and
his followers were not 'graduates of schools'), and the handful of
glosses that valorize poverty would all be congenial to mendicant as

[84] Ibid. 51/888 and 51/889–90.
[85] Ibid. 51/891–3.
[86] J. Bale, *Illustrium Maioris Britanniae Scriptorum* (Ipswich, 1548), f. 183ʳ.
[87] H. E. Allen, *Writings Ascribed to Richard Rolle and Materials for His Biography*
(Oxford, 1927), 190–1.

well as to Wycliffite use. The unprepossessing, portable, and worn nature of B 554 suggest that it did not spend its time on a shelf, but that it was put to use: learned and perhaps taught from. If, as I have suggested above, a particular mendicant may have contributed indirectly, by way of his Latin tables and questions on Lyra, to the material contents of B 554's glosses, it seems at least plausible that a mendicant compiler might have assembled or that a mendicant reader might have found useful a volume such as this one.

## VII. EDITORIAL METHOD

The Psalms, Canticles, and glosses in B 554 present special problems for an editor. I have handled these problems as follows:

The Psalms are numbered differently in the Vulgate and in the original Hebrew, because of different practices in both these texts regarding the divisions of particular psalms, as follows:

| Vulgate | Hebrew |
|---|---|
| 1–8 | 1–8 (these eight psalms having the same numbers in both versions) |
| 9 | 9–10 |
| 10–112 | 11–113 |
| 113 | 114–15 |
| 114–15 | 116 |
| 116–45 | 117–46 |
| 146–7 | 147 |
| 148–50 | 148–50 (these three psalms having the same numbers in both versions) |

I follow the Vulgate numbering of the Psalms in this edition, giving psalm numbers and verses in square brackets. Regarding the establishment of the text: I have collated the texts of the Psalms and Canticles in this edition against FM, since my focus here is the B 554 glosses rather than the primary biblical text, and because the Psalms and Canticles in WB LV are remarkably stable across their multiple manuscript witnesses.[88] B 554's text of Psalms and Canticles deviates little from FM, usually only by the omission of single words and

---

[88] See A. Hudson, 'The Origin and Textual Tradition of the Wycliffite Bible', in E. Solopova (ed.), *The Wycliffite Bible: Origin, History, and Interpretation* (Leiden, 2017), 133–61 at 133–6.

letters or because of scribal error due to eye-skip or dittography. I
have restored the correct readings in these cases, enclosing my
emendations in square brackets. In two instances, longer passages
are dropped in B 554, perhaps following interruptions in the scribe's
stint. These too I restore from FM, altering the orthography slightly
to bring it into line with that of the B 554 scribe. In transcribing, I
expand all abbreviations and suspensions and the ampersand silently.
The scribe's punctuation in the Psalms and Canticles is normally
careful (see my description above). On occasion, I have had,
however, to adjust it and I do so silently.

Concerning the glosses: the texts of the title glosses to the Psalms
are generally stable across manuscript copies of WB LV and are often
but not always copied in the margins of their manuscripts, where
they are sometimes labelled 'A glos'. Several manuscripts contain
these title glosses only through Psalm 72; this subgroup of glosses is
likely to have circulated separately from the rest of the glossarial
commentary. Other psalm glosses, however, migrate between the
margins and text areas of some copies of WB: for instance, whereas
K and V share variant readings in some of their non-title psalm
glosses, in K many of these glosses are rather awkwardly positioned
within the text and underlined, while in V they are kept in the
margins. This permeability of the text–margin divide is especially
apparent in M, where normally marginal glosses are intertextual and
normally intertextual glosses are marginal. In accounting for such
material in my apparatus, I try to be clear about each scribe's
manuscript-specific practice.

On the large pages of their four-volume folio edition, Forshall and
Madden reproduce most of the glosses they print to WB LV in the
margins and, where these are very extensive, have their printers wrap
the glosses around the biblical text in the bottom margins of their
pages. This arrangement has the advantage of imitating typographi-
cally the layout of a glossed medieval Bible. Its disadvantage lay in
the minuscule size of the typeface used to fit the glosses into the
margins of FM, which means not only reinforcing an awareness of
their subsidiary authority to WB but also dissuading all but
persistent readers from consulting them at any length. In this
edition, the Psalms and their glosses appear on facing pages. This
parity and the equivalent size of psalm and gloss typefaces invests
both sets of text with the complementary authority they evidently
had for the B 554 compiler, who viewed the glosses not simply as a

collection of by-the-way comments upon the Psalms and Canticles, but as a planned and consistent amplification of their textual and other meanings.

I mentioned in my discussion of the B 554 scribe's practice that he sometimes writes several glosses in a long sequence within crowded margins, linking them as a group by a single tie-mark to the first lemma of the sequence in the biblical text. In this edition, I have sometimes broken those sequences of glosses up, distributing them individually and more spaciously across the psalms or canticles they explain, using more gloss numbers than tie-marks in B 554 to link the separate glosses to their lemmata—hence the 1,363 glosses in this edition. In the Psalms, I position these additional gloss numbers as carefully as the B 554 scribe places his tie-marks: that is, as near as possible to the lemmata being explained by the glosses. This volume is not an effort to present a typographic facsimile of B 554's design. Rather, it seeks to translate that design into a different but analogous visual medium for conveying the B 554 compiler's purpose: to make a large body of exegetical material on a densely significant text of Scripture conveniently accessible in a reasonably compact space.

Given the difficulties of representing a manuscript Psalter with extensive marginal glosses in typographic form, the following layout is used in this edition: normally, the text of the Psalms appears on the verso and the Psalm Glosses on the facing recto. Sometimes it has been necessary, in order to keep particular psalm verses and their glosses proximate, to run the Psalms text onto the lower part of the facing recto; or the Psalm Glosses onto the lower part of the facing verso. In these cases, verses and glosses are separated from each other with a line.

Manuscript folio numbers appear in the margins throughout both the Psalms and the glosses in this edition. In two cases in the edited text, I have had to situate glosses at a slight remove from their folio placement in B 554. I mark these cases with an asterisk in the edited text and explain original manuscript placement in my explanatory notes.

Underlining that appears throughout the Psalms duplicates underlining used by the scribe in the manuscript to indicate alternate translations of words and phrases or words and phrases added to make the grammatical sense of the Middle English translation from the Latin Vulgate clearer. This kind of scribal

underlining is common in WB LV copies. It is usually done in B
554 lightly in black, but occasionally in red. Underlining that
appears throughout the glosses duplicates underlining used by the
scribe in the manuscript to identify lemmata. It is always done
lightly in red. Italics in the Psalms and glosses identifies words
written out in red in B 554—for example, psalm titles and authorial
attributions in the glosses.

The following symbols indicate throughout the edition my
adjustments to the Psalms and glosses in B 554 and provide
information about scribal practice in B 554 that could otherwise be
collected only by a direct encounter with the manuscript:

[ ]    enclose my editorial adjustments to the text
` ´    enclose text inserted by the scribe or another corrector either
       above or below the line of writing or in the margins

In the Psalms, superscript letters ($^a$, $^b$, $^c$, etc.) refer to the
apparatus to the B 554 psalms; in the glosses, superscript Roman
numerals ($^i$, $^{ii}$, $^{iii}$, etc.) refer to the apparatus to the B 554 glosses.

Forms of reference. Individual psalms are cited by psalm and
verse number: for example, 50: 3. When verses and their glosses are
cited together, I use a slash mark to separate them: for example, 50:
3/368. It is not always necessary, however, to provide both verse and
gloss number. In the Index of Scriptural References and Allusions
and the Index of Key Subjects, where coverage is limited to the
glosses, I provide only psalm and gloss number: for example, 50: 368.
In the Index of Proper Names and the Glossary, where coverage
includes the Psalms themselves and their glosses, psalm and verse
numbers are given in regular typeface (e.g. 50: 3) and gloss numbers
in bold (e.g. **368**). Throughout the Latin Sources and Explanatory
Notes, gloss numbers are in bold. When in this edition the word
'cue' or 'title' is not followed by a slash and gloss number—for
example, 17: title—the word refers to the rubricated psalm cue or
title in the Psalms text of B 554.

When I cite Jerome's Gallican and Hebrew versions, outside the
context of quotations from Lyra, I do so from the Stuttgart edition of
the Vulgate listed above, where these two versions appear on facing
pages. When I cite LXX, I do so from the Stuttgart edition of that
text as well, transliterating the Greek but without diacritics. Hebrew
cited in the notes I likewise transliterate without diacritics, following
Gruber.

When quoting the Bible in English, I use the Douay–Rheims translation, except of course where it is appropriate to quote from the Wycliffite translations, including the Psalms and Canticles text from WB LV that appear in B 554.

# BIBLIOGRAPHY

UNPRINTED PRIMARY SOURCES: MANUSCRIPTS

**Used in editing:**

British Library, MS Addit. 10046 (Pss. LV)
British Library, MS Addit. 10047 (Pss. 1–72 LV)
British Library, MS Addit. 31044 (Pss.–Ecclus. LV)
British Library, MS Cotton Claudius E.ii (ONT LV)
British Library, MS Harley 2249 (OT LV)
British Library, MS Royal 1.C.viii (ONT LV)
Cambridge, Corpus Christi College, Parker MS 147 (ONT LV)
Cambridge, Emmanuel College, MS 21 (ONT LV)
Cambridge, St John's College, MS E.14 (Pss.–Ecclus. LV)
Cambridge, University Library, MS Dd.1.27, vol. 1 (OT LV)
Cambridge, University Library, MS Mm.2.15, ONT LV
Dublin, Trinity College MS 70 (Pss. LV)
London, Lambeth Palace Library MS 25 (Gen.–Deut. EV)
London, Lambeth Palace Library MS 1033 (OT LV)
Oxford, Bodleian Library, MS Bodl. 277 (ONT LV)
Oxford, Bodleian Library, MS Bodl. 296 (Gen.–Pss. LV)
Oxford, Bodleian Library, MS Bodley 554 (Pss.–Canticles LV; base of this edition)
Oxford, Bodleian Library MS Fairfax 2 (ONT LV)
Oxford, Bodleian Library MS Laud misc. 182 (ONT extracts LV)
Oxford, Christ Church, MS 145 (ONT EV)
Oxford, Lincoln College, MS Lat. 119 (ONT LV)
Oxford, New College MS 66 (Gen.–Pss. LV)
Oxford, Queen's College MS 388 (ONT LV)

**Also used:**

Cambridge, Gonville and Caius College, MS 354/581 (*Rosarium*)
Chicago, Newberry Library, MS 13 (Augustine, *Enarrationes in Psalmos*, Pss. 1–50)
London, Lambeth Palace Library, MS Register of Archbishop Arundel, 1396–1414
Oxford, Bodleian Library, MS Bodley 788 (Wycliffite sermons)
Oxford, Bodleian Library, MS Bodley 959 (WB EV OT)
Oxford, Bodleian Library MS e museo 5 (Lyra's *Postilla super Psalterium*)
Oxford, Corpus Christi College MS 20 (WB LV OT)

Oxford, New College, MS 320 (WB LV Psalter)
Oxford, St John's College, MS 171 (Wyclif's *Postilla super totam Bibliam*, Job–Lamentations)
Oxford, Trinity College, MS 93 (ME summary of the Bible)
Philadelphia, University of Pennsylvania, Van Pelt Library MS 77 (Seneca's tragedies with commentary attributed to Nicholas Trevet)

PRINTED PRIMARY SOURCES

*The Anglo-Norman Gospel Harmony: A Translation of the 'Estoire de l'Evangile' (Dublin, Christ Church C6.1.1, Liber niger)*, trans. B. A. Pitts (Tempe, Arzx., 2014).
Augustine of Hippo, *De Doctrina Christiana*, PL 34: 15–122 (Paris, 1887).
———— *De Libero Arbitrio*, PL 32: 1221–1310 (Paris, 1841).
———— *Enarrationes in Psalmos*, PL 36 and 37 (Paris, 1865).
———— *Epistolae*, PL 33 (Paris, 1865).
———— *In Iohannis Evangelium*, PL 35: 1379–1976 (Paris, 1864).
———— *On Free Choice of the Will*, trans. A. S. Benjamin and L. H. Hackstaff (Indianapolis, Ind., 1964).
Bale, J., *Illustrium Maioris Britanniae Scriptorum* (Ipswich, 1548).
Bernard of Clairvaux, *Sermones in Cantica Canticorum*, ed. H. Hurter (Innsbruck, 1888).
———— *On the Song of Songs, II*, trans. Kilian Walsh (London, 1976).
*Biblia Sacra Vulgata*, 5th edn., ed. R. Weber, rev. R. Gryson (Stuttgart, 2007).
*Bibliorum Sacrorum cum Glossa Ordinaria*, 6 vols. (Venice, 1603).
*Bibliorum Sacrorum Latinae Versiones Antiquae*, ed. P. Sabatier, 2 vols. (Reims, 1743).
Cassiodorus, *Expositio in Psalterium*, PL 70: 9–1056 (Paris, 1865).
*Decretum Gratiani*, PL 187: 65– (Paris, 1861).
*The Earliest Advocates of the English Bible: The Texts of the Medieval Debate*, ed. M. Dove (Exeter, 2010).
*The Earliest Complete English Prose Psalter*, ed. K. D. Bülbring, EETS os 97 (1891; repr. 1987).
*The English Works of Wyclif hitherto Unprinted*, ed. F. D. Matthew, EETS os 74 (1880).
*English Wycliffite Sermons*, ed. A. Hudson and P. Gradon, 5 vols. (Oxford, 1983–96).
Eusebius, *Commentaria in Psalmos*, PG 23: 65–1396 (Paris, 1857).
———— *The Ecclesiastical History of Eusebius Pamphilus, Bishop of Cesarea, in Palestine, in Ten Books*, trans. C. F. Crusé (Philadelphia, 1833).
———— *Historia Ecclesiastica*, PG 20: 9–906 (Paris, 1857).

Gregory the Great, *Moralia in Iob*, PL 75: 509–1162 (Paris, 1862) and PL 76: 9–782 (Paris, 1857).

Hilton, Walter, *An Exposition of* Qui Habitat *and* Bonum Est *in English*, ed. Björn Wallner (Lund, 1954).

*The Holy Bible . . . Made from the Latin Vulgate by John Wycliffe and his Followers*, ed. J. Forshall and F. Madden, 4 vols. (Oxford, 1850).

*The Holy Bible, Translated from the Latin Vulgate* (Baltimore, 1914).

Isidore of Seville, *Etymologiarum sive Originum*, ed. W. M. Lindsay (Oxford, 1911).

———— The *Etymologies* of Isidore of Seville, trans. Stephen A. Barney, W. J. Lewis, J. A. Beach, and O. Berghof (Cambridge, 2006).

Jerome, *Liber de Nominibus Hebraicis*, PL 23: 815–904 (Paris, 1845).

———— *Tractatus sive Homiliae in Psalmos, in Marci evangelium, aliaque varia argumenta*, ed. G. Morin (Maredsous, 1897).

John of Damascus, *Expositio Fidei Orthodoxae*, PG 94: 790–1228 (Paris, 1864).

John of Trevisa, *On the Properties of Things: John Trevisa's Translation of Bartholomaeus Anglicus* De Proprietatibus Rerum*: A Critical Text*, ed. M. C. Seymour and G. M. Liegey, 3 vols. (Oxford, 1975–88).

*The Lanterne of Liȝt, Edited from MS. Harley 2324*, ed. L. M. Swinburn, EETS os 151 (1917).

*The Middle English Translation of the Rosarium Theologie: A selection, ed. from Cbr., Gonville and Caius Coll. MS 354/581*, ed. Christina Von Nolcken (Heidelberg, 1979).

*The Middle English Weye of Paradys and the Middle French Voie de Paradis: A Parallel-Text Edition*, ed. F. N. M. Diekstra (Leiden, 1991).

Nicholas of Lyra, *Postilla litteralis in Vetus et Novum Testamentum*, 3 vols. (Venice 1488).

*An Old English Miscellany containing a Bestiary*, ed. R. Morris, EETS os 49 (London, 1872).

Peter Lombard, *Commentarium in Psalmos*, PL 191: 55–1296 (Paris, 1854).

Pseudo-Jerome, *Breviarium in Psalmos*, PL 26: 821–1328 (1845).

*Rashi's Commentary on the Psalms*, ed. and trans. Mayer I. Gruber (Philadelphia, 2007).

*Remonstrance against Romish Corruptions in the Church*, ed. J. Forshall (London, 1851).

Rolle, R., *In Psalterium Dauidicum enarratio* (Cologne, 1536).

———— *The Psalter . . . with a Translation and Exposition by Richard Rolle of Hampole*, ed. H. R. Bramley (Oxford, 1884).

*Septuaginta*, ed. A. Rahlfs and R. Hanhart (Stuttgart, 2007).

Socrates Scholasticus, *Historia Ecclesiastica*, PG 67: 30–842 (Paris, 1864).

*Speculum Christiani: A Middle English Religious Treatise of the 14th Century*, ed. G. Holmstedt, EETS os 182 (London, 1933).

Thomas Aquinas, *Summa Theologica*, 2nd rev. edn., trans. Fathers of the English Dominican Province, 5 vols. (rept. Westminster, 1981).

———— *Truth, Translated from the Definitive Leonine Text*, trans. R. W. Mulligan, J. V. McGlynn, and R. W. Schmidt (Chicago, 1952).

*Les 'tituli Psalmorum' des manuscrits latins*, ed. P. Salmon, Collectanea Biblica Latina, 12 (Rome, 1959).

*Two Revisions of Richard Rolle's English Psalter Commentary*, ed. A. Hudson, 3 vols., EETS OS 340, 341, and 343 (2012–14).

*Two Wycliffite Texts*, ed. A. Hudson, EETS OS 301 (1993).

Wyclif, John, *Dialogus sive Speculum Ecclesie Militantis*, ed. A. W. Pollard (Oxford, 1886).


SECONDARY SOURCES


Allen, H. E., *Writings Ascribed to Richard Rolle* (Oxford, 1927).

Black, J., 'Psalm Uses in Carolingian Prayerbooks: Alcuin and the Preface to *De psalmorum usu*', *Medieval Studies*, 64 (2002), 1–60.

Brown, W. P. (ed.), *The Oxford Handbook of the Psalms* (Oxford, 2014).

Cain, A. *The Letters of Jerome: Asceticism, Biblical Exegesis, and the Construction of Christian Authority in Late Antiquity* (Oxford, 2009).

Colish, M. L., *Peter Lombard*, 2 vols. (Leiden, 1994).

Craun, E. D., *Ethics and Power in Medieval English Reformist Writing* (Cambridge, 2010).

Dahan, G. (ed.), *Nicolas de Lyre, franciscain du XIV^e siècle, exégète et théologien* (Turnhout, 2011).

Deanesly, M., *The Lollard Bible and Other Medieval Biblical Versions* (repr. Cambridge, 1966).

Dove, M., *The First English Bible: The Text and Contexts of the Wycliffite Versions* (Cambridge, 2007).

Driscoll, M. S., 'The Seven Penitential Psalms: Their Designation and Usages from the Middle Ages Onwards', *Ecclesia Orans*, 17 (2000), 153–201.

Dulles, A., *Models of the Church*, 2nd edn. (New York, 1991).

Emden, A. B., *A Biographical Register of the University of Oxford to A.D. 1500*, 3 vols. (Oxford, 1957–9).

Foster, J., *Alumni Oxonienses: The Members of the University of Oxford, 1500–1714*, 4 vols. (London, 1891–2).

Ghosh, K., *The Wycliffite Heresy: Authority and the Interpretation of Texts* (Cambridge, 2002).

Gillespie, V., 'Mystic's Foot: Rolle and Affectivity', in M. Glasscoe (ed.), *The Medieval Mystical Tradition in England*, ii (Exeter, 1982), 199–230.

Gosselin, E. A., 'A Listing of the Printed Editions of Nicholaus de Lyra', *Traditio*, 26 (1970), 399–426.

Hailperin, H., *Rashi and the Christian Scholars* (Pittsburgh, Pa., 1963).

Hanna, R., *A Descriptive Catalogue of the Western Medieval Manuscripts of St. John's College, Oxford* (Oxford, 2002).

———— *The English Manuscripts of Richard Rolle: A Descriptive Catalogue* (Exeter, 2010).

Hargreaves, H., 'The Latin Text of Purvey's Psalter', *MA* 24 (1955), 73–90.

Holsinger, B., 'The Vision of Music in a Lollard Florilegium: *Cantus* in the Middle English *Rosarium Theologie* (Cambridge, Gonville and Caius College MS 354/581)', *Plainsong and Medieval Music*, 8 (1999), 95–106.

Hudson, A., *Doctors in English: A Study of the Wycliffite Gospel Commentaries* (Liverpool, 2015).

———— 'Five Problems in Wycliffite Texts and a Suggestion', *MA* 80 (2011), 301–24.

———— 'Observations on the "Wycliffite Orthography"', in Simon Horobin and Aditi Nafde (eds.), *Pursuing Middle English Manuscripts and their Texts: Essays in Honour of Ralph Hanna* (Turnhout, 2017), 77–98.

———— 'The Origin and Textual Tradition of the Wycliffite Bible', in E. Solopova (ed.), *The Wycliffite Bible: Origin, History, and Interpretation* (Leiden, 2017), 133–61.

———— *The Premature Reformation: Wycliffite Texts and Lollard History* (Oxford, 1988).

Hunt, R. W., 'Manuscripts Containing the Indexing Symbols of Robert Grosseteste', *BLR* 4 (1953), 241–54.

Jurkowski, M., 'New Light on John Purvey', *English Historical Review*, 110 (1995), 1180–90.

Kelly, J. N. D., *Jerome: His Life, Writings, and Controversies* (New York, 1975).

Klepper, D. C., *The Insight of Unbelievers: Nicholas of Lyra and Christian Reading of Jewish Text in the Later Middle Ages* (Philadelphia, 2007).

Kuczynski, M. P., 'Extracts from a Revised Version of Richard Rolle's *English Psalter* in MS Longleat 3, an Early Version Wycliffite Bible', *MA* 85 (2016), 217–35.

———— 'A Fragment of Richard Rolle's *Form of Living* in MS Bodley 554', *BLR* 15 (1994), 20–32.

———— 'Glossing and Glosses', in E. Solopova (ed.), *The Wycliffite Bible: Origin, History, and Interpretation* (Leiden, 2017), 346–67.

———— 'An Important Lollard Psalter in Trinity College, Dublin', *Studies: An Irish Quarterly Review*, 99 (2010), 181–7.

———— 'An Unpublished Lollard Psalms *Catena* in Huntington Library MS 501', *Journal of the Early Book Society*, 13 (2010), 95–138.

Lindberg, C., 'The Manuscripts and Versions of the Wycliffite Bible—A Preliminary Survey', *Studia Neophilologica*, 42 (1970), 333–47.

Linde, C., *How to Correct the Sacra Scriptura?* (Oxford, 2012).

McIntosh, A., Samuels, M. L., and Benskin, M., *Linguistic Atlas of Late Medieval English*, rev. M. Benskin and M. Lang (Aberdeen, 1986), http://www.lel.ed.ac.uk/ihd/elalme/elalme.html.

McKinnon, J. W., 'Musical Instruments in Medieval Psalm Commentaries and Psalters', *Journal of the American Musicology Society*, 21 (1968), 3–20.

Madan, F., et al., *A Summary Catalogue of Western Manuscripts in the Bodleian Library at Oxford* (Oxford, 1895–1953).

Metlen, M., 'Letter of St. Jerome to the Gothic Clergymen Sunnia and Friþila concerning Places in their Copy of the Psalter which Had Been Corrupted from the Septuagint', *JEGP* 36 (1937), 515–42.

O'Neill, P. P., 'Old English *brondegūr*', *English Studies*, 62 (1981), 2–4.

Ong, W. J., *Orality and Literacy: The Technologizing of the Word*, 2nd edn. (London, 2002).

Pease, A. S., 'Notes on St. Jerome's Tractates on the Psalms', *JBL* 26 (1907), 107–31.

Peikola, M., 'The Wycliffite Bible and Central Midland Standard: Assessing the Manuscript Evidence', *Nordic Journal of English Studies*, 2 (2003), 29–51.

Pfaff, R. W., 'The *Tituli*', in M. Gibson, T. A. Heslop, and R. W. Pfaff (eds.), *The Eadwine Psalter: Text, Image, and Monastic Culture in Twelfth-Century Canterbury* (London, 1992), 88–93.

Rebenich, S., 'Jerome: The "Vir Trilinguis" and the "Hebraica Veritas"', *Vigiliae Christianae*, 47 (1993), 50–77.

Royster, J. F., 'A Middle English Treatise on the Ten Commandments', *Studies in Philology*, 6 (1910), 31–2.

Saenger, P., *A Catalogue of the Pre-1500 Western Manuscript Books at the Newberry Library* (Chicago, 1989).

Sharpe, R., *A Handlist of the Latin Writers of Great Britain and Ireland before 1540* (Turnhout, 2001).

Shereshevsky, E., 'Rashi's and Christian Interpretations', *Jewish Quarterly Review*, NS 61 (1970), 76–86.

Simon-Vandenbergen, A., 'No Doubt and Related Expressions', in M. Hannay and G. J. Steen (eds.), *Structural-Functional Studies in English Grammar: In Honour of Lachlan Mackenzie* (Amsterdam, 2007), 9–34.

Smalley, B., 'John Wyclif's *Postilla super totam bibliam*', *BLR* 4 (1953), 186–205.

———— *The Study of the Bible in the Middle Ages*, 3rd edn. rev. (Oxford, 1983).

———— 'Wyclif's *Postilla* on the Old Testament and his *Principium*', in *Oxford Studies Presented to Daniel Callus* (Oxford, 1964), 253–96.

Solopova, E., 'Manuscript Evidence for the Patronage, Ownership, and Use of the Wycliffite Bible', in E. Poleg and L. Light (eds.), *Form and Function in the Late Medieval Bible* (Leiden, 2013), 333–49.

————— *Manuscripts of the Wycliffite Bible in the Bodleian and Oxford College Libraries* (Liverpool, 2016).

————— 'A Previously Unidentified Extract about the Litany in a Wycliffite Psalter (Oxford, Bodleian Library, MS. Bodl. 554)', *BLR* 24 (2011), 217–23.

————— (ed.), *The Wycliffite Bible: Origin, History, and Interpretation* (Leiden, 2017).

Sutherland, A., *English Psalms in the Middle Ages, 1300–1450* (Oxford, 2015).

————— 'The Wycliffite Psalms', in Solopova (ed.), *The Wycliffite Bible: Origin, History, and Interpretation* (Leiden, 2017), 183–201.

Tanner, T., *Bibliotheca Britannico-Hibernica* (London, 1748).

Thomson, R. M., *A Descriptive Catalogue of the Medieval Manuscripts of Merton College, Oxford* (Cambridge, 2009).

Thomson, S. H., 'Grosseteste's Concordantial Signs', *Medievalia et Humanistica*, 9 (1955), 39–53.

Von Nolcken, C., 'Another Kind of Saint: A Lollard Reception of John Wyclif', in A. Hudson and M. Wilks (eds.), *From Ockham to Wyclif: Oxford Scholarship in the Later Fourteenth Century: Conference Papers* (Oxford, 1987), 429–43.

Wadding, Luke, *Annales Minorum seu Trium Ordinum a S. Francisco institutorum* (Rome, 1734).

Wakelin, D., *Designing English: Early English Literature on the Page* (Oxford, 2018).

# THE GLOSSED PSALTER

f. 1ʳ                     [PSALM 1]

*Beatus vir*

[þe firste salm.]ᵃ

[1] Blessid is þe man, þat ȝede not in þe councel of wickid men;¹ and stood not in þe weie of synneris, and sat not in þe chaier of pestilence.² [2] But his wille is in þe lawe of þe Lord; and he shal biþenke in þe lawe of hym dai and nyȝt. [3] And he shal be as a tre, which is plauntid bisidis þe rennyngis of watris;³ which tre shal ȝyue his fruyt in his tyme. And his leef shal not falle doun; and alle þingis whiche euere he shal do shulen haue prosperite. [4] Not so wickid men, not so; but <u>þei ben</u> as dust, which þe wynd castiþ awei fro þe face of [þe]ᵇ erþe. [5] Therfor wickid men risen not aȝen in doom;⁴ neiþer synneris in þe councelᶜ ⁵ of iust men. [6] For þe Lord knowiþ þe weie of iust men; and þe weie of wickid men shal perische.⁶

[PSALM 2]

*Quare fremuerunt gentes*⁷

[þe secounde salm.]ᵃ

[1] Whi gnastiden wiþ teeþ heþene men; and puplis þouȝten ueyn þingis? [2] þe kyngis of erþe stoden togidere; and pryncis camen togidere aȝenes þe Lord, and aȝenes his crist? [3] Breke we þe boondis of hem; and caste we awei þe ȝok of hem fro us. [4] He þat dwelliþ in heuenes shal scorne hem; and þe Lord shal bymowe hem. [5] Thanne he shal speke to hem in his ire; and he shal d[i]sturbleᵇ hem in his strong veniaunce. [6] Forsoþe I am maad⁸ of hym a kyng, on Sion his hooli hil; prechyng his comaundement. [7] The Lord seide to me, þou art my sone; I haue gendrid þee todai. [8] Axe þou of me, and I shal ȝyue to þee heþene men þyn eritage; and þi possessioun þe termes of erþe. [9] Thou shalt gouerne hem in an iren ȝerde; and þou shalt breke hem as þe vessel of a pottere. [10] And now, ȝe kyngis, vndurstonde; ȝe þat demen þe erþe, be ʽȝesʼᶜ lerud. [11] Serue⁹ ȝe
f. 1ᵛ  þe Lord with drede; and make ȝe ful ioie to hym | wiþ tremblyng.¹⁰
[12] Take ȝe¹¹ lore; lest þe Lord be wrooþ sumtyme, and lest ȝe

---

**Ps. 1**    ᵃ þe firste salm] *om.*    ᵇ þe] *om.*    ᶜ councel] *tie-mark nearly rubbed away*
**Ps. 2**    ᵃ þe secounde salm] *om.*; *no title in Hebrew or Hebr.*    ᵇ disturble] dusturble    ᶜ ȝes]
*added by a 2nd hand above the line of writing*

[PSALM 1 GLOSSES] f. 1ʳ

1. þat is, in þe false doctryn of vnfeiþful men. *Lire here.*

2. In Ebreu it is, <u>of scorneris</u>, for þe techeris of weiward doctryn ben scorneris verili, for þei techen errours vndur þe licnesse of treuþe. *Lire here.*

3. For þe floodis of Goddis grace and glorie comen to feiþful techeris of hooli chirche. *Lire here.*

4.ⁱ þat is, to her saluacioun, but more to dampnacioun of bodi and soule. *Lire here.*

5. In Ebreu and in Ieroms translacioun it is, <u>in þe congregacioun of iust men</u>. þis congregacioun is in heuenli blisse. *Lire here.*

6. God knowiþ bi knowing of appreuyng þe weie of iust men and bi knowyng of repreuyng þe weie of wickid men. *Lire here.*

[PSALM 2 GLOSSES]

7.ⁱ þe secounde salm, 'þat'ⁱⁱ haþ no title in Ebreu and in Ieroms translacioun, was maad of Dauiþ, as þe postlis witness[en]ⁱⁱⁱ in þe four[þ]eⁱᵛ chapitre of Dedis. And þis salm is vndurstonden of Crist God and man to þe lettre, as Poul in þe firste chapitre to Ebreus and þe postlis in þe fourþe chapitre of Dedis witnessen, and þe eld doctours of Ebreis. Forwhi preuyng bi gostli vndurstonding is not worþ, but oneli of literal vndurstondynge, as Austin seiþ in his pistle aȝenes Vyncent Donatist. *Lire here.*

8. In Ebreu and in Ieroms translacioun, <u>I haue ordeyned my kyng. I shal telle þe comaundement of God</u>. *Lire here.*

9. Bi deuocioun and reisyng of herte into God;

10. <u>wiþ tremblyng</u>: þis is addid lest þe ful ioiyng be turned into dissolucioun eþer wantounnesse, as þei doon þat syngen wantounli in þe chirche, whanne al þe song of þe chirche is ordeyned to stire deuocioun of cristen men. *Lire here.*

11. þat is, make ȝe ȝou soget mekeli to þe techyng of Crist. In f. 1ᵛ Ieroms translacioun it is, <u>worschipe ȝe pureli</u>, þat is God, wiþout feynyng, bi onour du to God oneli. Ebreis seien, <u>kisse ȝe þe sone</u>, þat is make ȝe du omage to Crist, of whos euerlastynge generacioun it is tretid in þis salm. þe firste Hebreu word here signefieþ boþe 'take ȝe',

**Ps. 1 glosses** ⁱ *this gloss also in margin of* V *(damaged)*
**Ps. 2 glosses** ⁱ *this gloss also in* CC_J_E.14*(damaged)*ikKLPQSUV*X* ⁱⁱ þat] *added by the scribe above the line of writing* ⁱⁱⁱ witnessen] witnessis ⁱᵛ fourþe] foure

perischen fro iust weie. [13] Whanne his `ire'^d brenneþ out in short tyme; blessid ben alle þei, þat tristen^12 in hym.

## [PSALM 3]

*Domine quid multiplicati sunt*
þe title of þe iij salm.

[1] *þe salm of Dauiþ, whanne he fledde fro þe face of Absolon his sone.*^a

[2] Lord, whi ben þei multiplied þat disturblen me? manye men risen aʒenes me. [3] Manye men seien of my soule, Noon heelþe is to hym in his God. [4] But þou, [Lord],^b art myn uptakere; my glorie, and enhaunsyng myn heed. [5] Wiþ my uois I criede to þe Lord; and he herde me fro his^c hooli hil. [6] I slepte, and was quenchid,^13 `and'^d I roos up; for þe Lord resseyuede me. [7] I shal not drede þousyndis of puple cumpassynge me; Lord rise þou up; my God, make þou me saaf. [8] For þou hast smyte alle men beynge aduersaries to me wiþout cause; þou hast al tobroke þe teeþ^14 of synneris. [9] Helþe is of þe Lord; and þi blessyng, <u>Lord</u>, is on þi pu[p]le.^e

## [PSALM 4]

*Cum inuocarem*^a ^15
þe title of þe iiij salm.^16

[1] [*To victorie in orguns; þe salm of Dauiþ.*]^b

[2] Whanne I inwardli clepide,^17 God of my riʒtfulness^c herde me; in tribulacioun þou hast alargid to me. Haue þou merci on me; and here þou my preier. [3] Sones of men, hou longe^18 ben ʒe of heuy herte? whi louen ʒe vanite, and seken a leesing? [4] And wite ʒe, þat þe Lord haþ maad meruelouse his hooli^19 man; þe Lord shal here me, whanne I shal crie to hym. [5] Be ʒe wrooþ, and nyle ʒe do synne; and for <u>þo þingis</u> whiche ʒe seien in ʒoure hertis and in ʒoure beddis, be ʒe

---

^d ire] *added by a 2nd hand in margin*
**Ps. 3**    ^a þe . . . sone] *this title also in* CC_J_E.14(*damaged*)ikKLPQSUVX    ^b Lord] *om.*
^c his] his his, *second* his *canc.*    ^d and] *added by the scribe above the line of writing*    ^e puple] pule

**Ps. 4**    ^a Cum inuocarem] *in the bottom margin, a red paraph to begin*    ^b To . . . Dauiþ] *om.,
a ME version of the title from Gall., the base for the titles in B 554; provided here from FM: 740,
variant (m) to the title they print, based on Hebr. and given in B 554 glossarially in the left
margin, underlined in red*    ^c riʒtfulness] *several MSS, including A, read* riʒtwisnesse, *but I do
not emend here**

and 'kisse ȝe', and 'worschipe ȝe'. þe secounde Hebreu word here signefieþ boþe 'lore' and 'clennesse' and 'sone'. *Lire here.*

12. þat is, ben pacient and dispeire not in turment, but abiden tristili rewardyng to-comynge. *Lire here.*

## [PSALM 3 GLOSSES]

13. As sopun up for sorewe. *Lire here*

14. þat is, of Achitofel and oþere bacbityng Dauiþ, þat seiden þat sauynge myȝte not be to Dauiþ, þat dide avoutrie and manquellyng. *Lire here.*

## [PSALM 4 GLOSSES]

15.[i] þe fourþe salm is doyng of þankingis to God bi Dauiþ, for God delyueride him fro Saul cumpassynge hym wiþ his oost þat he myȝte not ascape bi mannis weie, outakun þe meruelouse help of God.

To gostli vndurstonding, bi Saul is vndurstondun þe deuel, bi Dauiþ, a cristen man þat enforsiþ wiþ Goddis help to aȝenstonde þe deuelis assailyngis. And whanne þis man vndurstondiþ bi Goddis reuelacioun eþer inward comfort of soule þat he is herd of God, he dispisiþ þe deuel and þankiþ God. *Lire here.*

16. To victorie in orguns; the salm of Dauiþ: þis is þe title in Ebreu. In Ieroms translacioun þus: To þe ouercomere in salmes; the song of Dauiþ. [*Lire here.*][ii]

17. þat is, preiede God deuoutli. *Lire here.*

18. In Ieroms translacioun þus: Hou longe ȝe noble men louen vanyte shendfuli; and seken euere a leesyng. *Lire here.*

19. In Ieroms translacioun it is, his merciful man. *Lire here.*

20. In Ieroms translacioun þus: speke in hertis on ȝoure beddis; and euere be ȝe stille. *Lire here.*

---

compunct.[20] [6] Sacrifice ȝe þe sacrifice of riȝtfulnesse, and hope ȝe in þe Lord; manye seyn, Who shewide goodis to us? [7] Lord, þe liȝt of þi cheer is markid on us; þou | hast ȝoue gladnesse in myn herte.    f. 2ʳ

---

[8] þei ben multiplied of þe fruyt of whete [and]$^d$ of wyn; and of her oile.[21] [9] In pees in þe same þing; I shal slepe, and take reste. [10] For þou, Lord; hast set me syngulerli in hope.

[PSALM 5]

*Verba mea auribus*

þe title of þe fyueþe salm.

[1] *To þe ouercomere on þe eritagis, þe song of Dauiþ.*[a] [22]

[2] Lord, perseyue þou my wordis wiþ eeris; vndurstonde þou my cry.[23] [3] Mi kyng and my God; ȝyue þou tent to þe uois of my preier. [4] For, Lord, I shal preie to þee; here þou eerli my uois. [5] Eerli I shal stonde nyȝ þee and I shal se; for þou art God not willynge wickidnesse. [6] Neþer an yuel willid man[24] shal dwelle bisidis þee; neiþer vniust men shulen dwelle bifor þyn iȝen. [7] Thou hatist alle þat worchen wickidnesse; þou shalt leese alle þat speken leesyng. The Lord shal holde abhomynable a manquellere[25] and gileful man. [8] But, Lord, in þe multitude of þi merci I shal entre into þyn hous; I shal worshipe to þyn hooli temple in þi drede. [9] Lord, lede þou$^b$ forth me in þi riȝtfulnesse for myn enemyes; dresse þou my weie in þi siȝt. [10] Forwhi treuþe is not in her mouþ; her herte is veyn. [11] Her þrote is an open sepulcre, þei diden gilefuli wiþ her tongis; God, deme[26] þou hem. Falle þei doun fro her þouȝtis, upe þe multitude of her wickidnessis caste þou hem doun; for, Lord, þei han terrid þee to ire. [12] And alle þat hopen in þee be glad; þei shulen make fulli ioie wiþouten ende, and þou shalt dwelle in hem. And alle þat louen þi name shulen haue glorie in þee: [13] For þou shalt blesse a iust man. Lord, þou hast corounned us, as wiþ þe sheeld of thi good wille.

[PSALM 6]

*Domine ne in furore*

þe title of þe vj salm.

[1] *To þe ouercomere in salmes, þe salm of Dauiþ, on þe eiȝtþe.*[a] [27]

f. 2$^v$    [2] Lord, repreue þou not me in þi stronge ueniaunce; neþer chastise þou me in þyn ire. [3] Lord, haue þou merci on me for I am

---

$^d$ and] *om.*
**Ps. 5**    $^a$ þe . . . Dauiþ] *rubricated title extends into right margin, title gloss beneath*    $^b$ þou] þou me, me *canc.*
**Ps. 6**    $^a$ *title in the bottom margin of f. 2$^r$*

21. þis word <u>oile</u> is not in Ebreu neþer in Ieroms translacioun. *Lire* f. 2ʳ *here.*

## [PSALM 5 GLOSSES]

22.ⁱ Dauiþ made þe fifþe salm for prestis and dekenes shulden synge it, to gete Goddis help aʒenes enemyes of Goddis puple and þat God shulde defende his puple.

Bi allegorie, þis salm is þe preier of hooli chirche aʒenes vnfeiþful men asailyng þe lond of cristen men.

Bi moral vndurstondyng, it is þe preier of hooli chirche aʒenes feendis pursuynge cristen men bi her temptaciouns, and sekinge to caste doun cristen men fro þe getyng of euerelastynge eritage. *Lire here.*

23. In Ebreu it is, <u>my þouʒt</u>. *Lire here.*

24. þat is, ydolatrour. *Lire here.*

25. þat is, a shedere out of innocent blood. *Lire here.*

26. In condempnyng hem to peyne and deþ. Wherfor in Ieroms translacioun it is þus: <u>God condempne þou hem</u>. *Lire here.*

## [PSALM 6 GLOSSES] f. 2ᵛ

27.ⁱ Dauiþ made þe sixte salm to axe merci for his offence, bi which he comaundide þe puple to be noumbrid for pride and aʒenes þe lawe in xxx capitulo of Exodi, wiþout monei assigned þere of God.

To gostli vndurstonding, þis salm mai be expowned of ech synnere repentynge verili and bisechynge Goddis merci for his delyueraunce fro synne doon and fro peyne into which he is fallun, and aftir long and deuoute preier, he supposiþ resonabli þat he is herd of God, bi inward comfort ʒouun of God to him. Wherfor it is þe firste salm among seuene salmes of penaunce. *Lire here.*

---

**Ps. 5 glosses**    ⁱ *title gloss beneath rubric in margin; the first historical part of this gloss also in* CikKLOPQSUV*X*
**Ps. 6 glosses**    ⁱ *gloss at the top of f. 2ᵛ, left margin; the first historical part of this gloss also in* AbCikKLPQSUV*X*

sijk; Lord, make þou me hool, for alle my boones ben troblid. [4] And
my soule is troblid greetli; but þou, Lord, hou longe?²⁸ [5] Lord, be
þou conuertid, and delyuere my soule; make þou [me]ᵇ saaf, for þi
merci. [6] For noon is in deeþ²⁹ which is myndful of þee; but in helle
who shal knouleche to þee?³⁰ [7] I trauelide in my weilyng, I shal
waische my bed bi ech ny3t; I shal moiste, [eþer make weet],ᶜ my
bedstre wiþ my teeris. [8] Myn i3e is disturblid of woodnesse;³¹ I wax
eld among alle myn enemyes. [9] Alle 3e þat worchen wickidnesse,
departe fro me; for þe Lord haþ herd þe uois of my wepyng. [10] The
Lord haþ herd my bisech[y]ng;ᵈ þe Lord haþ resseyued my preier.
[11] Alle myn enemyes be ashamed, and be disturblid greetli; be þei
turned togidere, and be þei ashamed ful swiftli.

[PSALM 7]

*Domine Deus meus in te speraui*ᵃ ³²

*þe title of þe vij salm.*

[1] *For þe ignoraunce of Dauid, which he song to þe Lord on þe wordis of
Ethiopien, þe sone of Gemyny.*³³

[2] Mi Lord God, I haue hopid in þee; make þou me saaf fro alle
þat pursuen me, and delyuere þou me. [3] Lest ony tyme he as a lioun
rauysche my soule;³⁴ þe while noon is þat a3enbieþ, neþer þat makiþ
saaf. [4] Mi Lord God, if I dide þis þing;³⁵ if wickidnesse is in myn
hondis:³⁶ [5] If I 3eldide to men 3eldynge to me yuelis, falle I bi
disseruyng uoide fro myn enemyes.³⁷ [6] Myn enemy pursueþ my
soule, and take and defoule my lijf in erþe; and brynge my glorie into
dust. [7] Lord rise þou up in þyn ire; and be þou reisid in þe coostis of
myn enemyes. And, my Lord God, rise þouᵇ in þe comaundement,
f. 3ʳ   which þou hast comaundid;³⁸ [8] and þe synagoge of | puplis shal
cumpasse þee. And for þis go þou a3en an hi3. [9] þe Lord demeþ
puplis. Lord, deme þou me bi my ri3tfulnesse; and bi myn innocence
on me. [10] The wickidnesse of synneris be endid; and þou, God,
sekynge þe hertis and reynes³⁹ shalt dresse a iust man. [11] Mi iust
help is of þe Lord; þat makiþ saaf ri3tful men in herte. [12] The Lord
is a iust iuge, strong and pacient; wher he is wrooþ bi alle daies? [13] If
3e ben not conuertid, he shal florische his swerd;ᶜ ⁴⁰ he haþ bent his
bouwe, and made it redi. [14] And þerinne he haþ maad redi þe

28. þat is, hou longe shalt þou suffre þe sleing of þe puple and my turment? *Lire here.*

29. þat is, aftir deeþ. *Lire here.*

30. As if he seie, Noon bi knoulechyng of preisyng. *Lire here.*

31. þat is, for sorewe of herte. Wherfor in Ebreu and in Ieroms translacioun it is, <u>of bittirnesse</u>. *Lire here.*

## [PSALM 7 GLOSSES]

32.[i] þis `vij´[ii] salm[iii] mai be expowned gostli, þat it be þe preier of ech man set in bodili turment bi vniust persecucioun eþer in goostli turment bi wickid temptacioun of feendis, which man axiþ of God to be delyuerid and allegiþ his innocence and þe malice of pursueris. *Lire here.*

33.[iv] þat is, for þe synne of <u>þe ignoraunce of Dauiþ</u>, bi which he was occasioun of þe deeþ of prestis slayn of Saul and Doech for þe helpyng of Dauiþ which, þat is, for which ignoraunce to be forʒouun, he song þis salm to þe Lord, on <u>þe wordis of þe Ethiopien</u>, þat is, for þe wordis of Saul maad blak in fame and condiciouns. *Lire here.*

34. In departinge it fro þe bodi. *Lire here.*

35. þat is, if Y souʒte þe deþ of Saul;

36.[v] þat is, if I seke to do yuel aftirward. *Lire here.*

37. In Ebreu and in Ieroms translacioun it is þus: <u>and lefte myn enemyes voide</u>, in spoilyng Saul and hise men of her goodis. *Lire here.*

38.[v] To iugis to do riʒtful veniaunce of yuele men. *Lire here.*

39.[v] þat is, þouʒtis and delitingis. *Lire here.*

40.[v, vi] [þat is, make redi to smyte.]

41. þat is, þe instrumentis berynge deeþ. *Lire here.*

f. 3[r]

---

uessels[41] of deþ; he haþ fulli maad his arowis wiþ brennynge þingis. [15] Lo! he conseyuede sorewe; he peynefuli brouʒt forþ vnriʒtful-nesse, and childide wickidnesse. [16] He openyde a lake, and diggide

**Ps. 7 glosses** [i] *no tie-mark at the moral gloss* [ii] vij] *added by the scribe above the line of writing* [iii] salm] salm be, be *canc.* [iv] *this historical gloss also in* bCC_J_E.14*(damaged)* ikKLPQSUV*(nearly rubbed away)*X [v] *in K glosses 36, 38–40 interlinear, combined and underlined:* If wickidnesse þat is wille to do wickidnesse [*also verbatim in margin of* V] is in my hondis God sekinge þe hertis þat is þouʒtis and reynes þat is delitingis [*both of these as one gloss also in margin of* V] he shal floriʒsshe þat is make redi to smyte his swerd. [vi] *a missing marginal gloss; Lyra and Augustine both interpret* gladium suum *as a figure for divine justice.* þat is make redi to smyte, *the reading from* K, *may be the missing gloss*

it out; and he felde into þe diche which he made. [17] His sorewe shal be turned into his heed; and his wickidnesse shal come doun into his necke. [18] I shal knouleche to þe Lord bi his riȝtfulnesse; and I shal synge to þe name of þe hiȝeste Lord.

## [PSALM 8]

*Domine Dominus noster*
*þe title of viij salm.*

[1] *To þe ouercomere, for pressours, þe salm of Dauiþ.*[42]

[2] Lord, þou art oure Lord; þi name is [ful]ᵃ wondurful in al erþe. For þi greet doyng[43] is reisid aboue heuenys. [3] Of þe mouþ of ȝonge children, not spekynge and soukyng mylk, þou madist perfitli heriyng, for þyn enemyes;[44] þat þou distrie þe enemye and auengere. [4] For I shal se þyn heuenes, þe werkis of þi fyngris; þe moone and sterris, whiche þou hast foundid. [5] What is a man,[45] þat þou art myndeful of hym; eþer þe sone of a virgyn, for þou visitist hym? [6] Thou hast maad hym a litil lesse þan | aungelis; þou hast corounned hym wiþ glorie and onour, [7] and hast ordeyned hym aboue þe werkis of þyn hondis. [8] Thou hast maad suget alle þingis vndur hise feet; alle sheep and oxis, ferþermore and þe beestis of þe feeld; [9] þe briddis of þe eir, and þe fischis of þe see; þat passen bi þe paþis of þe see. [10] Lord, þou art oure Lord; þi name is wondurfulᵇ in al erþe.

f. 3ᵛ

## [PSALM 9]

*Confitebor tibi Domine in toto corde meo*
*þe title of þe ix salm.*

[1] *Into*[46] *þe ende, for þe priuytes of þe sone, þe salm of Dauiþ.*

[2] Lord, I shal knouleche[47] to þee in al myn herte;[48] I shal telle alle þi meruels. [3] Thou hiȝest, I shal be glad, and I shal be fulli ioiful in þee; I shal synge to þi name. [4] For þou turnest myn enemye abac; þei shulen be maad feble, and shulen perische fro þi face. [5] For þou hast [maad]ᵃ my doom and my cause; þou, þat demest riȝtfulnesse, hast sete on þe troone. [6] Thou blamedist heþene men, and þe wickid perischide; þou hast do awei þe name of hem into þe world, and into þe world [of world].ᵇ [7] The swerdis of þe enemye failiden into þe

Ps. 8    ᵃ ful] *om.*    ᵇ wondurful] ful wondurful
Ps. 9    ᵃ maad] *om.*    ᵇ of world] *om.*

## [PSALM 8 GLOSSES]

42.[i] þat is, to Crist ouercomere for þe meritis of hise passiouns, bi whiche he hadde ful victorie and coroun of glorie and enhaunsyng aboue alle creaturis, þis salm is maad of Dauiþ to his glorie and onour. And þis salm to þe lettre is vndurstondun of Crist, for in xxj chapitre of Matheu, Crist aleggiþ summe of þis salm seid of himsilf and so doiþ Poul, in ij chapitre to Ebreis; and þe eld doctours of Ebreis vndurstondun þis salm seid of Messias. *Lire here.*

43. þat is, Crist himsilf. *Lire here.*

44. To be ouercomun. *Lire here.*

45.[ii] þat is, mankynde in comparisoun of aungels kynde, as if he seie, A litil þing. *Lire here.*

## [PSALM 9 GLOSSES]                                    f. 3[v]

46.[i] þis salm was maad of Dauiþ for þe priuytes of þe sone, þat is, for þe dom of discrecioun, bi which feiþful men ben departid in meritis fro vnfeiþful men; and for þe doom of þe laste departing of good men and yuele into þe ende, þat is, dressinge us to holde þe ende of þe worlde and of blisse. *Lire here.*

47. Bi kno[u]leching[ii] of preisyng;

48. in al myn herte, þat is, vndurstonding and loue. *Lire here.*

49.[iii] þat is, þe lawe of þe gospel, which he tauȝte studiousli bi word and dede. *Lire here.*

---

ende; and þou hast distriede þe citees of hem. The mynde of hem perischide wiþ sown; [8] and þe Lord dwelliþ wiþouten ende. He made redi his troone in doom; [9] and he shal deme þe world in equyte, he shal deme puplis in riȝtfulnesse. [10] And þe Lord is maad refuyt, eþer help, to a pore man; an helpere in couenable tymes, in tribulacioun. [11] And þei þat knowen þi name, haue hope in þee; for þou, Lord, hast not forsake hem þat seken þee. [12] Synge ȝe to þe Lord, þat dwelliþ in Syon; telle ȝe hise studies[49] among heþene men.

**Ps. 8 glosses**      [i] *next to the title in the right margin; this gloss also in* AbCC_J_E.14*(damaged)*ikKLPQSUV*X*      [ii] *interlinear and underlined in* K, *where the phrase* as if he seie, a litil þing *is om.; complete in* V *(damaged)*
**Ps. 9 glosses**      [i] *this gloss also in* AbCC_J_E.14*(damaged)*ikKLPQSUV*X*; þe priuytes of] *om. in* k      [ii] knouleching] knoleching      [iii] *a variant gloss here interlinear and underlined in* K: telle ȝe hise studies þat is þe gospel

[13] God forȝetiþ not þe cri of pore men; for he haþ mynde,[50] and
f. 4ʳ sekiþ þe blood of hem. [14] Lord, | haue þou merci on me; se þou my
mekenesse[51] of myn enemyes. [15] Which enhaunsist me fro þe ȝatis
of deþ; þat I telle alle þi preisyngis in þe ȝatis of þe douȝtir of Syon.
[16] I shal be fulli ioieful in þyn helþe; heþene men ben faste set in þe
perischyng, which þei maden. In þis snare, whichᶜ þei hidden, þe foot
of hem [is]ᵈ cauȝte. [17] The Lord makynge domes shal be knowun;
þe synnere is takun in þe werkis of hise hondis. [18] Synneris be
turned togidere into helle; alle folkis þat forȝeten God. [19] For þe
forȝetyng of a pore man shal not be into þe ende; þe pacience of pore
men shal not perische into þe ende. [20] Lord, rise þou up, a man be
not comfortid;[52] folkis be demed in þi siȝt. [21] Lord, ordeyne þou a
lawemakere on hem; wite folkis, þat þei ben men. [22] Lord, whi hast
þou go fer awei? þou dispisist in couenable tymes in tribulacioun. [23]
While þe wickid is proud, þe pore man is brent; þei[53] ben taken in þe
councels, bi whiche þei þenken. [24] Forwhi þe synnere is preisid in
þe desiris of h[is]ᵉ soule; and þe wickid is blessid. [25] The synnere
wraþþide þe Lord; up þe multitude of his ire[54] he shal not seke.
[26] Godᶠ is not in his siȝt; hise weies ben defoulid in al tyme. God, þi
domes be takun awei fro his face; he shal be lord of alle hise enemyes.
[27] For he seide in his herte, I shal not be moued, fro generacioun
into generacioun wiþout yuel. [28] Whos mouþ is ful of cursyng, and
of bittirnesse, and of gile; trauel and sorewe is vndur his tunge. [29]
He sittiþ in aspies[55] wiþ ryche men in pryuytees; to sle þe innocent
f. 4ᵛ man. [30] Hise iȝen biholden on a pore man; he settiþ aspies in hid |
place, as a lioun[56] in his denne. He settiþ aspies, for to rauys[c]heᵍ a
pore man; for to rauysche a pore man, while he drawiþ[57] þe pore man.
[31] In his snare he shal make meke þe pore man; he[58] shal bowe
hymsilf, and shal falle doun, whanne he haþ be lord of pore men. [32]
For he seide in his herte, God haþ forȝete; he haþ turned awei his
face, þat he se not into þe ende. [33] Lord God, rise þou up, and þyn
hond be enhaunsid; forȝete þou not pore men. [34] For what þing
terride þe wickid man God to wraþþe? For he seide in his herte, God
shal not seke. [35] Thou seest, for þou biholdist trauel and sorewe; þat
þou take hem[59] into þyn hondis. The pore man is lefte to þee; þou
shalt be an helpere to þe fadirles and modirles. [36] Al[t]oʰ breke þou
þe arme of þe synnere and yuel willid; his synne shal be souȝt,[60] and it

ᶜ which] in which    ᵈ is] *om.*    ᵉ his] *the* er *of* her *erased but not corrected*    ᶠ God] *om. in* I,
*according to* FM, *though not indicated that the divine name here is an interpolation (see* FM ii.
*746)*    ᵍ rauysche] rauyshe    ʰ Alto] Also

50. Of her cry. [*Lire here.*]<sup>iv</sup>

51. þat is, turment doon of tirauntis to me. *Lire here.*     f. 4<sup>r</sup>

52. Bi power of iuge aboue oþere men, forwhi sich power shal be takun awei in þe fynal doom. *Lire here.*

53. þat is, Antecrist and hise sueris. *Lire here.*

54. þat is, of Goddis ire terrid aȝenes him; he shal not seke penaunce, but die in dispeir. *Lire here.*

55. To sle an innocent man in pryuyte is to make an innocent man a gilti man, where it is not vndurstondun liȝtli what owiþ to be coueitid eþer what to be fled. *Austin here.*

56. As a lioun: þe firste persecucioun of hooli chirche was violent, f. 4<sup>v</sup> whanne tirauntis compelliden cristen men, bi forfeture and exilyng and bi deþ, to make sacrifice to idols. þe secounde persecucioun was gileful, bi eretikis and false briþeren. þe þridde persecucioun bi Auntecrist shal be moost perelouse, for it shal be boþe violent and gileful. He shal haue violence in lordschip, gile in myraclis: as a lioun, as to violence; as in his denne, as to gile. *Austyn here.*

57. For he shal be bisy to drawe þo men bi gileful wordis to himsilf, whiche he mai not bowe bi turmentis. *Lire here.*

58. Shal boowe himsilf not wilfuli, but bi Goddis vertu; and shal falle fro þe lordschip; whanne he haþ be lord of pore men, þat is, of cristen men maad soget and spuyled in his tyme. *Lire here.*

59. þat is, Auntecrist and hise sueris; into þyn hondis: of þi riȝtfulnesse. *Lire here.*

60. þat is, his wickidnesse shal be discussid diligentli of þee, wher it be profitable ferþere to be purchyng of chosen men; and it shal not be founden profitable more herto, for þei shulen be purgid sufficientli. And so Antecrist wiþ hise sueris shal be caste doun into þe fier of helle. *Lire here.*

61. þat is, þou Antecrist and þi felowis. *Lire here.*

Eþer folkis, þat is, synneris and vnfeiþful men. *Austyn here.*

---

shal not be founden. [37] The Lord shal regne wiþouten ende, and into þe world of world; folkis,<sup>61</sup> ȝe shulen perische fro þe lond of hym. [38] The Lord haþ herd þe desir of pore men; þyn eere haþ herd þe

<sup>iv</sup> Lire here] *om.*

makynge redi of her hertc. [39] To deme for þe modirles and meke;
þat a man leie [to]ⁱ no more, to magnefie hymsilf on erþe.

[PSALM 10]

*In Domino confido*
*þe title of þe x salm.*

[1] *To þe victorie of Dauid.*

[2] I triste in þe Lord; hou seien ʒe to my soule, Passe þou ouer into
an hil, as a sparewe <u>doiþ</u>? [3] For lo! synneris han bent a bouwe; þei
han maad redi her arowis in an arowe-caas; for to schete in derknesse
riʒtful men in herte. [4] For þei han distried, whom þou [hast maad]ᵃ
perfit; but what dide þe riʒtful man? [5] The Lord is in his hooli
f. 5ʳ   temple; <u>he is</u> Lord, his seete is in heuene. Hise iʒen | biholden on a
pore man; his iʒelidis axen þe sones of men. [6] The Lord axiþ⁶² a iust
man and vnfeiþful man; but he, þat loueþ wickidnesse, hatiþ his
soule. [7] He shal reyne snaris on synful men; fier, brymstoon, and þe
spirit of tempestis ben þe part of þe cuppe of hem. [8] For þe Lord is
riʒtful, and louyde riʒtfulnessis; his cheer siʒ equyte, <u>eþer euennesse</u>.

[PSALM 11]

*Saluum me fac*
*þe title of þe xj salm.*

[1] *To þe victorie on þe eiʒtþe, þe song of Dauiþ.*

[2] Lord, make þou me saaf, for þe hooli failide; for treuþis ben
maad litil fro þe sones of men. [3] Thei spaken ueyn þingis, ech man
to his neiʒbore; <u>þei han</u> gileful lippis, þei spaken in herte [and herte].ᵃ
[4] The Lord distrie alle gileful lippis; and þe grete spekynge tunge.
[5] Whiche seiden, We shulen magnefie oure tunge, our lippis⁶³ ben of
us; who is oure lord? [6] For þe wrecchidnesse of nedi men, and for þe
weilyng of pore men; now I shal rise up, seiþ þe Lord. I shal sette in
helþe; I shal do tristili in hym. [7] The spechis of þe Lord ben chast⁶⁴
spechis; siluer examyned bi fier, preued fro erþe, purgid seuenfold. [8]
Thou, Lord, shalt kepe us; and þou shalt kepe us fro þis generacioun
wiþouten ende. [9] Wickid men goon in cumpas; bi þin hiʒnesse þou
hast multeplied þe sones of men.

---

ⁱ to] *om.*
**Ps. 10**     ᵃ hast maad] madist; *cf.* EV: formedest
**Ps. 11**     ᵃ and herte] *om.*

[PSALM 10 GLOSSES]

62. In Ieroms translacioun it is þus: þe Lord appreueþ a iust man; forsoþe his soule hatiþ a wicked man and louynge wickidnesse. *Lire here.*

[PSALM 11 GLOSSES]

63. þat is, wordis. *Lire here.*
64. Wiþout wem of falsnesse. *Lire here.*

[PSALM 12 GLOSSES]

65. In my puple þat shal come aftir me, in suffringe to be turmentid of Assiriens. *Lire here.*
66. In suffrynge my puple in þe seruage of Egipcians. *Lire here.*
67. Tretynge hou mai Y be delyuerid fro þe caitifte of Babiloyne. *Lire here.*
68. þat is, Antiok. [*Lire here.*]ⁱ

---

[PSALM 12]

*Usquequo Domine*

*þe title of þe twelueþe salm.*

[1] *To þe victorie of Dauiþ.*

[2] Lord, hou long forȝetist þou me⁶⁵ into þe ende? hou longe turnest þou awei þi face fro me?⁶⁶ [3] Hou longe shal I sette councels in my⁶⁷ soule; sorewe in myn herte bi dai? [4] Hou long shal myn enemye⁶⁸ be reisid on me? my Lord God, biholde þou, and here þou me. Liȝtne þou myn iȝen, lest ony time I slepe in deþ; [5] lest ony tyme myn enemy seie, | [I]ᵃ hadde þe maistrie aȝenes hym. Thei þat troblen me shulen haue ioie, if I shal be stirid; [6] forsoþe I hopide in þi merci. Myn herte shal fulli haue ioie in þyn heelþe; I shal synge to þe Lord, þat ȝyueþ goodis to me, and I shal seie salm to þe name of þe hiȝest Lord.

f. 5ᵛ

## [PSALM 13]

*Dixit insipiens*

þe title of xiij salm.

[1] *To þe victorie of Dauiþ.*

The vnwise man[69] seide in his herte, God is not. Thei ben corrupt, and ben maad abhomynable in her studies; noon is þat doiþ good, noon[70] is til to oon. [2] The Lord biheld fro heuene on þe sones of men; þat he se if ony is vndurstondynge, eþer sekinge God. [3] Alle bowiden awei, togidere þei ben maad vnprofitable; noon is þat doiþ good,[71] noon is til to oon.[a 72] The þrote of hem is an open sepulcre, þei diden gilefuli wiþ her tungis; þe venym of snakis is vndur her lippis. Whos mouþ is ful of cursyng and bittirnesse; her feet ben swifte to shede out blood. Sorewe and cursidnesse is in þe weies of hem, and þei knewen not þe weie[b] of pees; þe drede of God is not bifor her iȝen. [4] Wher alle men þat worchen wickidnesse shulen not knowe;[73] þat deuouren my puple, as mete of breed? [5] Thei clepiden not þe Lord; þei trembliden þere for drede, where was no drede. [6] For þe Lord is in a riȝtful generacioun. Thou hast shent þe councel of a pore man; for þe Lord is his hope. [7] Who shal ȝyue [fro][c] Syon helþe to Israel? Whanne þe Lord haþ turned awei þe caitifte of his puple; Iacob shal fulli be ioiful, and Israel shal be glad.

## [PSALM 14]

*Domine quis habitabit*

þe title of þe xiiij salm.

[1] *þe salm of Dauiþ.*

f. 6ʳ          Lord, who shal dwelle in þi tabernacle; eþer who shal res|te in þyn hooli hil? [2] He þat entriþ wiþout wem; and worchiþ riȝtfulnesse. [3] Which spekiþ treuþe in his herte; which dide not gile in his tunge. Neiþer dide yuel to his neiȝbore; and took not shenschip aȝenes his neiȝboris. [4] A wickid man is brouȝt to nouȝt in his siȝt; but he glorifieþ[74] hem þat dreden þe Lord. Which sweriþ[75] to his neiȝbore, and disseyueþ not; [5] which ȝaf not his monei to vsure; and took not

---

**Ps. 13**    [a] noon is til to oon] *a mark over* oon, *perhaps to signal a missing tie-mark*    [b] weie] weies, -s *canc.*    [c] fro] to

## [PSALM 13 GLOSSES]

69. þat is, Nabugodonosor and his oost seide þat God of [I]srael^i is not veri God and moost myȝti. *Lire here.*

70. þis [noon is til to oon]^ii is not here in Ebreu neþer in Ieroms translacioun. *Lire here.*

71. þat is, meritorie of blis, which meritorie good mai not be wiþout feiþ and charite;

72. noon is til to oon, so þat neþer oon is sich founden in hem, for it is inpossible to plese God wiþout feiþ; eþer þus, noon is til to oon, þat is, in alle puplis is not no but oon—þat is, þe puple of Iewis, þat haþ veri lawe and religioun of God, for þe lawe ȝouun in þe hil of Synay was ȝouen oneli to þe puple of Iewis. *Lire here.*

Eiþer til to oon, þat is, outakun oon, þat is, þe Lord Crist. *Austin here.*

73. þe riȝtfulnesse of God. Ȝhe, þei schulen knowe it bi feelyng of peyne ȝouen to hem. *Lire here.*

## [PSALM 14 GLOSSES]

74. þat is, onouringe hem openli. *Lire here.*

75. þat is, makiþ a good ooþ and holdiþ it. In Ieroms translacioun þus, which sweriþ to turmente himsilf in chastisyng his fleisch bi fastingis and wakyngis; and chaungiþ not in keping þe ooþ. Neþeles, an ooþ is set þere for a vow and eiþer eiþer byndiþ. *Lire here.*

76. þat is, shal not be remouyd fro his seruyce as vnworþi in present liyf, neþer fro meede in liyf to comynge. *Lire here.*

---

ȝiftis on þe innocent. He, þat doiþ þese þingis, shal not be moued^76 wiþouten ende.

---

**Ps. 13 glosses**     ^i Israel] osrael     ^ii noon is til to oon] *om.*

*Conserua me Domine*

þe title of þe xv salm.

[1] *Of þe meke and symple, þe salm of Dauid.*[77]

    Lord, kepe þou me, for I haue hopid in þee. [2] I seide to þe Lord,
þou art my God, for þou hast no nede of my goodis. [3] To þe seyntis
þat ben in þe lond of hym; he made wondurful alle my willis in hem.
[4] The sijknessis[78] of hem ben multiplied; aftirward þei haastiden. I
shal not gadere togi[de]re[a] þe conuenticulis, eþer litle couentis, of
hem of bloodis; and I shal not be myndeful of her names bi my lippis.
[5] The Lord is part of myn eritage, and of my passioun; þou art, þat
shalt restore myn eritage to me. [6] Coordis[79] felden to me in ful cleer
þingis;[80] for myn eritage is ful cleer to me.[81] [7] I shal blesse þe Lord,
þat ȝaf vndurstondyng to me; ferþermore and my reynes blameden
me til to nyȝt.[82] [8] I purueiede euere þe Lord in my siȝt; for he is on
þe riȝthalf to me, þat I be not moued. [9] For þis þing[83] myn herte was
glad, and my tunge ioied fulli; ferþermore and my fleisch shal reste in
hope. [10] For þou shalt not forsake my soule in helle; neiþer þou
shalt ȝyue þyn hooli to se corupcioun.[84] [11] Thou hast maad |
knowun to me þe weies of lijf; þou shalt fille me of gladnesse wiþ þi
cheer; delityngis ben in þi riȝthalf til into þe ende.[85]

f. 6ᵛ

*Exaudi Domine iusticiam meam*

þe title of þe xvj salm.

[1] *þe preier of Dauiþ.*

    Lord, here þou my riȝtfulnesse; biholde þou my preier. Perseyue
þou wiþ eeris my preier; not maad in gileful lippis. [2] Mi doom come
forþ of þi cheer; þyn iȝen se equytees. [3] Thou hast preued myn
herte, and hast visitid in nyȝt; þou hast examyned me bi fier, and
wickidnesse[86] is not founden in me. [4] That my mouþ speke not þe
werkis of men; for þe wordis of þi lippis I haue kept harde weies. [5]
Make þou parfite my goyngis in þi paþis; þat my steppis be not
moued. [6] I criede, for þou, God, herdist me; bowe doun þin eere to
me, and here þou my wordis. [7] Make wondurful þi mercies; þat

Ps. 15      ᵃ togidere] togire

[PSALM 15 GLOSSES]

77.[i] þat is, þis salm is maad of Dauiþ, to þe preisyng of þe meke and symple Crist. [*Lire here.*][ii]

78. þat is, þe siyknessis of heþene men ȝouun to idolatrie; in Ieroms translacioun þus: þe idols of hem shulen be multeplied; aftirward þei hastiden. *Lire here.*

79. þat is, þe lottis of apostlis þat weren sent bi lottis to preche þe gospel;

80. In ful clere þingis, þat is, in apostlis, whiche bifore oþere men weren liȝtned of þe hooli goost;

81. myn eritage: þat is, þe chirche of feiþful men, which is clepid þe eritage of Crist in lj capitulo of Ieremye;

82. my reynes: þat is, Iewis borun of my kynrede; til to nyȝt, þat is, til to deeþ.

Iewis blamyden Crist in liyf and seiden, 'þou hast a feend', in viij capitulo of Ioon [John 8: 48]; and þei seiden of Crist in xj capitulo of Matheu, 'Lo, a mandeuourere and drynkere of wyn, and þe frend of synneris and of pupplicans' [Matt. 11: 19]; and in þe passioun þei seiden to Crist in xxvij capitulo of Matheu, 'Fiȝ on þee þat distriest [þe][iii] temple of God' [Matt. 27: 40]. *Lire here.*

83.[iv] þat is, for my risyng aȝen. *Lire here.*

84. þat is, turnyng into aischis eþer into rot. Neþeles, Crist suffride corrupcioun of deþ. *Lire here.*

85.[v] þat is, til into wiþouten ende. *Lire here.*                    f. 6[v]

[PSALM 16 GLOSSES]

86. Dauiþ purposide not bi þis [salm][i] to seie himsilf giltles of al synne, but þat [he][ii] dide no wickid þing aȝenes Saul wherfor he ouȝte pursue Dauiþ. But twies Dauiþ sparide hym whanne he myȝte haue slayn hym, in þe firste book of Kingis xxiiij capitulo and xxvj capitulo. *Lire here.*

---

**Ps. 15 glosses**    *om.*[i] *this gloss also in* AbCC_J_E.14*(damaged)*ikKLPQSUV*X*; Of þe meke and symple, þe salm] of the orisoun (k); meke and symple Crist] meke and symple, þat is Crist (K)    [ii] Lire here] *om.*    [iii] þe] *something erased, not corrected*    [iv] *this gloss interlinear and underlined in* K *and in margin of* V *(damaged)*    [v] *this gloss interlinear and underlined in* K
**Ps. 16 glosses**    [i] salm] *om.*    [ii] he] *om.*

makist saaf men hopynge in þee. [8] Kepe þou me as þe appil of þe
iȝe; fro men aȝenstondyng þi riȝthond. Kyuere þou me vndur þe
schadewe of þi wyngis; [9] fro þe face of vnpitouse men, þat han
turmentid me. Myn enemyes han cumpasside my soule; [10] þei han
closid togidere her fatnesse; þe mouþ of hem spak pride. [11] Thei
castiden me forþ and han cumpassid me now; þei ordeyneden to bowe
doun her iȝen into erþe. [12] Thei, as a lioun maad redi to prey, han
take me; and as þe whelp of a lioun dwellynge in hid places. [13] Lord,
rise þou up, biforcome þou hym and disseyue þou hym; delyuere þou
my lijf fro þe vnpitouse, delyuere þou þi swerd[87] [14] fro þe enemyes
of þyn hond. Lord, departe þou hem fro a fewe men of þe lond in þe
lijf of hem; her wombe is fillid of þyn hid þingis. Thei ben fillid wiþ
f. 7ʳ sones; and þei leften her relifis[88] to her litil | children. [15] But I in
riȝtfulnesse shal appere to þi siȝt; I shal be fillid, whanne þi glorie shal
appere.

## [PSALM 17]

*Diligam te Domine*
þe title of þe xvij salm.

[1] *To victorie, þe word of þe Lord to Dauiþ; which spak þe wordis of þis
song, in þe dai in which þe Lord delyueride him fro þe hond of alle hise
enemyes, and fro þe hond of Saul; and he seide:*

[2] Lord, my strengþe, I shal loue þee; þe Lord is my stidfastnesse,
and my refuyt, and mi delyuerere. [3] Mi God is myn helpere; and I
shal hope into hym. Mi defendere, and þe horn of myn heelþe; and
myn uptak[er]e.[a] [4] I shal preise and inwardli clepe þe Lord; and I
shal be saaf fro myn enemyes. [5] The sorewis of deþ cumpassiden
me; and þe strondis of wickidnesse disturbliden me. [6] The sorewis
of helle cumpassiden me; þe snaris of deþ biforocupieden me. [7] In
my tribulacioun I inwardli clepide þe Lord; and I criede to my God.
And he herde my uois fro his hooli temple; and my cri in his siȝt
entride into hise eeris. [8] The erþe[89] was mouyd togidere, and
tremblide togidere; þe foundementis of hillis weren troblid togidere,
and weren moued togidere; for he was wrooþ to hem. [9] Smoke
stiede in þe ire of hym, and fier brente out fro his face; coolis weren
kyndlid of hym. [10] He bowide doun heuenes, and cam doun; and

---

Ps. 17    ᵃ uptakere] uptake

87. þat is, me þat am þi swerd to þe distriyng of vnfeiþful men. *Lire here.*

88. þat is, þe residue goodis. *Lire here.*

## [PSALM 17 GLOSSES]

89. þis is þe delyueraunce of Israel fro þe lond of [Egipt].ⁱ *Lire here.*

90. þat is, of tribulaciouns. *Lire here.*

91. þat is, werkis. *Lire here.*

92. þat is, encreessing his hoolynesse. *Lire here.*

---

derknesse was vndur hise feet. [11] And he stiede on cherubyn, and flei; he flei ouer þe pennes of wyndis. [12] And he settide derknessis his hiding-place, his tabernacle in his cumpas; derk watir was in þe cloudis of þe lower eir. [13] Ful cleer cloudis passiden in his siȝt; hail and þe coolis of fier. [14] And þe Lord þundride fro heuene; and þe hiȝeste ȝaf his vois, hail and þe coolis of fier camen doun. [15] And he sente | hise arowis and distriede þo men; he multiplied leitis, and  f. 7ᵛ disturblide þo men. [16] And þe wellis of watris apperiden; and þe foundementis of þe erþe weren shewid: Lord, of þi blamyng; of þe breþyng of þe spirit of þyn ire. [17] He sente fro þe hiȝeste place and took me; and he took me fro manye watris.⁹⁰ [18] He delyuerede me fro [my]ᵇ strongeste enemyes; and fro hem þat hatiden me, for þei weren comfortid on me. [19] Thei camen bifor me in þe dai of my turment; and þe Lord was maad my defendere. [20] And he ledde me out into breede; he made me saaf for he wolde me. [21] And þe Lord shal ȝelde to me bi my riȝtfulnesse; and he shal ȝelde to me bi þe clennesse of myn hondis.⁹¹ [22] For I kepte þe weies of þe Lord; and I dide not vnfeiþfuli fro my God. [23] For alle hise domes ben in my siȝt; and I puttide not awei fro me hise riȝtfulnessis. [24] And I shal be vnwemmed wiþ him; and I shal kepe me fro my wickidnesse. [25] And þe Lord shal ȝelde to me bi my riȝtfulnesse; and bi þe clennesse of myn hondis in þe siȝt of hise iȝen. [26] Wiþ þe hooli,⁹² þou shalt be hooli; and wiþ a man innocent, þou shalt be innocent. [27] And wiþ a

---

**Ps. 17 glosses**      ⁱ Egipt] Syrie(?) *erased, not corrected*

ᵇ my] *om.*

chosun man, þou `schal be chosyn'ᶜ; and wiþ a weiward man, þou shalt be weiward.⁹³ [28] For þou shalt make saaf a meke puple; and þou shalt make meke þe iȝen of proude men. [29] For þou, Lord, liȝtnest my lanterne;⁹⁴ my God, liȝtne þou my derknessis.⁹⁵ [30] For bi þee I shal be delyuerid fro temptacioun; and in my God⁹⁶ I shal go ouer þe wal. [31] Mi God, his weie is vndefoulid, þe spechis of þe Lord ben examyned bi fier; he is defendere of [alle]ᵈ men hopyngȝe⁹⁷ in hym. [32] For whi, who is God, outakun þe Lord? eþer who is

f. 8ʳ   God | outakun oure God? [33] God þat haþ gird me wiþ vertu; and haþ set my weie⁹⁸ vnwemmed. [34] Which made perfite my feet as of hertis; and ordeynynge me on hiȝe þingis. [35] Which techiþ myn hondis to batel; and þou hast set myn armes as a brasun bouwe. [36] And þou hast ȝoue to me þe kyueryng of þin helþe; and þi riȝthond haþ upetake me. And þi chastisyng amendide me into þe ende; and þilke chastisyng of þee shal teche me. [37] Thou alargidist my paaces vndur me; and my steppis ben not maad vnstidfast. [38] I shal pursue myn enemyes and I shal take hem; and I shal not turne til þei failen. [39] I shal al tobreke hem, and þei shulen not mowe stonde; þei shulen falle vndur my feet. [40] And þou hast gird me wiþ vertu to batel; and þou hast supplauntid, eþer disseyued, vndur me men risynge aȝenes me. [41] And þou hast ȝoue myn enemyes abak to me; and þou hast distried men hatynge me. [42] Thei crieden, and noon was þat made hem saaf; þei crieden to þe Lord, and he herd not hem. [43] And I shal al tobreke hem as dust bifor þe face of wynd; I shal do hem awei as þe clei of stretis. [44] Thou shalt delyuere me fro aȝenseiyngis of þe puple; þou shalt `set'ᵉ me into þe heed of folkis. [45] The puple, which I knew not⁹⁹ seruyde me; in þe heryng of eere it obeiede to me. [46] Alien sones lieden to me, alien sones wexiden elde;¹⁰⁰ and crokiden¹⁰¹ fro þi paþis. [47] The Lord lyueþ, and my God be blessid; and þe God of myn heelþe be enhaunsid.¹⁰² [48] God, þat ȝauest veniaunces to me, and makist suget puplis vndur me;

f. 8ᵛ   my delyuerere fro my wraþful enemyes. [49] And þou shalt | enhaunce me fro hem, þat risen aȝenes me; þou shalt delyuere me fro a wickid man. [50] Therfor, Lord, I shal knoulecheᶠ ¹⁰³ to þee among naciouns; and I shal seie salm to þi name. [51] Magnefiynge

ᶜ schal be chosyn] *added by a 2nd hand in margin*    ᵈ alle] *om.*    ᵉ set] *added by a 2nd hand in margin*    ᶠ shal knouleche] shal k- knouleche, k- *canc.*

93. þou semest weiward to a weiward man, for he seiþ 'þe weie of þe Lord is not riȝtful' [Ezek. 18: 35]. *Austin here.*

94. <u>Mi lanterne</u>: þat is, þe kyndli wit of mannis vndurstonding set in a bodi of erþe, which lanterne God liȝtneþ whanne he addiþ þe liȝt of grace to þe liȝt of kynde. For grace makiþ þe kynde perfite;

95. <u>my derknessis</u>: þat is, medeful werkis quenchid bi dedli synne, þat ben quykened and liȝtned whanne grace is rekyuerid; eþer, kyndli liȝt comparisound to God is derknesse, þerfor he axeþ it to be liȝtned wiþ Goddis grace. *Lire here.*

96.[ii] þat is, in þe vertu of my God. *Lire here.*

97. While þis hope comeþ of grace and gode werkis, ellis it were not hope but presumpcioun. *Lire here.*

98. Doynge awei fro me þe wem of avoutrie wiþ Bersabee and of þe manquellinge of Vrie, whiche wemmes weren purgid bi þe pacience which þe Lord God ȝaf to Dauiþ in þe persecucioun of Absolon. *Lire here.*    f. 8ʳ

99. Bi knowing of appr[e]uyng[iii] for þe idolatrie of hem. *Lire here.*

100. For þei sworen to serue Dauiþ and hise successouris, and þouȝ þei obeieden wel in þe bigynnyng, aftirward þei bowiden awei fro ob[e]dience;[iv]

101. in Ebreu it is þus: <u>And þei shulen drede in her closyngis</u>; and in Ieroms translacioun þus: <u>And þei shulen be drawun togidere in her angwischis</u>. For þei þat wolen rebelle closen hemsilf and her þingis in wallid citees and places, and dreden to be assailid of hem, aȝenes whiche þei rebellen. *Lire here.*

102. Not in himsilf, but in creaturis preisynge him. *Lire here.*

103. Bi knouleching of þin heriyng, for salmes made of Dauiþ    f. 8ᵛ weren spred forþ to alle naciouns bileuynge in Crist. *Lire here.*

---

þe helþis of his kyng; and doynge merci to his crist Dauiþ, and to his seed til into þe world.

---

## [PSALM 18]

*Celi enarrant gloriam*
*þe title of þe xviij salm.*

[1] *To victorie, þe salm of Dauiþ.*[a] `In Ieroms translacioun þus: To þe
ouercomere, þe song of Dauiþ.´[b]

[2] Heuenes[104] tellen out þe glorie of God; and þe firmament telliþ
þe werkis of hise hondis. [3] The dai telliþ out to þe dai a word; and
þe ny3t shewiþ kunnyng to þe ny3t. [4] No langagis ben, neþer
wordis; of whiche þe uoices of hem ben not herd. [5] The soun of hem
3ede out into al erþe; and þe wordis of hem 3eden out into þe endis of
þe world. [6] In þe sunne[105] he haþ [set][c] his tabernacle; and he as a
spouse comynge forþ of his chaumbre. He fulli ioiede, as a giaunt, to
renne his weie; [7] his goynge out was fro hi3este heuene. And his
goynge a3en was to þe hi3este þerof; and noon is þat hidiþ hymsilf fro
his heete.[106] [8] The lawe of þe Lord is wiþout wem, and conuertiþ
soulis; þe witnessyng of þe Lord is feiþful, and 3yueþ wisdom to litle
children.[107] [9] The ri3tfulnessis of þe Lord ben ri3tful, gladynge
hertis; þe comaundement of þe Lord is cleer, li3tnynge i3en. [10] The
hooli drede[108] of þe Lord dwelliþ into þe world of world; þe domes of
þe Lord ben trewe, iustefied into hemsilf. [11] Desirable more þan
gold and a stoon myche preciouse; and swettere þan hony and
honycoomb. [12] Forwhi þi seruaunt kepiþ þoo; myche [3eldyng][d]
is in þo to be kept. [13] Who vndurstondiþ trespassis? make þou me
cleene fro my pryuy synnes; [14] and of alien[109] synnes spare þi
f. 9ʳ  seruaunt. If þe forseid defautis ben not, Lord, of | me, þanne I shal be
wiþout wem; and I shal be clensid of þe moost synne.[110] [15] And þe
spechis of my mouþ shulen be þat þo plese; and þe þenkyng of myn
herte euere in þi si3t. Lord, myn helpere; and myn a3enbiere.

## [PSALM 19]

*Exaudiat te Dominus*
*þe title o[f]*[a] *þe xix salm.*

[1] *To victorie, þe salm of Dauiþ.*[111]

[2] The Lord here þee in þe dai of tribulacioun; þe name of God of

---

**Ps. 18**    [a] *this title also in* bikKLPQSV    [b] In Ieroms translacioun . . . song of Dauiþ]
*added to the rubricated title in margin by the scribe, rather than being written separately as a gloss;*
*this phrase lacking in* k    [c] set] shewid    [d] 3eldyng] *om.*
**Ps. 19**    [a] of] on

[PSALM 18 GLOSSES]

104. [Heuenes],[i] þat is, apostlis;
firmament, þat is, hooli chirche, as to hooli doctours;
þe dai, þat is, þe newe testament, telliþ out to þe dai, þat is, cristen
puple, a word, þat is, Goddis sone maad man; and þe nyȝt, þat is, þe
elde testament, shewiþ kunnyng, þat is, þe mysterie of Crist, to þe
nyȝt, þat is, to Iewis. *Lire here.*

105. In þe sunne: in Ebreu and in Ieroms translacioun þus: To þe
sunne he haþ set his tabernacle among hem. Crist is þe sunne of
riȝtfulnesse whos tabernacle is his manheed, which is a tabernacle of
þe godheed. And God þe fadir haþ set þis tabernacle among hem, þat
is, apostlis and oþere disciplis, wiþ whiche he dwellide homeli. *Lire
here.*

106.[ii] þat is, þe brennyng charite of Crist. *Lire here.*

107. þat is, to meke men. [*Austin*][iii] here.

108. þat is, sones reuerence ioyned wiþ loue. *Lire here.*

109. þat moun be arettid to him for necligence of amendyng bi
constreynyng, as to prelatis and prynces. *Lire here.*

110. þat is, in deþ Y shal be founden cleene of ech dedli synne. *Lire* f. 9ʳ
*here.*

[PSALM 19 GLOSSES]

111.[i] þat is, þis salm was maad of Dauiþ, to gete victorie for his
oost. *Lire here.*

112. þat is, heuene. *Lire here.*

113. þat is, acceptable to God. *Lire here.*

---

Iacob defende þee. [3] Sende he helpe to þee fro þe hooli[112] place; and
fro Syon defende he þee. [4] Be he myndeful of al þi sacrifice; and þi
brent sacrifice be maad fat.[113] [5] Ȝyue he to þee aftir þyn herte; and
conferme he al þi councel. [6] We shulen be glad in þyn heelþe; and
we shulen be magnefied in þe name of oure God. [7] The Lord fille
alle þyn axyngis; now I haue knowe, þat þe Lord hath maad saaf his
crist. He shal here hym fro his hooli heuene; þe heelþe of his riȝthond

---

**Ps. 18 glosses**    [i] Heuenes] *om.*    [ii] *a short form of this gloss,* þat is, charite, *interlinear
and underlined in* K    [iii] Austin] Lire; *a variant gloss interlinear and underlined in* K: litle eþer
meke children; *also in margin of* V
**Ps. 19 glosses**    [i] *this gloss also in* AbCGikKLPSVX

is in poweris.[114] [8] These[115] in charis and þese in horsis; but we shulen inwardli clepe in þe name of oure Lord God. [9] The`i'[b] ben bounden, and felden doun; but we han rise, and ben reisid. [10] Lord, make thou saaf þe kyng; and here thou us in þe dai in which we inwardli clepen þee.

[PSALM 20]

*Domine in uirtute tua*

*þe title of þe twentiþe salm.*

[1] *To victorie, þe salm of Dauiþ.*

[2] Lord,[116] þe kyng shal be glad in þi vertu; and he shal [ful out][a] haue ioie greetli on þi heelþe. [3] Thou hast ȝoue to hym [þe][b] desir of his herte; and þou hast not defraudid hym of þe wille[117] of hise lippis. [4] For þou hast biforcome hym in þe blessyngis of swetnesse; þou hast set on his heed a coroun of preciouse stoon. [5] He axide of þee lijf, and þou ȝauest to hym; þe lengþe of daies into þe world, and into þe world of world. [6] His glorie is greet | in þyn heelþe; þou shalt putte glorie and greet fairnesse on hym. [7] For þou shalt ȝyue hym into blessyng into þe world of world; þou shalt make hym glad in ioie wiþ þi cheer. [8] For þe kyng hopith in þe Lord; and in þe merci of þe hiȝeste; he shal not be moued. [9] Thyn hond[118] be founden to alle þyn enemyes; þi riȝthond fynde alle hem þat haten þee. [10] Thou shalt putte hem as a furneis of fier in þe tyme of þi cheer; þe Lord shal disturble hem in his ire, and fier shal deuoure hem. [11] Thou shalt leese[119] þe fruyt of hem fro erþe; and þou shalt leese þe seed of hem[120] fro þe sones of men. [12] For þei bowiden yuelis aȝenes þee; þei thouȝten councelis, whiche þei myȝten not stablische. [13] For þou shalt putte hem abak; in þi relifs þou shalt make redi þe cheer of hem.[121] [14] Lord, be þou enhaunsid in þi vertu; we shulen synge and seie openli þi vertues.

f. 9ᵛ

[PSALM 21]

[Deus][a] *Deus meus respice in me*[b]

*þe title of xxj salm.*

ᵇ Thei] The, i *added by the scribe above the line of writing*

Ps. 20    ᵃ fulout] fulli    ᵇ þe] *om.*

Ps. 21    ᵃ Deus] Domine    ᵇ Deus Deus meus respice in me] *at the bottom of the page*

114. þat is, bi hooli aungelis myȝti, þat ben at þe riȝthalf of his fadir. *Lire here.*

115.ᶦᶦ þat is, oure aduersaries tristen. *Lire here.*

## [PSALM 20 GLOSSES]

116. <u>Lord</u>: God þe fadir; <u>þe king</u>: þat is, Crist, kyng of kingis and Lord of lordis. *Lire here.*

117. þat is, of hise preieris declaryng bi lippis his innere wille. *Lire here.*

118. þat is, vertu of [his]ᶦ worching punysching synne. Bi þe lefte f. 9ᵛ hond is vndurstondun lesse punyschyng and bi þe riȝthond greuousere punysching. *Lire here.*

119. <u>Leese þe fruyt</u>: þat is, þou shalt take awei fro hem hoolich temporal goodis, whiche þei vsiden lustfuli;

120. <u>and þe seed of hem</u>, þat is, sueris; <u>fro þe sones of men</u>, þat is, fro þe felouschipe of seyntis, putte hem abak in castinge hem fro þi face doun to helle;

121. <u>in þi relifs</u>, þat is, in fendis þat ben al lefte of þee, as vnmyȝti to turne to good; <u>make redi þe cheer of hem</u>, in sendynge hem to þe felouschipe of fendis. *Lire here.*

## [PSALM 21 GLOSSES]

122. <u>þe morewtid hynde</u> is Cristis manheed, þat roos aȝen in þe moreutid of Estir dai.

þis salm to þe lettre is verified of Crist in xxvij capitulo of Matheu, xix capitulo of Ioon, and ij capitulo to Ebreis. [*Lire here.*]ᶦ

123. A þou <u>God</u> þe fadir, <u>my God</u>, for resoun of my manheedᶦᶦ maad of þee, <u>biholde þou on me</u> set in tribulacioun eþer turment. Neþeles, þis word <u>biholde þou on me</u> is not in Ebreu neþer in Ieroms translacioun;

---

[1] *To ouercome, for þe morewtid*¹²² *hynde; þe salm of Dauid.*

[2] God,¹²³ my God, biholde þou on me, whi hast þou forsake me?

---

ᶦᶦ*a variant gloss interlinear and underlined in* K: þese, þat is aduersaries, tristen in charis; *also in margin of* V *(damaged)*
**Ps. 20 glosses**    ᶦhis] *om.*
**Ps. 21 glosses**    ᶦLire here] *om.; this gloss also in* GikKSV*(damaged)*    ᶦᶦmanheed] manheed of, of *canc.*

þe wordis of my trespassis[124] ben fer fro myn heelþe.[125] [3] Mi God, I
shal crie bi dai, and þou shalt not here; and bi nyȝt, and not to
vnwisdom to me. [4] Forsoþe þou, þe preisyng of Israel, dwellist in
hoolynesse. [5] Oure fadris hopiden in þee, þei hopiden and þou
delyueridist hem. [6] Thei crieden to þee, and þei weren maad saaf;
þei hopiden in þee, and þei weren not shent. [7] But I am a worm,[126]
and not man;[127] þe shenship of men, and þe outcastyng of þe puple.
[8] Alle men seynge me scorneden me; þei spaken wiþ lippis, and
stiriden þe heed. [9] He hopide in þe Lord, delyuere he hym; make he
f. 10ʳ  hym saaf, for he wole hym. | [10] For þou [it]ᶜ art þat drowist me out
of þe wombe, þou art myn hope fro þe tetis of my modir. [11] Into þee
I am caste forþ fro þe wombe.[128] Fro þe wombe of my modir þou art
my God; [12] departe þou not fro me. For tribulacioun is next; for
noon is þat helpiþ. [13] Many calues[129] cumpassiden me; fatte bolis
bisegiden me. [14] Thei openyden her mouþ on me; as doiþ a lioun
rauyshynge and rorynge. [15] I am shed out as watir; and alle my
boonys ben scaterid. Myn herte is maad as wexe fletynge abrood; in þe
myddis of my wombe. [16] Mi vertu driede as a tijlstoon, and my
tunge cleuyde to my chekis; and þou hast brouȝt forþ me into þe dust
of deþ.[130] [17] For manye doggis[131] cumpassiden me; þe councel of
wickid men bisegide me. Thei deluyden myn hondis and my feet. [18]
þei noumbriden alle my boonys. Soþeli þei lokiden and bihelden me.
[19] þei departiden my cloþis to hemsilf, and þei senten lot on my
cloþ. [20] But þou, Lord, dilaie not þyn help fro me; biholde þou toᵈ
my defence. [21] God, delyuere þou my lijf fro swerd;[132] and delyuere
þou myn oon aloone fro þe hond of þe dogge.[133] [22] Make þou me
ʽsaafʾᵉ fro þe mouþ of a lioun;[134] and my mekenesse fro þe hornes of
vnycornes.[135] [23] I shal telle þi name to my briþeren; I shal preise þee
in þe myddis of þe chirche. [24] Ȝe þat dreden þe Lord, herie hym; al
þe seed of Iacob,[136] glorifie ȝe him. [25] Al þe seed of Israel dredeᶠ
hym; for he forsook not neiþer dispiside þe preier of a pore man.
Neiþer he turnyde awei his face fro me; and whanne I criede to him,
he herde me. [26] Mi preisyng is at þee in a greet chirche; I shal ȝelde
my vowis in þe siȝt of men dredynge hym. [27] Pore men[137] shulen
f. 10ᵛ  ete, and shulen be fillid, | and þei shulen herie þe Lord, þat sekiþ
hym; þe hertis of hem shulen lyue into þe world of world. [28] Alle þe
endis of erþe shulen biþenke; and shulen be conuertid to þe Lord.

ᶜ it] om.    ᵈ to] into    ᵉ saaf] added by the scribe above the line of writing    ᶠ drede] drede ȝe

124. þe wordis of my trespassis: Crist clepiþ þe synnes of þe puple hise for þe vnyte of membris and of þe heed, for he made þo synnes hise in a maner in suffring peyne for þo synnes. But in Ebreu and in Ieroms translacioun it is þus: þe wordis of my roryng eþer of my cry. For Crist in þe cros criede, seiynge wiþ greet vois, 'God, my God, whi hast þou forsake me?' [Matt. 27: 46];

125. fer fro helþe of bodi, for he was not kept fro bodili deþ. *Lire here.*

126. þat is, vile and abhomynable in þe siȝt of Iewis;

127. and not man, þat is, not vsinge resoun but more dryuyng of þe deuel, for þei seiden 'þou hast a deuel' [John 7: 20]. *Lire here.*

128. þat is, Y am ooned to þee in þe persoone of þe sone, fro þe bigynnyng of concepcioun. *Lire here.*    f. 10ʳ

129. þat is, Iewis seid calues, for wildenesse and pride of[iii] fleisch; and bolis, for þei weren auarouse and fatte in richessis. *Lire here.*

130. þat is, into deþ, bi which bodies ben dryuun into dust. Neþeles, Cristis bodi was kept fro corrupcioun bi hastynesse of his risyng aȝen, as it is seid in þe xv salm. *Lire here.*

131. þat is, Iewis, hauynge hemsilf not as men to me, but as wode doggis. *Lire here.*

132. þat is, violent deþ, þat is wont to be maad bi swerd; for þouȝ Crist suffride moost peyne in bodi, he diede wilfuli. *Lire here.*

133. þat is, fro þe power of helle, þat deuouriþ gredili as a dogge doiþ;

134. mouþ of a lioun: þat is, cruel Iewis;

135. hornes of vnycornes: þat is, fro pride and presumpcioun of knyȝtis, þat gessiden to kepe me wiþinne þe sepulcre. *Lire here.*

136. þat is, alle sueris of his feiþ and werkis. *Lire here.*[iv]

137. þat is, veri meke men. *Lire here.*

138. þat is, fillid wiþ richessis and onouris: and siche ben cristen   f. 10ᵛ
prynces, þat eten Cristis bodi deuoutli;

---

And alle þe meynees of heþene men; shulen worschip in his siȝt. [29] For þe rewme is þe Lordis; and he shal be Lord of heþene men. [30] Alle þe fatte men[138] of erþe eeten and worschipiden; alle men, þat

[goen]<sup>g</sup> doun into erþe, shulen falle doun<sup>139</sup> in his siȝt. [31] And my
soule shal lyue to hym;<sup>140</sup> and my seed shal serue hym.<sup>141</sup> [32] A
generacioun to-comynge shal be teld to þe Lord; and heuenes shulen
telle his riȝtfulnesse to þe puple þat shal be borun, whom þe Lord
made.

[PSALM 22]

*Dominus regit me*
*þe title of xxij salm.*

[1] *þe salm eþer þe song of Dauiþ.*

The Lord gouerneþ me, and no þing shal faile to me. [2] In þe place
of pasture þere he haþ set me. He nurschide me on þe watir of
refreischyng: [3] he conuertide my soule. He ledde me forþ on þe
paþis of riȝtfulnesse; for his name. [4] Forwhi þouȝ I shal go in þe
myddis of shadewe of deþ, I shal not drede yuelis, for þou art wiþ me.
Thi ȝerde<sup>142</sup> and þi staf; þo han comfortide me. [5] Thou hast maad
redi a boord in my siȝt; aȝenes hem þat troblen me. Thou hast maad
fat myn heed wiþ oile; and my cuppe, fillinge greetli, is ful cleer. [6]
And þi merci shal sue me; in alle þe daies of my lijf. And þat I dwelle
in þe hous of þe Lord; into þe lengþe of daies.

[PSALM 23]

*Domine est terra*<sup>143</sup>
*þe title of xxiij salm.*

[1] *þe song of Dauiþ.*

The erþe and þe fulnesse þerof is þe Lordis; þe world, and alle þat
dwellen þerinne is þe Lordis. [2] For he foundide it on þe sees;<sup>144</sup> and
f. 11<sup>r</sup>  m`a´de<sup>a</sup> it | redi on floodis. [3] Who shal stie into þe hil of þe Lord;
eþer who shal stonde in þe hooli place of hym? [4] The innocent in
hondis,<sup>145</sup> and cleene in herte; which took not his soule in veyn, neþer
swoor in gile to his neiȝbore. [5] This man shal take blessyng of þe
Lord; and merci of God his helþe. [6] This is þe generacioun of men
sekynge hym; of men sekynge þe face of God of Iacob. [7] Ȝe
prynces,<sup>146</sup> take up ȝoure ȝatis, and ȝe euerelastynge ȝatis be reisid;

<sup>g</sup> goen] *om.*
**Ps. 23**      <sup>a</sup> made] mde, *corrected by the scribe above the line of writing*

139. falle doun, bi reuerence of onour to God oneli; for in Ebreu
and in Ieroms translacioun it is þus: and þei shulen bowe þe knee,
which is propirli a signe of onour du to God oneli;

140. And my soule shal lyue to him, for Dauiþ hadde feiþ of Crist
to comynge;

141. in Ebreu and in Ieroms translacioun it is þus: and his liyf shal
not lyue, and þis is þe ende of þe vers biforgoynge; for bi þis þat Crist
puttide^v forþ himsilf to deþ mekeli and charitabli for mankynde, he
disseruyde sich onour, þat alle men worshipe hym. *Lire here.*

### [PSALM 22 GLOSS]

142. þat is, þi defendingis eþer protecciouns. *Lire here.*

### [PSALM 23 GLOSSES]

143.^i þis salm is seid of þe glorifiyng and rising aȝen of Crist. *Austin
here.*

144. Not þat þe see is outirli lowere þan þe erþe, siþen þe erþe is þe
loweste and heuyest element, but þat summe partis of erþe, as brynkis
of þe see þat stonden aboue þe watir, ben hiȝere þan þe see. *Lire here.*

145.^ii þat is, werkis. *Lire here.*                                  f. 11^r

146. In Ebreu and in Ieroms translacioun þus: ȝe ȝatis reise ȝoure
heedis, þat is, departe ȝoure hiȝere partis bi Goddis vertu. *Lire here.*

147. þat is, of poweris of aungelis. *Lire here.*

---

and þe kyng of glorie shal entre. [8] Who is þis kyng of glorie? þe Lord
strong and myȝti, þe Lord myȝti in batel. [9] Ȝe prynces, take up
ȝoure ȝatis, and ȝe euerelastynge ȝatis be reisid; and þe kyng of glorie
shal entre. [10] Who is þis kyng of glorie? þe Lord of vertues,[147] he is
þe kyng of glorie.

---

^v puttide] puttide p-, p- *canc.*
**Ps. 23 glosses**      ^i *this gloss also in* AbCGikKLPQSUVX      ^ii *this gloss interlinear and
underlined in* K *and in margin of* V

[PSALM 24]

*Ad te [Domine]*<sup>a</sup> *leuaui animam*<sup>148</sup>

þe title of xxiiij salm.

[1] *To Dauiþ.*

Lord, to þee I haue reisid my soule. [2] My God, I triste in þee, be I not ashamed. [3] Neiþer myn enemyes scorne me; for alle men þat suffren þee<sup>149</sup> shulen not be shent. [4] Alle men doynge wickid þingis superfluy; be shent. Lord, shewe þou þi weies to me; and teche þou me þi paþis. [5] Dresse þou me in þi treuþe and teche þou me, for þou art God my sauyour; and I suffride<sup>150</sup> þee al dai. [6] Lord, haue þou mynde of þi merciful doyngis; of þi mercies þat ben fro þe world.<sup>151</sup> [7] Haue þou not mynde on þe trespassis o[f]<sup>b</sup> my ȝongþe; and on myn vnkunnyngis. Thou, Lord, haue mynde on me bi þi merci; for þi goodnesse. [8] The Lord is swete<sup>152</sup> and riȝtful; for þis he shal ȝyue a lawe<sup>153</sup> to men trespassyng in þe weie. [9] He shal dresse deboner men in doom; he shal teche mylde men hise weies.<sup>c</sup> |

f. 11<sup>v</sup>

[10] Alle þe weies<sup>154</sup> of þe Lord ben merci and treuþe; to men sekynge his testament and hise witnessyngis. [11] Lord, for þi name þou shalt do merci to my synne; for it is myche. [12] Who is a man þat dredith þe Lord? he ordeyneth to hym a lawe [in þe weie]<sup>d</sup> which he chees. [13] His soule shal dwelle in goodis; and his seed<sup>155</sup> shal enherite þe lond.<sup>156</sup> [14] The Lord is a sadnesse<sup>157</sup> to men dredynge hym; and his testament is, þat it be shewid to hem. [15] Myn iȝen ben euere to þe Lord; for he shal breide awei my feet fro þe snare. [16] Biholde þou on me and haue þou merci on me; for I am [oon]<sup>e</sup> aloone and pore. [17] The tribulaciouns of myn herte ben multe-plied; delyuere þou me of my nedis. [18] Se thou my mekenesse and my trauel; and forȝyue þou alle my trespassis. [19] Biholde þou myn enemyes, for þei ben multiplied; and þei haten me bi wickid hatrede. [20] Kepe þou my soule,<sup>158</sup> and delyuere þou me; be I not ashamed, for I hopide in þee. [21] Innocent men and riȝtful cleuyden to me; for I suffride þee. [22] God, delyuere þou Israel; fro alle hise tribulaciouns.

---

**Ps. 24**    <sup>a</sup> Domine] *om.*    <sup>b</sup> of] on    <sup>c</sup> weies] weieies    <sup>d</sup> in þe weie] *om.*    <sup>e</sup> oon] *om.*

[PSALM 24 GLOSSES]

148.[i] þis is a symple preier, þat Dauiþ made for his delyueraunce fro þe pursuyng of Saul. *Lire here.*

Crist in þe persoone of þe chirche spekiþ in þis salm, for þo þingis þat ben seid in þis salm perteynen more to cristen puple conuertid to God. *Austin here.*

149.[ii] þat is, persecuciouns for þee. *Lire here.*

150.[iii] þat is, for þee Y suffride contynueli þe persecuciouns of Saul. *Lire here.*

151. þat is, fro þe bigynnyng of þe world. *Lire here.*

152. þat is, merciful;

153. A lawe: þat is, if þei repenten verili þei gete merci; ellis, þat þei be punyschid wiþouten ende. *Lire here.*

154. Alle þe weies, þat is, werkis, of þe Lord, þat ben summe weies f. 11ᵛ to com into þe knowyng of him; ben merci and treuþe, þat is, riȝtfulnesse. For þouȝ merci apperiþ more in summe werkis of him, as in rewardyng of good men, neþeles riȝtfulnesse is þere also, in as myche as God ordeynede þat euerlastynge meede shulde be ȝoldun to hem for siche werkis. And þouȝ riȝtfulnesse apperiþ more in summe werkis, as in dampnyng of yuel men, neþeles merci is þere, in as myche as God punyschiþ lesse þanne he is euene worþi. For þe offence is greet wiþouten ende and so greet in sorewe shulde þe peyne be, if it myȝte. *Lire here.*

155. þat is, lyuynge men;

156. þat is, heuene. *Lire here.*

157. In Ebreu and in Ieroms translacioun þus: þe councel eþer priuyte of þe Lord is to men dredynge hym; and it turneþ into þe same, for he þat ȝyueþ a good councel to men confermeþ and stablischiþ hem. *Lire here.*

158. þat is, lijf. *Lire here.*

---

Ps. 24 glosses    [i] *the first historical part of this gloss also in* AbCikKLPQSUV    [ii] *this gloss interlinear and underlined in* K *and in margin of* V    [iii] *in margin of* V: þat is, for þee

[PSALM 25]

*Iudica me Domine*
*þe title of xxv salm.*
[1] *To Dauiþ.*[159]

Lord, deme þou me, for I entride in myn innocence; and I hopynge in þe Lord shal not be maad vnstidfast. [2] Lord, proue þou me and asaie me; brenne þou my reynes[160] and myn herte. [3] Forwhi þi merci is b`i´for[a] myn iȝen; and I pleside in þi treuþe. [4] I sat not wiþ councel of uanyte;[161] and I shal not entre wiþ men doynge wickid þingis. [5] I hatide þe chirche of yuele men; and I shal not sitte wiþ wickid men. [6] I shal waische myn hondis among innocentis; and, Lord, I shal cumpasse þin auter. [7] That | I here þe vois of heriynge; and þat I telle out alle þi meruelis. [8] Lord, I haue loued þe fairenesse of þyn hous; and þe place of þe dwellyng of þi glorie.[b] [9] God, leese[162] þou not my soule wiþ vnfeiþful men; and my lijf wiþ men of bloodis. [10] In whose hondis wickidnessis ben; þe riȝthond of hem is fillid wiþ ȝiftis. [11] But I entride in myn innocence; aȝenbie þou me and haue merci on me. [12] Mi foot[163] stood in riȝtfulnesse; Lord, I shal blesse þee[164] in chirchis.

f. 12ʳ (margin)

[PSALM 26]

*Dominus illuminacio*
[1] *þe title of xxvj salm. To Dauiþ.*[165]

The Lord is myn liȝtnyng and myn heelþe; whom[166] shal I drede? The Lord is defendere of my lijf; for whom shal I tremble? [2] The while noiful men neiȝen on me; for to ete my fleischis. Myn enemyes þat trobliden me; þei weren maad sijk and felden doun. [3] Thouȝ castels[167] stonden togidere aȝenes me; myn herte shal not drede.[168] Thouȝ batel risiþ aȝenes me; in þis þing I shal haue hope. [4] I axide of þe Lord o þing, I shal seke þis þing; þat I dwelle in þe hous of þe Lord alle þe daies of my lijf. That I se[169] þe wille of þe Lord; and þat I visite his temple. [5] For he hid me in his tabernacle in þe dai of yuelis; he defendide me in þe hid place of his tabernacle. [6] He enhaunside me in a stoon; and nov he enhaunside myn heed ouer myn enemyes. I cumpasside and offride in his tabernacle a sacrifice of

Ps. 25    [a] bifor] bofor, *corrected by the scribe above the line of writing*    [b] *a unique gloss here interlinear and underlined in* K: þe fairnesse of þin hous, þat is cristen mannes soule

[PSALM 25 GLOSSES]

159.[i] þe xxv salm shal be expowned of þe staat of Dauiþ, whanne aftir þe deþ of Saul he entride into þe rewme bi Goddis answere and dwellide in Ebron wiþ men cleuyng to hym. *Lire here.*

160. Brenne þou my reynes, þat is, my delitingis and þouȝtis, þat Y þenke noon yuel and þat noon yuel delite me. *Austyn here.*

Eþer in kepynge me fro fleischli synnes and gostli synnes. *Lire here.*

161. þat is, consentide not wiþ hem þat sitten þere. *Austin here.*

162. þat is, suffre þou not to be lost; wiþ men of bloodis, þat is,  f. 12ʳ shederis out eþer eteris of myche blood. Siche ben manquelleris and rauenours, lyuyng of oþere mennis trauel and blood. *Lire here.*

163. þat is, affeccioun. [*Lire here.*][ii]

164. Blesse þee in chirchis: To blesse þe Lord in chirchis is to lyue so þat þe Lord be blesside bi þe vertues of eche man. For he þat blessiþ God bi tunge and cursiþ bi dedis blessiþ not þe Lord in chirchis. þei in whose vertues þat þat[iii] þei seien is not founden, maken God to be blasfemyd. *Austyn here.*

[PSALM 26 GLOSSES]

165.[i] Dauiþ made þis salm aftir Sauls deþ bifor his anoyntyng. *Lire here.*

166. Whom shal I drede: A dedli man is cumpassid wiþ dedli men of armes, and he drediþ not but is sikur. A dedli man is defendid of God vndedli. Shal he drede and tremble? *Austyn here.*

167. þat is, oostis. *Lire here.*

168. Noon no but 'God'[ii] mai[iii] take awei temporal þingis. God shal not take awei goostli ȝiftis, no but þou forsake him. *Austin here.*

169. þat is, knowe. *Lire here.*

---

criyng; I shal synge and I shal seie salm to þe Lord. [7] Lord, here þou my vois bi which I criede to þee; haue þou merci on me, and here me. [8] Myn herte seide to þee, My face souȝte þee; Lord, I shal | seke eft  f. 12ᵛ þi face. [9] Turne þou not awei þi face fro me; bowe þou not awei in

**Ps. 25 glosses**   [i] *next to the title in the left margin; this gloss also in* AbCGikKLPQSUVX   [ii] *Lire here] om.; this gloss also in margins of* GOQS, *interlinear and underlined in* K   [iii] *þat] þat þ-, þ- canc.*
**Ps. 26 glosses**   [i] *next to the title in the right margin; this gloss also in* AbCGikKLPQSUVX   [ii] *God] added by the scribe above the line of writing*   [iii] *mai] mai take mai, take mai canc.*

ire fro þi seruaunt. Lord, be þou myn helpere, forsake þou not me; and, God, myn helþe, dispise þou not me. [10] For my fadir and my modir¹⁷⁰ han forsake me; but þe Lord haþ take me. [11] Lord, sette þou `a´ᵃ lawe to me in þi weie; and dresse þou me in þi paþ for myn enemyes. [12] Bitake þou not me into þe soulis of hem þat troblen me;¹⁷¹ for wickid witnessis han rise aȝenes me, and wickidnesse liede to itsilf. [13] I bileue to se þe goodis of þe Lord; in þe lond of hem þat lyuen. [14] Abide þou þe Lord, do þou manli; and þyn herte be comfortid, and suffre þou þe Lord.

[PSALM 27]

*Ad te Domine clamabo*

[1] *þe title of xxvij salm. To Dauiþ.*¹⁷²

Lord, I shal crie¹⁷³ to þee; my God, be þou not stille fro me, be þou not stille ony tyme fro me; and I shal be maad lijk to hem, þat goon doun into þe lake. [2] Lord, here þou þe vois of my bisechyng, while I preie to þee; while I reise myn hondis to þyn hooli temple. [3] Bitake þou not me togidere wiþ synneris; and leese þou not me wiþ hem þat worchen wickidnesse. Whiche speken pees wiþ her neiȝbore; but yuelis ben in her hertis. [4] Ȝyue¹⁷⁴ þou to hem upe þe werkis of hem; and vpe þe wickidnesse of her fyndyngis. Ȝyue þou to hem upe þe werkis of her hondis; ȝelde þou her ȝeldyng to hem. [5] For þei vndurstoden not þe werkis of þe Lord, and bi þe werkis of hise hondis þou shalt distrie hem; and þou shalt not bilde hem. [6] Blessid be þe Lord; for he herde þe vois of my bisechyng. [7] The Lord is myn helpere and my defendere; and myn herte hopide in hym, and I am helpid. And | my fleisch flouride aȝen; and of my wille Y shal knowleche to hym. [8] The Lord is þe strengþe of his puple; and he is defendere of þe sauyngis of his crist. [9] Lord, make þou saaf þi puple, and blesse þou þyn eritage; and reule þou hem and enhaunce þou hem til into wiþouten ende.

f. 13ʳ

[PSALM 28]

*Afferte domino*

[1] *þe title of xxviij salm. þe salm eþer þe song of Dauiþ.*¹⁷⁵

Ȝe sones of God, brynge to þe Lord; brynge ȝe to þe Lord þe sones

---

**Ps. 26**    ᵃ a] *added by the scribe above the line of writing*

170. þat is, Adam and Eue <u>han forsaken me</u>, set forþ to    f. 12ᵛ
wrecchidnessis of present liyf. For bi her trespassyng orignyal
synne is brouȝt forþ to alle men, bi which a man haþ enclynyng to
yuel, and hardnesse to good. *Lire here.*

171. þat is, into þe willis of fendisⁱᵛ þat ben aduersaries to me. *Lire
here.*

## [PSALM 27 GLOSSES]

172.ⁱ Dauiþ made þis salm of þe persecucioun of Absolon aȝenes
him, whanne Dauiþ fledde fro Ierusalem for drede of him.

Gostli, þis salm mai be expowned of ech cristen man, set in
tribulacioun of bodi eþer of soule. *Lire here.*

þis salm is þe vois of Crist himsilf. *Austin here.*

173. þat is, preie of greet desire. *Lire here.*

174. Dauiþ seide þis, not for loue of veniaunce, but of riȝtfulnesse.
*Lire here.*

þis is not desire of yuel wille, butⁱⁱ tellyng out of þe peyne of hem,
and so is þat vois of 'Crist in'ⁱⁱⁱ þe gospel, 'Woo to þee Coroȝaym'
[Matt. 11: 21]. [*Austin*]ⁱᵛ here.

## [PSALM 28 GLOSSES]                    f. 13ʳ

175.ⁱ Dauiþ made þis salm in þe endyng of þe tabernacle, which he
made to putte þe arke þerinne, as Ierom seiþ on þe prologe of þe
Sauter. *Lire here.*

176. þis was doon in þe goingⁱⁱ out of Egipt, whanne þe Lord made
Israel to go þorouȝ þe see, and drenchide Egipcians;

---

of rammes. [2] Brynge ȝe to þe Lord glorie and onour; brynge ȝe to þe
Lord glorie to his name; herie ȝe þe Lord in his hooli large place. [3]
The vois of þe Lord on watris,¹⁷⁶ God of maieste þundride; þe Lord

---

ⁱᵛ of fendis] of fendis of fendis *the dittography not canc.*
**Ps. 27 glosses**      ⁱ *next to the title in the left margin; the first historical part of this gloss also in*
AbCGikKLPQSU*X*; *the second* Austin *part of the gloss in margin of* V      ⁱⁱ but] *corrected by the*
*scribe on an erasure*      ⁱⁱⁱ Crist in] *added by the scribe above the line of writing*      ⁱᵛ Austin]
*obscured by a splatter of red wax or ink*
**Ps. 28 glosses**      ⁱ *next to the title in the right margin; this gloss also in* AbCGikKLPQUV*X*
ⁱⁱ going] goinge, -e *canc.*

on manye watris. [4] þe vois of þe Lord in vertu;[177] þe vois of þe Lord
in greet doyng. [5] The vois of þe Lord brekynge cedris; and þe Lord
shal breke þe cedris of þe Liban.[178] [6] And he shal al tobreke hem to
dust as a calf of þe Liban; and þe derlyng[179] was [as]ᵃ þe sone of an
vnycorn. [7] The vois of þe Lord departynge þe flawme of fier; [8] þe
vois of þe lord shakynge desert; and þe Lord shal stire togidere þe
desert of Cades.[180] [9] The vois of þe Lord makynge redi hertis,[181] and
he shal shewe þicke þingis; and in his temple alle men shulen seie
glorie. [10] The Lord makiþ to enhabite þe grete flood;[182] and þe Lord
shal sitte kyng wiþouten ende. The Lord shal ȝyue vertu to his puple;
þe Lord shal blesse his puple in pees.

### [PSALM 29]

[*Exaltabo te Domine*]ᵃ

[1] þe title of xxix salm. þe salm of song, for þe halewyng of þe hous[183] of
Dauiþ.

[2] Lord, I shal enhaunce þee, for þou hast uptake me; and þou
delitidist not myn enemyes on me. [3] Mi Lord God, I criede to þee;
and þou madist me hool. [4] Lord, þou leddist out my soule fro helle;
f. 13ᵛ  | þou sauedist me fro hem þat goon doun into þe lake. [5] Ȝe seyntis[184]
of þe Lord, synge to þe Lord; and knouleche ȝe to þe mynde of his
hoolynesse. [6] For ire is in his dignacioun;ᵇ [185] and lijf is in his wille.
Wepyng shal dwelle at euentid; and gladnesse at [þe]ᶜ moreutid. [7]
Forsoþe I seide in my plentee;[186] I shal not be moued wiþouten ende.
[8] Lord, in þi wille; þou hast ȝoue vertu to my fairenesse. Thou
turnedist awei þi face fro me; and I am [maad]ᵈ disturblid.[187] [9] Lord,
I shal crie to þee; and I shal preie to my God. [10] What profite is in
my blood; while Y go doun into corrupcioun? Wher dust[188] shal
knoulech to þee; eþer shal telle þi treuþe? [11] The Lord herde and
hadde merci on me; þe Lord is maad myn helpere. [12] Thou hast
turned my weilyng into ioie to me; þou hast torent my sak and hast
cumpassid me wiþ gladnesse. [13] That my glorie synge to þee, and I
be not compunct; my Lord God, I shal knouleche to þee wiþouten
ende.

Ps. 28    ᵃ as] *om.*
Ps. 29    ᵃ Exaltabo te Domine] *om.*    ᵇ dignacioun] *most MSS read* indignacioun *(cf. Gall.*
indignatione); B 554 *shares this reading with* A*    ᶜ þe] *om.*    ᵈ maad] *om.*

177. þe vois of þe Lord in vertu: þis was whan he ʒaf þe lawe in Syna, wiþ grete drede and lordlynesse. *Lire here.*

178.[iii] þat is, þe princes of Iewis. *Lire here.*

179. þat is, Moises, loued of God and men, was not afeerd but sikur as an vnycorn; Ieroms translacioun haþ þus: And he shal scatere hem; and þe sone as þe sone of an vnycorn, and al is o sentence. *Lire here.*

180. þis was whanne God took veniaunce of Chore, Dathan, and Abiron and her felowis. *Lire here.*

181. Ebreis seien, sleynge hyndis; Ierom seiþ, brynging forþ hyndis as a mydwif doþ. þe Ebreu word here signefieþ boþe sleyng and bryngyng forþ as a mydwif doiþ, and makyng redi. Bi þe comyn translacioun it is expowned of þe lond of Neptalym, þat bryngiþ forþ fruytis bifore oþere londis, as an hert renneþ swiftliere þan oþere beestis. And þerfor sacrifices weren maad at Pask of þe newe cornes, and þanne þe dekenes sungen þe heriyngis of God. *Lire here.*

182. þat is, þe lond distried bi þe grete flood. *Lire here.*

[PSALM 29 GLOSSES]

183.[i] Not in which Dauiþ dwellide but of þe temple bildid of Salomon, which temple is seid[ii] here þe hous of Dauiþ, for he wolde bilde it and he dis[c]ryuyde[iii] it, and made redi þe costis þerof. *Lire here.*

Dauiþ made þe xxix salm, to preise and þanke God of his merci and grace for he forʒaf þe synne of avoutrie and of mansleyng, for whiche he disseruyde to be slayn and dampned, outakun Goddis merci.

Gostli, þis salm mai be expowned of ech cristen man, þat knowiþ bi Goddis reuelacioun eþer resonable euydence þat God haþ forʒoue a greuouse synne to him. Wherfor he doiþ þankyngis to God, in preisynge þe goodnesse of God and in knoulechyng his freelte. *Lire here.*

184. þat is, ʒe prestis and dekenes halewid and assigned to Goddis worshiping. *Lire here.* f. 13ᵛ

185. In Ebreu and in Ieroms translacioun þus, for his ire is at a moment. *Lire here.*

186. þat is, in þe bigynnyng of my rewme, whanne Y hadde plentee of bodili goodis and gostli. *Lire here.*

187. For bi Sathanas Y am caste doun into greuouse synnes. *Lire here.*

188. þat is, of my bodi turned into aischis. *Lire here.*

ⁱⁱⁱ *this gloss interlinear and underlined in K and in margin of* V
**Ps. 29 glosses** ⁱ *the first historical part of this gloss also in* AbCGikKLPQSUVX ⁱⁱ seid] st- seid, st- *canc.* ⁱⁱⁱ discryuyde] distryuyde

## [PSALM 30]

*In te Domine speraui*

[1] þe title of xxx salm. To victorie, þe salm[189] of Dauiþ.

[2] Lord, I hopide in þee, be I not shent wiþouten ende; delyuere þou me in þi riȝtfulnesse. [3] Bowe doun þyn eere to me; haaste þou to delyuere me. Be þou to me into God defendere, and into an hous of refuyt; þat þou make me saaf. [4] For þou art my strengþe and my refuyte; and for þi name þou shalt lede me forþ, and shalt nur[i]sche[a] me. [5] Thou shalt lede me out of þe snare which þei hidden to me; for þou art my defendere. [6] I bitake my spirit into þyn hondis; Lord God of treuþe, þou hast aȝenbouȝte me. [7] Thou hatist hem þat kepen vanytees[190] superfluy. Forsoþe I hopide in þe Lord; | [8] I shal haue fulli ioie, and shal be glad in þi merci. For þou biheldist my mekenesse; þou sauydist my lijf fro nedis. [9] And þou closidist not me togidere wiþinne þe hondis of þe enemy; þou hast set my feet in a large place. [10] Lord, haue þou merci on me, for I am troblid; myn iȝe is troblid in ire, my soule and my wombe ben troblid. [11] Forwhi my lijf failide in sorewe; and my ȝeeris in weilynges. Mi uertu is maad feble in pouert; and my boonys ben disturblid. [12] Ouer alle myn enemyes I am maad shenship gretli to my neiȝboris; and drede to my knowun. Thei þat sien me wiþoutforþ, fledden fro me; [13] I am ȝouen to forȝetyng, as a deed man fro herte. I am maad as a lorun uessel; [14] for I herde dispisynge of manye men dwellynge in cumpas. In þat þing þe while þei camen togidere aȝenes me; þei counceliden to take my lijf. [15] But, Lord, I hopide in þee; I seide, þou art my God; [16] my times[191] ben in þyn hondis. Delyuere þou me fro þe hondis of myn enemyes; and fro hem þat pursuen me. [17] Make þou cleer þi face on þi seruaunt; Lord, make þou me saaf in þi merci; [18] be I not shent, for I inwardli clepide þee. Unpitouse men be ashamed, and be led forþ into helle; [19] gileful lippis be maad doumbe. That speken wickidnesse aȝenes a iust man; in pride, and in mysusyng. [20] Lord, þe multitude of þi swetnesse is ful greet; which þou hast hid to men dredynge þee. Thou hast maad a perfit þing to hem, þat hopen[192] in þee; in þe siȝt of þe sones of men.[193] [21] Thou shalt hide hem in þe pryuyte of þi face;[194] fro | disturblyng of men. Thou shalt defende hem in þi tabernacle; fro aȝenseiyng of tungis.

f. 14ʳ

f. 14ᵛ

**Ps. 30** ᵃ nurische] nursche

## [PSALM 30 GLOSSES]

189.[i] Dauiþ made þis salm in þe persecucioun of Saul, in doynge þankyngis for he hadde ascapid manye perelis and in preiynge to ascape present perels and to-comynge, whiche he dredde. *Lire here.*

190.[ii] He þat hopiþ in riches, in onour, eþer in mannis power, eþer in a my3ti frend, kepiþ vanyte. *Austin here.*

191. þus it is in Ebreu, þou3 Latyn bookis han here <u>my lottis</u>. *Lire here.*   f. 14[r]

192. Bi du hope þat comeþ of grace and of good werkis;

193. <u>in þe si3t of sones of men</u>, for þei dreden not neþer ben ashamed to shewe her hope bifore men, 3he, þat pursuen hem. *Lire here.*

Crist wolde þat his signe be set in þe forheed, as in þe seete of shame, þat a cristen man be not ashamed of þe shenshipis of Crist. Now, it is not `shenschip´[iii] to be clepid a cristen man, but it is shenschip to lyue as a cristen man. þerfor knouleche þou bifore men, þat þou art verili a cristen man. *Austyn here.*

194. þat is, bifor þi face, which is hid to men of þis world. *Lire here.*

195. In delyueringe me wondurfuli in Ceila. *Lire here.*   f. 14[v]

196. In Ieroms translacioun it is, <u>Y seide of myn astonying</u>. *Lire here.*

197.[iv] Cri to God is not bi vois, but bi herte. Manye beynge stille wiþ lippis crieden; manye makinge noise wiþ mouþ, while þe herte was turned awei, my3ten gete no þing. *Austyn here.*

---

[22] Blessid be þe Lord; for he haþ maad wondurful his merci to me in a strengþid citee.[195] [23] Forsoþe I seide in þe passyng of my soule;[196] I am caste out fro þe face of þyn i3en. Therfor þou herdist þe uois of my preier; while I criede[197] to þee. [24] Alle 3e hooli men of þe Lord, loue hym; for þe Lord shal seke treuþe, and he shal 3elde plenteuousli to hem[b] þat doen pride. [25] Alle 3e þat hopen in þe Lord, do manli; and 3oure herte be comfortid.

**Ps. 30 glosses**   [i] *this gloss also in* ACikKLPQSUVX   [ii] *this gloss also in margin of* D_70   [iii] shenschip] *in margin by the scribe; the* Austyn *part of this gloss also in margin of* D_70   [iv] *this gloss also in margin of* D_70

[b] plenteuousli to hem] to hem plenteuousli, *marked for transposition*

## [PSALM 31]

*Beati quorum remisse*

[1] þe title of xxxj salm. Lernyng to Dauiþ.[198]

   Blessid ben þei whos wickidnessis ben forȝouen; and whose synnes
ben hilid.[199] [2] Blessid is þe man to whom þe Lord arettide not[200]
synne; neþer gile is in his spirit. [3] For I was stille,[201] my boones[202]
wexiden elde; while I criede[203] al dai. [4] For bi dai and nyȝt þyn hond
was maad greuouse on me; I am turned in my wrecchidnesse, while þe
þorn[204] is set in. [5] I made my synne knowun to þee; and I hidde not
myn vnriȝtfulnesse. I seide,[205] I shal knouleche aȝenes me myn
vnriȝtfulnesse to þe Lord; and þou hast forȝoue þe wickidnesse of
my synne. [6] For þis þing ech hooli man shal preie[206] to þee; in
couenable tyme. Neþeles in þe grete flood of manye watris;[207] þo shulen
not neiȝe to þee. [7] Thou art my refuyt fro tribulacioun þat cumpasside
me; þou, my fulli ioiynge, delyuere me fro hem þat cumpassen me.[208]
[8] I shal ȝyue vndurstondyng to þee, and I shal teche þee; in þis weie in
which þou shalt go, I shal make stidfast myn iȝen on þee. [9] Nile ȝe be
f. 15ʳ  maad as an hors and mule; to whiche | is noon vndurstondyng. Lord,
constreyne þou þe chekis of hem wiþ a bernacle and bridil; þat neiȝen
not to þee. [10] Manye betyngis ben of þe synnere; but merci shal
cumpasse hym þat hopiþ in þe Lord. [11] Ȝe iust men be glad and make
fulli ioie in þe Lord; and alle ȝe riȝtful of herte[209] haue glorie.

## [PSALM 32]

*Exultate iusti in Domino*

þe xxxij salm haþ no title.[a]

   [1] Ȝe iust men, haue fulli ioie in þe Lord; preisyng togidere
bicomeþ riȝtful men. [2] Knouleche ȝe to þe Lord in an harpe; synge
ȝe to hym in a sautre of ten stryngis. [3] Synge ȝe to hym a newe song;
seie ȝe wel salm to hym in criynge. [4] For þe word of þe Lord is
riȝtful; and alle hise werkis ben in feiþfulnesse. [5] He loueþ merci
and doom; þe erþe is ful of þe merci of þe Lord. [6] Heuenys ben
maad stidfast bi þe word of þe Lord; and al þe uertu[210] of þo bi þe
spirit of his mouþ. [7] And he gaderiþ togidere þe watris of þe see as
in a bowge; and settiþ depe watris in tresours. [8] Al erþe drede
þe Lord; soþeli alle men enhabityng þe world be moued of hym.

Ps. 32      [a] The xxxij psalm of Dauid *in A* k

## [PSALM 31 GLOSSES]

198.[i] Dauiþ made þis salm whanne God shewide to him þat his synne of auoutrie wiþ Bersabee and of manquellyng of Vrie was forȝouun to him. *Lire here.*

199. þat is, þat God biholdiþ not þo, to punysche bi euerelastinge peyne. *Lire here.*

200. To punysche euerelastingli. *Lire here.*

201. In knouleching of synnes, and criede my meritis. [*Austin*][ii] here.

202. þat is, vertues. *Austin here.*

203. þis was not knouleching of synnes, but cry of angwisch and drede, lest Goddis doom apperide on him in ony open punysching. *Lire here.*

204.[iii] þat is, of contricioun; is set yn, for at þe word of Nathan þe profete he was contrite, and knoulechide his synne. *Lire here.*

205. Y seide: He pronounsiþ not now, he bihetiþ þat he shal pronounce; and God forȝueþ now. Y seide Y shal pronounce, and þou hast forȝoue. In þis he shewide þat he pronounside not ȝit bi mouþ, but he pronounside bi herte. *Austin here.*

þe pite eþer merci of God is greet, for at biheest aloone of knouleching, he forȝyueþ þe synne. Forwhi, wille is demed for worchyng. *Cassiodore here and þe comyn glos here.*

206. In Ieroms translacioun it is, preieþ. *Lire here.*

207. þat is, of grete temptaciouns; synne[ri]s[iv] bi turnynge aȝen to synne[v] shulen not neiȝe to þee. *Lire here.*

208. þat is, fro fendis þat tempten me. *Lire here.*

209. þei ben riȝtful in herte þat dressen her herte aftir Goddis f. 15[r] wille, þat no þing þat God doiþ displese hem. *Austin in xxxij salm on þe firste vers.*

## [PSALM 32 GLOSSES]

210. In Ieroms translacioun it is, al þe ournyng of þo; bi ournyng is vndurstondi[þ][i] sterris. *Lire here.*

---

**Ps. 31 glosses** [i] *next to the title in the left margin; this gloss also in* ACikKLPSUVX
[ii] Austin] Lire   [iii] *the first part of this gloss, through* contricioun, *interlinear and underlined in* K
[iv] synneris] synnes   [v] synne] synne s-, s- *canc.*
**Ps. 32 glosses** [i] vndurstondiþ] vndurstondis

[9] For he seide, and þe þingis weren maad; he comaundide, and þingis weren maad of nouȝt. [10] The Lord distrieþ þe councel[s]ᵇ of folkis, forsoþe he repreueþ þe þouȝtis of puplis; and he repreueþ þe councels of prynces. [11] But þe councel²¹¹ of þe Lord dwelliþ wiþouten ende; þe þouȝtis of his herte <u>dwellen</u> in generacioun and into generacioun. [12] Blessid is þe folk whos Lord is his God; þe puple which he chees into eritage to hymsilf. [13] The Lord bihelde fro heuene; he siȝ alle þe sones of men. [14] Fro his dwellyng place maad redi bifore; he bihelde on alle men, þat enhabiten þe erþe. [15]

f. 15ᵛ Whiche made syngulerli,²¹² eþer ech bi hymsilf, þe soulis | of hem; which vndurstondiþ alle þe werkis of hem. [16] A kyng is not saued bi myche uertu;²¹³ and a giaunt shal not be saued in þe mychelnesse of his uertu. [17] An hors is false to heelþe; forˈsoþeˈᶜ he shal not be saued in þe abundaunce, eþer <u>plentee</u>, of his uertu. [18] Lo! þe iȝen of þe Lord ben on men²¹⁴ dredynge hym; and in hem þat hopen on his merci. [19] That he delyuere her soulis fro deþ; and feede hem in hungur. [20] Oure soule suffriþ þe Lord;²¹⁵ for he is oure helpere and defendere. [21] For oure herte shal be glad in hym; and we shulen haue hope in his hooli name. [22] Lord, þi merci be maad on us; as we hopiden in þee.

## [PSALM 33]

*Benedicam Dominum*

[1] *þe title of xxxiij salm. To Dauiþ, whanne he chaungide his mouþ²¹⁶ bifor Abymelech, and he droof out Dauiþ, and he ȝede forþ.*ᵃ

[2] I shal blesse þe Lord in al tyme; euere his heriynge [is]ᵇ in my mouþ. [3] Mi soule shal be presid²¹⁷ in þe Lord; mylde men here, and be glad. [4] Magnefie ȝe þe Lord²¹⁸ wiþ me; and enhaunce we his name into [it]ᶜsilf. [5] I souȝte þe Lord, and he herde me; and he delyueride me fro alle my tribulaciouns. [6] Neiȝe ȝe to him, and be ȝe liȝtned; and ȝoure faces shulen not be shent. [7] This pore man criede,²¹⁹ and þe Lord herd hym; and sauyde hym fro alle hise tribulaciouns. [8] The aungel of þe Lord sendiþ in þe cumpas of men dredynge hym; and heᵈ shal delyuere hem. [9] Taaste ȝe, and se, for þe Lord is swete; blessid is þe man þat hopiþ in hym. [10] Alle ȝe hooli men of þe Lord, drede hym; for no nedynesse is to men dredynge hym. [11] Riche men weren nedi, and weren hungry; but

---

ᵇ councels] councel    ᶜ forsoþe] *corrected in margin by the scribe*
**Ps. 33**    ᵃ *this title also in* GikKPV; *om. in* k: and he droof out Dauiþ, and heȝede forþ    ᵇ is] *om.*    ᶜ it] him    ᵈ he] he t-, t- *canc.*

211. þou3 þe sentence of God is chaungid sumtyme, Goddis councel is neuere chaungid. For his councel is taken propirli aftir `his´[ii] ordenaunce as it is in hymsilf, but his sentence is takun sumtyme upe þe meritis eþer synnes of men. *Lire here.*

212. In Ieroms translacioun þus: <u>makynge togidere þe hertis of hem</u>. þis þat he seiþ, <u>togidere</u>, shal be referrid to þe vnyte of kynde soulis, for alle resonable soulis ben of þe same kynde, and þe Ebreu word set here signefieþ boþe syngulerte and plurelte. And seuenti translatours token þe firste signyficacioun, and Ierom took þe secounde signyficacioun, and in þis place, as Y suppose, þe seuenti translatours token betere þan Ierom. *Lire here.*

213.[iii] þat is, of his oost, no but he haue wiþ þis Goddis f. 15ᵛ proteccioun. *Lire here.*

214. To kepe hem diligentli; <u>and</u> is set here for 'þat is'. *Lire here.*

215.[iv] þat is, abidiþ pacientli his good plesaunce. *Lire here.*

### [PSALM 33 GLOSSES]

216. þat is, his word. *Lire here.*

217. þat is, if ony þing worþi to be preisid is in me, al be 3ouen to God of whom Y haue it; eiþer þus, Y charge not of þe preisyngis of men, but Y desire to be preisid of God. *Lire here.*

218. <u>Magnefie 3e þe Lord</u>: If 3e louen God, rauysche 3e alle men to his loue þat ben ioyned to 3ou and alle men þat ben in 3oure hous; rauysche 3e whiche 3e moun bi excityng, bi heryng, bi preiyng, bi disputing, bi 3eldyng of resoun wiþ myldenesse and pacience; rauysche 3e Goddis loue, and seie 3e, 'Magnefie 3e þe Lord', et cetera. *Austyn here.*

219. þat is, Y þat am outlawid, pore and fleynge aboute. *Lire here.*[i]

220. Vndurstonde þou, do he þis þat sueþ in þe salm: <u>forbede þi</u> f. 16ʳ <u>tunge fro yuel</u> of blasfemye and of Goddis dispisyng. *Lire here.*

---

men þat seken þe Lord shulen not faile of al good. [12] Come, 3e sones, here 3e me; I shal teche 3ou þe drede of | þe Lord. [13] Who is f. 16ʳ a man, þat wole lijf; loueþ to se goode daies?²²⁰ [14] Forbede þi tunge

fro yuel; and þi lippis speke not gile. [15] Turne þou awei fro yuele,
and do good; seke þou pees, and parfitli sue þou it. [16] The iȝen of þe
Lord ben on iust men; and his eeren ben to her preieris. [17] But þe
cheer[221] of þe Lord is on men doynge yuelis;[222] þat he leese þe mynde
of hem fro erþe. [18] Iust men crieden and þe Lord herde hem; and
delyueride hem fro alle her tribulaciouns. [19] The Lord is nyȝ hem
þat ben of troblid herte; and he shal saue meke men in spirit. [20]
Manye tribulaciouns ben of iust men; and þe Lord shal delyuere hem
fro alle þese. [21] The Lord kepiþ alle þe boonys[223] of hem; oon of þo
shal not [be][e] br[o]kun.[f] [22] The deeþ of synneris[224] is worst; and þei
þat haten a iust man[g] shulen trespasse. [23] The Lord shal aȝenbie þe
soulis of hise seruauntis; and alle þat hopen[225] in hym shulen not
trespasse.[226]

[PSALM 34]

*Iudica Domine nocentes me*[a]

[1] *þe title of xxxiiij salm. To Dauiþ.*[227]

Lord, deme[228] þou hem þat anoien me; ouercome þou hem þat
fiȝten aȝenes me. [2] Take þou armeris and sheeld; and rise up into
help to me. [3] Schede out þe swerd, and close togidere aȝenes hem
þat pursuen me; seie þou to my soule, I am þyn heelþe. [4] Thei þat
seken my lijf; be shent and ashamed. Thei þat þenken yuelis to me; be
turned awei bacward, and be shent. [5] Be þei made as dust bifor þe
face of [þe][b] wynd; and þe aungel of þe Lord make hem streiȝt. [6]
Her weie be maad derknesse and slidirnesse; and þe aungel of þe Lord
pursue hem. [7] For wiþout cause þei hidden to me þe deþ of her
f. 16ᵛ  snare; in ueyn þei dispisiden my soule. [8] The | snare which he
knowiþ not come to hym, and þe takyng which he hidde take hym;
and fall he into þe snare in þat þing. [9] But my `soul'[c] shal fulli haue
ioie in þe Lord; and shal delite on his helþe. [10] Alle my boonys
shulen seie, Lord, who is lijk þee?[229] Thou delyuerist a pore man fro
þe hond of hise strengere; a nedi man and pore fro hem þat dyuerseli
rauyschen hym. [11] Wickid witnessis risynge, axiden me þingis
whiche I knew not. [12] Thei ȝeldiden to me yuelis[230] for goodis;
bareynesse to my soule. [13] But whanne þei weren diseseful to me; I
was cloþid in an haire. I mekide my soule in fastyng; and my preier

      [e] be] *om.*    [f] brokun] brekun    [g] man] man i-, i- *canc.*
**Ps. 34**    [a] Iudica Domine nocentes me] *below the bottom line of the page, 13 lines from the title*
      [b] þe] *om.*    [c] soul] *added by the scribe above the line of writing*

221. þat is, of ire and trobling;

222. þerfor in Ebreu it is, þe ire of þe lord is on men doynge yuel to punysche hem. *Lire here.*

223. Bi boonys, in whiche þe strengþe of bodi stondiþ, ben vndurstondun vertues, in whiche þe strengþe of soule stondiþ, which þe Lord kepiþ vnhurt fynali in chosun men. *Lire and Austin here.*

224. þe deþ of synneris: in Ebreu and in Ieroms translacioun þus: Malice shal sle wickid men, and hem þat haten a iust man, for þe malice of a man is euere cause of his gostli deþ, and sumtyme of bodili deþ. *Lire here.*

225. Bi hope formed wiþ charite;

226. not trespasse, þat is, fynali. [*Lire here.*]<sup>ii</sup>

[PSALM 34 GLOSSES]

227.<sup>i</sup> Dauiþ made þis<sup>ii</sup> salm aȝenes þe persecucioun of Saul.

Gostli, þis salm is expowned of Crist, in parti for himsilf and in parti for hise membris. *Lire here.*

228.<sup>iii</sup> Lord deme, by doom of condempnyng. *Lire here.*

229. þat is, shulen shewe bi stiryngis of ful out ioiyng þe kyndnesse of my sauyng. *Lire here.*  f. 16<sup>v</sup>

230.<sup>iv</sup> þei ȝeldiden yuelis, et cetera: Y brouȝte plentee, þei ȝeldiden bareynnesse; Y brouȝte liyf, þei ȝeldiden deþ; Y brouȝte onour, þei ȝeldiden dispisyng; Y brouȝte medecyn, þei ȝeldiden woundis. Crist curside þis bareynnesse in þe fige tre: leeuys weren, and no fruyt was. Wordis weren, and good dedis weren not. *Austin here.*

---

shal be turned wiþinne my bosum. [14] I pleside so as oure neiȝbore as oure broþer; I was maad meke so as morenyng and soreuful. [15] And þei weren glad, and camen togidere aȝenes me; turmentis weren gaderid on me, and I knew not. [16] Thei weren scaterid, and not compunct; þei temptiden me, þei scorneden me wiþ mouwing; þei gnastiden on me wiþ her teeþ. [17] Lord, whanne þou shalt biholde, restore þou my soule fro þe wickidnesse of hem; restore þou myn

<sup>ii</sup> Lire here] *om.*

**Ps. 34 glosses** <sup>i</sup> *next to the title in the left margin; this gloss also in* bCGikKPQUVX
<sup>ii</sup> þis] þis sa-, sa- *canc.* <sup>iii</sup> *next to the first verse in the left margin* <sup>iv</sup> *this gloss also in margin of* D_70

oon[231] aloone fro liouns.[232] [18] I shal knouleche to þee in[d] a greet
chirche; I shal herie þee in a sad puple. [19] Thei þat ben aduersaries
wickidli to me, haue not ioie on me; þat haten me wiþout cause, and
bekenen wiþ iȝen. [20] For soþeli þei spaken pesibli to me; and þei
spekynge in wraþfulnesse of erþe[233] þouȝten giles. [21] And þei
maden large her mouþ on me; þei seiden, Wel, wel! oure iȝen han
seyn. [22] Lord, þou hast seyn, be þou not stille; Lord, departe þou
not fro me, [23] Rise up and ȝyue tent to my doom; my God and my
f. 17[r]   Lord, biholde into my cause. | [24] Mi Lord God, deme þou me bi þi
riȝtfulnesse; and haue þei not ioie on me. [25] Seie þei not in [her][e]
hertis, Wel, wel! to oure soule; neiþer seie þei, We shulen deuoure
hym. [26] Shame þei and drede þei togidere; þat þanken for my[n][f]
yuelis. Be þei cloþid wiþ shame and drede; þat speken yuele þingis on
me. [27] Haue þei ful ioie and be þei glad þat wolen my riȝtfulnesse;
and seie þei euere, þe Lord be magnefied, whiche wolen þe pees of his
seruaunt. [28] And my tunge shal biþenke[234] þi riȝtfulnesse; al dai[235]
þyn heriyng.

## [PSALM 35]

*Dixit iniustus*

[1] *þe title of xxxv salm.* In Ebreu þus: *To victorie to Dauiþ, þe seruaunt
of þe Lord.* In Ieroms translacioun þus: *For þe uictorie of Dauiþ, þe
seruaunt of þe Lord.*[236]

[2] The vniust man seide, þat he trespasse in hymsilf; þe drede of
God is not bifore his iȝen. [3] For he dide gilefuli in þe siȝt of God;
þat his wickidnesse be founden to hatrede. [4] The wordis of his
mouþ ben wickidnesse and gile, he nolde vndurstonde to do wel. [5]
He þouȝte wickidnesse in his bed, he stood nyȝ al weie not good;
forsoþe he hatide not malice. [6] Lord þi merci is in heuene; and þi
treuþe is til to cloudis. [7] Thi riȝtfulnesse is as þe hillis of God; þi
domes ben myche depþe of watris. Lord, þou shalt saue men and
beestis; [8] as þou, God, hast multeplied þi merci. But þe sones of
men;[237] shulen hope in þe hilyng of þi wyngis.[238] [9] Thei shulen be
fillid greetli of þe plentee of þyn hous; and þou shalt ȝyue drynke to
hem wiþ þe stif streem of þi likyng. [10] For þe welle of lijf is at þee;
f. 17[v]   and in þi liȝt we shulen se liȝt.[239] | [11] Lord, sette forþ `þi'[a] merci to
hem þat knowen þee; and þi riȝtfulnesse to hem þat ben of riȝtful

[d] in] *canc. then restored by the scribe*    [e] her] *om.*    [f] myn] my
**Ps. 35**    [a] þi] *added by the scribe above the line of writing*

231. þat is, lijf;

232.<sup>v</sup> Fro liouns, þat is, fro cruel men, in maner of liouns. *Lire here.*

233. þat is, erþeli men, þat han o þing in þe herte and an oþere in þe mouþ. *Lire here.*

234. þat is, shal knouleche it in mouþ and herte. *Lire here.*     f. 17<sup>r</sup>

235.<sup>vi</sup> Al dai: What euere þou doist, do wel. þat is, kepe charite to God and man and þou hast heried God. Whanne þou syngest an ympne, þou heriest God. What doiþ þi tunge, no but also þi conscience herieþ God? In þe innocence of þi werkis, make þee redi to herie God al dai. *Austin here.*

### [PSALM 35 GLOSSES]

236.<sup>i</sup> Dauiþ made þis salm of himsilf, aȝenes þe persecucioun of Saul. *Lire here.*

237.<sup>ii</sup> þat is, lyuynge resonabli and iustli. *Lire here.*

þei ben seid men, þat axen God temporal goodis and desiren fleischli goodis and bodili helþe. þei ben seid sones of men, þat axen euerelastinge goodis and beren þe ymage of Crist. *Austin here.*

238. þat is, veri blis & hid at þee. *Lire here.*

239. þat is, in þe liȝt of glorie, we shulen se þe liȝt of þi beyng. *Lire here.*

240. þe foot of pride, þat is, þe foot of proude Saul and of hise   f. 17<sup>v</sup>
felowis; come not to me, to defoule me for her wille; [and]<sup>iii</sup> þe hond of þe synnere, þat is, councelyng yuelis to me; moue me not, fro euennesse of treuþe and of riȝtfulnesse;

eþer þus: þe foot of pride come not to me, þat is, þe fend þat felde doun bi pride, make me not suget to him bi dedli synne; and þe hond of þe synnere, þat is, þe power of þe fend obstynat in synne, moue me not, fro þe staat of grace, and euere eiþer was grauntid to him fynaly. *Lire here.*

---

herte. [12] The foot of pride<sup>240</sup> come not to me; and þe hond of þe synnere moue me not. [13] There þei felden doun þat worchen wickidnesse; þei ben caste out, and myȝten not stonde.

---

<sup>v</sup> *tie-mark placed above* aloone *by rubricator error for* liouns     <sup>vi</sup> *this gloss also in margin of* D_70
**Ps. 35 glosses**     <sup>i</sup> *next to the first verse in the left margin; this gloss also in* AbCGikKLPQSUVX     <sup>ii</sup> *the* Austin *part of this gloss also in margin of* D_70     <sup>iii</sup> and] *in*

[PSALM 36]

*Noli emulari*

[1] *þe title of xxxvj salm. To Dauiþ.*

Nile þou sue wickid men; neþer loue²⁴¹ þou men doynge wickidnesse. [2] For þei shulen wexe drie swiftli as hei; and þei shulen falle
doun soone as þe wortis of eerbis. [3] Hope þou in þe Lord, and do
þou goodnesse; and enhabite þou þe lond, and þou shalt be fed wiþ
hise richessis. [4] Delite þou in þe Lord; and he shal ȝyue to þee þe
axyngisᵃ ²⁴² of þyn herte. [5] Shewe þi weie to þe Lord, and hope þou
in hym; and he shal do. [6] And he shal lede out þi riȝtfulnesse as liȝt,
and þi doom as myddai; [7] be þou suget to þe Lord, and preie þou
hym. Nile þou sue hym þat haþ prosperite in his weie;²⁴³ a man
doynge `vn´riȝtfulnesses.ᵇ [8] Ceesse þou of ire and forsake wood-
nesse; nyle þou sue, þat þou do wickidli. [9] For þei þat doon wickidli,
shulen be distried; but þei þat suffren þe Lord,²⁴⁴ shulen enherite þe
lond. [10] And ȝit a litil, and a synnere shal not be;²⁴⁵ and þou shalt
seke his place and shalt not fynde. [11] But mylde men shulen
enherite þe lond; and shulen delite in þe multitude of pees. [12] A
synnere shal aspie a riȝtful man; and he shal gnaste wiþ hise teeþ on
hym. [13] But þe Lord shal scorne þe synnere; for he biholdiþ þat his
dai comeþ. [14] Synneris drowen out swerd; þei benten her bouwe.
f. 18ʳ To disseyue a pore man and nedi; to strangle | riȝtful men [of]ᶜ herte.
[15] Her swerd entre into þe herte of hemsilf; and her bouwe be
brokun. [16] Betere is a litil þing to a iust man; þan manye richessis of
synneris. [17] For þe armes of synneris shulen be al tobrokun; but þe
Lord confermeþ iust men. [18] The Lord knowiþ þe daies of men
vnwemmed; and her eritage shal be wiþouten ende. [19] Thei shulen
not be shent in þe yuel tyme, and þei shulen be fillid in þe daies of
hungur; [20] for synneris shulen perische. Forsoþe anoon as þe
enemyes of þe Lord ben onourid and enhaunsid; þei failynge shulen
faile as smoke. [21] A synnere²⁴⁶ shal borewe, and shal not paie; but a
iust man haþ merci, and shal ȝyue. [22] For þei þat blessen þe Lord
shulen enherite þe lond; but þei þat cursen hym shulen perische. [23]
The goyng of [a]ᵈ man shal be dressid anentis þe Lord; and he shal
wilne his weie.²⁴⁷ [24] Whanne he falliþ, he shal not be hurtlidᵉ doun;

---

**Ps. 36**    ᵃ axyngis] axyyngis    ᵇ doynge vnriȝtfulnesses] vndoynge riȝtfulnesses,
*corrected by canc. and insertion above the line of writing by the scribe*    ᶜ of] in    ᵈ a] *om.*
ᵉ hurtlid] burtlid, *corrected by the scribe with overwriting*

[PSALM 36 GLOSSES]

241. þou3 þe kynde shal be loued, þei shulen neþer be sued neþer be loued in þat þei ben yuele. *Lire here.*

242.[i] þe axyngis of fleisch ben aboute þe helþe of fleisch, but þe axingis of herte ben aboute euerelastynge goodis. *Austin here.*

Iust men axen not outirli of God, no but goodis of grace and of vertu, whiche ben euere 3ouun to hem þat axen, whanne þei axen for hemsilf and feiþfuli and wiþ perseueraunce, as iust men doon. But þei axen not temporal goodis, no but vndur a condicioun: þat is, if þo ben spedeful to Goddis onour, and to þe helþe of hem eþer of oþere men, and in þis maner God heriþ hem. *Lire here.*

243.[ii] þat is, haþ þe yuel þat he purposiþ. *Lire here.*

244.[iii] þat is, abiden pacientli his good wille. *Lire here.*

245.[iv] To vss to purge good men, as he is now; but he shal be in peyne wiþouten ende. *Austin here.*

246. Synneris shulen resseyue peyne euere in helle for her synnes,   f. 18[r] and þei shulen not paie, for þei shulen dwelle as myche bounden as bifore, þat is, to euerelastyng peyne. *Lire here.*

247. þat is, approue it and ordeyne it to þe merit of euerelastynge liyf;

248. Whanne he falliþ, bi venyal synne;

shal not be [h]urtlid[v] doun, for bi þis he falliþ not[vi] doun fro þe staat of grace;

his hond, þat is, kepiþ him bi grace; eþer þou3 he falliþ bi dedli synne, he shal be restorid bi penaunce. *Lire here.*

249.[vii] Neþer his seed sekynge breed: Hooli chirche, Cristis bodi, þat conteyneþ alle iust men and good aungelis, seiþ, Y was 3ongere, et cetera, sekynge breed, þat is, Goddis word, þat goiþ neuere awei fro þe mouþ of a iust man; and a iust man doiþ euere Goddis wille, and þenkiþ in his lawe. *Austin here.*

---

for þe Lord vndursettiþ his hond.[248] [25] I was 3ongere, and soþeli I wexide eld, and I si3 not a iust man forsakun; neþer his seed sekynge breed.[249] [26] Al dai he haþ merci and leeneþ; and his seed shal be in

**Ps. 36 glosses**   [i] *this gloss also in margin of* D_70L2   [ii] *this gloss also in margin of* L2   [iii] *a variant gloss here interlinear and underlined in* K: þei þat suffren þe Lord, þat is mekeli his wille *(cf. note iv to* **32: 215** *above)*   [iv] *this gloss also in margin of* L2   [v] hurtlid] burtlid   [vi] not] not f-, f- *canc.*   [vii] *a dot above* sekynge *for an undrawn tie-mark; this gloss also in margin of* D_70

blessyng. [27] Bowe þou awei fro yuel and do good; and dwelle þou
into þe world `of world'.[f 250] [28] For þe Lord loueþ doom, and shal
not forsake hise seyntis; þei shulen be kept wiþouten ende. Vniust
men shulen be punyshid; and þe seed of wickid men shal perische.
[29] But iust men shulen enherite þe lond; and shulen enhabite
þeronne into þe world of world.[251] [30] The mouþ of a iust man shal
biþenke wisdom; and his tunge shal speke doom. [31] The lawe of
f. 18ᵛ   his | God is in his herte; and hise steppis shulen not be disseyued.
[32] A synnere biholdiþ a iust man; and sekiþ to sle hym. [33] But þe
Lord shal not forsake hym in hise hondis; neþer shal dampne hym,
whanne it shal be demed aȝenes hym. [34] Abide þou þe Lord and
kepe þou his weie, and he shal enhaunse þee, þat bi eritage þou take
þe lond; whanne synneris shulen perische, þou shalt se.[252] [35] I siȝ a
wickid man enhaunsid aboue; and reisid up as þe cedris of Liban. [36]
And I passide, and lo! he was not; I souȝte hym and his place is not
founden.[253] [37] Kepe þou innocence and se equyte; for þo ben relikis
to a pesible man. [38] Forsoþe vniust men shulen perische; þe relifs
of wickid men shulen perische togidere. [39] But þe helþe of iust men
is of þe Lord; and he is her defendere in þe tyme of tribulacioun. [40]
And þe Lord shal helpe hem, and shal make hem fre, and he shal
delyuere hem fro synneris; and he shal saue hem, for þei hopiden in
hym.

## [PSALM 37]

*Domine ne in furore*

[1] *þe title of xxxvij salm. þe salm of Dauiþ, to biþenke of þe sabat.*[254]

[2] Lord, repreue þou not me in þi strong ueniaunce; neiþer
chastise þou me in þyn ire. [3] For þyn arewis ben ficchid in me; and
þou hast confermed þyn hond on me. [4] Noon helþe is in my fleisch
for þe face of þyn ire; no pees is to my boonys for þe face of my
synnes.[255] [5] For my wickidnessis ben goon ouer myn heed; as an
heuy birþun, þo ben maad heuy on me. [6] Myn heelid woundis[256]
weren rotun, and ben brokun; for þe face of myn vnwisdom. [7] I am
maad a wrecche, and I am bowid doun til into þe ende; aldai I
f. 19ʳ   entride soreuful. [8] For my leendis ben | fillid wiþ scornyngis;[257]
and heelþe is not in my fleisch. [9] I am turmentid and maad low ful
gretli; I roride for þe weilyng of myn herte. [10] Lord, al my desir[258]

---

[f] of world] *added by the scribe in margin*

250. þat is, herbi þou shalt gete euerelastinge blisse. *Lire here.*

251. þat is, wiþouten ende, for where þe world is doubled in þe elde testament, it signefieþ wiþouten ende. *Lire here.*

252. Men in blis seen þe dampnacioun of yuele men, and it is to hem a mater of fulli ioiynge, in as myche as þei han ascapid it bi þe grace of Goddis merci. *Lire here.* f. 18ᵛ

253. þat is, for he is hid in þe depþe of helle. *Lire here.*

## [PSALM 37 GLOSSES]

254.ⁱ Ierom addiþ þis word, of þe sabat, but it is not in Ebreu; neþer Ebreis seien ony þing þerof. *Lire here.*

Dauiþ made þis salm for remembraunce of hise greet synnes, and speciali for remembraunce of avoutrie wiþ Bersabee and of manquel-linge of Vrie, and of þe synne in noumbring of þe puple; and firste of þe synne of noumbryng of þe puple, til þidur: Y am maad a wrecche, et cetera; and þere he remembriþ þe synne of avoutrie wiþ Bersabe. *Lire here.*

255.ⁱⁱ þat is, for my synnes; and bi þis he shewide, þat he sorewide more for his synne, þan for his peyne. *Lire here.*

256. Myn heelid woundis: for þe synne of avoutrie cam aȝen in sum maner, wiþ þe synne of noumbring of þe puple. *Lire here.*

257. In Ieroms translacioun it is, wiþ shenschip eþer sclaundir. *Lire* f. 19ʳ *here.*

258.ⁱⁱⁱ þi desir is þi preier. If þe desir is contynuel eþer wiþout ceessyng, þe preier is contynuel. þe brennyng of charite is þe cri of herte. If charite dwelliþ euere in þee, þou criest euere to God. *Austin here.*

---

is bifor þee; and my weilyng is not hid fro þee. [11] Myn herte is disturblid in me, my vertu forsook me; and þe liȝt of myn iȝen forsook me, and it is not wiþ me. [12] Mi frendis and my neiȝboris neiȝiden and stoden aȝenes me. And þei þat weren bisidis me stoden a fer; [13] and þei diden violence, þat souȝten my lijf. And þei þat souȝten yuelis to me, spaken vanytees; and þouȝten giles al dai. [14] But I as a deef man herde not; and as a doumb man not openyng his

**Ps. 37 glosses**   ⁱ *this gloss also in* ikKV   ⁱⁱ for] for þe face of   ⁱⁱⁱ *this gloss also in margin of* D_70

mouþ. [15] And I am maad as a man not herynge; and not hauynge
reprouyngis in his mouþ. [16] For, Lord, I hopide in þee; my Lord
God, þou shalt here me. [17] For I seide, lest ony tyme myn enemyes
haue ioie on me; and þe while my feet ben mouyd, þei spaken grete
þingis on me. [18] For I am redi to betyngis; and my sorewe²⁵⁹ is
euere redi in my siȝt. [19] For I shal telle my wickidnesse; and I shal
þenke for my synne. [20] But myn `enemyes'ᵃ lyuen, and ben
confermed on me; and þei ben multeplied, þat haten me wickidli.
[21] Thei þat ȝelden yuelis for goodis bacbitiden me; for I suede
goodnesse. [22] Mi Lord God, forsake þou not me; go þou not
awei fro me. [23] Lord God of myn heelþe; biholde þou into myn
helpe.

[PSALM 38]

*Dixi custodiam*

[1] *þe title of xxxviij salm. For victorie to Iditum, þe song of
Dauiþ.*²⁶⁰

[2] I seide, I shal kepe my weies; þat I trespasse not in my tunge.
I settide keping to my mouþ; whanne a syn[n]ereᵃ stood aȝenes |
me. [3] I was doumb and was mekid ful greetli, and was stille fro
goodis; and my sorewe was renulid. [4] Myn herte was hoot
wiþinne me; and fier shal brenne out in my þenkyng. [5] I spak
in my tunge; Lord, make þou myn ende knowun to me. And þe
noumbre of my daies what it is; þat I wite, what failiþ to me. [6]
Lo! þou hast set my daies mesurable;²⁶¹ and my substaunce is as
nouȝt bifor þee. Neþeles al vanyte; ech man lyuynge. [7] Neþeles a
man passiþ inᵇ ymage;²⁶² but also he is disturblid veynli. He
tresoriþ; and he not to whom he shal gadere þo þingis. [8] And
now which is myn abidyng? wher not þe Lord? and my sub-
staunce²⁶³ is at þee.²⁶⁴ [9] Delyuere þou me fro alle my wickidnessis; þou hast ȝoue me shenship to þe vnkunnynge. [10] I was
doumb and openyde not my mouþ; for þou hast maad, [11] remoue
þou þi woundis²⁶⁵ fro me. Fro þe strengþe of þin hond I failide in
blamyngis; [12] for wickidnesse þou hast chastisid man. And þou
madist his lijf to faile as an ireyne;²⁶⁶ neþeles ech man is disturblid
in veyn. [13] Lord, here þou my preier and my bisechyng; perseyue

---

Ps. 37      ᵃ enemyes] *added by the scribe in margin*
Ps. 38      ᵃ synnere] synere      ᵇ in] in his, his *canc.*

259.<sup>iii</sup> For Y woot þat Y disseruyde betyngis for my synne of avoutrie wiþ Bersabee, and of manquellynge of Vrie. *Lire here.*

Sumtyme synneris ben not betun in þis liyf, for her sauyng is dispeirid. But it is nede þat þei be betun here, to whiche euerelastinge liyf, þat is blis, is made redi. Men maken sorewe for her betingis, but þei maken not sorewe whi þei ben betun. But Dauiþ made sorewe not so, but for þe leesing of riȝtfulnesse, not for þe leesyng of money. *Austin here.*

### [PSALM 38 GLOSSES]

260.<sup>i</sup> þus it is in Ieroms translacioun and þe Ebreu acordiþ þerwiþ. *Lire here.*

Dauiþ made þis salm for hymsilf, whanne he was pursued of Absolon his sone, aftir þat he herde þe dispisyngis of Semey. And goostli it<sup>ii</sup> mai be expowned of ech cristen man beynge in temporal turment for hise synnes, which suffriþ it pacientli and tristiþ in Goddis merci, and bisechiþ it deuoutli and contynueli. *Lire here.*

261. þat is, shorte; and þerfor in Ierom it is,<sup>iii</sup> shorte; and my substaunce, þat is, liyf, for in Ieroms translacioun it is, my liyf. *Lire here.*    f. 19<sup>v</sup>

262.<sup>iv</sup> In Ebreu it is, in derknesse. [*Lire here.*]<sup>v</sup>

263. þat is, riches;

264. For þe riches of iust men is kept at God. *Lire here.*

265. þat is, þese peynes ȝouun of þee to me. *Lire here.*

266. In Ebreu and in Ieroms translacioun it is, as a mouȝte. *Lire here.*

267.<sup>vi</sup> Fro present liyf bi deþ. *Lire here.*

268. þat is, in staat to disserue blis. *Lire here.*

---

þou wiþ eeris my teeris. Be þou not stille, for I am a comelyng at þee; and a pilgrym, as alle my fadris. [14] Forȝyue þou to me, þat I be refreischid bifor þat I go;<sup>267</sup> and I shal no more be.<sup>268</sup>

<sup>iii</sup> *the* Austin *part of this gloss also in margin of* D_70
**Ps. 38 glosses**    <sup>i</sup> *a tie-mark in the title but not at the gloss, which is in the bottom margin* <sup>ii</sup> it] *corrected by the scribe on an erasure; the first historical part of this gloss also in* AbCGikKLPQSUVX    <sup>iii</sup> is] is sch-, sch- *canc.*    <sup>iv</sup> *this gloss interlinear and underlined in* K, *the phrase* In Ebreu it is *om.; also in margin of* V *(damaged)*    <sup>v</sup> Lire here] *om.*    <sup>vi</sup> *this gloss also in margin of* k2 *(the only Psalms gloss in this MS)*

## [PSALM 39]

*Expectans*

[1] þe title of nyne and þrittiþe salm. For victorie, þe song of Dauiþ.[269]

[2] I [a]bidynge[a] abood þe Lord; and he ȝaf tent to me. [3] And he herde my preieris; and he ledde out me fro þe lake of wrecchidnesse, and fro þe filþe of draste. And he ordeynede my feet | on a stoon;[270] and he dresside my goyngis.[271] [4] And he sente into my mouþ a newe song; a song to oure God. Manye men shulen se and shulen drede; and shulen haue hope in þe Lord. [5] Blessid is þe man of whom þe name of þe Lord is his hope; and he bihelde not into vanytees, and into false woodnessis. [6] Mi Lord God, þou hast maad þi meruelis manye; and in þi[272] þouȝtis noon is þat is lijk þee. I telde and I spak; and þei ben multeplied aboue noumbre.[273] [7] Thou noldist sacrifice and offryng; but þou madist perfitli eeris to me. Thou axidist not brent sacrifice and sacrifice for synne; [8] þanne I seide, Lo! I come. In þe heed of þe book it is writun of me, [9] þat I shulde [d]o[b] þi wille; my God, I wolde; and þi lawe in þe myddis of myn herte. [10] I telde þi riȝtfulnesse in a greet chirche; lo! I shal not refreyne my lippis, Lord, þou wistist. [11] I hidde not þi riȝtfulnesse in myn herte; I seide þi treuþe and þyn helþe. I hidde not þi merci and þi treuþe; fro a myche councel.[274] [12] But þou, Lord, make not[275] fer þi merciful doyngis fro me; þi mercy and treuþe euere token me up. [13] Forwhi yuelis, of whiche is no noumbre, cumpassiden me; my wickidnessis token me, and I myȝte not þat I shulde se. Tho ben multeplied aboue þe heeris of myn heed; and myn herte forsook me. [14] Lord, plese it to þee, þat þou delyuere me; Lord, biholde þou to helpe me. [15] Be þei shent and aschamed togedere; þat seken my lijf, to take awei it. Be þei turned abak, and be þei aschamed; þat wolen yuelis to me. [16] Bere þei her confusioun anoon;[c] þat seien to me, Wel! wel![276] [17] Alle men þat seken | þee, be fulli ioieful and be glad on þee; and seie þei, þat louen þin helþe, þe Lord be magnefied euere. [18] Forsoþe I am a beggere and pore; þe Lord is bisi of me. Thou art myn helpere and my defendere; my God, tarie þou not.[277]

## [PSALM 40]

*Beatus qui intelligit*

[1] þe title of fourtiþe salm. For victorie, þe song of Dauiþ.[278]

---

**Ps. 39**    [a] abidynge] bidynge    [b] do] þo    [c] anoon] anoon anoon, *the dittography not canc.*

[PSALM 39 GLOSSES]

269.ⁱ þis salm is expowned of Crist in x capitulo to Ebreis, in parti of Crist himsilf, and in parti of his bodi hooli chirche. þe firste vers is seid of hooli chirche, in þe persoone of hooli fadris desirynge Cristis incarnacioun. *Lire here.*

270.ⁱⁱ þat is, Crist. *Lire here.*                                     f. 20ʳ

271. þat is, my dedis into euerelastynge liyf. *Lire here.*

272. In Ebreu and in Ieroms translacioun þus: And þi þouȝtis ben for us, bi whiche þou disposidist fro wiþout bigynnyng þe mysterie of þin incarnacioun. *Lire here.*

273. þat is, werkis of þi meruels ben multeplied; þerfor in Ieroms translacioun þus: þi meruelis ben mo, þan þat þo mowun be teld. *Lire here.*

274. In Ieroms translacioun þus: fro a myche chirche. *Lire here.*

275. Here Crist preieþ for þe staat of his gostli bodi; fro me, þat is, fro my gostli bodi, for which he preiede ofte in þe gospel. *Lire here.*

276. þat is, scorn. [*Lire here.*]ⁱⁱⁱ

277. Tarie þou not: No man bihete to himsilf, þat þat þe gospel  f. 20ᵛ bihetiþ not. My briþeren, Y biseche ȝou, perseyue ȝe hooli scripturis, if þo disseyueden ony þing, if þo seiden ony þing, and it bifelde in oþere maner þan þo seiden; it is nede þat til into þe ende alle þin[gi]sⁱᵛ be doon so, as þo seiden. Oure scripturis biheten not to us in þis world, no but tribulaciouns, angwischis, encreessyngis of sorewis, and plente of temptaciouns. *Austyn here.*

[PSALM 40 GLOSSES]

278.ⁱ þis salm is expowned of Cristis passioun and risynge aȝen. *Lire here.*

279. Blessid is he þat vndurstondiþ, þat is, rediþ wiþinne bi feiþ formed wiþ charite þe richessis of Cristis godhed, vndur þe pouert which he bar in þe forme of oure manheed; on a nedi man and pore,

---

[2] Blessid is he²⁷⁹ þat vndurstondiþ on a nedi man and pore; The Lord shal delyuere him in þe yuel dai. [3] The Lord kepe

**Ps. 39 glosses**          ⁱ *next to the title in the left margin; this gloss also in* AbCGikKLPQSV*X*     ⁱⁱ *this gloss also in* V     ⁱⁱⁱ Lire here] *om.; this gloss also interlinear and underlined in* K *and in margins of* OV     ⁱᵛ þingis] þins
**Ps. 40 glosses**      ⁱ *this gloss also in* AbCikKLPQSV*X*

hym, and quykene hym, and make hym bl[e]sful<sup>a</sup> in þe lond; and
bitake not hym into þe wille of hise enemyes. [4] The Lord bere
help to hym on þe bed of his sorewe; þou hast ofte turned²⁸⁰ al his
bedstre in his sijknesse. [5] I seide, Lord, haue þou merci on me;²⁸¹
heele þou my soule, for I synnede aȝenes þee. [6] Myn enemyes²⁸²
seiden yuelis to me; Whanne shal he die, and his name shal
perische? [7] And if he entride²⁸³ for to se, he spak veyn þingis;
his herte gaderide wickidnesse to hymsilf. He ȝede wiþoutforþ; and
spak to þe same þing.²⁸⁴ [8] Alle myn enemyes bacbitiden pryueli
aȝenes me; aȝenes me þei þouȝten yuelis to me. [9] Thei
ordeyneden an yuel word aȝenes me; Wher he þat slepiþ,²⁸⁵ shal
not leic to, þat he rise aȝen? [10] Forwhi þe man of my pees, in
whom I hopide,²⁸⁶ he þat eet my looues;²⁸⁷ made greet disseit on
me. [11] But þou, Lord, haue merci on me, and reise me aȝen; and
I shal ȝelde to hem. [12] In þis þing I knew þat þou woldist me;²⁸⁸
for myn enemye shal not<sup>b</sup> haue ioie on me. [13] Forsoþe, þou hast
take me up for innocence; and hast confermed me in þi siȝt
f. 21ʳ  wiþouten ende. [14] Blessid be þe Lord God of Israel, fro þe |
world and into þe world; be it doon, be it doon.

## [PSALM 41]

*Quemadmodum desiderat*

[1] *Þe title of xlj salm. To victorie, to þe sones of Chore. Þus it is in
Ebreu. But in Ieroms<sup>a</sup> translacioun þus: For þe victorie, of þe wisest of
þe sones of Chore.*²⁸⁹

[2] As an hert²⁹⁰ desiriþ to þe wellis of watris; so þou, God, my
soule desiriþ to þee. [3] Mi soule þirstide²⁹¹ to God strong, quyk;
whanne shal I come and appere bifore þe face of God? [4] Mi
teeris weren looues to me<sup>b</sup> bi dai and nyȝt; while it is seid to me
ech dai, Where is þi God? [5] I biþouȝte of þese þingis, and I
shedde out in [me]<sup>c</sup> my soule;²⁹² for I shal passe into þe place of
þe wondurful tabernacle, til to þe hous of God. In þe vois of ful
out ioiyng and knoulechyng; is þe sown of þe etere.²⁹³ [6] Mi
soule, whi art þou sori; and whi disturblist þou me? Hope þou in

---

Ps. 40      <sup>a</sup> blesful] blisful      <sup>b</sup> shal not] shal not not, *the dittography not canc.*
Ps. 41      <sup>a</sup> Ieroms] Ieroms þus, þus *canc.*      <sup>b</sup> to me] to me to me, *the dittography not canc.*
<sup>c</sup> me] *om.*

þat is, Crist, þat was borun in pouer[t],[ii] as of a pore modir, and in a pore place, and was wlappid in pore cloþis, and lyuyde in pouert, for he hadde not where to reste his heed; also he diede in pouert, as spuylid of his cloþis,[iii] and he was leid in an oþere mannis sepulcre. *Lire here and Austyn here in sentence.*

280. þat is, be he so comfortid and maad hool of God, þat he haue no more nede. *Lire here.*

281. Dauiþ seiþ þis of himsilf, for þe synne of avoutrie and oþere. *Lire here.*

282. <u>Myn enemyes, et cetera</u>: here he spekiþ of Crist. *Lire here.*

283. þat is, ony of myn enemyes;

284. eþer Iudas speciali. *Lire here.*

285. þat is, liggiþ deed in þe sepulcre. *Lire here.*

286. þat is, as it semyde, eþer in my membris Y hopide in hym. *þe glos here.*

287. In Ieroms translacioun þus, <u>þat eet my breed, shal reise þe foot</u> aȝenes me. *Lire here.*

288. þat is, louedist eiþer appreuydist me. *Lire here.*

[PSALM 41 GLOSSES]                    F. 21[r]

289.[i] þis salm is expowned of þe staat of þe pupl[e][ii] of Israel, beynge in þe caitifte of Babiloyne, and desiryng to come to Ierusalem. *Lire here.*

290. <u>As an hert</u> sleeþ a serpent, and þirstiþ more, and renneþ scharpliere to þe welle, so sle þou þe serpent of wickidnesse, and þou shalt desire more þe welle of treuþe; as hertis swymmynge helpen hemsilf togidere, so bere we togidere oure birþuns, oon of an oþere. *Austyn here.*

291.[iii] þat is, souereynli desiride. <u>Strong</u>: þus it is in Ebreu[iv] and in Ierom[s][v] translacioun, þouȝ oure bookis han <u>welle</u>, bi errour of writeris eþer of vnwise amenderis. *Lire here.*

292. þat is, in preiynge wiþ teeris. *Lire here.*

293. In Ieroms translacioun þus: <u>Of þe multitude halewyng feestis.</u> *Lire here.*

---

[ii] pouert] pouer    [iii] cloþis] cloþid, *corrected by the scribe on an erasure*
**Ps. 41 glosses**    [i] *next to the title in the left margin*    [ii] puple] pupli; *this gloss also in* AbCGikKLPQSUV*X*    [iii] *a dot above* strong *for an undrawn tie-mark*    [iv] Ebreu] Ebreus, -s *canc.*    [v] Ieroms] Ierom; *a variant gloss here interlinear and underlined in K:* My soule þirstede to God, þat is a qwik welle

God, for ȝit I shal knouleche to hym; he is þe helþe of my cheer,
[7] and my God. Mi soule is disturblid at mysilf; þerfor, God, I
shal be myndeful of þee fro þe lond of Iordan;²⁹⁴ and fro þe litil
hil Hermonyim. [8] Depþe clepiþ depþe;²⁹⁵ in þe vois of þi
wyndows.²⁹⁶ Alle þin hiȝe þingis and þi wawis; passiden ouer
me. [9] The Lord sente his merci in þe dai; and his song in þe
nyȝt. At me is a preier to þe God of my lijf; [10] I shal seie to
God, þou art my takere-up. Whi forȝetist þou me; and whi go I
soreuful, while þe enemye turmentiþ me? [11] While my boo[ny]sᵈ
ben brokun togidere; myn enemyes, þat troblen me, dispisiden me.
While þei seien to me bi alle daies: Where is þi God? [12] Mi
soule, whi art þou sori; and whi disturblist | þou me? Hope þou
in God, for ȝit I shal knoulech to hym; he is þe helþe of my
cheer,²⁹⁷ and my God.

f. 21ᵛ

## [PSALM 42]

*Iudica me Deus*

[1] *þe two and fourtiþe salm.*²⁹⁸

God, deme þou me,²⁹⁹ and departe þou my cause fro a folk not
hooli; delyuere þou me fro a wickid man and gileful. [2] For þou artᵃ
God, my strengþe; whi hast þou put me abac, and whi go I soreuful,
while þe enemy turmentiþ me? [3] Sende out þi liȝt and þi treuþe;
þo ledden me forþ,³⁰⁰ and brouȝten into þyn hooli hil, and into þi
tabernaclis. [4] And I shal entre to þe auter of God; to God, þat
gladiþ my ȝongþe. [5] God, my God, I shal knowleche to þee in an
harpe; my soule, whi art þou sori, and whi troblist þou me? [6] Hope
þou in God, for ȝit I shal knouleche to hym; he is þe helþe of my
cheer, and my God.

ᵈ boonys] bookis
**Ps. 42**      ᵃ art] art my

294. <u>Of Iordan</u>: No man renneþ to remyssioun of synnes, no but he þat displesiþ himsilf; no but in mekinge himsilf to God, he knouleche þat he is a synnere. *Austyn here.*

295.[vi] þat is, o turment bryngiþ in an oþere. *Lire here.*

296. <u>þi wyndows</u>: þe wyndows of God ben seid þe wyndowis of heuene, þat semen bi summe licnesse to be openyd, in þe vois of þundur and leit, and of grete [r]eynes[vii] comynge doun in siche. And bi þis licnesse is signefied þe multitude and greetnesse of turmentis, þat camen of þe puple of Israel for her wickidnesse bi þe iust doom of God, in þe tyme of caitifte of Babiloyne. *Lire here.*

297. þat is, he ȝyueþ to me þe gladnesse of helþe. *Lire here.*          f. 21[v]

[PSALM 42 GLOSSES]

298.[i] þis xlj and xlij salm ben not departid in Ebreu, and þerfor it haþ no title. But in Ieroms translacioun it is departid fro þe xlj salm.

Also, þe xlj and xlij salm mai be expownyd gostli of ech deuoute persoone þat biholdiþ þe wrecchidnesse of present liyf and arettiþ himsilf to be in þe caitifte of Babiloyne, þat is interpretid confusioun eþer shenschip. And þerfor he desiriþ wiþ al his loue to be delyuerid fro þis wickid world, and to be brouȝt to his lond þat is henne. And þerfor sich a deuoute persoone weiliþ þat he is in þe wrecchidnesse of present liyf, and bisechiþ to be brouȝt to þe glorie of heuenli liyf, where he shal se God 'face to face' [1 Cor 13: 12]. *Lire on þe title of þe xlj salm.*

299. þat is, delyuere þou me [b]i[ii] þi iust doom. *Lire here.*

'Lord entre þou not into doom wiþ þi seruaunt, for ech man lyuyng shal not be maad iust in þi siȝt' [Ps 142: 2]. For who euere lyueþ here, lyue he neuere so iustli, wo to him if God entriþ wiþ him into doom. þerfor be þou bisy to be iust, and hou euere iust þou art, knoulech þee a synnere, and euere hope þou merci. If þou ȝyuest breed and art sori þerfor, þou hast lost boþe þe breed and meede. þerfor do þou almes wilfuli þat he þat seeþ, seie ȝit while þou spekist, 'Lo, Y am present'. þis is mannis riȝtfulnesse in þis liyf: fastyng, preier, and almes. If þou wolt þat þi preier fle to heuene, make þou redi fastyng and almes. *Austin here.*

300. þat is, shulen lede forþ. þe profete spekiþ here of þing to comyng bi þe maner of þing passid for þe certeynte of profesie. And þis maner of speking is ofte vside in profetis. *Lire here.*

[vi] *this gloss interlinear and underlined in* K; *also in margin of* V, *with the variant* yuel *for* turment      [vii] reynes] peynes
**Ps. 42 glosses**      [i] *the first historical part of this gloss also in* ikKV      [ii] bi] þi

# [PSALM 43]

*Deus auribus nostris*

[1] *þe title of xliij salm. To victorie, lernyng to þe sones of Chore.*[301]

God, we herden wiþ oure eeris; oure fadris telden to us. The werk which þou wrouȝtist in þe daies of hem; and in elde daies. [2] Thyn hond loste heþene men, and þou plauntidist hem;[302] þou turmentidist puplis and castidist hem[a] out. [3] For þe children of Israel weldiden þe lond not bi her swerd; [4] and þe arm of hem sauyde not hem. But þi riȝthond, and þyn arm, and þe liȝtnyng of þi cheer <u>sauyde hem</u>;[303] for þou were plesid in hem. [5] Thou art þisilf my king and my God; þat sendist helþis to Iacob. [6] Bi þee[304] we shulen wyndewe oure
f. 22[r]  enemyes wiþ horn; and in þi name we shulen dispise hem þat risen | aȝenes us. [7] For I shal not hope in my bouwe; and my swerd shal not saue me. [8] For þou hast saued us fro men t[urmen]tynge[b] us; and þou hast schent men hatynge us. [9] We shulen be preisid in God al dai; and in þi name we shulen knoulech to þee into þe world. [10] But now þou hast putte us abac, and hast schent us; and þou, God, shalt not go out in oure vertues.[305] [11] Thou hast turned us awei bihynde aftir oure enemyes; and þei þat hatiden us, rauyschiden dyuerseli to hemsilf. [12] Thou hast ȝoue us as scheep of metis; and among heþene men þou hast scaterid us. [13] Thou hast seeld þi puple wiþout prijs;[306] and multitude was not in þe chaungyngis of hem. [14] Thou hast 'set'[c] us schenschip to oure neiȝboris; mouwyng and scorn to hem þat ben in oure cumpas. [15] Thou hast [set][d] us into licnesse to heþene men; stiryng [of][e] heed among puplis. [16] Al dai my shame is aȝenes me; and þe schenschipe of my face hilide me. [17] Fro þe uois of dispisere and yuelspekere; fro þe face of enemye and pursuere. [18] Alle þese þingis camen on us, and we han not forȝete þee; and we diden not wickidli in þi testament. [19] And oure herte ȝede not awei bihynde;[307] and þou hast bowid awei oure paþis fro þi weie.[308] [20] For þou hast maad us low in þe place of turment;[309] and þe shadewe of deþ hilide us. [21] If we forȝaten þe name of oure God; and if we helden forþ oure hondis to an alien God. [22] Wher God shal not seke þese þingis? for he knowiþ þe hid þingis of herte. Forwhi we ben slayn al dai for þee;[310] we ben demed as sheep of sleyng. [23] Lord,
f. 22[v]  rise up,[311] whi slepist þou? rise up, | and putte not awei into þe ende.

---

**Ps. 43**   [a] hem] hem doun, doun *canc.*   [b] turmentynge] temptynge   [c] set] shent,
*corrected by the scribe above the line of writing*   [d] set] *om.*   [e] of] þe

[PSALM 43 GLOSSES]

301.[i] þis xliij salm was maad of þe persecucioun, which þe[ii] puple of Iewis suffride vndur Antiok, as þe book of Machabeis tellen.

Gostli þis salm mai be expowned of ech feiþful man, set in greet turment of soule eiþer of bodi, þat suffriþ pacientli and haþ mynde of þe formere benefices of God ȝouun to him, and declariþ þe yuelis whiche he suffriþ bifor God, and axiþ mekeli and deuoutli to be delyuerid of þo bi Goddis merci and vertu. *Lire here.*

302. þat is, þe children of Israel in þe lond of heþene men. *Lire here.*

303.[iii] þat is, ȝaf to hem þe lond. *Lire here.*

304. þat is, bi þi vertu we shulen make oure enemyes to fle, þorou power ȝouun of þee to us. *Lire here.*

305. In Ebreu and in Ieroms translacioun it is, in oure oostis. *Lire here.* f. 22[r]

306. þat is, so manye Iewis weren ȝouen for litil priys, þat þei weren arettid as nouȝt; and multitude, þat is, of monei eþer of bieris. *Lire here.*

307. Bi apostasie fro feiþ;

308. Oure paþis fro þi weie, þat is, it semeþ bi þe turmentis whiche we suffren, þat þou hast putte us awei fro þee. *Lire here.*

309. In Ebreu and in Ieroms translacioun it is, in þe place of dragouns; Iewis fledden þanne to desert places, and hadden turment on turment. *Lire here.*

310. þat is, for keping of þi lawe;

311. Lord rise þou up: þe profete spekiþ of God bi mannis custom, for he þat wole help a man oppressid, risiþ to helpe him;

whi slepist þou: God is seid to haue himsilf at þe maner of a slepere, whanne he suffriþ yuele men to be lordis and iust men to be troblid;

putte þou not awei, þat is, oure preieris, into þe ende, þat is, fynali. *Lire here.*

[24] Whi turnest þou awei þi face? þou forȝetist oure pouert and oure tribu[la]cioun.[f] [25] For oure lijf is maad low in dust; oure wombe is

Ps. 43 glosses    [i] *next to the title in the left margin*    [ii] þe] þe þe; *this gloss also in* AbCGikKLPQSUVX    [iii] *tie-mark placed over* cheer

[f] tribulacioun] tribucioun

glued togidere in þe erþe. [26] Lord, rise up þou and helpe us; and aȝenbie us for þi name.

## [PSALM 44]

*Eructauit cor meum*

[1] *þe title of xliiij salm. To þe ouercomere for þe lilies, þe moost loued song of lernyng of þe sones of Chore.*[312]

[2] Myn hert haþ teld out a good word; I seie my werkis to þe king.[313] Mi tunge is a penne of a writere, writing swiftli.[314] [3] Crist, þou art fairere in schap þan þe sones of men; grace is spred abrood in þi lippis; þerfor God blesside þee[315] wiþouten ende. [4] Be þou gird wiþ þi swerd;[316] on þyn hipe moost myȝtili. [5] Biholde þou in þi schaplynesse and þi fairnesse; come þou forþ wiþ prosperite and regne þou. For treuþe and myldnesse and riȝtfulnesse; and þi riȝthond[317] shal lede forþ þee wondurfuli. [6] Thi scharpe arowis schulen falle into þe hertis of þe enemyes of þe kyng; puplis schulen be vndur þee.[318] [7] God, þi seete[319] is into þe world of world; þe ȝerde of þi rewme is a ȝerd of riȝt[a] reulyng, eiþer of equyte. [8] Thou louydist riȝtfulnesse and hatidist wickidnesse; þerfor þou, God, þi God, anoyntide þee wiþ þe oile of gladnesse,[320] more þan þi felowis. [9] Mirre and gumme and cassia, of þi cloþis, of þe housis of yuer;[321] of whiche þe douȝtris of kyngis delitiden þee. [10] A queen[322] stood nyȝ on þi riȝtside in cloþyng ouergildid; cumpassid wiþ dyuersite. [11] Douȝtir, here þou and se, and bowe doun þyn eere; and for|ȝete þi puple, and þe hous of þi fadir.[323] [12] And þe kyng shal coueite þi fairenesse; for he is þi Lord God, and þei shulen worschipe hym.[324] [13] And þe douȝtris of Tire[325] in ȝiftis; alle þe riche men of þe puple shulen biseche þi cheer. [14] Al þe glorie of þat douȝtir of þe kyng is wiþinne in goldun hemmes; [15] she is cloþid aboute wiþ dyuersitees. Virgyns shulen be brouȝt to þe kyng aftir h[ir];[b] [326] hir neiȝboressis shulen be brouȝt to þee. [16] Thei shulen be brouȝte in gladnesse and ful out ioiynge; þei shulen be brouȝt into þe temple of þe kyng.

f. 23[r]

Ps. 44    [a] riȝt] riȝtful    [b] hir] hym

## [PSALM 44 GLOSSES]

312.ⁱ þus it is in Ieroms translacioun and þe Ebreu acordiþ. þis salm is seid of Crist and of hooli chirche, modir and virgyn, for Poul in þe firste capitulo to Ebreis aleggiþ þisⁱⁱ salm seid of Crist to þe lettre. *Lire here.*

313. To þe kyng, þat is, to þeⁱⁱⁱ preisyng of Ihesu Crist king of kyngis;

314. writinge swiftli, þat is, of þe hooli goost, which in techyng haþ no nede to space of tyme;

315. blesside þee ⁱᵛ: þis blessyng is ȝuyng of glorie of þe bodi, and takyng up to heuene;

316. wiþ þi swerd: bi swerd is vndurstondun Goddis word;

317. þi riȝthond, þat is, þi godheed;

318. arowis, þat is, apostlis; enemyes, þat is, vnfeiþful men and heþene þat weren conuertid bi þe postlis preching; vndur þee, þat is, vndur þin obedience, Crist;

319. þi seete, þat is, kingis mageste, and þerfor in Ebreu and in Ieroms translacioun is set God, þi troone: a troone is seid propirli þe seete of kyngis maieste;

into þe world of world, þat is, wiþouten ende; a rewme is departid for tirauntrie bi þis, þat a tiraunt sekiþ his owne profite bi oppressyng of soietis, but a kyng sekiþ þe comyn good of soietis, bi his reulyng bi þe lyne of treuþe and of riȝtfulnesse. [*Lire here.*]ᵛ

A kyng is seid of gouernyng, treuli he reuliþ not, þat amendiþ not. *Austin here.*

320. Oile of gladnesse, þat is, wiþ þe fulnesse; felowis, þat is, more þan alle creaturis able to vndurstonde;

321. housis of yuer, þat is, of boxis of yuer eþer of alabastre;

322. a queen, þat is, hooli chirche, Cristis spousesse; ouergildid, þat is, in þe fairnesse of wisdom; wiþ dyuersite, of gostli ȝiftis and vertues. *Lire here.*

323. þat is, þe puple of Iewis, and þe synagoge eiþer þe temple;  f. 23ʳ

324. and þei shulen worshipe hym: in Ieroms translacioun it is, and worship þou hym;

325. and þe douȝtris of Tire in ȝiftis, þat is, þe citees of heþene men conuertid to feiþ bi þe prechyng of apostlis, shulen offre ȝiftis to Crist deuoutli;

326. virgyns shulen be brouȝt to þe kyng aftir hir, et cetera: inᵛⁱ

---

Ps. 44 glosses  ⁱ *interlinear and then down the right margin*  ⁱⁱ þis] þis se-, se- *canc.; this gloss also in* AbCGikKLPQSUVX  ⁱⁱⁱ þe] þe þe  ⁱᵛ þee] *corrected by the scribe with overwriting*  ᵛ Lire here] *om.*  ᵛⁱ in] in Ierom, Ierom *canc.*

[17] Sones ben borun to þee³²⁷ for þi fadris; þou shalt ordeyne hem prynces on al erþe. [18] Lord, þei shulen be myndeful of þi name; in ech generacioun and into generacioun. Therfor puplis shulen knouleche to þee wiþouten ende; and into þe world of world.

[PSALM 45]

*Deus noster refugium*

[1] *þe title of xlv salm. To þe ouercomere, þe song of þe sones of Chore, for ʒongis.*³²⁸

[2] Oure God, þou art refuyt and vertu; helpere in tribulacions, þat han founde us gretli. [3] Therfor we shulen not drede³²⁹ while þe erþe shal be troblid; and þe hillis shulen be borun ouer into þe herte of þe see. [4] The watris of hem sownyden and weren troblid; hillis weren troblid togidere in þe strengþe of hym. [5] The fer[s]nesseᵃ of flood³³⁰ makiþ glad þe citee of God; þe hiʒeste God haþ halewid his tabernacle. [6] God in þe myddis þerof shal not be mouyd;ᵇ God shal helpe it eerli in þe grei morewtid. [7] Heþene men weren disturblid togidere, and rewmes weren bowid doun; God ʒaf his f. 23ᵛ    vois, þe erþe was | moued. [8] The Lord of uertues is wiþ us; God of Iacob is oure uptakere. [9] Come ʒe and se þe werkis of þe Lord; whiche wondris he haþ set on þe erþe.³³¹ [10] He doynge awei batelis til to þe ende of þe lond; shal al tobrise bouwe, and shal breke togidere armuris, and shal brenne scheeldis bi fier. [11] ʒyue ʒe tent and se ʒe, þat I am God; I shal be enhaunsid among heþene men; and I shal be enhaunsid in erþe. [12] The Lord of vertues is wiþ us; God of Iacob is oure uptakere.

[PSALM 46]

*Omnes gentes*

[1] *þe title of xlvj salm. To victorie, a salm to þe sones of Chore.*³³²

[2] Alle ʒe folkis,³³³ make ioie wiþ hondis; synge ʒe hertli to God in þe uois of ful out ioiynge. [3] For þe Lord is hiʒ and ferdful; a greet kyng on al erþe. [4] He made puplis soget to us; and heþene men vndur oure feet. [5] He cheesᵃ his eritage to us; þe fairenesse

Ps. 45    ᵃ fersnesse] fernesse    ᵇ *a dot above* mouyd *for an undrawn tie-mark*
Ps. 46    ᵃ chees] chees chees, *the dittography not canc.*

Ebreu and in Ieroms translacioun þus: in browdid cloþis eiþer in cloþis faire peyntid and dyuersli ourned she shal be led to þe kyng; virgyns suen hir; hir frendessis shulen be led to þee;

327. Sones shulen be borun to þee: here þe profete spekiþ to Crist, whose fadris ʼbiʼ [vii] mankynde weren patriarkis, hooli kyngis, and profetis; þou shalt ordeyne hem prynces, þat is, in goostli þingis. *Lire here.*

## [PSALM 45 GLOSSES]

328.[i] þe sones of Chore maden þis salm whanne þei weren sauyd bi myracle, while Chore her fadir perischide and manye oþere in xvj capitulo of Numeri. For whanne þe erþe openyde and Chore and hise felowis ȝeden doun into helle, hise sones stoden bi Goddis vertu in þe eir in þe myddis of þe openyng, til þe erþe was closid aȝen vndur her feet. [*Lire here.*][ii]

329. þerfor we shulen not drede, þat is, we dreden not, seynge openli þe help of þi grace; eþer shulen not drede while þe erþe shal be troblid, þat is, þouȝ a liyk caas eþer more orrible bifalle, and þouȝ hillis falle doun into þe see. *Lire here.*

330. þe fersnesse of flood, þat is, þe fers rennyng of Iordan makiþ glad þe puple of Iewis;

þe hiȝeste God haþ shewid þe hoolynesse of his arke signefied bi þe tabernacle; for whanne prestis ʼberingeʼ [iii] þe arke settiden feet in Iordan, þe watir aboue stood stille, and whanne þei weren goon out of Iordan, þe watir helde his cours;

shal not be moued, þat is, so þat he forsake it and wiþdrawe his help. *Lire here.*

331. In Ebreu and in Ieroms translacioun it is, wildirnessis, for þe   f. 23ᵛ
citee of Ierico was set vndur cursyng to be bildid aȝen. *Lire here.*

## [PSALM 46 GLOSSES]

332.[i] þe sones of Chore in þis salm diden þankingis to God bi spirit of profesie, for victorie to comynge vndur Iosue of puplis enhabityng þe lond of Chanaan *Lire here.*

333. þat is, alle þe lynagis of Israel. þerfor in Ebreu and in Ieroms

---

[vii] bi] ben, *canc. and corrected in margin by the scribe*
Ps. 45 glosses    [i] *next to the first verses in the right margin; this gloss also in* AbCGikKLPQSUVX    [ii] Lire here] *om.*    [iii] beringe] settiden, *canc. and corrected by the scribe above the line of writing*
Ps. 46 glosses    [i] *next to the title in the right margin; this gloss also in* AbCGikKLPQSUVX

of Iacob, whom he louyde.[334] [6] God stiede in hertli song; and þe
Lord in þe vois of a trumpe. [7] Synge ȝe to oure God, synge ȝe;
synge ȝe to oure[b] kyng, synge ȝe. [8] For God is kyng of al erþe;
synge ȝe wiseli. [9] God shal regne on heþene men; God sittiþ
on his hooli seete. [10] The prynces of puplis ben gaderid togidere
wiþ God of Abraham; for þe stronge goddis of erþe[335] ben reisid
gretli.

*Magnus Dominus*

[1] *þe title of xlvij salm. þe song of salm, of þe sones of Chore.*[336]

[2] The Lord is greet and worþi to be preisid ful myche; in þe
citee of oure God, in þe hooli hil of hym. [3] It is foundid[337] in þe
f. 24ʳ  ful out ioiyng of al erþe; þe hil of[a] | Sion; þe sidis of þe norþ, þe
citee of þe grete kyng.[338] [4] God shal be knowun in þe housis
þerof; whanne he shal take it.[339] [5] For lo! þe kyngis of erþe[340]
weren gaderid togidere; þei camen into o place. [6] Thei seynge so
wondriden; þei weren disturblid,[341] þei weren mouyd togidere, [7]
tremblyng took hem. There sorewis as of a womman trauelyng of
child; [8] in a greet spirit[342] þou shalt al tobreke þe schippis of
Tharsis. [9] As we herden so we sien, in þe citee of þe Lord of
vertues, in þe citee of oure God; God haþ foundid þat citee
wiþouten ende.[343] [10] God, we han resseyued þi merci; in þe
myddis of þi temple. [11] Aftir þi name, God, so þyn heriyng[344] is
spred a brood into þe endis of erþe; þi riȝthond is ful of
riȝtfulnesse. [12] The hil of Sion be glad, and þe douȝtris of
Iudee[345] be fulli ioieful; for þi domes, Lord. [13] Cumpasse ȝe Sion
and biclippe ȝe it; telle ȝe in þe touris þerof. [14] Sette ȝe ȝoure
hertis in þe vertu of hym;[346] and departe ȝe þe housis of him, þat ȝe
telle out in an oþere generacioun. [15] For þis is God, oure God,
into wiþouten ende, and into þe world of world; he schal gouerne
us into worldis.[347]

translacioun it is, <u>Alle ȝe puplis touche wiþ hondis</u>, þat is, instrumentis of musik, in whiche Goddis preisyngis weren songen of
dekenes;

334. <u>Iacob whom he louyde</u>: in Ebreu it is, <u>Iacob whom he louyde,
hadde glorie of þis</u>. *Lire here.*

335. <u>Goddis of erþe</u>, þat is, þe iugis of Israel þat ben seid 'goddis' in
xxij capitulo of Exodi. *Lire here.*

## [PSALM 47 GLOSSES]

336.<sup>i</sup> þis salm is expowned of Crist to þe lettre, and in his comyng
he glorified more wiþout comparisoun þe citee of Ierusalem, þan it
was euere glorified bifore. For in Ierusalem he was offrid of his modir,
and þere he tauȝte and diede and dide manye myraclis. *Lire here.*

337. In cristen feiþ, bi prechynge and doynge myraclis þere, and
aftirward bi hise apostlis. *Lire here.*

338. þat is, þese maken þe citee of oure king;                    f. 24<sup>r</sup>

339. In Ieroms translacioun þus: <u>God is knowun in þe housis þerof,
in helping</u>. *Lire here.*

340. <u>þe kyngis</u>, þat is, þe þre kingis þat onouriden Crist;

341. <u>þei weren disturblid</u>, þat is, Eroude and hise felowis. *Lire here.*

342. In Ebreu and in Ieroms translacioun it is, <u>in þe spirit of
brennyng</u>. *Lire here.*

343. For Crist, God and man, foundide it in cristen feiþ, which
founding is stidfast wiþouten ende. *Lire here.*

344. þe heriyng of God mai not be, no but in hise seyntis, for þei
þat lyuen yuele preisen not him; but þouȝ þei prechen bi tunge, þei
blasfemen bi liyf. Soþeli þei herien, þat lyuen wel. *Austin here.*

345. þat is, of citees of Iudee in whiche Crist prechide. *Lire here.*

346. þat is, of Crist. *Lire here.*

<u>In þe vertu of him</u>, þat is, in charite, which no man ouercomeþ.
For 'Loue is strong as deþ' [Song 8: 6]; for as no man aȝenstondiþ
deþ, þat nededli man dieþ, so þe world mai no þing aȝenes charite.
*Austyn here.*

347. Ebreis seien, <u>he shal reule us sweteli</u>; Ierom seiþ, <u>he shal reule
us in deþ</u>; and þe Ebreu word here mai signefie þese þre maneris, but
þe comyn translacioun here þat haþ <u>into worldis</u> is þe beste. *Lire
here.*

Ps. 47 glosses     <sup>i</sup> *next to the title in the right margin; this gloss also in* AbCGikKLPQ-
SUV*X*

## [PSALM 48]

*Audite hec, omnes gentes*

[1] þe title of xlviij salm. In Ebreu þus: *To victorie, a salm to þe sones of Chore.* In Ieroms translacioun þus: *To þe ouercomere, þe song of þe sones of Chore.* Al is o sentence.[348]

[2] Alle ȝe folkis, here þese þingis; alle ȝe þat dwellen in þe world, perseyue wiþ eeris. [3] Alle þe sones of erþe and þe sones of men; togidere þe riche man and [þe][a] pore into oon. [4] Mi mouþ shal speke | wisdom; and þe þenkyng of myn herte shal speke prudence. [5] I shal boowe doun myn eere into a parable; I shal opene my resoun set forþ in a sawtree. [6] Whi schal I drede in þe yuel dai?[349] þe wickidnesse of myn heele[350] shal cumpasse me.[351] [7] Whiche tristen in her owne vertu;[352] and han glorie in þe mul[ti]tude[b] of her richessis. [8] A broþer aȝenbieþ not, shal a man aȝenbie?[353] and he shal not ȝyue to God his plesyng.[354] [9] And he shal not ȝyue þe prijs of raunsum of his soule; and he shal trauele wiþouten ende, [10] and he shal lyue ȝit into þe ende. [11] He shal not se perischyng, whanne he shal se wise men diyng; þe vnwise man and fool shulen perische togidere. And þei shulen leeve her richessis to aliens; [12] and þe sepulcris of hem[355] ben þe housis of hem wiþouten ende. The tabernaclis of hem ben in generacioun and generacioun; þei clepiden her names in her londis. [13] A man, whanne he was in onour, vndurstood not; he is comparisound to vnwise beestis, and [he][c] is maad lijk to þoo. [14] This weie of hem is sclaundir `to´[d] hem; and aftirward þei shulen plese togidere in her mouþ.[356] [15] As scheep þei ben set in helle; deþ shal gnawe hem. And iust men shulen be lordis of hem in þe morewtid; and þe help of hem shal wexe eld in helle, for þe glorie of hem. [16] Neþeles God shal aȝenbie my soule fro þe power of helle; whanne he shal take me. [17] Drede þou not whanne a man is maad riche; and whanne þe glorie of his hous is multiplied. [18] For whanne he shal die, he shal not take alle þingis;[357] and his glorie shal not go | doun wiþ him. [19] For his soule shal be blessid in his lijf;[358] he shal knoulech to þee, whanne þou hast do wel to hym. [20] He shal entre til into þe

f. 24ᵛ (margin)
f. 25ʳ (margin)

---

**Ps. 48**    ᵃ þe] *om.*    ᵇ multitude] multude    ᶜ he] *om.*    ᵈ to] of, *canc. and corrected by the scribe above the line of writing*

## [PSALM 48 GLOSSES]

348.[i] Alle þe spechis of God ben heelful, to hem þat vndurstonden wel; but þo ben per[e]louse[ii] to hem, þat wolen wriþe to þe weiwardnesse of herte. Whanne þei nylen be amendid, þei wolen þat God be peruertid eþer maad vniust. þei demen not þat þing riȝtful þat God wole haue doon, but þat þat þei wolen. Also, gruccheris blasfemen God. *Austin on þe title of xlviij salm.*

349. In þe yuel dai, þat is, in þe dai of doom;                    f. 24ᵛ

350.[iii] þat is, werkis;

351. þe wickidnesse, et cetera: In þis Y haue drede for to drede in doom: if wickidnesse cumpassiþ me, as a net wlappiþ in a brid eþer a beeste takun. Bi þis it is vndurstondun þat þei þat ben asoilid of wickidnesse, shulen not haue for to drede in þe doom. *Lire here.*

352. In her owne vertu, þat is, temporal power in hemsilf and in her frendis;

353. shal a man aȝenbie, as if he seie, Nay;

354. his plesyng, þat is, sacrifice eiþer offryng bi which God shal be plesid to him. *Lire here.*

355. In Ebreu and in Ieroms translacioun þus: And þe innere þingis of hem. *Lire here.*

356. For þei avaunten hem of sich lust[f]ul[iv] liyf, as if þei han gete blis possible to man. *Lire here.*

357. þat is, he shal bere no þingis. *Lire here.*

358. þat is, he shal be preisid of flatereris. *Lire here.*                    f. 25ʳ

---

generacioun[s]ᵉ of hise fadris; and til into wiþouten ende he shal not se liȝt. [21] A man, whanne he was in onour, vndurstood not; he is comparisound to vnwise beestis, and is maad lijk to þoo.

---

**Ps. 48 glosses**    [i] *next to the title in the right margin*    [ii] perelouse] perolouse    [iii] *this gloss interlinear and underlined in* K, *with the variant* werk    [iv] lustful] lustul; *this gloss interlinear and underlined in* K, *with the variant* bosting; *the same variant gloss marginal in* V

ᵉ generaciouns] generacioun

[PSALM 49]

*Deus deorum*

[1] *þe title of xlix salm. þe salm of Asaph.*<sup>359</sup>

God, þe Lord of goddis,<sup>360</sup> spak; and clepide þe erþe,<sup>361</sup> fro þe risyng of þe sunne til to þe goynge doun. [2] The shap of his fairenesse fro Sion, [3] God shal come openli; oure God, and he shal not be stille. Fier<sup>362</sup> shal brenne an hiȝ in his siȝt; and a strong tempeste in his cumpas. [4] He clepide heuene aboue; and þe erþe, to deme his puple. [5] Gadere ȝe<sup>363</sup> to hym hise seyntis; þat ordeynen his testament aboue sacrifices. [6] And heuenes shulen telle his riȝtfulnesse; for God is þe iuge. [7] My puple, here þou, and I shal speke to Israel; and I shal witnesse to þee, I am God, þi God. [8] I shal not repreue þee in þi sacrifices;<sup>364</sup> and þi brent sacrifices ben not<sup>365</sup> euere bifor me. [9] I shal not take calues of þyn hous; neiþer geet-buckis of þi flockis. [10] For alle þe wielde beestis of woodis ben myn; werkbeestis and oxis in hillis. [11] I haue knowe alle þe volatils of heuene; and þe fairnesse of þe feeld is wiþ me. [12] If I shal be hungry, I shal not seie to þee; for þe world and þe fulnesse þerof is myn. [13] Wher I shal ete þe fleischis of bolis? eþer shal I drynke þe blood of geet-buckis? [14] Offre þou to God | þe sacrifice of heriyng; and ȝelde þyn avowis to þe hiȝest God. [15] And inwardli clepe þou me in þe dai of tribulacioun; and I shal delyuere þee, and þou shalt onoure me. [16] But God seide to þe synnere, Whi tellist þou out of my riȝtfulnessis; and takist my testament bi þi mouþ? [17] Soþeli þou hatidist lore; and hast cast awei my wordis bihynde. [18] If þou siest a þeef, þou hast runne wiþ him; and þou settidist þi part wiþ avouteris. [19] Thi mouþ was plenteuouse of malice; and þi tunge medlide togidere giles.<sup>366</sup> [20] Thou sittynge spakist aȝens þi broþer, and þou settidist sclaundir aȝens þe sone of þi modir; [21] þou didist þese þingis, and I was stille. Thou gessidist wickidli þat I shal be lijk þee; I shal repreue þee, and [I]<sup>a</sup> shal sette aȝens þi face. [22] Ȝe þat forȝeten God, vndurstonde þese þingis; lest sumtyme `he'<sup>b</sup> rauysche, and noon be þat shal delyuere. [23] The sacrifice of heriyng shal onoure me; and þere is þe weie wherinne I shal schewe to him þe helþe of God.

f. 25<sup>v</sup>

---

**Ps. 49**   <sup>a</sup> I] *om.*   <sup>b</sup> he] ȝe, *canc. and corrected by the scribe above the line of writing*

[PSALM 49 GLOSSES]

359.<sup>i</sup> þis salm is expowned of Crist to þe lettre, of his firste comyng into þe world, of ȝyuyng of þe lawe of þe gospel, and of his laste comyng to þe general doom. *Lire here.*

360. þat is, of hooli men, maad goddis bi grace. *Lire here.*

361. Here is þe ende of þe firste vers in Ebreu and in Ieroms translacioun. *Lire here.*

362. For litle manaassis of men þou doist yuel, for euerelastynge manaassis of God þou doist not good. Wherof art þou slow, but `for´ þou bileuest not. *Austin<sup>ii</sup> here.*

363. þis is seid to hooli aungelis. *Lire here.*

364. þouȝ þo ben lefte. *Lire here.*

365. þus it is in Ebreu and in Ieroms translacioun bi trewe vndurstondyng. *Lire here.*

366. In Ebreu it is, <u>blasfemye</u>, for þe synne of blasfemye comeþ   f. 25<sup>v</sup> forþ of greet reisyng of pride. *Lire here.*

[PSALM 50 GLOSSES]

367.<sup>i</sup> þat is, whanne aftir þe deþ of Vrie, Dauiþ weddide Bersabee. *Lire here.*

368. As Austyn seiþ, merci is nedeful to wrecchis, and þerfor in bisechyng greet merci, he knoulechiþ his greet wrecchidnesse, and þe greuouste of his synne;

369. And bi þ[e]<sup>ii</sup> mychilnesse, et cetera: in bisechyng þe mychilnesse of merciful doyngis, he shewiþ þe mychefoldnesse of his synne: for firste Dauiþ synnyde in avoutrie; þe secounde tyme in willynge to

---

[PSALM 50]

*Miserere mei Deus*

[1] þe title of þe fiftiþe salm. To victorie, þe salm of Dauiþ; [2] whanne Nathan þe profete cam to hym, whanne he entride<sup>367</sup> to Bersabee.

[3] God, haue þou merci on me; bi þi greet merci.<sup>368</sup> And bi þe mychelnesse<sup>369</sup> of þi merciful doyngis; do þou awei my wickidnesse.

---

Ps. 49 glosses    <sup>i</sup> *interlinear and then down the right margin; this gloss also in* ikKPV <sup>ii</sup> *but for* þou bileuest not. Austin *corrected by the scribe above the line of writing and on an erasure*
Ps. 50    <sup>i</sup> *this gloss also in* ikKV    <sup>ii</sup> þe] þi

[4] More waische þou me fro my wickidnesse; and clense þou me fro my synne. [5] For I knoulech my wickidnesse; and my synne is euere aȝenes me. [6] I haue synned to þee aloone,[370] and I haue do yuel bifor þee; þat þou be iustefied in þi wordis, and ouercome whanne f. 26ʳ þou art demed.[371] [7] For lo! | I was conseyued in wickidnessis; and my modir conseyuede me in synnes. [8] For lo! þou louedist treuþe; þou hast schewid to me þe vncerteyn[372] þingis and pryuy þingis of þi wisdom. [9] Lord, bisprynge þou me wiþ isope, and I shal be clensid; waische þou me, and I shal be maad white more þan snow. [10] Ȝyue þou ioie and gladnesse to myn heryng; and boonys maad meke shulen ful out make ioie. [11] Turne awei þi face fro my synnes; and do awei alle my wickidnessis. [12] God, make þou a cleene herte in me; and make þou newe a riȝtful spirit in myn entrailis. [13] Caste þou not me awei fro þi face; and take þou not awei fro me þyn hooli spirit.[373] [14] Ȝyue þou to me þe gladnesse of þyn heelþe; and conferme þou me wiþ þe pryncipal spirit. [15] I shal teche wickid men þi weies; and vnfeiþful men shulen be conuertid to þee. [16] God, þe God of myn helþe, delyuere þou me fro bloodis;[374] and my tunge shal ioifuli synge þi riȝtfulnesse.[375] [17] Lord, opene þou my lippis; and my mouþ shal telle þi preisyng. [18] For if þou haddist wolde sacrifice, Y hadde ȝoue; treuli þou shalt not delite in brent sacrifices.[376] [19] A sacrifice to God is a spirit troblid;[377] God, þou shalt not dispise a contrite herte and maad meke. [20] Lord, do þou benygneli in þi good wille to Sion; þat þe wallis[378] of Ierusalem be bildid. [21] Thanne þou shalt take plesauntli þe sacrifice of riȝtfulnesse, offryngis and brent sacrifices; þanne þei schulen putte calues on þin auter.[379]

## [PSALM 51]

*Quid gloriaris*[a]

[1] *þe title of lj salm. To victorie, þe salm of Dauiþ,* [2] *whanne Doech*
f. 26ᵛ *Ydumei cam and telde to | Saul and seide to hym, Dauiþ cam into þe hous of Achymelech.*[380]

---

Ps. 51    [a] Quid gloriaris] *on f. 26ᵛ, following the rubricated title*

holde priuy his synne; þe þridde tyme in willynge to make a fals eir to hide his synne; þe fourþe tyme, whanne he myȝte not do þis, he made Vrie his trewest knyȝt to be slayn bi tresoun; þe fyueþe tyme, for manye mo seruauntis of Dauiþ weren slayn for cause of Vries deeþ. *Lire here.*

370. As to iuge; for Dauiþ was kyng, he hadde no iuge þat myȝte punysche him `no but God´;[iii]

do yuel bifore þee: vndurstonde, forȝyue þou synne. *Lire here.*

371. Whanne þou art demed: in Ebreu it is, þou shalt be clensid whanne þou art demed, þat is, þou shalt appere cleene in fillyng þi biheest, þouȝ manye men demen þe contrarie. *Lire here.*

372. þat is, þe biheest maad to Dauiþ of successioun of rewme in       f. 26ʳ hise sones, and of Cristis birþe, þat he shulde be borun of þe seed of Dauiþ. *Lire here.*

373. Of profesie. *Lire here.*

374. þat is, fro peyne of deeþ, which Y disseruyde, for þe shedyng out of bloodis of Vrie and of oþere men slayn for occasioun of him. *Lire here.*

375. þat is, þi riȝtfulnesse temprid wiþ merci. *Lire here.*

376. For þe sacrifices of þe elde lawe weren not acceptable to God of hemsilf, no but oneli of þe feiþ and deuocioun of þe offreris, and bi du contricioun biforgoyng. *Lire here.*

377.[iv] þat is, sori for synne. *Lire here.*

378. þat is, þe wallis of þe temple in Ierusalem, be[v] bildid bi my sone. *Lire here.*

379.[vi] Dereworþest briþeren, reule ȝe ȝoure housis, ȝoure sones, and ȝoure meynees. As it perteyneþ to us to speke to ȝou in þe chirche, so it perteyneþ to ȝou to do in ȝoure housis, þat ȝe ȝelde good resoun of hem þat ben soget to ȝou. God loueþ chastisyng. It is weiward and false innocence to ȝyue fredom to synnes. Ful perelousli to deþ þe sone feeliþ þe softnesse of þe fadir, þat he feele aftirward þe sharp punyschyng of God. *Austyn in þe ende of þe fiftiþe salm.*

[PSALM 51 GLOSSES]          f. 26ᵛ

380.[i] Gostli, þis salm mai be expownyd of ech wickid bacbitere, whiche bi hise bacbityngis excitiþ a myȝti man to pursue innocentis,

---

[iii] no but God] *added by the scribe in margin*     [iv] *this gloss interlinear and underlined in* K *and in margin of* V     [v] be] be bil-, bil- *canc.*     [vi] *in the bottom margin*
**Ps. 51 glosses**     [i] *next to the title in the right margin*

[3] What hast þou glorie in malice;[381] which art myȝti in wickidnesse? [4] Al dai þi tunge þouȝte vnriȝtfulnesse; as a scharp rasour
þou hast to gile. [5] Thou louedist malice more þan benygnyte; þou
louydist wickidnesse more þan to speke equyte. [6] Thou louedist alle
wordis of castynge doun; wiþ a gileful tunge. [7] Therfor God shal
distrie[382] þee into þe ende, he shal drawe þee out bi þe roote, and he
schal make þee to passe awei fro þi tabernacle, and þi roote fro þe lond
of lyuynge men. [8] Iust men schulen se and shulen[b] drede; and þei
shulen leiȝe on him, and þei shulen seie, [9] Lo! þe man þat settide not
God his helpere. But he hopide in þe multitude of hise richessis; and
hadde maistrie in his vanyte. [10] Forsoþe I, as a fruytful olyue tree in
þe hous of God; hopide in þe merci of God wiþouten ende, and into
þe world of world.[383] [11] I shal knoulech to þee into þe world, for þou
hast do;[384] and I shal abide þi name, for it is good in þe siȝt of þi
seyntis.

## [PSALM 52]

*Dixit insipiens*

[1] *þe title of lij salm. To þe ouercomere bi þe queer, þe lernyng of
Dauiþ.*[385]

The vnwise man seide in his herte; God is not.[386] [2] Thei ben
corrupt, and maad abhomynable in her wickidnessis; noon is þat doiþ
good. [3] God bihelde fro heuene on þe sones of men; þat he se, if ony
is vndurstondyng, eþer sekynge God. [4] Alle bowiden awei, þei ben
f. 27ʳ  maad vnprofitable togidere; noon | is þat doiþ good, þer is not til to
oon. [5] Wher alle men, þat worchen wickidnesse, shulen not wite;
whiche deuouren my puple as þe mete of breed? [6] Thei clepiden not
God; þere þei trembliden for drede, where no drede was. For God
haþ scaterid þe boonys of hem, þat plesen men;[387] þei ben schent, for
God haþ forsake hem. [7] Who shal ȝyue fro Sion helþe to Israel?
whanne þe Lord haþ turned þe caitifte of his puple, Iacob shal ful out
make ioie, and Israel shal be glad.

---

[b] se and shulen] *corrected by the scribe on an erasure*

for which doyng he getiþ euerelastinge peyne, and sumtyme temporal peyne also. *Lire here.*

381. In Ebreu and in Ieroms translacioun þus: What hast glorie þou my3ti in malice; þe merci of God is al day; þi tunge þou3te tresouns; as a scharp rasour þou didist gile;

my3ti in malice, þat is, what hast þou glorie, in þat þat þou didist my3tili þi malice in werk, in þe sleinge of prestis and of her wyues and children;

þe merci of God, þat suffriþ al dai, in present liyf, ou3te to haue wiþdrawe þee fro so greet malice;

tresouns: for þis Doech settide tresouns as wiþout ceessyng to Dauiþ and hise frendis, in accusynge hem falsli to Saul. *Lire here.*

382. þis is not preier a3enes yuele men, but profesie what shal bifalle to yuele men. It is not seid bi yuel wille, but bi spirit of profesie. *Austin here.*

383. þis is rehersyng of þe same sentence, þat signefieþ wiþouten ende. *Austin here.*

384. Merci to me. *Lire here.*

[PSALM 52 GLOSSES]

385.[i] þis salm mai bi expowned of þe turment of Iewis bi þe rewme of Grekis, in whiche manye Iewis weren slayn and manye taken prisoneris, and moost in þe tyme of Antiok þe noble, as þe bookis of Machabeis tellen.

Gostli, þis salm mai be expowned of ech synnere obstynat in hise yuelis, whiche þou3 he knoulechiþ God bi wordis, denyeþ hym bi dedis; whos malice God examyneþ and punyschiþ, and delyueriþ þe innocent man fro his hond. *Lire here.*

386. Iewis seiden þis of Crist. Paynyms, eretikis, and false cristen men seien þis. Whanne þou seist þat wickidnesse plesiþ God, þou denyest God. *Austyn here.*

387. God haþ scaterid þe boonys of hem: in Ebreu and in Ieroms f. 27[r] translacioun þus: God haþ scaterid þe boonys of men bisechynge eiþer cumpassinge þee; and þis is referrid to Antiok and his oost, þat bisegiden and distrieden þe citees of Iudee;

þat plesen men, þat is, þe vertu of hem þat deliten in þe flateryngis of men,[ii] and chargen not of Goddis plesaunce. *Lire here.*

**Ps. 52 glosses** [i]*next to the title in the left margin; this gloss also in* ikKPV [ii]men] *corrected by the scribe on an erasure*

*Deus in nomine tuo*

[1] þe title of liij salm. *To þe victorie in orguns eþer in salmes. þe lernyng of Dauiþ*, [2] wh[anne]ᵃ ʒifeis camen, and seiden to Saul wh[er] Dauiþ is not hid at us.³⁸⁸

[3] God, in þi name make þou me saaf; and in þi vertu deme þou me. [4] God, here þou my preier; wiþ eeris perseyue þou þe wordis of my mouþ. [5] For aliens han rise aʒens me, and stronge men souʒten my lijf; and þei settiden not God bifor her siʒt. [6] For, lo! God helpiþ me; and þe Lord is uptakere of my soule.³⁸⁹ [7] Turne þou awei yuelis to myn enemyes; and leese þou hem in þi treuþe.³⁹⁰ [8] Wilfuli I shal make sacrifice to þee; and, Lord, I schal knoulech to þi name for it is good. [9] For þou delyueridist me fro al tribulacioun; and myn iʒe dispiside on myn enemyes.³⁹¹

*Exaudi Deus orationem meam*

[1] þe title of liiij salm. In Ebreu þus: *To victorie in orguns, þe lernyng of Dauiþ*. In Ieroms translacioun þus: *To þe ouercomere in salmes of Dauiþ lerned*.³⁹²

[2] God, here þou my preier, and dispise þou not my bisechyng; [3] ʒyue þou tent to me and here þou me. I am soreuful in myn excercisyng;³⁹³ and I am distur|blid [4] of þe face of þe enemy, and of þe tribulacioun of þe synnere. For þei bowiden wickidnessis `in'toᵃ me; and in ire þei weren diseseful to me. [5] Myn herte w`a´sᵇ disturblid in me; and þe drede of deþ felde on me. [6] Drede and tremblyng camen on me; and derknessis³⁹⁴ hiliden me. [7] And I seide, Who shal ʒyue to me feþeris as of a culuer; and I shal fle and shal take reste? [8] Lo! I ʒede fer awei and fledde; and I dwellide in wildirnesse. [9] I abood hym, þat made me saaf fro þe litilnesse, eþer drede, of spirit; and fro tempest. [10] Lord, caste þou doun, departe þou þe tungis³⁹⁵ of hem; for I siʒ wickidnesse and aʒenseiynge in þe citee. [11] Bi dai and nyʒt wickidnesse shal cumpasse it on þe wallis

f. 27ᵛ

---

**Ps. 53** ᵃ whanne] anne *nearly rubbed away*
**Ps. 54** ᵃ into] *corrected by the scribe above the line of writing* ᵇ was] *corrected by the scribe above the line of writing*

## [PSALM 53 GLOSSES]

388. þis salm mai be expowned gostli aȝenes worste accuseris, excitynge myȝti men aȝenes innocentis, whose tresouns innocentis ascapen bi Goddis goodnesse. *Lire here.*

389. þat is, kepere of my liyf. *Lire here.*

390. þat is, turne awei fro me yuelis þouȝt of myn enemyes aȝenes me, and turne þoo on her heedis. *Lire here.*

391. þat is, Y tristynge in goodness and vertu, not in my meritis, arettide for nouȝt þe tresouns of hem aȝenes me. *Lire here.*

## [PSALM 54 GLOSSES]

392.[i] Dauiþ made þis liiij salm in doynge þankyngis to God, whanne he fledde fro Ceila and was sauyd fro the hondis of Saul, þat wolde bisege hym in Ceila; and fro þe hondis of þe puple of Ceila, þat disposide to bitraie hym.

Gostli, þis salm mai be expowned of ech iust man set in persecucioun, aȝenes whom gileful castis ben maad, ȝhe, of vnkynde men. Wherfor he preieþ deuoutli to be delyuerid fro þese, whom þe Lord heriþ, and punyschiþ hise aduersaries. *Lire here.*

þe heriyng of God owiþ not to go awei fro þe herte and mouþ of a cristen man, neþer in prosperitees neiþer in aduersitees. Crist is þe sone of Dauiþ bi fleisch, and þe Lord of Dauiþ bi godheed. *Austin on þe title of liiij salm.*

393. In myn excersisyng, þat is, bi excercisyng of armuris þat delyueride þe puple of Ceila. And neþeles, þei as vnkynde wolen bitraie me into þe hondis of Saul. *Lire here.*

Ech yuel man lyueþ eiþer herfor þat he be amendid, eþer þat a good man be excersisid bi him. þe deuel and hise aungelis ben gouernours of þis world, þat is, of louyeris of þis world, þat is, of vnfeiþful men and wickid men. *Austin here.*

394. þat is, hard aduersitees. *Lire here.* f. 27v

395. þat is, make þou dwelleris of Ceila to speke so hedeli and discordyngli, þat þei moun not perfourme her tresoun in bitakynge me into þe hondis of Saul. *Lire here.*

**Ps. 54 glosses** [i] *the first historical part of this gloss also in* bCGikKLPQSV*X*

þerof; and trauel [12] and vnriȝtfulnesse ben in þe myddis þerof.
And vsure and gile failide not; fro þe stretis þerof. [13] For if myn
enemye hadde cursid me; soþeli I hadde suffrid. And if he þat hatide
me, hadde spoke grete þingis on me; in hap I hadde hid me fro hym.
[14] But þou art a man of o wille;[396] my ledere and my knowun. [15]
Which[397] tokist togidere swete-metis wiþ me; we ȝeden wiþ consent
in þe hous of God. [16] Deþ come on hem;[398] and go þei doun quyk
into helle. For weiwardnessis ben in þe dwellynge place of hem; in
þe myddis of hem. [17] But I criede to þe[e],[c] Lord; and þe Lord
sauyde me. [18] In þe euentid and morewtid and in myddai I shal
telle and shewe; and he shal here my vois. [19] He shal aȝenbie my
soule in pees fro hem,[399] þat neiȝen to me; for among manye þei
weren wiþ me. [20] God shal here; and he þat is bifor þe worldis shal

make hem low. For | chaungyng[400] is not to hem, and þei dredden
not God; [21] he holdiþ forþ his hond in ȝeldyng. Thei defouliden
his testament, [22] þe cheris þerof[401] weren departid fro ire; and his
herte neiȝide.[402] The wordis þerof weren softere þan oile; and þo ben
dartis. [23] Caste þ[i cu]re[d] on þe Lord, and he shal fulli norische
þee; and he shal not ȝyue wiþouten ende floteryng[403] to a iust man.
[24] But þou, God, shalt lede hem forþ; into þe pit of deþ.
Menquelleris and gilours shulen not haue half her daies;[404] but,
Lord, I shal hope in þee.

## [PSALM 55]

*Miserere mei Deus*

[1] *þe title of lv salm.* In Ebreu *þus: To þe ouercomyng on þe doumb
culuer of fer drawyng awei, þe comeli*[405] *song of Dauiþ, whanne Filisteis
helden hym in Geþ.* In Ieroms translacioun *þus: To þe ouercomere for þe
doumb culuer, for it [ȝede]*[a] *awei fer, Dauiþ meke and symple* made þis
salm, *whanne Palastynes helden hym in Geþ.*[406]

---

[c] þee] þe      [d] þi cure] *something erased but not corrected*
**Ps. 55**      [a] ȝede] *om.*

396. Dauiþ spekiþ to þe puple of Ceila, vndur þe name of a man þat hadde schewid frendschip to him. *Lire here.*

397. In Ebreu and in Ieroms translacioun þus: Whiche hadden swete priuyte eþer councel togidere; in þe hous of God we ȝeden wiþ noise, þat is, wiþ greet cumpenye. *Lire here.*

398. Deþ come on hem, þat is, þei ben worþi þat deþ come on hem; quyke into helle, as Chore and Dathan and Abiron in xvj capitulo of Numeri, for þei weren vnkynde to þe benefices of Moises and rebelliden aȝenes him. So diden þe dwelleris of Ceila to Dauiþ himsilf. *Lire here.*

Whanne þou woost þat þat is yuel þat þou doist, and neþeles þou doist it, wher þou gost not quyk doun to helle? þis is seid of proude lederis as Datan and Abiron. þei goon quyke doun to helle, þat knowen þat þat þei doon to be yuel. Loue we enemyes, repreue we hem, chastise we hem, curse we hem, and also departe we hem fro us wiþ loue, for[ii] Poul seiþ, 'If ony man obeieþ not to oure word bi a pistle, marke ȝe hym'[iii] [2 Thess 3: 14]. *Austyn here.*

399. þat is, fro þe traitours of Ceila, þat neiȝen to me in signe of frenschip. *Lire here.*

400.[iv] þat is, fro synne to penaunce. *Lire here.*                    f. 28ʳ

401. þat is, þe puple of Ceila. *Lire here.*

402. þat is, in cheer þei weren pesible to Dauiþ, and þei hadden þe contrarie in þe herte. *Lire here.*

403. þat is, þe persecucioun of Saul to Dauiþ, bi which he was compellid to fle fro place to place. *Lire here.*

404. þat is, schulen not lyue bi þe half part of her kyndli liyf. *Lire here.*

## [PSALM 55 GLOSSES]

405. þis dyuersite, for þis Ebreu word 'myktam' signefieþ a special eþer comeli song, and also meke and symple eþer perfit; and Ebreis taken þe firste signyficacioun and Ierom takiþ þe secounde signyficacioun. *Lire here.*

406.[i] Dauiþ made þis lv salm whanne he fledde fro þe face of Saul and cam to Achis þe kyng of Geth, and whanne þei wolden kille Dauiþ, he feyned him wood, and so he was sauyd.

---

[ii] for] for oure, oure *canc.*    [iii] bi a pistle, marke ȝe hym] marke ȝe hym bi a pistle *(transposed)*    [iv] *in margin of* V: fro synne to vertue, vertue *altered (possibly by a 2nd hand above the line of writing) to* penaunce
**Ps. 55 glosses**    [i] *in the bottom margin*

[2] God, haue þou merci on me, for a man[407] haþ defoulid me; al dai he inpungnede and troblide me. [3] Myn enemyes defouliden me al dai; for manye fiȝteris[408] weren aȝenes me. [4] Of þe hiȝnesse of dai I shal drede; but God I shal hope in þee. [5] In God I schal preise my wordis; I hopide in God, I shal not drede what þing fleisch[409] shal[b] do to me. [6] Al dai þei cursiden my wordis;[410] aȝenes me al her þouȝtis weren into yuel. [7] Thei shulen dwelle and shulen hide; þei shulen aspie myn heele. As þei abididen my lijf,[411] [8] for nouȝt shalt þou make hem saaf; in ire þou shalt breke togidere puplis. God, [9] I shewide my lijf to þee; þou hast set my teeris in þi siȝt. As [and][c] in þi biheest, Lord;[412] | [10] þanne myn enemyes shulen be turned abak. In what euere dai I shal ynwardli clepe þee; lo! I haue knowe, þat þou art my God. [11] In God I shal preise a word; in þe Lord I shal preise a word. I shal hope in God; I shal not drede, what þing a man shal do to me. [12] God, þin avowis ben in me; whiche I shal ȝelde heriyngis to þee.[413] [13] For þou hast delyuerid my lijf fro deþ, and my feet fro slidyng; þat I plese bifor God[414] in þe liȝt of hem þat lyuen.

f. 28ᵛ

## [PSALM 56]

*Miserere mei Deus*

[1] *þe title of lvj salm.* In Ebreu þus: *To þe victorie, leese þou not þe semeli song eþer þe swete song of Dauiþ, whanne he fledde fro þe face of Saul into þe denne.*[a] In Ieroms translacioun þus: *For victorie, þat þou leese not Dauiþ meke and symple, whanne he fledde fro þe face of Saul into þe denne.*[415]

[2] God, haue þou merci on me, haue þou merci on me; for my soule tristiþ in þee. And I shal hope in þe schadewe of þi wyngis; til wickidnesse passe. [3] I shal crie to God alþerhiȝeste; to God þat dide wel to me.[416] [4] He sente fro heuene and delyuyrede me; he ȝaf into schenschip hem þat defoulen me. God sente his merci and his treuþe, [5] and delyueride my soule[417] fro þe myddis of whelpis of liouns; I slepte disturblid. þe sones of men, þe teeþ of hem ben armuris and arowis; and her tunge is a sharp swerd. [6] God, be þou

---

ᵇ shal] shal shal, *the dittography not canc.*   ᶜ and] *om.*
**Ps. 56**   ᵃ *this title also in* ikKPV

Gostli, þis salm mai be expowned of ech feiþful man, which whanne he is set in þe perel of deþ, preieþ God deuoutli for his delyueraunce. And whanne he is herd of God, he doiþ þankyngis to God, as a kynde man owiþ.

Also, Dauiþ fledde firste into þe denne of Odollam, and þerof spekiþ þe hundrid and xlj salm, as Ierom seiþ on þe prologe of þe Sauter. Þe secounde tyme Dauiþ fledde into a denne, whanne Saul pursuyde him on ful hard and brokun stoonys, and herof spekiþ þe ʼlvjʼ ⁱⁱ salm. *Lire here.*

407. þat is, men, for manye Filisteis helden him, and hurliden and defouliden him, as a man worþi þe deþ. *Lire here.*

408. In Ebreu and in Ieroms translacioun þus: <u>Manye fiȝteris aȝenes me þou hiȝeste</u>, þat is, þou Hiȝest delyuere me, delyuere me fro þis multitude, fro whiche Y mai not defende me. þe secounde vers bigynneþ þus: <u>In what euere dai Y shal drede; forsoþe Y shal hope in þee</u>. *Lire here.*

409. þat is, fleischli man. Dauiþ excludiþ here þat drede þat castiþ doun into dispeir;

410. <u>þei cursiden my wordis</u>, þat is, þei turnyden into my condempnyng, alle wordis seid of me to my preisyng. *Lire here.*

411. In Ebreu and in Ieroms translacioun þus: <u>abidynge my soule</u>, þat is, hopyng to take awei my soule fro þe bodi. And þe vers suynge bigynneþ þus: <u>For nouȝt shalt þou make hem saaf</u>, as if he seie, Nay; <u>in ire God þou shalt breke togidere puplis</u>, þat is, of Filisteis;

412. [In Ebreu þus: ]ⁱⁱⁱ <u>þou hast noumbrid my stiryng eþer my priuyere þingis; sette þou my teer in þi bowge</u>. As [and]ⁱᵛ in þi biheest, Lord: In Ebreu þus: <u>Wher not in þi noumbre?</u> In Ieroms translacioun þus: <u>But not in þi tellyng</u>. *Lire here.*

413. þat is, to heriyng of þi name. *Lire here.*                    f. 28ᵛ

414. In Ebreu and in Ieroms translacioun þus: <u>þat Y go bifor God</u>. *Lire here.*

## [PSALM 56 GLOSSES]

415. Gostli, þis salm mai be expowned as þe formere, for in liyk maner it is in euere eiþer. *Lire here.*

416.ⁱ In Ieroms translacioun it is, <u>to God my vengere</u>. *Lire here.*

417. In Ieroms translacioun þus: <u>My soule slepte in þe myddis of ferse liouns</u>. *Lire here.*

---

ⁱⁱ lvj] *added by the scribe below the line of writing; this gloss also in* AbCGikKLPQSV*X*
ⁱⁱⁱ In Ebreu þus] *om.*    ⁱᵛ and] *om.*
**Ps. 56 glosses**    ⁱ *next to the title in the left margin*

enhaunsid⁴¹⁸ aboue heuenys; and þi glorie aboue al erþe. [7] Thei
maden redi a snare to my feet; and þei greetli bowiden my lijf.⁴¹⁹
Thei deluyden a diche bifor my face; and þei felden doun into it. [8]
God, myn herte is redi, myn herte is redi; I shal synge and I shal seie

f. 29ʳ  salm. [9] Mi glorie, rise þou | up; sautree and harp, rise þou up; I
shal rise up eerli. [10] Lord, I shal knoulech to þee among puplis;
and I shal seie salm among heþene men. [11] For þi merci is
magnefied til to heuenys; and þi treuþe til to cloudis. [12] God, be
þou enhaunsid aboue heuenys; and þi glorie ouer al erþe.

## [PSALM 57]

*S[i] [u]e[re]ᵃ utique.*

[1] *þe title of lvij salm. In Ebreu þus: To victorie; leese þou not þe swete
song eþer þe semeli song of Dauiþ. In Ieroms translacioun þus: To þe
ouercomere, þat þou leese not Dauiþ meke and simple.*⁴²⁰

[2] Forsoþe if ȝe speken riȝtfulnesse verili; ȝe sones of men, deme
riȝtfuli. [3] For in herte ȝe worchen wickidnesse in erþe; ȝoure
hondis maken redi vnriȝtfulnesses.⁴²¹ [4] Synneris weren maad aliens
fro þe wombe; þei erriden fro þe wombe, þei spaken false þingis. [5]
Woodnesse⁴²² is to hem bi þe licnesse of a serpent; as of a deef snake,
and stoppynge hise eeris. [6] Which shal not here þe uois of
charmeris; and of a venym-makere charmynge wiseli. [7] God
schal al tobreke þe teeþ of hem in her mouþ; þe Lord shal breke
togidere þe grete teeþ of liouns. [8] Thei shulen come to nouȝt, as
watir rennynge awei; he⁴²³ bente his bouwe til þei ben maad sijk. [9]
As wex þat fletiþ awei,⁴²⁴ þei schulen be takun awei; fier felde⁴²⁵
aboue; and þei sien not þe sunne. [10] Bifor þat ȝoure þornes
vndurstoden þe ramne;⁴²⁶ he swolewiþ hem so in ire, as lyuynge
men. [11] The iust man shal be glad, whanne he shal se veniaunce;
he shal waissche hise hondis⁴²⁷ in þe blood of a synnere. [12] [And]ᵇ a
man shal seie treuli, for fruyt is to a iust man; treuli god is
demynge⁴²⁸ hem in erþe.

---

**Ps. 57**    ᵃ Si uere] *partly rubbed away*    ᵇ And] *om.*

418. þat is, þi preisyng be magnefied of hooli aungelis. *Lire here.*

419. þat is, þei wolden gretli bowe my liyf, in castynge me doun into deþ. *Lire here.*

## [PSALM 57 GLOSSES]

420.ⁱ Dauiþ made þis lvij salm, whanne Saul at þe tellyng of 3ifeis 3ede out wiþ þre þousynde of chosen men to seke Dauiþ in þe firste book of Kingis, xxvj capitulo, and Dauiþ took awei þe spere and þe cuppe of Saul slepynge. *Lire here.*

421. þat is, maken fair and colouren bi false and apperyng ri3tfulnesse. In Ieroms translacioun þus: þei se3e þe wickidnessis of 3oure hondis. *Lire here.*

422. In Ebreu it is, venym is to hem. *Lire here.*

423. þis mai be referrid to God, þat makiþ redi þe sleynge of yuele men to be doon in du tyme. *Lire here.*

He bente his bouwe: in Ieroms translacioun þus, beende þei her bouwe til þei ben al tobrokun;

424. As wexe þat fletiþ: in Ebreu þus, as a long clooþ maad rotun þei shulen be doon awei; in Ieroms translacioun þus, as a worm maad rotun passe þei forþ;

425. fier felde, et cetera: in Ebreu and in Ieroms translacioun þus, a child borun out of tyme of a womman felde doun; which child si3 not þe sunne;

426. Bifor þat 3oure þornes, et cetera: in Ieroms translacioun þus, Bifore þat 3oure þornes wexe into a ramne, þat is, bifor þat þei comen to þe malice of a ram[n]e,ⁱⁱ þat is, of elde men;

tempest as in ire shal rauysche hem as lyuynge men: in Ebreu þus, as lyuynge so in ire he swolewiþ hem, and þis is referrid to God;

þat is, bifor þat 3oure litilⁱⁱⁱ children hadden so greet vndurstondyng, þat þei my3ten do as yuele as elde sones. *Lire here.*

427. þat is, shal make iust hise werkis in þe punyschyng of a synnere, which is occasioun of amendyng of his liyf. *Lire here.*

428. þat is, 3yuynge þe sentence for hem not oneli in tyme to comynge, but ofte also in present tyme. *Lire here.*

---

**Ps. 57 glosses**  ⁱ *next to the title in the right margin, no tie-mark; this gloss also in* bCGikKLPQSVX  ⁱⁱ ramne] ramme; *cf. in margin of* O, *f. 219ᵛ*: þe raume eþer þe þorn ⁱⁱⁱ litil] litil lich litil, lich *canc. but the dittography is not corrected*

[PSALM 58]

*Eripe me*

f. 29ᵛ *þe title of lviij salm.* In Ieroms translacioun þus: | [1] *To þe ouercomere, þat þou leese not Dauiþ, meke and symple; whanne Saul sente and kepte þe hous, to sle hym.*ᵃ In Ebreu þus: *To þe ouercomyng, leese þou not þe semeli song of Dauiþ, and so forþ.*⁴²⁹

[2] Mi God, delyuere þou me fro myn enemyes; and delyuere þou me fro hem þat risen aȝenes me. [3] Delyuere þou me fro hem þat worchen wickidnesse; and saue þou me fro menquelleris.⁴³⁰ [4] For lo! þei han take my soule;⁴³¹ stronge men felden in on me. [5] Neiþer my wickidnesse, neþer my synne;⁴³² Lord, I ran wiþout wickidnesse,⁴³³ and dresside. [6] Rise þou up into my metyng and se; and þou, Lord God of vertues, art God of Israel. Ȝyue þou tent to visite alle folkis; do þou not merci to alle⁴³⁴ þat worchen wickidnesse. [7] Thei shulen be turned at euentid, and þei as doggis shulen suffre hungur;⁴³⁵ and þei shulen cumpasse þe citee. [8] Lo! þei shulen speke in her mouþ, and a swerd in her lippis; for who herde?⁴³⁶ [9] And þou, Lord, shalt scorne hem; þou shalt brynge alle folkis to nouȝt.⁴³⁷ [10] I shal kepe my strengþe to þee; for God is myn uptake[re],ᵇ [11] my God, his merci shal come bifor me. [12] God shewide to me on myn enemyes, sle þou not hem; lest ony tyme my puplis forȝete.⁴³⁸ Scatere þou hem in þi vertu; and, Lord, my defendere, putte þou hem doun. [13] Putte þou doun þe trespas of her mouþ, and þe word of her lippis; and be þei takun in her pride. And of cursyng and of leesyng; [14] þei shulen be schewid in þe endyng. In þe ire of endyng, and þei shulen not be;⁴³⁹ and þei shulen wite, þat þe Lord shal be Lord of Iacob⁴⁴⁰ and of þe endis of erþe.

f. 30ʳ [15] Thei | shulen be turned at euentid, and þei as doggis shulen

**Ps. 58**    ᵃ *this title also in* bikKPV    ᵇ uptakere] uptake

429.ⁱ Gostli, þis lviij salm mai be expowned of ech iust man set in angwisch, which disserueþ to be delyuerid bi hise preieris and hise enemyes to be punyschid.

Bi allegorie, þis salm mai be expowned of Crist, þat was kept in þe sepulcre; but not wiþstondynge þis, he roos aȝen bi Goddis myȝt, and Iewis þat maden hym to be kept in þe sepulcre weren takun prisoneris bi Romayns for peyne of þis, and weren scaterid þorouȝ þe world.

Neþeles at euentid of þis world, þei shulen be conuertid to Crist, and þei shulen suffre hungur bi þe feruent loue of cristen feiþ, as doggis berkyng aȝenes eresies and prechynge þe feiþ of Crist wiþ greet feruour and desire. *Lire here.*

430. þat is, fro men redi to shede out þe blood of innocentis. *Lire here.*

431. þat is, mysilf, for þei arettiden þat þei hadden take Dauiþ. *Lire here.*

432. Vnderstonde þou disseruyden þis persecucioun;

433. in Ieroms translacioun þus, and þei rennen and ben maad redi; and bi þis it is referrid to Saul and hise knyȝtis, þat runnen aboute as maad redi to þe sleyng of Dauiþ; and dresside my werkis.ⁱⁱ *Lire here.*

434. Do þou not merci to alle, et cetera: Summe wickidnesse is and if a man doiþ it, it mai not be þat God haue merci on hym; þilke wickidnesse is defendyng of synnes. If he doiþ ony good, he wole þat it be arettid to himsilf; if he doiþ ony yuele, he wole þat it be arettid to God and seiþ, If God nolde, Y hadde not do it. *Austyn here.*

Of certeyn malice, and ben obstynat þerinne; for siche ben vnworþi of merci. *Lire here.*

435. þat is, sekynge wiþ greet desire to sle Dauiþ; þerfor in Ebreu þus: and berke þei as doggis. [*Lire here.*]ⁱⁱⁱ

436. As if noon herde of hem; þerfor in Ieroms translacioun þus: as if no man herde. *Lire here.*

437. þat is, þat doon wickidli as þese men doon. *Lire here.*

438. To haue merci on her pursueris. *Lire here.*

439. þat is, in pride. *Austin here.*

440. In translating þe rewme to Dauiþ and to his hous. *Lire here.*

suffre hungur; and þei shulen cumpasse þe citee.⁴⁴¹ [16] Thei shulen
be scaterid abrood for to ete;⁴⁴² soþeli if þei ben not fillid, and þei
shulen grucche. [17] But I shal synge⁴⁴³ þi strengþe; and eerli I shal
enhaunce þi merci. For þou art maad myn vptakere; and my refuyt
in þe dai of my tribulacioun. [18] Myn helpere, I shal synge to þee;
for þou art God, myn uptakere, my God, my merci.⁴⁴⁴

## [PSALM 59]

*Deus repulisti nos*

[1] *þe title of lix salm.* In Ebreu þus:ᵃ *To victorie on þe witnessyng of
roose, þe swete song of Dauiþ to teche,* [2] *whanne he fauȝte aȝenes Aram of
floodis and Sirie of Soba; and Ioab turnyde aȝen, and smoot Edom in þe
valei of salt pittis, twelue þousynde.* In Ieroms translacioun þus: *To þe
ouercomere for lilies,*⁴⁴⁵ *þe witnessyng `of´*ᵇ *meke and perfite Dauiþ, to
teche, whanne he fauȝte aȝenes Sirie of Mesopotamye, and Soba, and so
forþ.*⁴⁴⁶

[3] God, þou hast put awei us, and þou hast distried us; þou were
wrooþ, and þou hast do merci to us. [4] Thou mouydist þe erþe, and
þou disturblidist it; make þou hool þe sorewis þerof, for it is mouyd.
[5] Thou schewidist harde þingis to þi puple; þou ȝauest drynke to us
wiþ þe wyn of compunccioun.⁴⁴⁷ [6] Thou hast ȝoue a signefiyng to
hem þat dreden þee; þat þei fle fro þe face of þe bouwe.⁴⁴⁸ That þi
derlyngis be delyuerid; [7] make þou saaf wiþ þi riȝthond.⁴⁴⁹ and here
þou me. [8] God spak bi his hooli; I shal be glad and I shal departe
f. 30ᵛ  Siccymam,⁴⁵⁰ and I shal mete þe grete valei of tabernaclis. | [9]
Galaad is myn and Manasses is myn; and Effraym is þe strengþe of
myn heed. Iuda is my kyng; [10] Moab is þe pot⁴⁵¹ of myn hope. Into
Ydumee I shal strecche forþ my shoo; aliens⁴⁵² be maad soget to me.
[11] Who shal lede me into a citee maad strong; who shal lede me til
into Ydumee? [12] Wher not þou, God, þat hast putte awei us; and
shalt þou not, God, go out in oure vertues?⁴⁵³ [13] Lord, ȝyue þou to
us helpe of tribulacioun; for þe helþe of man is veyn. [14] In God we
shulen make vertu; and he shal brynge to nouȝt hem þat disturblen us.

---

**Ps. 59**     ᵃ In Ebreu þus] *rubricated and then underlined, presumably to indicate that it
should not have been copied in red*     ᵇ of] and, *canc. and corrected by the scribe above the line of
writing; this title also in* ikKV

441. In sekinge liyflode bi beggynge. *Lire here.*     f. 30ʳ

442. þat is, to seke liyflode. *Lire here.*

443. þat is, shal preise in deuoute songis. *Lire here.*

444. þat is, al þing þat Y am, it is of þi merci. [*Austin*]ⁱᵛ *here.*

[PSALM 59 GLOSSES]

445. þat is, þe cumpenyes of wise men of þe lawe. [*Lire here.*]ⁱ

446.ⁱⁱ Gostli, þis salm mai be expowned of ech man verili repentynge, þat biholdiþ þe rewme of his soule distried bi synnes passid, and moreneþ þerfor, and preieþ for þe restoryng þerof, to þe staat of vertu and of grace. Herto he is helpid bi þis bi very knoulechyng, signefied bi Iuda, which is interpretid knoulechyng, and bi kepyng fro turnyng aȝen to synne, vndurstondun by Manasses, þat is interpretid forȝetyng, for he owiþ forȝete to worche synnes passed; and bi multepliyng of good werk, signefied bi Effraym, þat is interpretid wexinge eþer plentee, and bi witnessyng of his owne conscience, signefied bi Galaad, þat is interpretid an heep of witnessyng. Sich a man makiþ suget `to´ⁱⁱⁱ himsilf þe coueitise of fleisch and of iȝen and þe pride of liyf, signefied bi Moab, Ydume, and Filistia. *Lire here.*

447. Ierom haþ, wiþ þe wyn of morenyng; al is oon, for morenyng is compunccioun of synnes. *Lire here.*

448. Of þi riȝtfulnesse, which is shewid to smyte synneris. *Lire here.*

449.ⁱᵛ þe puple of Israel. *Lire here.*

450.ᵛ þat is, þe lond of Sichem. *Lire here.*

451. þat is, Y hope in God þat þe lond of Moab shal be suget to me     f. 30ᵛ
to serue me, as a pot which a man vsiþ to his seruyce; in Ebreu þus, Moab is þe pot of my waischyng, þat is, þe puple of Moab shal be so suget to me, as a pot maad redi to waischyng. *Lire here.*

452. In Ebreu þus: Filistia is associed to me, þat is, is addid to my rewme, for it was tributarie to Dauiþ. *Lire here.*

453. þat is, oure oostis, as if he seie, ȝhis, for ellis we myȝten no þing do. *Lire here.*

---

ⁱᵛ Austin] Lire
**Ps. 59 glosses** ⁱ Lire here] *om.* ⁱⁱ *in the bottom margin* ⁱⁱⁱ to] *added by the scribe both above the line of writing and in margin* ⁱᵛ *this gloss also in margin in* IMOQ *and intertextually in* A *and* U ᵛ *this gloss interlinear and underlined in* K *and in margin of* V

## [PSALM 60]

*Exaudi Deus deprecacionem meam*

[1] *þe title of lx salm. To þe victorie on orgoun, to Dauiþ hymsilf.*⁴⁵⁴

[2] God, here þou my bisechyng; ȝyue þou tent to my preier. [3] Fro þe endis of þe lond I criede to þee; þe while myn herte was angwischid, þou enhaunsidist me in a stoon. Thou leddist me forþ, [4] for þou art [maad]ᵃ myn hope; a tour of strengþe fro þe face of þe enemy. [5] I shal dwelle in þi tabernacle into worldis; I shal be kyuerid in þe hilyng of þi wyngis. [6] For þou, my God, hast herd my preier; þou hast ȝoue eritage⁴⁵⁵ to hem þat dreden þi name. [7] Thou shalt adde, eþer encreesse, daies on þe daies of þe kyng; hise ȝeeris til into þe dai of generacioun and of generacioun. [8] He dwelliþ wiþouten ende in þe siȝt of God; who shal seke⁴⁵⁶ þe merci and treuþe of hym? [9] So I shal seie salm to þi name into þe world of world; þat I ȝelde my vowis fro dai into dai.

## [PSALM 61]

*Nonne Deo subiecta erit*

[1] *þe title of lxj salm. To þe victorie ouer Iditum, þe salm of Dauiþ.*⁴⁵⁷

f. 31ʳ     [2] Wher my soule | shal not be suget to God; for myn heelþe is of hym. [3] Forwhi he is boþe my God and myn helþe; my takere-up, I shal no more be mouyd. [4] Hou longe fallen ȝe on a man? alle ȝe sleen;⁴⁵⁸ as to a wal boowid, and a wal of stoon wiþout morter caste doun. [5] Neþeles þei þouȝten to putte awei my prijs, I ran in þirst; wiþ her mouþ þei blessiden, and in her herte þei cursiden.⁴⁵⁹ [6] Neþeles, my soule, be þou suget to God; for my pacience⁴⁶⁰ is of hym. [7] For he is my God and my sauyour; myn helpere, I shal not passe out. [8] Myn helþe and my glorie is in God; God is þe ȝyuere of myn helpe, and myn hope is in God. [9] Al þe gaderyng togidere of þe puple, hope ȝe in God, schede ȝe out ȝoure hertis bifor hym; God is oure helpere wiþouten ende. [10] Neþeles þe sones⁴⁶¹ of men ben veyn; þe sones of men ben lieres in balaunces, þat þei disseyue of vanyte into þe same þing. [11] Nile

Ps. 60      ᵃ maad] *om.*

## [PSALM 60 GLOSSES]

454.[i] Dauiþ made þis lx salm aftir þat he hadde ascapid þe hondis of Saul, cumpassinge him at þe maner of a coroun. Also, Dauiþ biforseiþ bi profecie benefices of God, þat shulen be ȝouun to him aftirward. *Lire here.*

455. þat is, þe rewme of Israel, to me and to my sones suynge me. *Lire here.*

456. þat is, who mai declare eþer telle? þis is þe word of Dauiþ knoulechynge þat Goddis merci and treuþe is so greet aboute him, þat it mai not be teld out. *Lire here.*

## [PSALM 61 GLOSSES]

457.[i] Dauiþ made þis lxj salm whanne he was in þe persecucioun of Saul, and[ii] aftir þat he was comun aȝen fro þe lond of Moab to þe lond of Iuda, at þe word of Gad þe profete. Dauiþ made þe tenþe salm in þis comynge aȝen, but he made þis salm aftir þat he hadde dwellide sumdeel in þe lond of Iuda.

Gostli, þis lxj salm mai be expowned of ech cristen man, which for obedience to God suffriþ pacientli vniust persecuciouns, and repreuiþ þe vices of pursueris and remembriþ bifor God, and abidiþ þe equyte of Goddis ȝeldyng for euere eiþer. *Lire here.*

458. Alle ȝe sleen, þat is, ȝe seken to sle me, ȝe manaassen deþ to[iii] me, as a wal nyȝ to falling; in Ebreu þus: as a wal bowid, and a wal of stoon wiþout morter fallinge doun, þat is, ȝe manaassen deþ to me, as siche wallis manaassen deþ to men passinge bisidis hem. *Lire here.*  f. 31[r]

459. In Ebreu þus: þei telden a leesyng; in Ierom þus: sones plesiden in a leesing. [*Lire here.*][iv]

460. For my pacience is of him: þe world is a furneis. 'Wickid men ben chaf' [Ps 1: 4]; iust men ben gold. þe fier is tribulacioun, þe goldsmyȝt is God. þerfor Y do þat þe goldsmyȝt wole; Y suffre where þe goldsmyȝt settiþ me. *Austin here.*

461. In Ebreu þus: þe sones of men ben lieris in balaunces for to stie; and þei and vanyte ben togidere, þat is, ben of þe same weiȝte. For siche men ben no þing worþ, as þilke vanyte is no þing worþ. *Lire here.*

---

**Ps. 60 glosses** [i] *next to the title in the right margin; this gloss also in* bCGikKLPQSVX
**Ps. 61 glosses** [i] *next to the title in the left margin; the first historical part of this gloss also in* bCGikKLPQSVX    [ii] and] and þis    [iii] to] to n-, n- *canc.*    [iv] Lire here] *om.*

ȝe haue hope in wickidnesse,⁴⁶² and nyle ȝe coueite raueyns; if
richessis ben plenteuouse, nyle ȝe sette þe [herte]ᵃ þerto. [12] God
spak onys, I herde þese twei þingis, þat power is of God, [13] and,
þou Lord, merci is to þee; for þou shalt ȝelde to ech man bi hise
werkis.

### [PSALM 62]

*Deus Deus meus*

[1] *þe title of lxij salm. þe salm of Dauiþ, whanne he was in desert of
Iudee.*⁴⁶³

[2] God, my God, I wake to þee⁴⁶⁴ ful eerli. Mi soule þirstide toᵃ
þee; my fleisch þirstide to þee ful manyefold. [3] In a lond forsakun
wiþout weie and wiþout watir, so I apperide to þee in hooli;⁴⁶⁵ þat I
shulde se þi vertu and þi glorie. [4] For þi merci is betere þan lyues;
my lippis shulen herie þee. [5] So I shal blesse þee in my lijf; and in þi
name I shal reise⁴⁶⁶ myn hondis. | [6] Mi soule be fillid as wiþ innere
fatnesse and outirmere fatnesse; and my mouþ shal herie wiþ lippis of
ful out ioiynge. [7] So I hadde mynde of þee on my bed, in morewtidis
I shal þenke of þee; [8] for þou were myn helpere. And in þe kyueryng
of þi wyngis I shal make ful out ioie, [9] my soule cleuyde aftir þee; þi
riȝthond took me up. [10] Forsoþe þei souȝten in veyn my lijf, þei
shulen entre into þe lowere þingis of erþe; [11] þei shulen be bitakun
into þe hondis of swerd, þei shulen be maad þe partis of foxis. [12]
But þe kyng shal be glad in God; and alle men shulen be preisid þat
sweren⁴⁶⁷ in hym, for þe mouþ of hem, þat speken wickid þingis, is
stoppid.

### [PSALM 63]

*Exaudi Deus orationem meam cum deprecor*

[1] *þe title of lxiij salm.* In Ebreu þus: *To þe victorie, þe salm of Dauiþ.*
In Ierom þus: *To þe ouercomere, þe song of Dauiþ.*⁴⁶⁸

[2] God, here þou my preier whanne I biseche; delyuere þou my
soule fro þe drede of þe enemy. [3] Thou hast defendide me fro þe
couent of yueledoeris; fro þe multitude of hem þat worchen wickidnesse. [4] For þei scharpiden her tungis as a swerd, þei benten a

Ps. 61    ᵃ herte] *om.*
Ps. 62    ᵃ to] into

462. Wickidnesse is veyn. No þing is my3ti, no but ri3tfulnesse. Treuþe may be hid at a tyme; it mai not be ouercomun. Wickidnesse mai blosme at a tyme; it mai not dwelle.ᵛ *Austin here.*

[PSALM 62 GLOSSES]

463.ⁱ Dauiþ made þis salm whanne he was in þe pursuynge of Saul, aftir þat he was turned a3en into þe lond of Iudee, and was in desert of Iudee.

Gostli, þis salm mai be expowned of ech iust man set in persecucioun of men, which neþeles is nurschid bi Goddis comfortingis; and hise aduersaries shulen be distried fynali, for which þing he shal be glad in þe Lord, not for þe loue of his owne veniaunce, but of Goddis ri3tfulnesse. *Lire here.*

464. For in þe bigynnyng of þe morewtid, he roos up to Goddis preisyngis. þis is a3enes prynces, þat wolen slepe til to hi3-dai. *Lire here.*

465. þat is, desir eþer halewid herte. *Austyn here.*

466. Cristis hondis weren reisid and strecchid forþ in þe cros for us, þat oure hondis be strecchid forþ to good werkis. *Austin here.*

467. þat sweren in him: For an ooþ maad duli is a dede of vertu, for it    f. 31ᵛ is foundid on þe reuerence of Goddis treuþe. þerfor it is seid in x capitulo of Deutero, 'þou shalt swere bi þeⁱⁱ name of God' [Deut 10: 20]. *Lire here.*

Alle shulen be preisid þat sweren in him, þat is, þat biheete and avowen her liyf to him and 3elden, and ben maad cristen men. *Austin here.*

[PSALM 63 GLOSSES]

468.ⁱ Elde Ebreis expownen þis salm of Danyel, þat was sent into þe lake of liouns bi enuye and false councel of þe princesⁱⁱ and was delyuerid bi Goddis vertu.

Gostli, þis salm mai be expowned of ech iust man, suffrynge false calenge of wickidⁱⁱⁱ men til to þe deþ, which neþeles is delyuerid sodenli of God for his ri3tfulnesse, and hise aduersaries ben condempned. *Lire here.*

---

ᵛ dwelle] *corrected by the scribe on an erasure*
**Ps. 62 glosses**    ⁱ *next to the title in the left margin and concluding in the bottom margin; this gloss also in* bCikKLPQSV.X    ⁱⁱ þe] þe þe
**Ps. 63 glosses**    ⁱ *next to the title in the left margin; the historical part of this gloss also in* ikKV
ⁱⁱ princes] princies    ⁱⁱⁱ wickid] wickidnesse, -nesse *canc.*

bouwe, a bittir þing;⁴⁶⁹ [5] for to schete in pryuytees hym þat is
vnwemmyd. [6] Sodenli þei shulen schete hym, and þei shulen not
drede; þei maden stidfast to hemsilf a wickid word. Thei telden, þat
þei shulden hide snaris; þei seiden, Who shal se hem? [7] Thei
souȝten wickidnessis; þei souȝten and failiden in sekynge. A man
neiȝe to deep⁴⁷⁰ herte; [8] and God shal be enhaunsid. The arowis of
f. 32ʳ litle men⁴⁷¹ ben maad þe woundis of hem; [9] and þe tungis | of hem
ben maadᵃ sijk aȝenes hem. Alle men weren disturblid þat sien hem;
[10] and ech man dredde. And þei telden þe werkis of God; and
vndurstoden þe dedis of God. [11] The iust man shal be glad in þe
Lord, and shal hope in hym; and alle men of riȝtful herte shulen be
preisid.

## [PSALM 64]

*Te decet ymnis Deus in Sion*

[1] *þe title of lxiiij salm. To victorie, þe salm of þe song of Dauiþ.*⁴⁷²

[2] God, heriyng⁴⁷³ bicomeþ þee in Sion; and a vow shal be ȝoldun
to þee in Ierusalem. [3] Here þou my preier; ech man⁴⁷⁴ shal come to
þee. [4] The wordis of wickid men⁴⁷⁵ hadden þe maistrie ouer us; and
þou shalt do merci to oure wickidnessis. [5] Blessid is he whom þou
hast chose, and hast take; he schal dwelle in þi forȝerdis.⁴⁷⁶ We shulen
be fillid wiþ þe goodis of þyn hous; þi temple is hooli, [6] wondurful
in equyte. God, oure helþe, here þou us; þou art hope of alle coostis of
erþe, and in þe see afer. [7] And þou makist redi hillis in þi vertu, and
art gird wiþ power; [8] which disturblist þe depþe of þe see, þe sown
of þe wawis þerof. Folkis shulen be disturblid, [9] and þei þat dwellen
in þe endis⁴⁷⁷ shulen drede of þi signes; þou shalt delite⁴⁷⁸ þe
outgoyngis of þe morewtid and euentid. [10] Thou hast visitid þe
lond, and hast greetli fillid it; þou hast multeplied to make it riche.
The flood of God was fillid wiþ watris; þou madist redi þe mete of
hem, for þe makynge redi þerof is [so].ᵃ [11] Thou fillynge greetli þe
streemys⁴⁷⁹ þerof, multeplie þe fruytis þerof; þe lond bryngynge forþ
fruytis shal be glad in goteris⁴⁸⁰ of it. [12] Thou shalt blesse þe
f. 32ᵛ coroun⁴⁸¹ of þe ȝeer of | þi good wille; and þi feeldis shulen be fillid
wiþ plentee of fruytis. [13] The faire þingis of desert shulen wexe fat;
and litle hillis shulen [be]ᵇ cumpassid wiþ ful out ioiynge. [14] The

Ps. 63    ᵃ ben maad] ben maad ben maad, *first* ben maad *canc.*
Ps. 64    ᵃ so] *om.*    ᵇ be] *om.*

469. In Ebreu it is, <u>a bittir word</u>. *Lire here.*

470. þe Latyn word mai be boþe 'hiȝ' and 'deep', but in Ebreu it is <u>deep</u>. *Lire here.*

471.<sup>iv</sup> þat is, of enuyouse men;

<u>þe arowis of litle men</u>: in Ebreu þus: <u>þe Lord sheet hem wiþ a sudeyn arowe; þe strokis of hem ben maad; her tungis sclaundriden hem</u>; in Ierom þus: <u>þerfor þe Lord shal schete hem wiþ a sodeyn dart; her woundis shulen be maad wiþ her dart; þei shulen falle aȝenes hemsilf bi her tunges</u>. þis is expowned of þe arowe of Goddis riȝtfulnesse, bi whiche þe aduersaries of Danyel weren slayn and deuouride of þe liouns. *Lire here.*

[PSALM 64 GLOSSES] f. 32<sup>r</sup>

472.<sup>i</sup> þer is no more in Ebreu and in Ieroms translacioun. *Lire here.*

þis lxiiij salm spekiþ of þe comyng aȝen of Iewis prisoneris in Babiloyne into þe lond of biheest, and of þe plentee of fruytis of þat lond.

Gostli, þis salm mai be expowned of ech man repentinge verili, as goyng awei fro þe prisonyng of Babiloyne, and hastynge wiþ alle hise strengþis to þe plentee of good werkis, boþe in hymsilf and in oþere men. *Lire here.*

473. In Ebreu þus: <u>silence of heriyng is to þee in Syon</u>, þat is, Goddis heriyng, hou myche euere it is maad of man, failiþ wiþout noumbre fro Goddis greetnesse preisid. *Lire here.*

474. þat is, of ech nacioun, men shulen come to worschipe þee, whanne þe temple is bildid aȝen;

475. <u>þe wordis of wickid men</u>, þat is, þe dedis of men of Babiloyne. *Lire here.*

476. þese forȝerdis<sup>ii</sup> weren places of þe temple, where sacrifices and preieris and redyngis of þe lawe weren maad. *Lire here.*

477. þat is, of al erþe. *Lire here.*

478. þat is, shalt make þe offryngis of þe sacrifice of þe morewtid and of þe euentid delitable to feiþful men, deuoute to þee. *Lire here.*

479. In Ebreu and in Ierom it is, <u>þe forewis þerof</u>. *Lire here.*

480. þat is, in reynes droppinge doun fro heuene bi Goddis ordenaunce. *Lire here.*

481. þat is, þe sercle. [*Lire here.* ]<sup>iii</sup>

<sup>iv</sup> *this gloss interlinear and underlined in* K *and in margin of* V
**Ps. 64 glosses** <sup>i</sup> *the textual part interlinear at the end of the title and into the right margin; the historical part in the bottom margins; also in* bCGikKLPQSVX <sup>ii</sup> forȝerdis] *in margin of* I, *or* hallis <sup>iii</sup> Lire here] *om.; this gloss interlinear in* V

weþeris of scheep ben cloþid, and valeis shulen be plenteuouse of
wheete; þei shulen crie, and soþeli þei shulen seie herijng.

## [PSALM 65]

*Iubilate Deo omnis terra*

[1] *þe title of lxv salm. To victorie,*[482] *þe song of salm.*[483]

Al [þe][a] erþe,[484] make 3e ioie hertli to God, [2] seie 3e salm to his
name; 3yue 3e glorie[485] to his heriyng. [3] Seie 3e to God, Lord, þi
werkis ben ful dredeful; in þe multitude of þi vertu þyn enemyes
shulen lie[486] to þee. [4] God, al þe erþe wo[r]schipe[b] þee and synge
to þee; seie it salm to þi name. [5] Come 3e and se 3e þe werkis of
God; ferdful in councels on þe sones of men. [6] Which turnyde þe
see into drie lond; in þe flood þei shulen passe wiþ [foot],[c] þere we
shulen be glad in hym. [7] Which is Lord in his vertu wiþouten
ende, hise i3en biholden on folkis; þei þat maken scharp[487] be not
enhaunsid in hymsilf. [8] 3e heþene men, blesse oure God; and make
3e herd þe vois of his preising. [9] That haþ set my soule to lijf, and
3af not my feet into stiryng.[488] [10] For þou, God, hast preued us;
þou hast examyned us bi fier, as siluer is examyned. [11] Thou
leddist us[d] into a snare, þou puttidist tribulaciouns in oure bak; [12]
þou settidist men on oure heedis. We passiden bi fier and watir;[489]
and þou leddist us out into refreischyng. [13] I shal entre into þyn
hous in brent sacrifices; I shal 3elde to þee my vowis, [14] whiche my
'lippis'[e] spaken distynctli. And my mouþ spak in my tribulacioun;
[15] I shal offre to | þee brent sacrifices ful of merowe, wiþ þe
brennynge of rammes;[490] I shal offre to þee oxis wiþ buckis of geet.
[16] Alle 3e þat dreden God, come and here, and I shal telle; hou
grete þingis he haþ do to my soule. [17] I criede to hym wiþ my
mouþ; and I ioiede fulli vndur my tunge. [18] If I bihelde
wickidnesse[491] in myn herte; þe Lord shal not here. [19] Therfor
God herde; and perseyuyde þe vois of my bisechyng. [20] Blessid be
God; þat remouyed not my preier, and[492] his merci fro me.

f. 33ʳ

---

Ps. 65    ᵃ þe] *om.*    ᵇ worschipe] woschipe    ᶜ foot] flood    ᵈ us] us out, out *canc.*
ᵉ lippis] *added by the scribe above the line of writing*

[PSALM 65 GLOSSES]

482. In Ierom it is, to þe ouercomere. *Lire here.*          <sup>f. 32ᵛ</sup>

483.ⁱ þis lxv sa[l]mⁱⁱ is doyng of þankingis for þe delyueraunce of þe puple of Iewis fro Egipt.ⁱⁱⁱ

Gostli, þis salm mai be expowned of ech man led out of þe seruage of synne as of Egipt, þat is, of derknesse, and herieþ God for his wondurful delyueraunce. For it is more to make a wickid man iust, þan to make of nouȝt heuene and erþe, as Austyn seiþ on Ioon. And for ascapyng of greuouse trauelis, þat ben in þe werkis of synneris, and also for Goddis comfort, which ofte is feelid more aftir veri penaunce for synnes, þan bifor þe doynge of synnes. *Lire here.*

484. Al erþe, þat is, alleⁱᵛ men dwellynge in erþe, make ȝe ioie hertli. þis is ioie of þe herte, which mai not al be holdun stille, þat ne it be schewid in outward signe. *Lire heere.*

Eþer make ȝe ioie hertli, þat is, breke ȝe out into þe vois of ioies, þouȝ ȝe moun not of wordis. For sich ioie is not maad bi wordis, but sown aloone of hem þat ioieᵛ is ȝoldun, as of þi herte trauelynge and bryngyngeᵛⁱ forþ into vois þe gladnesse of þing conseyued, þat mai not be declarid bi wordis. *Austyn here.*

485. Ȝyue ȝe glorie, et cetera, þat is, while drede is putte awei, herie ȝe hym bifor alle men; forwhi, glorie is cleer knowyng wiþ preisyng. *Lire here.*

Nathanael in whom no gile was, was wysᵛⁱⁱ in þe lawe and he was not chosun to þe office of apostle, lest kunnynge men wolden gesse hemsilf chosun for þe merite of her kunnyng, so her kunnyng shulde be preisid and þe preisyng of Cristis grace shulde be maad lesse. *Austin here.*

486. þat is, lieden. *Lire here.*

487. In aȝenstonding God. *Lire here.*

488. þat is, suffrid not me falle doun bi idolatrie. *Lire here.*

489. þat is, temporal angwischis and prosperitees. [þe glos]ᵛⁱⁱⁱ here.

490. þat is, wiþ rammes al brent to þin onour. *Lire here.*          <sup>f. 33ʳ</sup>

491. þat is, louyde wickidnesse. *Austin here.*

Eþer if Y was gilti to me of dedli synne. *Lire here.*

492.ⁱˣ Took not awei. [*Lire here.*]

**Ps. 65 glosses**   ⁱ *in the bottom margin, a red paraph to begin the spiritual gloss; the historical part of this gloss also in* bCGikKLPQV*X*   ⁱⁱ salm] sam   ⁱⁱⁱ Egipt] Egipit   ⁱᵛ alle] allen   ᵛ ioie] ioien   ᵛⁱ bryngynge] brynge   ᵛⁱⁱ wys] wiys, -i- *canc.*   ᵛⁱⁱⁱ þe glos] Lire   ⁱˣ *also in margin of* U, *attributed to Lyra*

[PSALM 66]

*Deus misereatur nostri*

[1] *þe title*[493] *of lxvj salm.* In Ebreu þus: *To þe victorie in orguns, þe salm of song.* In Ierom þus: *To þe ouercomere in salmes, þe song of writing of a delitable þing wiþ metre.*

[2] God haue merci[494] on us, and blesse us;[495] liȝtne he his cheer on us, and haue merci on us. [3] That we knowe þi weie in erþe; þin heelþe in alle folkis. [4] God, puplis knoulech to þee; alle puplis knoulech to þee. [5] Heþene men be glad and make fulli ioie, for þou demest puplis in equyte; and dressist heþene men[496] in erþe. [6] God, puplis knouleche to þee, alle puplis knoulech to þee; [7] þe erþe ȝaf his fruyt.[497] God, oure God blesse us,[498] [8] God blesse us; and al þe coostis of erþe drede hym.[499]

[PSALM 67]

*Exurgat Deus et dissipentur*

[1] *þe title of lxvij salm. To victorie, þe salm of song of Dauid.*[500]

[2] God rise up, and hise enemyes be scaterid; and þei[501] þat haten hym fle fro his face. [3] As smoke failiþ, faile þei; as wex fletiþ fro þe face of fier, so perische synneris fro þe face of God. [4] And | iust men ete, and make fulli ioie in þe siȝt of God; and delite þei in gladnesse. [5] Synge ȝe to God, seie ȝe salm to his name; make ȝe weie to him þat stieþ on þe goynge doun,[502] þe Lord is name to hym. Make ȝe fulli ioie in his siȝt, enemyes shulen be disturblid fro þe face of him, [6] which [is][a] þe fadir of fadirles and modirles children; and þe iuge of widewis. God is in his hooli place; [7] God þat makiþ men of o wille to dwelle in þe hous. Which lediþ out bi strengþe hem þat ben bounden;[503] in lijk maner hem þat maken sharp, þat dwellen in sepulcris. [8] God, whanne þou ȝedist out in þe siȝt of þi puple; whanne þou passidist forþ in `þe´[b] desert. [9] The erþe was mouyd, for heuenes droppiden doun fro þe face of God of Synai;[504] fro þe face of God of Israel. [10] God, þou shalt departe wilful reyn to þyn eritage;[505] and it was sijk; but þou madist it parfite. [11] Thi beestis[506] shulen dwelle þerinne; God, þou hast maad redi in þi swetnesse to þe pore man. [12] The Lord schal ȝyue a word; to hem þat prechen þe gospel wiþ myche

Ps. 67    [a] is] *om.*    [b] þe] *by the scribe above the line of writing*

f. 33[v]

[PSALM 66 GLOSSES]

493.<sup>i</sup> þis `lxvj´<sup>ii</sup> salm is profesie of Cristis incarnacioun and his conuersacioun among men, þat was souereynli desirid of hooli fadris. *Lire here.*

494. In sendynge us þe sauyour. *Lire here.*

495. Blesse us: Whanne þe Lord blessiþ us, we encreessen, and whanne we blessen þe Lord, we encreessen. He is not encreessid bi oure blessyng, neiþer is decreesid bi oure cursyng. God is oure erþetiliere bi aungelis, bi profetis, and bi apostlis; and þe postlis ben erþetilieres. If Y seie, no man bileue; if Crist seiþ, wo to hym þat bileueþ not. *Austyn here.*

496. þat is, into þe weie of euerelastinge helþe. [*Lire here.*]<sup>iii</sup>

497. þe erþe ȝaf his fruyt, þat is, þe blessid virgyn brouȝt forþ hir sone. *Lire here.*

498. God oure God blesse us [, et cetera]<sup>iv</sup>: He seiþ blesse in synguler noumbre, to signefie þe vnyte of beyng eiþer of substaunce of God þe trynyte; and he seiþ þries God, to shewe þre persoones in trinite þat ben alle euene in power, wit, and good wille. *Lire here.*

499. þat is, bi sones drede, þat stondiþ wiþ charite. *Lire here.*

[PSALM 67 GLOSSES]

500.<sup>i</sup> þis salm is profesie of benefices to comynge, to be ȝouun bi Crist. Firste it tretiþ of Cristis risyng aȝen and of ascencioun aftirward, and of benefices suynge to þo. *Lire here.*

501. þat is, fendis obstynat in synne. *Lire here.*

502. Ebreis seyn þis is þe veri lettre: þat stieþ into heuene. *Lire* f. 33ᵛ *here.*

503. In Ierom þus, boundun; soþeli in þe cruel, þat is, men obstynat in vnfeiþfulnesse, dwelliden in drienessis, þat is, wantiden þe humour of vertu and grace. *Lire here.*

504. þat is, of God comynge<sup>ii</sup> doun into þe hil of Synay;

505. to þin eritage,<sup>iii</sup> þat is, shalt moist wilful hooli chirche wiþ þe reyn of þi grace;

506. þi beestis, þat is, þi feiþful men. *Lire here.*

**Ps. 66 glosses** <sup>i</sup> *this gloss also in* ikKV   <sup>ii</sup> lxvj] *by the scribe above the line of writing*   <sup>iii</sup> Lire here] *om.*   <sup>iv</sup> et cetera] *om.*
**Ps. 67 glosses** <sup>i</sup> *next to the title in the right margin; this gloss also in* ikKV   <sup>ii</sup> comynge] comynge comynge   <sup>iii</sup> *a dot above* eritage *for an undrawn tie-mark*

vertu. [13] The kyngis of vertues[507] ben maad loued of þ[e][c] derlyng;
and to þe fairnesse of þe hous, to departe spuylis. [14] If ȝe slepen
among þe myddil of sortis,[508] eþer eritages, þe feþeris of þe culuer ben
of siluer; and þe hyndrere þingis of þe bak þerof ben in þe
schyn[yn]g[d] of gold. [15] While þe kyng of heuene demeþ kyngis
þeronne, þei shulen be maad whittere þan snow in Selmon; [16] þe hil

f. 34[r] of God is a fat hil.[509] | The crudid[510] hil is a fat hil; [17] wherto
bileuen ȝe falsli, croddid hillis? The hil in which it plesiþ wel[e] God to
dwelle þerinne; for þe Lord shal dwelle into þe ende.[511] [18] The
chare of God is manyefold wiþ ten þousynde, a þousynde of hem þat
ben glad; þe Lord was in hem, in Syna, in þe hooli.[512] [19] Thou
stiedist an hiȝ, þou tokist caitifte;[513] þou resseyuydist ȝiftis among
men. Forwhi þou tokist hem þat bileuyden not; for to dwelle in þe
Lord God. [20] Blessid be þe Lord ech dai; þe God of oure helþis shal
make an esy weie to us. [21] Oure God is God to make men saaf; and
outgoynge fro deþ is of þe Lord God.[514] [22] Neþeles God shal breke
þe heedis of hise enemyes; þe cop of þe heer of hem þat goon in her
trespassis. [23] The Lord seide, I schal turne fro Basan;[f] and I shal
turne into þe depþe of þe see. [24] That þi foot be dippid in blood; þe
tunge of þi doggis be dippid in blood of þe enemyes of hym. [25] God,
þei sien þi goyngis yn; þe goyngis yn of my God, of my kyng, which is
in þe hooli.[515] [26] Prynces ioyned wiþ syngeris camen bifore; in þe

507. þe kyngis of vertues: In Ieroms translacioun þus, þe kyngis of
oostis shulen be acordid in pees, for bi þe prechyng of apostlis and of
oþere disciplis of Crist, not oneli comyn men, but also manye kyngis
and prynces and myȝti men weren acordid in pees wiþ Crist, bi takyng
of cristen feiþ. And þis it is þat is seid here: þe king of vertues, þat is,
myȝti kyngis, ben maad loued of þe derlyng, þat is, of Crist himsilf,
which is þe derlyng of þe fadir in þe þridde chapitre of Matheu. *Lire
here.*

508. If ȝe slepen among þe myddil sortis, þat is, resten among þe
statis of þe chirche fiȝtynge aȝenes synnes and of þe chirche hauynge
victorie, þe [feþeris][iv] of þe culuer, þat is, þe vertues of hooli chirche,
ben of siluer, for present liyf is led in þe clennesse of conscience;

[c] þe] þi    [d] schynyng] schyng    [e] wel] wel to    [f] Basan] Basan and

[iv] feþeris] penne, *the translator probably erroneously reproducing Gall.* pennae

and þe hyndrere þingis of þe bac þerof ben in þe shynyng of gold, þat is, ben endid in charite. *Lire here.*

Eþer þus: Bitwixe þe myddil sortis, þat is, bitwixe twei testamentis; If ȝe slepen among þe myddil eritagis, þat is, dwellen in þe hope of heuenli euerelastyngnesse, and resten now fro coueitise of erþeli blis eþer prosperite; If ȝe slepen, þat is, dien, among þe myddil eritagis: þis is þe beste deþ, þat a man contynuynge in þe refreynyng of coueitisis fro erþeli þingis, and in þe hope of heuenli eritage, close þe laste dai of þis liyf. *Austyn here.*

Eþer þus: þe culuer is hooli chirche, maad of siluer, þat is, tauȝte bi Goddis spechis; þe feþeris of þe culuer ben þe techeris of hooli chirche;

If ȝe slepen, þat is, resten, among þe myddil of sortis, þat is, in þe autorite of twei testamentis, eþer among twei eritagis, oon erþeli and þe toþer heuenli, in not coueitinge greetli erþeli eritage and in abidyng pacientli heuenli eritage; eþer if ȝe contynuen til to þe deþ in dispisyng of erþeli goodis, and in þe desiryng of heuenli goodis; if ȝe slepen þus, þanne þe feþeris of þe culuer shulen be maad of siluer, þat is, þe techeris of þe chirche shulen be lerned in hooli scripture; and þe hyndrere þingis of þe bak, þat is, þe laste tymes of þe chirche in þe comyn risyng aȝen, eþer þe ende of ech iust man, shulen shyne in þe licnesse of gold, þat is, of wisdom and charite. *þe glos here.*

509. In Ebreu and in Ierom here bigynneþ þe vers suynge, þe hil of God is a fat hil. *Lire here.*

510. In Ebreu and in Ierom it is, þe hiȝ hil; bileuen ȝe falsli cruddid    f. 34ʳ
hillis?, þat is,ᵛ þat þe places of helþe ben wiþout hooli chirche. *Lire here.*

511. In Ierom it is, into wiþouten ende . *Lire here.*

512. þat is, þe Lord hadde felouschip of manye `þousynde´ ⱽⁱ hooli aungelis, in ȝyuynge of þe lawe on þe hooli hil Synay. *Lire here.*

513. þat is, hem þat weren holdun prisoneris in þe hiȝere part of helle and leddist hem wiþ þee to heuene. *Lire here.*

514. In Ebreu is set here þe name of þe Lord, thetragramaton, þat signefieþ þe pure beynge of God wiþout consideracioun of creature, and an oþere word, adonay, þat signefieþ 'Lord' comynli; and for þese twei wordis Ierom translatiþ here of þe Lord God. *Lire here.*

515. þat is, in briȝt heuene, apperid to hooli aungelis and men. *Lire here.*

ᵛ is] is of, of *canc.*    ⱽⁱ þousynde] *in margin by the scribe*

myddis of ȝonge dameselis[516] syngynge in tympans. [27] In chirchis
blesse ȝe God; blesse ȝe þe Lord fro þe wellis of Israel. [28] There
Beniamyn, a ȝong man;[517] in þe rauyschynge of mynde. The prynces
of Iuda weren þe duykis of hem; þe prynces of Ȝabulon, þe prynces of
Neptalym. [29] God, comaunde þou to þi vertu.[518] God, conferme
þou þis þing, which þou hast wrouȝt in us. [30] Fro þi temple, which
f. 34ᵛ  is in Ierusalem; kyngis shulen offre ȝiftis | to þee. [31] Blame þou þe
wielde beestis[519] of [þe]ᵍ rehed, þe gaderyng togidere of bolis is among
þe kiyn of puplis; þat þei exclude hem þat ben preued bi siluer.[520]
Distrie þou folkis[521] þat wolen batels, [32] legatis shulen come fro
Egipt; Ethiopie shal come bifore þe hondis þerof to God. [33]
Rewmes of [þe]ʰ erþe, synge ȝe to God; seie ȝe salm to þe Lord.
Synge ȝe to God; [34] þat stiede on þe heuene of heuene[522] at þe eest.
Lo! he shal ȝyue to his vois þe vois of vertu,[523] [35] ȝyue ȝe glorie to
God on Israel; his greet doyng and his vertu is in þe cloudis. [36] God
is wondurful in hise seyntis; God of Israel, he shal ȝyue vertu and
strengþe to his puple; blessid be God.

## [PSALM 68]

*Saluum me fac Deus*

[1] þe title of lxviij salm. In Ebreu þus: *To þe victorie, on þe roosis of
Dauid. In Ierom þus: To þe ouercomere, for þe sones of Dauiþ.*[524]

[2] God, make þou me saaf; for watris[525] entriden til to my soule.
[3] I am set in þe slym of þe depþe; and substaunce is not.[526] Iᵃ cam
into þe depþe of þe see; and þe tempest drenchide me.[527] [4] I
trauelide criyng, my cheekis weren maad hoose; myn iȝen failiden,[528]
þe while I hope into my God. [5] Thei þat hatiden me wiþout cause;
weren multeplied aboue þe heeris of myn heed. Myn enemyes þat
pursuyden me vniustli weren comfortid; I paiede þanne þo þingis,

---

516. þat is, deuoute virgyns heriynge God. *Lire here.*
517. þat is, Poul, þe laste of apostlis. *Lire here.*
518. þat is, to hooli aungelis, þat þei kepe and defende us. *Lire here.*
f. 34ᵛ  519. Wielde beestis, þat is, þe prynces of Romayns mouyd wiþ

---

ᵍ þe] *om.*    ʰ þe] *om.*
**Ps. 68**    ᵃ I] *written in a gap on the line, by a 2nd hand*

veynglorie; eþer þus, þe prynces of R[o]mayns<sup>vii</sup> þat ben clepid wielde
beestis for cruelte, ben þe gaderyng togidere of bolis, for þei
enforsiden to distrie cristen men not oneli bi turmentis, but also bi
flateryngis, in bihetyng to hem onouris, richessis, and lijk þingis, so
þat þei wolden forsake cristen feiþ;

520. þat þei exclude hem þat ben preued bi siluer, þat is, to exclude
hem fro þe treuþe of feiþ, þat ben more preued in þe feiþ, þan siluer is
preued in þe furneis. *Lire here.*

þe gaderyng togidere of bolis, þat is, of proude eretikis; among þe
kiyn of puplis, þat is, soulis able to be disseyued; bi siluer, þat is,
Goddis spechis; þat þei exclude hem, þat is, departe feiþful men þat
ben able to teche Goddis spechis fro þe eeris of puplis. *Austyn here.*

521. Distrie þou folkis, þat is, Romayns, þat maden soget al þe
world to hem bi batels; Ethiopie shal come bifore, þat is, Ethiopie shal
ʒyue hir hondis to God bi resseyuyng of cristen feiþ, bifor þat Egipt
be conuertid to feiþ;

522. on þe heuene of heuene: to þe hiʒest part of briʒt heuene. *Lire
here.*

523. þe vois of vertu, þat is, to þe prechyng of apostlis, þe vois of
myraclis to conferme it; on Israel, þat is, for goodis whiche he haþ
doon to cristen men; and his vertu is in þe cloudis, þat is, apostlis and
oþere disciplis sent to preche þe gospel. *Lire here.*

[PSALM 68 GLOSSES]

524.<sup>i</sup> As Cassiodore and Austin seyn here, þis lxviij salm to þe lettre
is seid of Crist, of his passioun in himsilf and in hise membris, for
Crist himsilf and þe postlis aleggen þus þis salm in þe newe
testament. *Lire here.*

525. þat is, tribulaciouns and persecuciouns til to þe departyng of
þe soul fro þe bodi. *Lire here.*

526. And substaunce is not, þat is, richessis ben not to Crist in his
deþ, neþer kyndli vertu of abidyng in þe deed bodi and biried;

527. of þe see, þat is, of persecucioun; and þe tempest drenchide
me, þat is, þe bit[er]nesse<sup>ii</sup> of passioun, bi which he diede in þe cros;

528. myn iʒen failiden, for hise bodili iʒen weren quenchid in deþ.
*Lire here.*

<sup>vii</sup> Romayns] Remayns
**Ps. 68 glosses** <sup>i</sup> *next to the title in the left margin; this gloss also in* ikKV   <sup>ii</sup> biternesse]
bitnesse

whiche I rauyschide not.[529] [6] God, þou knowist myn vnkunnyng;
and my trespassis ben not hid fro þee.[530] [7] Lord, Lord of vertues;
f. 35ʳ þei þat abiden | þee, be not aschamed in me. God of Israel; þei, þat
seken þee, be not schent on me. [8] For I suffride schenschip `for´[b]
þee; shame hilide my face. [9] I am maad a straunger to my briþeren;
and a pilgrym to þe sones of my modir. [10] For þe feruent loue of þin
hous eet me; and þe schenschipis of men seiynge schenschipis to þee,
felden on me. [11] And I hilide my soule wiþ fastyng; and it was maad
into schenschipe to me. [12] And I puttide on my clooþ an heire; and I
am maad to hem into a parable.[531] [13] Thei þat saten in þe ȝate,
spaken aȝenes me; and þei þat drunken wijn, sungen of me. [14] But
Lord, I <u>dresse</u> my preier to þee; God, I bide þe tyme of good
plesaunce. Here þou me in þe multitude of þi merci; in þe treuþe of
þyn helþe. [15] Delyuere þou me fro þe clei, þat I be not faste set
in;[532] delyuere þou me fro hem þat haten me, and fro depþis of watris.
[16] þe tempest of wat[ir][c] drenche not me,[533] neþer þe depþe
swolowe me; neþer þe pit make streiȝt his mouþ on me.[534] [17]
Lord, here þou me, for þi merci is benygne; upe þe multitude of þi
merciful doyngis biholde þou into me. [18] And turne not awei þi face
fro þi child;[535] for I am in tribulacioun, here þou me swiftli. [19] Ȝyue
þou tent to my soule and delyuere þou it; for myn enemyes delyuyere
þou me. [20] Thou knowist my schenschip and my dispisyng; and my
shame.[536] [21] Alle þat troblen me ben in þi siȝt; myn herte abood
schenschip and wrecchidnesse. And I abood hym þat was sori
togidere, and noon was;[537] and þat shulde comforte, and I foond
f. 35ᵛ not. | [22] And þei ȝauen galle into my mete; and in my þirste þei
ȝauen to me drynke wiþ vynegre.[538] [23] The boord of hem be maad
bifore hem into a snare; and into ȝeldyngis and into sclaundir. [24]
Her iȝen be maad derk, þat þei se not; and euere bowe doun þe bak of
hem.[539] [25] Schede out þyn ire on hem; and þe strong veniaunce of
þin ire take hem. [26] The abitacioun[d] of hem be maad forsakun; and
noon be þat dwelle in þe tabernaclis of hem. [27] For þei pursuyden
hym whom þou hast smyte; and þei addiden on þe sorewe of my
woundes. [28] Adde[540] þou wickidnesse on þe wickidnesse of hem;
and entre þei not into þi riȝtfulnesse. [29] Be þei doon awei fro þe
book of lyuynge men; and be þei not writun[541] wiþ iust men. [30] I am
pore and soreuful; God, þin helþe t[oo]k[e] me up. [31] I shal herie þe

[b] for] in, *canc. and corrected in margin by the scribe*　　　[c] watir] watris　　　[d] abitacioun]
abitaticioun　　　[e] took] take

529. Crist paiede peynes for þe synnes of mankynde, whiche he hadde not do. *Lire here.*

530. þis is vndurstondun of Cristis bodi, not of his owne persoone. þe vnkunnyng and synnes of hise membris he clepiþ hise, for þe vnyte of þe heed and of þe membris, and for he made satisfaccioun for þese. *Lire here.*

531. þat is, into scornyng. *Lire here.*                                 f. 35<sup>r</sup>

532. þat is, þat Y dwelle not longe in sepulcre. *Lire here.*

533. þat is, holde me not long in deþ. *Lire here.*

534. In Ebreu it is, stoppe not his mouþ on me. *Lire here.*

535. þat is, fro þi seruaunt ful obedient, Ihesu Crist. *Lire here.*

536. In Ierom it is, my sclaundir. *Lire here.*

537. Disciplis and oþere men weren sori fleischli but not gostli for þe synne of Iewis, as Crist was sori. *Austin here.*

538. Iewis þat crucifieden Crist goynge in erþe synnyden lesse þan    f. 35<sup>v</sup>
þ[ei]<sup>iii</sup> þat dispisen him sittynge in heuene;
þe boord of hem be maad, et cetera: he d[e]s[i]riþ<sup>iv</sup> not þis, but profecieþ þis, not þat it be maad, but for it shal be maad; þerfor be it maad, for it mai not ellis be, no but þese þingis bifalle to siche men;

539. Her iȝen be maad derk, for þei sien wiþout cause be it maad to hem þat þei se not. Whanne þei han ceessid to know heuenli þingis, it is nede þat þei be blyndid and þenke of lowere þingis, and þis it is to haue þe bac crokid. *Austin here.*
Her iȝen be maad derk, for þei þat dwelliden weren scaterid þorou þe world, and weren blyndid in her vnfeiþfulnesse, as Poul seiþ in xj capitulo to Romayns;
bowe doun, bi þe birþun of synnes leid to. *Lire here.*

540. þat is, þou shalt adde, þat is, suffre to be addid. *Lire here.*

541. Not þat þei ben writun þere. þis is seid bi þe hope of hem, for þei gessiden hemsilf writun; þat is, be it knowun to hem þat þei ben not þere. *Austin here.*

---

name of God wiþ song; and I shal magnefie hym in heriyng. [32] And it shal plese God more þan a newe calf; bryngynge forþ hornes and clees. [33] Pore men se and be glad; seke ȝe God, and ȝoure soule shal lyue. [34] For þe Lord herde pore men; and dispiside not hise

<sup>iii</sup> þei] þat   <sup>iv</sup> desiriþ] diseriþ

bounden men. [35] Heuenys⁵⁴² and erþe, herie him; þe see, and alle
crepynge beestis in þoo, herie him. [36] For God shal make saaf Sion;
and þe citees of Iuda shulen be bildid. And þei shulen dwelle þere;
and þei shulen gete it bi eritage. [37] And þe seed of hise seruauntis
shal haue it in possessioun; and þei þat louen his name, shulen dwelle
þerinne.

## [PSALM 69]

*Deus in adiutorium*

[1] *þe title of lxix salm. To þe victorie of Dauiþ, to haue mynde.*⁵⁴³

f. 36ʳ    [2] God, biholde þou in|to myn helpe; Lord, haaste þou to helpe
me. [3] Be þei shent and ashamed; þat seken my lijf. [4] Be þei turned
abak;⁵⁴⁴ and shame þei, þat wolen yuelis to me. Be þei turned aweiᵃ
anoon and shame þei; þat seien to me, Wel! wel! [5] Alle men þat
seken þee, make fulli ioie and be glad in þee; and þei þat louen þyn
helþe seie euere, þe Lord be magnefied. [6] Forsoþe I am a nedi man
and pore; God, helpe þou me. Thou art myn helpere and my
delyuerere; Lord, tarie þou not.

## [PSALM 70]

*In te Domine speraui*

[1] *þe title of lxx salm.*⁵⁴⁵

Lord, I hopide in þee, be I not shent wiþouten ende; [2] in þi
riȝtfulnesseᵃ delyuere þou me, and rauysche me [ou]t.ᵇ Bowe doun
þin eere to me; and make me saaf. [3] Be þou to me into God a
defendere; and into a strengþid place, þat þou make me saaf. For þou
art my stidfastnesse; and my refuyt. [4] My God, delyuere þou me fro
þe hond of þe synnere; and fro [þe hond of]ᶜ a man doynge aȝenes þe
lawe, and of þe wickid man. [5] For þou, Lord, art my pacience; Lord
þou art myn hope fro my ȝongþe. [6] In þee I am confermyd⁵⁴⁶ fro þe
wombe; þou art my defendere fro þe wombe of my modir. Mi
syngynge is euere in þee; [7] I am maad as a greet wondur to
manye men; and þou art a strong helpere to me. [8] Mi mouþ be
fillid wiþ heriyng; þat I synge þi glorie, al dai⁵⁴⁷ þi greetnesse. [9]
Caste þou not awei me in þe tyme of eldnesse; whanne my vertu failiþ,

---

**Ps. 69**      ᵃ awei] *corrected by the scribe on an erasure*
**Ps. 70**      ᵃ riȝtfulnesse] *cf. note to 4: 2 above*      ᵇ out] not      ᶜ þe hond of] *om.*

542. þat is, heuenli citeseyns;

and erþe, þat is, men dwellynge in erþe;

þe see, et cetera, not þat siche vnresonable creaturis herien him propirli, but for þo ben maad of Goddis heriyng to men, þat herien him bi hise creaturis. *Lire here.*

### [PSALM 69 GLOSSES]

543.[i] Dauiþ made þis salm whanne he was in þe persecucioun of Absolon his sone. *Lire here.*

544. Twei kyndis ben of pursueris, þat is, of dispisers and of f. 36ʳ flatereris. þe tunge of þe flaterere pursueþ more þan þe hond of þe sleere. *Austin here.*

### [PSALM 70 GLOSSES]

545.[i] þis salm haþ no title in Ebreu neþer in Ieroms translacioun. *Lire here.*

Gostli, þis salm mai be expowned of ech feiþful man, beynge in greet tribulacioun, which telliþ bifor God perels neiȝyng to hym, and axiþ to be delyuerid swiftli fro þo perelis, and bihetiþ to do þankyngis to God deuoutli and feiþfuli. *Lire here.*

546.[ii] In Ierom þus: Of þee Y am susteyned fro þe wombe, not þat he was halewid in his modris wombe, but he was defendid of God in his modris wombe. *Lire here.*

547. þat is, wiþout ceessing in prosperites[iii] and in aduersitees. *Austin here.*

---

forsake þou not me. [10] For myn enemyes seiden of me; and þei þat kepten my lijf maden councel togidere. [11] Seiynge, God haþ for| f. 36ᵛ sake hym; pursue ȝe and take hym; for noon is þat shal delyuere. [12] God, be þou not [maad]ᵈ afer fro me; my God, biholde þou into myn

**Ps. 69 glosses** [i] *next to the title in the left margin; this gloss also in* bCGikKLPQSVX  
**Ps. 70 glosses** [i] *next to the title in the left margin; the first textual part of this gloss also in* CikKV [ii] *a variant gloss here interlinear and underlined in* K: In þe I am confermed, þat is defendid; *in margin of* V: þat is not halewid but defendid [iii] prosperites] prospertites; *a compressed version of this gloss also in margin of* V *(damaged)*

ᵈ maad] *om.*

helpe. [13] [Men þat bacbiten my soule, be shent, and faile þei; and be þei hilid wiþ schenschip and schame, þat seken yuels to me. [14] But I shal hope euere; and I shal adde euere ouer al þi preising. [15] Mi mouþ shal telle þi riȝtfulnesse; al dai þin helþe.]ᵉ For I knew not lettrure,⁵⁴⁸ [16] I shalᶠ entre into þe poweres of þe Lord; Lord, I shal biþenke on þi riȝtfulnesse aloone. [17] [G]od,ᵍ þou hast tauȝte me fro my ȝongþe and til to now; I shal telle out þi meruelis. [18] And til into þe eldnesse and þe laste age; God, forsake þou not me. [T]ilʰ I telle þyn arm;⁵⁴⁹ to ech generacioun þat shal come. Til I telle þi myȝt [19] and þi riȝtfulnesse, God, til into þe hiȝest grete dedis whiche þou hast do; God, who is lijk þee? [20] Hou grete tribulaciouns manye and yuele hast þou schewid to me; and þou conuertid hast quykened me, and hast efte brouȝte me aȝen fro þe depþis of erþe. [21] [T]houⁱ hast multeplied þi greet doyng; and þou conuertid hast comfortid me. [22] Forwhi and I shal knoulech to þee, þou God, þi treuþe in þe instrumentis of salm; I shal synge in an harpe to þee, þou art þe hooli of Israel. [23] Mi lippis shulen make fulli ioie, whanne I shal synge to þee; and my soule, which þou aȝenbouȝtist. [24] But and my tunge shal þenke al dai on þi riȝtfulnesse; whanne þei shulen be shent and ashamed, þat seken yuelis to me.

## [PSALM 71]

*Deus iudicium tuum regi da*

[1] *þe title of lxxj salm. In Ebreu it is þus: To Salomon. In Ierom it is þus: Into Salomon.*⁵⁵⁰

[2] God,⁵⁵¹ ȝyue þi doom to þe kyng; and þi riȝtfulnesse to þe sone of a kyng. To deme þi puple in riȝtfulnesse; and þi pore men in doom. f. 37ʳ [3] Mounteynes⁵⁵² resseyue pees to þe puple; and litle hillis resseyue | riȝtfulnesse.⁵⁵³ [4] He shal deme þe pore men of þe puple, and he shal make saaf þe sones of pore men; and he shal make lowe þe false calenger.⁵⁵⁴ [5] And he shal dwelle wiþ þe sunne, and bifor þe moone;⁵⁵⁵ in generacioun and into generacioun. [6] He shal come doun as reyn into a flees; and as goteris droppynge on þe erþe. [7] Riȝtfulnesse shal come forþ in hise daies, and þe abundaunce of pees; tilᵃ þe moone be takun awei.⁵⁵⁶ [8] And he shal be Lord fro þe see til to þe see; and fro þe flood til to þe endis of þe world. [9] Ethiopiens

---

ᵉ Men þat bacbiten . . . al dai þin helþe] *nearly three verses om.*      ᶠ shal] shal not, not *canc.*
ᵍ God] *initial capital om.*      ʰ Til] *initial capital om.*      ⁱ Thou] *initial capital om.*
**Ps. 71**      ᵃ til] til to

548. Bi mannis techyng. For he hadde knowyng of dyuyn þingis, f. 36ᵛ
not bi excercise of studie, but bi Goddis reuelacioun. [*Lire here.*]ⁱᵛ

Eþer lettrure, þat is, men hauynge glorie of þe lettre, and
presumynge weiwardli of her strengþis, as frentik men doon. An
oþere lettre is þus: For Y knew not marchaundies. Marchaundie
wiþout leesyng, fraude, and periurie is leueful as oþere craftis ben, but
repreueble marchauntis ben here, þat han glorie and presumynge of
her daies. [*Austin here.*]ᵛ

549. þat is, þe gretnesse of þi vertu. *Lire here.*

[PSALM 71 GLOSSES]

550.ⁱ Bi Ierom, Austyn, and Cassiodore, þis lxxj salm is profecie of
Crist veri kyng, and not of prosperite of þe rewme vndur Salomon.
For manye þingis conteyned in þis salm moun not be seid couenabli of
Salomon, but oneli of Crist. *Lire here.*

551. þat is, God þe fadir ȝyue þu to Crist king power of demyng.
*Lire here.*

552. þat is, aungelis;

553. litle hillis, þat is, apostlis and oþere disciplis of Crist. *Lire here.*

Eþer mounteynes, þat is, men in excellent holynesse, þat ben able
to teche also oþere men;

litil hillis ben good sugetis suynge bi obedience þe excellence of
hem. *Austin here.*

554. þat is, Auntecrist; eþer he shal caste doun tirauntis, pursueris f. 37ʳ
of feiþful men. *Lire here.*

555.ⁱⁱ þat is, wiþout bigynnyng and endyng. *Lire here.*

556. þat is, dedlynesse be takun awei; eþer til þe chirche be
enhaunsid bi þe glorie of risyng aȝen. *Austin here.*

þe moone, þat is, gostli peesⁱⁱⁱ þat stondiþ in pesyblenesse of
conscience, þat dwelliþ in iust men wiþouten ende, as þe moone is
vncorruptible. *Lire here.*

---

ⁱᵛ Lire here] *om.*    ᵛ Austin here] *om.; a variant gloss here interlinear and underlined in* K:
For I knew not lettrure, þat is not bi mannes teching but bi Goddis reuelacion; *this variant
gloss also in margin of* V *(damaged)*
**Ps. 71 glosses**    ⁱ *in the bottom margin; also in* CikKV    ⁱⁱ *interlinear and underlined in* K
ⁱⁱⁱ til þe mone, þat is gostli pees, *interlinear and underlined in* K *and in margin of* V *(damaged)*

shulen falle doun bifore hym;[557] and hise enemyes shulen licke þe
erþe. [10] The kyngis of Tharsis and iles shulen offre ȝiftis; þe kyngis
of Arabie and of Saba shulen brynge ȝiftis. [11] And alle kingis shulen
worschipe hym; alle folkis shulen serue hym. [12] For he shal delyuer
a pore man fro þe myȝti; and a pore man to whom was noon helpere.
[13] He shal spare a pore man and nedi; and he shal make saaf þe
soulis of pore men. [14] He shal aȝenbie þe soulis of[b] hem fro vsuris,
and wickidnesse; and þe name of hem is onorable[558] bifore hym. [15]
And he shal lyue, and me shal ȝyue to hym of þe gold of Arabie; and
þei shulen euere worschipe [of][c] hym, al dai þei shulen blesse him.
[16] Stidfastnesse[559] shal be in þe erþe, in þe hiȝest places of
mountey[nes];[d 560] þe fruyt þerof shal be enhaunsid aboue þe Liban;
and þei shulen blosme fro þe citee, as þe hei of erþe doiþ. [17] His
name be blessid into worldis; his name dwelliþ bifore þe sunne. And
f. 37ᵛ   alle þe lynagis of erþe shulen be blessid in hym; alle folkis shulen |
magnefie hym. [18] Blessid be þe Lord God of Israel; which aloone
makiþ meruelis. [19] And blessid be þe name of his maieste wiþouten
ende; and al erþe shal be fillid wiþ his maieste; be it doon, be it doon.
[20] The preieris of Dauiþ,[561] sone of Ysaie, ben fillid.

[PSALM 72]

*Quam bonus Israel Dominus*

[1] *þe title of lxxij salm. þe salm of Asaph. In Ierom þus: þe song of
Asaph.[562]*

God of Israel is ful good; to hem þat ben of riȝtful herte. [2] But my
feet[563] weren mouyd almest; my steppis weren shedout almest. [3] For
I louyde feruentli on wickid men;[564] seynge þe pees of synneris. [4]
For biholdyng is not to þe deþ of hem; and stidfastnesse in þe
sijknesse of hem. [5] Thei ben not in þe trauel of men; and þei shulen
not be betun wiþ men. [6] Therfor pride helde hem; þei weren
[h]illid[a] wiþ her wickidnesse and vnfeiþfulnesse. [7] The wickidnesse
of hem cam forþ as of fatnesse; þei ȝeden into desir of herte. [8] Thei
þouȝten and spaken weiwardnesse; þei spaken wickidnesse an hiȝ.[565]
[9] Thei puttiden her mouþ into heuene;[566] and her tunge passide in
erþe.[567] [10] Therfore my puple shal be conuertid here; and fulle
daies[568] shulen be founden in hem. [11] And þei seiden [How woot

ᵇ of] of pore men and nedi, pore men and nedi *canc.*   ᶜ of] *om.*   ᵈ mounteynes] -nes
*obscured by a splatter of red wax or ink*
**Ps. 72**   ᵃ hillid] fillid

557. þat is, shulen swiftli be conuertid to þe feiþ of Crist. *Lire here.*

558. þat is, worþi to be onourid. *Lire here.*

559. In Ebreu it is, <u>Abundaunce of wheete shal be</u>; in Ierom it is, <u>Whete worþi to be in mynde shal be in erþe</u>;

560. <u>Whete</u>, þat is, þe sacrament of þe auter, <u>shal be in þe hiȝeste places of hillis</u>, þat is, of bischopis aboue her heedis. *Lire here.*

561. þis vers is of þis salm, as Ierom and Ebreis witnessen. And f. 37ᵛ þouȝ manye salmes of Dauiþ suen aftirward, þe preiers of Dauiþ ben seid fillid in þis salm, for it is tretid in þis salm of þe rewme of Crist, to which alle þe salmes of Dauiþ ben maad as to þe ende, and þe ende bryngiþ fillyng: þis is þe soilyng of sum men.

Eþer þus betere to þe lettre: þis was þe laste salm þat Dauiþ made, þouȝ it be set in þe myddis of þe book. For þe salmes ben writun here bi þe ordre of fyndyng, and þerfor þe hundrid and xlii[i]jⁱᵛ salm, þat was þe firste eþer oon of þe firste, is set almost in þe ende as it is founden. *Lire here.*

[PSALM 72 GLOSSES]

562.ⁱ Asaph made þis lxxij salm, to schewe þe goodnesse of Goddis puruyaunce, þat strecchiþ fro þe ende til to þe ende strongli, and disposiþ alle þingis softli; þouȝ þe contrarie semeþ to þe vnkunnyng men, for þei seen þat yuele men han temporal prosperite and good men han tribulacioun. *Lire here.*

563. þat is, Y felde awei almost fro riȝtful feelyng of þe goodnesse of Goddis puruyaunce; he spekiþ þis in þe persoone of þe siyk puple;

564. <u>wickid men</u>, þat is, Y was stirid bi couetise to sue hem. *Lire here.*

565.ⁱⁱ þat is, blasfemye aȝenes God. *Lire here.*

566. þat is, comaundyng hemsilf to be worschipid as God. *Lire here.*

567. þat is, so myche þei passiden þe markis of resoun, as if þei weren not erþeli men, but goddis of heuene;

568. <u>and fulle daies</u>, of wakyngis and þenkyngis. *Lire here.*

ⁱᵛ xliiij] xliij
**Ps. 72 glosses** ⁱ *next to the title in the left margin; also in* bCGikKLPQSVX ⁱⁱ *interlinear and underlined in* K *and in margin of* V

God];[b] and wher kunnyng is an hiȝ?[569] [12] Lo! þilke synneris and
hauynge abundaunce in þe world; helden richessis. [13] And I seide,
þerfor wiþout cause I iustefied myn herte;[570] and waischide myn
hondis among innocentis. [14] And I was betun al dai; and my
chastisyng[c] was in þe morewtidis. [15] If I seide, I shal telle þus;[571]

f. 38[r]   lo! I repreuyde þe nacioun of þi sones. [16] I gesside þat I | shulde
knowe þis;[572] trauel is bifor me. [17] Til I entre into þe seyntuarie of
God;[573] and vndurstonde in þe laste þingis of hem.[574] [18] Neþeles for
giles þou hast putte to hem;[575] þou castidist hem doun; while þei
weren reisid.[576] [19] Hou ben þei maad into desolacioun, eþer
discomfort; þei failiden sodenli, þei perischiden for her wickidnesse.
[20] As þe dreem of men þat risen; Lord, þou shalt dryue her ymage
to nouȝt in þi citee. [21] For myn herte is enflawmed.[577] and my
reynes ben chaungid; [22] and I am dryuun to nouȝt, and I wiste not.
[23] As a werke-beeste Y am maad[d] at þee;[578] and I am euere wiþ þee.
[24] Thou heldist my riȝthond, and in þi wille þou leddist me forþ;
and wiþ glorie þou tokist me up. [25] Forwhi what is to me in
heuene;[579] and what wolde I of þee on erþe? [26] Mi fleisch and myn
herte failide;[580] God of myn herte, and my part is God wiþouten ende.
[27] For lo! þei þat drawen awei fer hemsilf fro þee[581] shulen perische;
þou hast loste alle men þat doen fornycacioun fro þee.[582] [28] But it is
good to me to cleue to God;[583] and to sette myn hope in þe Lord God.
That I telle alle þi prechyngis; in þe ȝatis of þe douȝtir of Sion.[584]

569.[iii] þat is, in hiȝ heuene. *Lire here.*

570. In eschewinge þe[iv] synne of herte, and þe synnes of werk. *Lire
here.*

571. þat is, Y helde þis opynyoun in desirynge temporal prosperite
wiþ synneris. *Lire here.*

f. 38[r]   572. þat is, þat Y myȝte knowe þe treuþe of þe forseid þingis, bi
sekyng of resoun. *Lire here.*

[b] How woot God] *om.*   [c] chastisyng] chastisyngis, -is *canc.*   [d] maad] maad maad

[iii] *interlinear and underlined in* K   [iv] þe] my þe

573. þat is, to þe vndurstonding shewid of God;

574. and vndurstonde þe laste þingis of hem, þat is, þat Y vndurstonde þe peynes and meedis of liyf to comynge. *Lire here.*

575. In þe ende of temporal prosperite, in wiþdrawing hem fro<sup>v</sup> present liyf;

576. while þei weren reisid, þat is, while þei weren ȝit in encreessyng of her temporal prosperite. *Lire here.*

577. Myn herte is enflawmyd, wiþ pure loue of God;

chaungid, bi refreynyng of þe coueitise of fleish;

dryuun to nouȝt, of þis þat Y louyde, God of al myn herte, and refreyned þe ferse stiryng of leccherie, it suyde þat Y am dryuun to nouȝt in my reputacioun;

and Y wiste not, þat is, Y arettide me vnkunnyng, for in as myche as a man is ioyned more to God bi charite, and is wiþdrawun fro fleischli lust, bi so myche he arettiþ himsilf lesse bi mekenesse, and knowiþ more his ignoraunce;

578. þerfor it sueþ, As a werk-beeste, et cetera, þat is, in comparisoun of þi kunnyng þat passiþ more mannis knowing, þan mannis knowing passiþ þe kunnyng of an vnresonable beeste;

Y am euere wiþ þee, for whanne a man goiþ into his owne litilnesse and ignoraunce, he bitakiþ himsilf hoollich to Goddis disposicioun, and he biholdiþ it and kepiþ þat man. *Lire here.*

579. What is to me in heuene, as if he seie, neiþer in heuene neiþer in erþe is ony creature, þat sufficiþ to me for my blis: þat stondiþ in God aloone;

580. myn herte failide, in þe biholdyng of þi goodnesse, þat mai not be comprehendid of vertu þat haþ ende;

581.<sup>vi</sup> fro þee, bi dedli synne;

582. fornycacioun fro þee, þat is, bi synne of idolatrie;

583. to cleue to God, bi feiþ and charite;

584. in þe ȝatis of þe douȝtir of Syon: þis is neþer in Ebreu neþer in Ierom, but was addid of sum expositour. [*Lire here.*]<sup>vii</sup>

<sup>v</sup> fro] fro temporal prosperite, temporal prosperite *canc.*    <sup>vi</sup> *also in margin of* V    <sup>vii</sup> Lire here] *om.*

[PSALM 73]

*Ut quid Deus repulisti*ᵃ

[1] þe title of lxxiij [salm].ᵇ þe lernyng of Asaph.⁵⁸⁵

God, whi hast þou put awei ʻus'ᶜ into þe ende;⁵⁸⁶ þi stronge
veniaunce is wrooþ on þe sheep of þi lesewe? [2] Be þou myndeful of
þi gaderyng togidere; which þou haddist in possessioun fro þe
bigynnyng.⁵⁸⁷ Thou aȝenbouȝtist þe ȝerde of þyn eritage; þe hil of
Syon in which þou dwellidist þerinne. [3] Reise þyn hondis into þe
pridis of hem; | hou grete þingis þe enemye dide wickidli in þe
hooli.⁵⁸⁸ [4] And þei þat hatiden þee; hadden glorie in þe myddis of þi
solempnyte. Thei settiden her signes, eþer baneris, signes on þe
hiȝeste, [5] as in þe outgoynge;⁵⁸⁹ and þei knewen not.⁵⁹⁰ As in a wode
of trees þei hewiden doun wiþ axis [6] þe ȝatis þerof into itsilf; þei
castiden doun it wiþ an ax, and a brood fallyng-ax. [7] Thei brenten
wiþ fier þi seyntuarie; þei defouliden þe tabernacle of þi name in erþe.
[8] The kynrede of hem seiden togidere in her herte: Make we alle þe
feeste daies of God to ceesse fro [þe]ᵈ erþe. [9] We han not seyn oure
signes,⁵⁹¹ nov no profete is; and he shal no more knowe us. [10] God,
hou long schal þeᵉ enemye seie dispit? þe aduersarie terriþ to ire þi
name into þe ende. [11] Whi turnest þou awei þyn hond, and to drawe
out þi riȝthond fro þe myddis of þi bosum, til into þe ende?⁵⁹² [12]
Forsoþe God oure kyng bifor worldis; wrouȝte helþe in þe myddis of
erþe.⁵⁹³ [13] Thou madist sad þe see bi þi vertu; þou hast troblid þe
heedis of draguns⁵⁹⁴ in watris. [14] Thou hast brokun þe heedis of þe
dragoun; þou hast ȝoue hym to mete to þe puplis of Ethiopiens.⁵⁹⁵

[PSALM 73 GLOSSES]

585.ⁱ þis lxxiij salm spekiþ of þe caitifte of Babiloyne, which caitifte
ʻAsaph'ⁱⁱ biforsiȝ to-comynge; and in þis salm he preieþ for delyueraunce þerof.

Gostli, þis salm mai be expowned of cristen puple, þat it be þe
preier of hooli chirche for cristen puple, which is holdun sum tyme bi

Ps. 73    ᵃDeus repulisti] repulisti Deus, *marked for transposition*    ᵇsalm] *om.*    ᶜus]
*added by the scribe above the line of writing*    ᵈþe] *om.*    ᵉþe] þe emye, emye *canc.*

Ps. 73 glosses    ⁱ*in the bottom margin*    ⁱⁱAsaph] *added by the scribe above the line of*
*writing*

fendis in þe seruage of synne. And for delyueraunce of þis puple, þe chirche aleggiþ firste þe frenschip of God, bi which he resseyuede cristen puple to þe grace of baptym. þe secounde tyme þe chirche[iii] aleggiþ þe obstynat malice of fendis. þe þridde tyme þe chirche aleggiþ þe myȝt of God, to þe iustefiyng of synneris. þe fourþe tyme þe chirche aleggiþ þe wrecchidnesse of þe puple, as longe as it is holdun in þe caitifte of synne, which is signefied bi Babiloyne, þat is interpretid confusioun. *Lire here.*

586. Into þe ende, þat is, suffryng so longe þe caitifte of þe puple;

587. fro þe bigynnyng, of þe goyng out of Egipt. *Lire here.*

588. þat is, in þe temple assigned to Goddis worschiping. *Lire here.*  f. 38ᵛ

589. Of batel, whanne victorie was had;

590. and Caldeis knewen not þat God ȝef to hem so greet victorie for þe synnes of þe puple of Israel; but þei arettiden it to her owne power. *Lire here.*

591. We han not seyn oure signes: þe apostatas of Iewis þat forsoken her lawe and reneyeden her God and passiden to Caldeis, seiden þus, 'We siȝen not oure signes' [Ps 73: 9], þat is, siche as weren ȝouun to oure fadris in þe going out of Egipt; now no profete is, þat shal telle to us þe wille of God, and so we owen to forsake him as he haþ forsake us; he shal no more knowe us, þat is, he shal not appreue oure dedis, for þei gessiden þat God hadde al putte awei þe puple of Iewis. þouȝ Ieremye þe profete was in þe tyme of þis caitifte, neþeles þei arettiden him no profete of þe lord, but a false profete. *Lire here.*

592. þat is, so longe;

593. helþe in þe myddis of erþe, in brynging þe puple of Israel in myraclis and grete wondris in þe lond of biheest and into Ierusalem. *Lire here.*

594. þe heedis of dragouns, þat is, þe prynces of Egipcians clepid dragouns, whiche God drenchide in þe see;

595. to þe puple of Ethiopiens, þat is, to briddis of rauenouse kynde, þat ben fed wiþ careyns, whiche briddis ben clepid men of Ethiopie for þe licnesse of blacnesse; and for in sum part of Ethiopie men eten dragouns and serpentis, and Egipcians ben clepid here draguns. *Lire here.*

---

[iii] chirche] chirchiþ; *a summary version of the first historical part of this gloss also in margin of* K

[15] Thou hast broke wellis and strondis; þou madist drie þe floodis of Ethan.[596] [16] The dai is þyn and þe ny3t is þyn; þou madist þe morewtid and þe sunne. [17] Thou madist al þe endis of erþe; somer and veertyme, þou formedist þo. [18] Be þou myndeful of þis þing, þe enemye haþ seid shenschipe to þe Lord; and þe vnwijs puple[f] haþ

f. 39[r]  excitid[597] to ire þi name. [19] Bitake þou not to bees|tis men knoulechynge to þee; and for3ete þou not into þe ende þe soulis of þi pore men. [20] Biholde into þi testament; for þei [þat][g] ben maad derk of erþe, ben fillid wiþ þe housis of wickidnesses. [21] A meke man be not turned awei maad aschamed; a pore man and nedi shulen herie þi name. [22] God, rise up, deme þou þi cause; be þou myndeful of þi schenschipis, eþer vpbreidyngis, of þo þat ben al dai of þe vnwise man. [23] For3ete þou not þe voices of þyn enemyes; þe pride of hem þat haten þee, stieþ euere.

[PSALM 74]

*Confitebimur tibi Deus*[a]

[1] þe [title][b] *of lxxiiij salm. To þe ouercomere; leese þou not þe salm of þe song of Asaph.*[598]

[2] God, we shulen knoulech to þee, we shulen knouleche; and we shulen inwardli clepe þi name. We shulen telle þi meruelis; [3] whanne I shal take tyme, I shal deme ri3tfulnessis.[599] [4] The erþe is meltid, and alle þat dwellen þerinne; I confermyde þe pileris þerof. [5] I seide to wickid men, Nyle 3e do wickidli; and to trespassouris, Nyle 3e enhaunce þe horn. [6] Nile 3e reise an hi3 3oure horn; nyle 3e speke wickidnesse a3enes God. [7] For neþer fro þe eest, neþer fro þe west, neþer fro desert hillis;[600] [8] for God is þe iuge. He mekiþ þis man and enhaunsiþ him; [9] for a cuppe of cleene wyn ful of medlyng is in þe hond of þe Lord. And he bowide of þis into þat; neþeles þe dra[f]t[c] þerof is not anyntischid; alle synneris of erþe shulen drynke þerof. [10] Forsoþe I shal telle[601] into þe world; I shal synge to God of

f. 39[v]  Iacob. [11] And I shal breke[602] alle | þe hornes[603] of synneris; and þe hornes[604] of þe iust man shulen be enhaunsid.

[f] vnwijs puple] puple vnwijs     [g] þat] *om.*
Ps. 74     [a] tibi Deus] Deus tibi, *marked for transposition*     [b] title] *om.*     [c] draft] drast

596. Ethan is þe propir name of a desert, and Ethan signefieþ strengþe; þe floodis of Ethan: in Ieroms translacioun it is, stronge floodis. *Lire here.*

597. þat is, haþ disseruyde for blasfemyes doon to þi name þat þi riȝtfulnesse be excitid to do veniaunce on hem. *Lire here.*

## [PSALM 74 GLOSSES]                   f. 39ʳ

598.ⁱ þis lxxiiij salm is þe salm of þe song of Asaph, þat þou leese not þe puple of Israel bi caitifte, as þou didist in þe caitifte of Babiloyne. þis þat is set bifore, to þe ouercomere, as Ierom seiþ, eiþer to þe ouercomyng, as Ebreis seyn, signefieþ þe enforsing of dekenes in þe syngyng of þis salm. As þe salm biforgoynge is þe preier of Asaph for delyueraunce of þe caitifte of Babiloyne, so þisⁱⁱ salm is discryuyng of þe puple turned aȝen into þe lond of her birþe vndur king Cirus.

Gostli, þis salm mai be expowned of ech man repentynge verili, which is goon out of þe caitifte of synne and knoulechiþ þe riȝtfulnesse of God and his merci, and dispisiþ þe power of fendis, and doiþ þankingis to God. *Lire here.*

599. þat is, Y God shal sette þe sentencis of riȝtfulnesse in execucioun in du tyme, in delyueringe iust men fro turmentis and in punyschyng wickid men. *Lire here.*

600. þat is, bi no side þou maist ascape Goddis doom. *Lire here.*

601. þat is, þe vertu and preisyng of God. *Lire here.*

602. þis is seid of God, for he takiþ veniaunce of synneris. *Lire here.*

603. þat is, pridis and poweris. *Lire here.*                   f. 39ᵛ

604. þat is, poweris. [*Lire here.*]ⁱⁱⁱ

**Ps. 74 glosses**   ⁱ *next to the title in the right margin*   ⁱⁱ þis] þis j-, j- *canc.; the beginning of the first historical part of this gloss also in margin of* K   ⁱⁱⁱ Lire here] *om.*

[PSALM 75]

*Notus in Iudea Deus*

[1] þe title of lxxv salm. *To þe victorie in orguns,*[605] þe salm of þe song of
Asaph.[606]

[2] God is knowun in Iudee; his name is greet in Israel. [3] And his
place is maad in pees; and his dwellyng is in Sion. [4] There he brak
poweris; bouwe, sheeld, swerd, and batel. [5] And þou, God, liȝtnest
wondurfuli fro euerelastynge hillis;[607] [6] alle vnwise men of herte
weren troblid. The[i]ª slepten her sleep;[608] and alle men founden no
þing of richessis in her hondis. [7] Thei þat stieden on horsis; slepten
for þi blamyng, þou God of Iacob. [8] Thou art ferdful, and who schal
aȝenstonde þee? fro þat tyme þyn ire.[609] [9] Fro heuene þou ma[d]istᵇ
doom herd; þe erþe tremblide and restide. [10] Whanne God roos up
into doom; to make saaf alle þe mylde men of erþe. [11] For þe þouȝt of
man shal knouleche to þee;[610] and þe relifs of þouȝt shulen make a feeste
dai to þee. [12] Make ȝe a vow and ȝelde ȝe to ȝoure Lord God; alle þat
bryngen ȝiftis in þe cumpas of it. To God ferdful,[611] [13] and to hym þat
takiþ awei þe spirit of prynces; to þe ferdful at þe kyngis of erþe.

[PSALM 76]

*Voce mea ad Dominum clamaui*

[1] þe title of lxxvj salm. *To þe ouercomere on I[d]i[t]umª; þe salm of
Asaph.*[612]

[2] Bi my uois I criede to þe Lord; bi my vois to God, and he ȝaf
tent to me. [3] In þe dai of my tribulacioun I souȝte God wiþ myn

[PSALM 75 GLOSSES]

605. In Ierom it is, to þe ouercomere in ditees. *Lire here.*
606.ⁱ Asaph biforsiȝ in spirit þe turmenting of þe rewme of Iuda bi
Sennacherib, and hou God shulde smyte Sennacherib, in killyng bi
his aungel an hundrid þousynde and lxxxv þousynde of his oost; and
of þis doyng, Asaph [made]ⁱⁱ þis lxxv salm.

**Ps. 75**      ª Thei] The      ᵇ madist] makist
**Ps. 76**      ª Iditum] Itidum

**Ps. 75 glosses**      ⁱ *in the top margin*      ⁱⁱ made] *om.; the second spiritual part of this gloss also
in margin of* K

Goostli, þis salm mai be expowned of ech feiþful comynte eþer synguler persoone, which is delyuerid bi God wondurfuli fro greet turment temporali eþer gostli, and for þis is stirid deuoutli to þe heriyng of God. *Lire here.*

607.[iii] Fro euerelastinge hillis, þat is, aungelis þat ben vndedli. In Ebreu it is, fro þe hillis of raueyn; in Ierom it is, fro þe hillis of caitifte eþer of caitif[s]', and þanne it shal be referrid to þe hil of Syon and to þe hil of Moria; for Sennacherib purposide to spoile and take prisoneris men dwellinge in þo. *Lire here.*

608.[iv] þat is, weren deed. *Lire here.*

609.[v] þat is, anoon whanne þou demest þe punysching of ony man, it comeþ forþ in effect bi þe maner of þi sentence. *Lire here.*

610. For þe þou3t of man shal knoulech to þee: in Ierom þus, For þe morenyng of man shal knoulech to þee; þou shalt be gird wiþ þe relifs of morenyng. þis is referrid to kyng E3echie, þat morenyde and was cloþid in sak for þe synnes of himsilf and of his puple;

in Ebreu þus: For þe ire of man shal knoulech to þee; and þou shalt girde eþer shalt wiþholde þe relifs of ire, þat is, þe ire of Sennacherib shal be occasioun to knouleche to þee bi confessioun of preisyng;

shalt wiþholde, et cetera, for he fledde and helde ire a3enes Iudee, and þou3te to come wiþ a newe oost to distrie it, but bi Goddis ordenaunce he was slayn of hise owne sones. *Lire here.*

611. In Ebreu and in Ieroms translacioun, þis word, to þe ferdful, is þe ende of þe vers bifor goynge. To þe ferdful, þat is, to God þat made ferdful doom of Sennacherib and hise oost. And þe vers suynge bigynneþ þus: And to him, þat is [fro][vi] him, takiþ awei þe spirit, þat is, liyf. *Lire here.*

## [PSALM 76 GLOSSES]                                    f. 40[r]

612.[i] Asaph bi þe spirit of profesie made þis lxxvj salm of þe comyng of þe caitifte of Babiloyne, and of þe endyng þerof.

Gostli, þis salm mai be expowned of ech feiþful congregacioun eþer of a synguler persoone, which is in tribulacioun temporali eiþer gostli, and preieþ God deuoutli to be delyuerid þerof. And hou myche euere he is anoied of mannis freelte, neþeles he hopiþ to be delyuerid of God bi ensaumple of seyntis biforgoynge, whiche God delyuyride fro

---

[iii] caitifs] caitifte *by dittography*   [iv] *also in margin of* V   [v] *the tie-mark over* heuene *in verse* 9, *but cf.* LY   [vi] fro] to
**Ps. 76 glosses**   [i] *in the bottom margin of the next leaf, f.* 40[r]

f. 40ʳ   hondis;⁶¹³ in þe ny3t toward hym, and I am not disseyued. | Mi soule
forsook to be comfortid; [4] I was myndeful of God⁶¹⁴ and I delitide,
and I was excercisid; and my spirit failide. [5] Myn i3en bifortoken
wakyngis;⁶¹⁵ I was disturblide and I spak not. [6] I thou3te elde daies;
and I hadde in mynde euerelastynge 3eeris. [7] And I þou3te in þe
ny3t wiþ myn herte; and I was excercised, and I clenside my spirit. [8]
Wher God shal caste awei wiþouten ende; eþer shal he not leie to, þat
he be more plesid 3it? [9] Eiþer shal he kit awei his merci into þe
ende;⁶¹⁶ fro generacioun into generacioun? [10] Eiþer shal God for3ete
to do mercy; eþer shal he wiþholde hise mercies in his ire? [11] And I
seide, now I bigan;⁶¹⁷ þis is þe chaungyng of þe ri3thond of þe hi3
God. [12] I hadde mynde on þe werkis of þe Lord; for I shal haue
mynde fro þe bigynnyng of þi meruelis. [13] And I shal þenke in alle
þi werkis; and I shal be excercisid, eþer occupied, in þi fyndingis. [14]
God, þi weie was in þe hooli; what God is greet as oure God? [15] þou
art God, þat doist meruelis. Thou madist þi vertu knowun among
puplis; [16] þou a3enbou3tist in þyn arm⁶¹⁸ þi puple, þe sones of Iacob
and of Ioseph. [17] God, watris sien þee, watris sien þee, and dredden;
and depþis of watris weren disturblid. [18] The multitude of þe sown
of watris; cloudis⁶¹⁹ 3auen vois. Forwhi þyn arowis passen; [19] þe
vois of þi þundur was in a wheel. Thi li3tnyngis shyneden to þe world;
þe erþe was mouyde, and tremblide. [20] Thi weie in þe see, and þi
f. 40ᵛ   paþis in manye watris; and þi steppis shulen not be | knowen. [21]
Thou leddist forþ þi puple as scheep; in þe hond of Moises and of
Aaron.

## [PSALM 77]

*Attendite populae meus*

[1] *þe title of lxxvij salm. þe lernyng of Asaph.*⁶²⁰

    Mi puple, perseyue 3e my lawe; bowe 3oure eere into þe wordis of
my mouþ. [2] I shal opene my mouþ in parablis; I shal speke parfite
resouns⁶²¹ fro þe bigynnyng. [3] Hou grete þingis han we herd, and
we han knowe þo; and oure fadris telden to us. [4] Tho ben not hid fro

---

þe hondis of tirauntis in translatynge hem to heuenli blis bi þe glorie
of martirdoom, and sum tyme in keping also in present liyf at a tyme,
to þe confermyng of cristen men in þe feiþ. Whiche seynge þat
martris weren delyuerid bi myracle fro þe hondis of tirauntis, weren
confermyd more bi þis in þe feiþ. *Lire here.*

613. Y souȝte God wiþ myn hondis: in Ierom þus, Y souȝte God, myn hond is holdun forþ in þe nyȝt; and it shal not haue reste. *Lire here.**

614. Y was myndeful of God: in Ierom and in Ebreu þus, Y þouȝte on God and Y was disturblid; Y spak and my spirit failide. *Lire here.*

615. þat is, Y wakide bifor þe tyme of rising at þe morewtid. *Lire here.*

616. þat is, hoollich. *Lire here.*

617. In Ebreu and in Ierom þus, And Y seide, it is my feblenesse, þat is, sich playnyng which Y biforseide comeþ forþ of mannis feblenesse. *Lire here.*

618. þat is, strengþe. *Lire here.*

619. For þe Lord made leitis and þundris to come forþ of þe piler of fier and of þe cloude, aȝenes Egipcians. *Lire here.*

[PSALM 77 GLOSSES]                                        f. 40ᵛ

620.ⁱ Asaph made þis lxxvij salm to shewe, bi scripturis and elde stories, þat þe rewme of Israel perteynede to Dauiþ and hise eiris bi Goddis chesing.

Gostli, þis salm is expowned of þe rewme of Crist figurid bi þe rewme of Dauiþ, wherfor in þis salm he excitiþ þe vndurstonding of Iewis as to þe moost excellent mysterie. þe secounde tyme he shewiþ þe goodnesse of Crist and þe vnkyndnesse of þe Iewis, fro þat place, Hou grete þingis han we herd, til þidur, And he puttide awei þe tabernacle of Joseph. For Crist, in as myche as he is God, ȝaf to þo Iewis alle þe benefices teld here.

þouȝ þe vnkyndnesse of Iewis generali is repreuyd in þis salm, þe vnkyndnesse of prestis is repreuyd speciali, for þe prestis weren mo[re]ⁱⁱ vnkynde to God and procuriden his deþ, and wolden mystake to hem þe rewme of Iudee, þat was seid speciali þe rewme of Crist. And fro þis place, he puttide awei þe tabernacle of Joseph, til to þe ende of þe salm, Asaph descryueþ þe alargyng of þe rewme of Crist and encreessyng of hooli chirche. *Lire here.*

621. In Ebreu and in Ierom it is, Y shal speke elde derke figuris. *Lire here.*

---

**Ps. 77 glosses**    ⁱ *next to the title in the left margin; the first historical part of this gloss also in margin of* K    ⁱⁱ *more*] mouyd

þe sones of hem; in an oþere generacioun. And þei telden þe heriyngis of þe Lord, and þe vertues of hym; and hise meruels, whiche he dide. [5] And he reiside witnessyng in Iacob; and he settide lawe in Israel. Hou grete þingis comaundide he to oure fadris, to make þo knowun to her sones; [6] þat an oþere generacioun knowe. Sones, þat shulen be borun, and shulen rise up; shulen telle out to her sones. [7] That þei sette her hope in God, and for3ete⁶²² not þe werkis of God; and þat þei seke hise comaundementis. [8] Lest þei be maad a shrewid generacioun; and terrynge to wraþþe, as þe fadris of hem. A generacioun þat dressiþ not his herte; and his spirit was not bileuyd⁶²³ wiþ God. [9] The sones of Effraym,⁶²⁴ bendynge a bouwe and sendinge arowis; weren turned in þe dai of batel. [10] Thei kepten not þe testament of God; and þei nolden go in his lawe. [11] And þei for3aten hise benefices; and hise meruels, whiche he shewide to hem. [12] He dide meruelis bifor þe fadris of hem in þe lond of Egipt; in þe feeld of Taphneos. | [13] He brak þe see, and ledde hem þorou; and he ordeinede þe watris as in a bouge. [14] And he ledde hem forþ in a cloude of þe dai; and al ny3t in þe li3tnyng of fier. [15] He brak a stoon in desert; and he 3af watir to hem as in a myche depþe. [16] And he ledde watir out of þe stoon; and he ledde [forþ]ᵃ watris as floodis. [17] And þei leiden to 3it to do synne a3enes hym; þei excitiden hi3 God into ire, in a place wiþout watir. [18] And þei temptiden God in [her]ᵇ hertis; þat þei axiden metis to her lyues. [19] And þei spaken yuelis of God; þei seiden, Wher God mai make redi a boord⁶²⁵ in desert? [20] For he smoot a stoon,⁶²⁶ and watris flowiden; and streemes 3eden out in abundaunce. Wher also he may 3yue breed;⁶²⁷ eþer make redi a boord to his puple? [21] Therfor þe Lord herde, and dilaiede; and fier was kyndlid in Iacob, and þe ire of God stiede on Israel. [22] For þei bileuyden not in God; neþer hopiden in his helþe. [23] And he comaundide to þe cloudis aboue; and he openyde þe 3atis of heuene. [24] And he reyneyde to hem manna for to ete; and he 3af to hem breed of heuene. [25] Man eet þe breed of aungelis; he sente to hem metis in abundaunce. [26] He turnyde ouer þe souþ wynd fro heuene; and he brou3te in bi his vertu þe west wynd. [27] And he reynyde fleischis as dust on hem; and he reynyde volatils feþerid, as þe grauel of þe see. [28] And þo felden doun in þe myddis of her castels; aboute þe tabernaclis of hem. [29] And þei eeten, and weren fillid gretli, and he brou3te her desir to hem; [30] þei weren not defraudid of her desir.

f. 41ʳ

**Ps. 77**      ᵃ forþ] out      ᵇ her] *om.*

622. þat is, þat þei holden stidfastli in mynde þe werkis of God. *Lire here.*

623. For þei bileuyden not to hise heestis. *Lire here.*

624. þus it is in Ebreu and in Ieroms translacioun. *Lire here.*

625. þat is, a delicat filling of fleisch;                    f. 41ʳ

626. For he smoot, et cetera: bi þis þei arguyden þat God ouȝte to do þis, bi þe signe of ȝuyng of watir of þe stoon;

627. he mai ȝyue breed, þat is, delicat mete of fleisch, for manna was ȝouun bifor þis tyme in xvj capitulo of Exodi;

make redi a boord, þat is, a schynynge and delicat feeste; in Ebreu and in Ierom it is eþer, make redi fleisch to his puple. *Lire here.*

628. þat is, þe veniaunce of God to punysche hem myȝtili. *Lire*    f. 41ᵛ
*here.*

629.ⁱⁱⁱ þat is, þe riche men fillid wiþ richessis. *Lire here.*

630. Not þei which he killide, but þei þat dredden to be slayn bi ensaumple of hem. *Austin and Lire here.*

631. In doynge awei hollich as þei disseruyden. *Lire here.*

632. þat is, freel and enclynaunt to falling;

a spirit goinge, to deþ bi þe departing fro þe bodi; not þat mannis spirit dieþ, which is vncorruptible, but for þe man maad of bodi and spirit dieþ, which is corruptible;ⁱᵛ

---

| ȝit her metis weren in her mouþ; [31] and þe ire⁶²⁸ of God stiede on    f. 41ᵛ
hem. And he killide þe fatte men⁶²⁹ of hem; and he lettide þe chosun men of Israel. [32] In alle þese þingis þei synneden ȝit; and bileuyden not in þe meruelis of God. [33] And þe daies of hem failiden in vanyte; and þe ȝeeris of hem failiden wiþ haaste. [34] Whanne he killide hem, þei⁶³⁰ souȝten hym; and turnyden aȝen, and eerli þei camen to hym. [35] And þei biþouȝten, þat God is þe helpere of hem; and þe hiȝ God is þe aȝenbiere of hem. [36] And þei louyden hym in her mouþ; and wiþ her tunge þei lieden to him. [37] Forsoþe þe herte of hem was not riȝtful wiþ hym; neþer þei weren hadde feiþful in his testament. [38] But he is merciful, and he shal be maad merciful to þe synnes of hem; and he shal not distrie hem.⁶³¹ And he dide greetli, to turne awei his ire; and he kyndlide not al his ire. [39] And he biþouȝte, þat þei ben fleisch; a spirit goynge, and not turnynge aȝen.⁶³² [40] Hou ofte maden þei hym wrooþ in desert; þei stiriden hym into ire in a

---

ⁱⁱⁱ *in margin of* V: þat is, þe riche men *(damaged)*     ⁱᵛ corruptible] vncorruptible

place wiþout watir. [41] And þei weren turned, and temptiden God; and þei wraþþiden þe hooli of Israel. [42] Thei biþou3ten not on his hond;⁶³³ in þe dai in whiche he a3enbou3te hem fro þe hond of þe trobˋlˊere.ᶜ [43] As he settide hise signes in Egipt; and hise grete wondris in þe feeld of Taphneos. [44] And he turnyde þe floodis⁶³⁴ of hem and þe reynes of hem into blood; þat þei shulden not drynke. [45] He sente a fleisch-flie⁶³⁵ into hem, and it eet hem; and he sente a paddook, and it loste hem. [46] And he | 3af þe fruytis of hem to rust;⁶³⁶ and he 3af þe trauelis of hem to locustis.⁶³⁷ [47] And he killide þe vynes of hem bi hail; and þe moore-trees of hem bi a forst. [48] And he bitook þe beestis of hem to hail; and þe possessioun of hem to fier. [49] He sente into hem þe ire of his indignacioun; indignacioun, and ire, and tribulacioun, sendyngis in bi yuele aungelis. [50] He made weie to þe paþ of his ire, and he sparide not fro þe deþ of her lyues; and he closide togidere in deþ þe beestis of hem. [51] And he smoot al þe firste gendrid þing in þe lond of Egipt; þe firste fruytis of al þe trauel of hem in þe tabernaclis of Cham.⁶³⁸ [52] And he took awei his puple as scheep; and he ledde hem forþ as a floc in desert. [53] And he ledde hem forþ in hope, and þei dredden not;⁶³⁹ and þe see hilide þe enemyes of hem. [54] And he brou3te hem into þe hilᵈ of his halewyng; into þe hil which his ri3thond gat. And he castide out heþene men fro þe face of hem; and bi lot he departide to hem þe lond in a coord of delyng. [55] And he made þe lynagis of Israel to dwelle in þe tabernaclis of hem. [56] And þei temptiden, and wraþþiden hi3 God; and þei kepten not hise witnessyngis. [57] And þei turneden awei hemsilf, and þei kepten not couenaunt; as her fadris weren turned into a schrewid bouwe. [58] Thei stiriden hym ˋinˊtoᵉ ire in her litle hillis; and þei terriden hym to indignacioun⁶⁴⁰ [i]nᶠ her grauun ymagis. [59] God herde, and forsook;⁶⁴¹ and brou3te to nou3t Israel gretli. [60] And he puttide awei þe tabernacle of Silo; his tabernacle where he dwellide among men. | [61] And he bitook þe vertu⁶⁴² of hem into caitifte; and þe fairenesse of hem into þe hondis of þe enemy.⁶⁴³ [62] And he closide togidere his puple in swerd; and he dispiside his eritage. [63] Fier eet þ[e]ᵍ 3onge men [of hem];ʰ and þe virgyns of hem weren not beweilid. [64] The prestis of hem felden doun bi swerd; and þe widewis of hem weren not biwept. [65] And þe

f. 42ʳ

f. 42ᵛ

---

ᶜ troblere] trobere, *corrected by the scribe above the line of writing*　　ᵈ hil] hooli hil　　ᵉ into] on to, on *canc. and corrected by the scribe above the line of writing*　　ᶠ in] on　　ᵍ þe] þo　　ʰ of hem] *om.*

and not turnynge aȝen, for þe spirit departide fro þe bodi turneþ not aȝen to it, bi þe weie of kynde. *Lire here.*

A man bi himsilf mai go in wickidnesse; he mai not bi himsilf turne aȝen, no but bi grace. *Austin here.*

633. þat is, his power. *Lire here.*

634. Goostli, to turne watir into blood, signefieþ þis: to feele eþer vndurstonde fleischli of þe causis of þingis. *Austin here.*

635. þat is, a multitude of fleisch flies and a multitude of paddockis. *Lire here.*

A fleisch-flie, is a dogge maneris; a paddocke, is moost ianglyng vanyte. [þe glos]ᵛ here.

636. þat is, a brennynge wynd. *Lire here.**

Rust, noieþ priueli: þis is, þat a man triste gretli of hymsilf, whanne a man gessiþ hymsilf to be sum þing, whanne he is nouȝt. [*Austin here.*]ᵛⁱ

637.ᵛⁱⁱ A locuste is malice hirtynge wiþ þe mouþ, þat is, bi false witnessynge; hail is wickidnesse takynge awei oþere mennis þingis; a forste is vice, bi which þe charite of neiȝbore waxiþ coold; fier signefieþ þe greetnesse of wraþfulnesse; þe deeþ of beestis signefieþ þe los of chastite. *Austin here.*

638. þat is, of Egipcians comynge of Cham. *Lire here.*                    f. 42ʳ

639. þouȝ þei dredden, þis dredde was not so greet þat it lettide hem to sue Moises. *Lire here.*

640. þat is, to veniaunce. *Lire here.*

641. þe puple for her malice. *Lire here.*

642. For Filisteis killiden þe puple and token prisoneris;                    f. 42ᵛ

643. þe fairenesse, þat is, þe arke of þe testament which þe Filisteis token. *Lire here.*

644. In Ebreu and in Ierom it is, as strong. *Lire here.*

645. þat is, þe citee of Silo in which þe arke was set in þe tabernacle;

646. of Effraym, þat is, to þe dignytee of þe kyng. *Lire here.*

---

Lord was reisid, as slepyng; as myȝti⁶⁴⁴ greetli fillid of wyn. [66] And he smoot hise enemyes on þe hyndrere partis; he ȝaf to hem euerelastynge shenschip. [67] And he puttide awei þe tabernacle⁶⁴⁵ of Ioseph; and he chees not þe lynage of Effraym.⁶⁴⁶ [68] But he chees

---

ᵛ þe glos] Austyn    ᵛⁱ Austyn here] *om.*    ᵛⁱⁱ *in the bottom margin of f. 41ʳ, not on the same leaf with the sequence of lemmata*

þe lynage of Iuda; <u>he chees</u> þe hil of Sion, whiche he louyde. [69] And
he as an vnicorn bildide his hooli place; in þe lond, which he foundide
into worldis. [70] And he chees Dauiþ his seruaunt, and took hym up
fro þe flockis of scheep; he took hym fro bihynde⁶⁴⁷ scheep wiþ
lambren. [71] To feede Iacob⁶⁴⁸ his seruaunt; and Israel his eritage.
[72] And he fedde hem⁶⁴⁹ in þe innocence of his herte; and he ledde
hem forþ in þe vndurstondyng[is]ⁱ ⁶⁵⁰ of hise hondis.

<h1 style="text-align:center">[PSALM 78]</h1>

*Deus uenerunt gentes*

[1] *þe title of lxxviij salm. þe salm of Asaph.* In Ierom it is: *þe song of*
Asaph.⁶⁵¹

God, heþene men camen into þyn eritage; þei defouliden þyn
hooli temple, þei settiden Ierusalem into þe kepyng⁶⁵² of applis. [2]
Thei settiden þe slayn bodies of þi seruauntis, metis to þe volatils
of heuenys; þe fleischis of þi seyntis to þe beestis of [þe]ᵃ erþe. [3]
Thei schedden out þe blood of hem, as watir in þe cumpas of
f.43ʳ Ierusalem; and | noon was þat biriede. [4] We ben maad
schenschipe to oure neiȝbores; mouwyng and scornyng to hem,
þat ben in oure cumpas. [5] Lord, hou longe shalt þou be wrooþ
into þe ende? shal þi veniaunce be kyndlid as fier? [6] Schede out
þyn ire into heþene men, þat knowen not þee; and into rewmes, þat
clepiden not þi name. [7] For þei eeten Iacob;⁶⁵³ and maden desolat
his place. [8] Haue þou not mynde on oure elde wickidnessis; þi
mercies bifortake us soone, for we ben maad pore gretli. [9] God,
oure helþe, helpe þou us, and, Lord, for þe glorie of þi name
delyuere þou us; and be þou merciful to oure synnes for þi name.
[10] Lest perauenture þei seie among heþene men, Where is þe
God of hem? and be he knowun among naciouns bifor oure iȝen.
The veniaunce of þe blood of þi seruauntis, which is sched out;⁶⁵⁴
[11] þe weilyng of feterid men entre in þi siȝt. Upe þe greetnesse of
þyn arm; welde þou þe sones of slayn men.⁶⁵⁵ [12] And ȝelde þou
to oure neiȝboris seuenfold in þe bosum of hem; þe schenschipe of
hem, whiche þei diden schenschipefuli to þee, þou Lord. [13] But
we <u>þat ben</u> þi puple, and þe scheep of þi lesewe; shulen knouleche

ⁱ vndurstondyngis] vndurstondyng
Ps. 78     ᵃ þe] *om.*

647. In Ieroms translacioun it is, <u>he took hym suynge sheep wiþ lambren</u>. *Lire here.*

648. þat is, þe puple of Israel comynge of Iacob. *Lire here.*

649. þat is, gouernyde hem;
<u>in þe innocence</u>, þat is, in þe clennesse of conscience. *Lire here.*

650. þat is, he dide prudentli in hise werkis. *Lire here.*

## [PSALM 78 GLOSSES]

651.[i] þis lxxviij [salm][ii] spekiþ of þe distriyng of Ierusalem and of þe temple, which distriyng was maad bi Nabugodonosor, and of þe reparelyng þerof bi Cirus kyng of Perses.

Goostli, þis salm mai be expowned þat it be þe preier of hooli chirche aȝenes vnfeiþful men, defoulynge chirchis and hooli places, and sleynge cristen puple and distriyng hir lond. For which þing hooli chirche, in þe bigynnyng of þis salm, biweiliþ þis distriyng; and þe secounde tyme it bisechiþ deuoutli and mekeli for restoryng, þere: <u>Shede out, et cetera</u>, in bisechyng Goddis riȝtfulnesse aȝenes vnfeiþful men, and his merci anentis feiþful men; and at þe laste, it þankiþ God in þe hope of heriyng, þere: <u>But we, et cetera</u>. *Lire here.*

652. In Ebreu it is, <u>into an heep</u>; in Ierom it is, <u>in heepis of stoonys</u>, for þe keperis of applis maken a greet heep of stoonys, to se þeronne al aboute þe gardyn. *Lire here.*

653. þat is, deuouriden þe goodis of þe puple comynge of Iacob, f. 43[r] and killide and took prisoneris of þis puple. *Lire here.*

654. 'Be knowun among naciouns' [Ps 78: 10]. *Lire here.*

655. þat is, nyȝ þe deþ bi ouer greet turment. þerfor Ierom haþ <u>þe sones of perischyng</u>, þat is, þat ben disposid to perisching. *Lire here.*

to þee into þe world. In generacioun and into generacioun; we shulen telle þin heriyng.

**Ps. 78 glosses**    [i] *in the bottom margin; the second spiritual part of this gloss also in margin of* K    [ii] salm] *om.*

[PSALM 79]

*Qui regis Israel intende*

[1] þe title of lxxix salm. *To victorie; þis salm is þe witnessyng of Asaph for lilies.*[656]

[2] Thou þat gouernest Israel, ȝyue tent; þat ledist forþ Ioseph[657] as
f. 43ᵛ a scheep. Thou þat sittist on che|rubym; be schewid [3] bifor
Effraym, Beniamyn, and Manasses. Stire þi power, and come þou;
þat þou make us saaf. [4] God of vertues, turne þou us; and schewe þi
face, and we shulen be saaf. [5] Lord God of vertues; hou longe shalt
þou be wrooþ on þe preier of þi seruaunt?[658] [6] Hou longe shalt þou
feede us wiþ þe breed of teeris; and shalt ȝyue drynke to vs wiþ teeris
in mesure? [7] Thou hast set us into aȝenseiyng to oure neiȝboris; and
oure enemyes han scorned us. [8] God of vertues, turne þou us; and
schewe þi face, and we shulen be saaf. [9] Thou translatidist a vyne[659]
fro Egipt; þou castidist out heþene men, and plauntidist it. [10] Thou
were ledere of þe weie in þe siȝt þerof; and þou plauntidist þe rootis
þerof, and it fillid þe lond.[660] [11] The schadewe þerof hilide hillis;
and þe braunchis þerof filliden þe cedris of God. [12] It streiȝte forþ
hise siouns til to þe see, and þe generaciouns þerof til to þe flood. [13]
Whi hast þou distried þe wal þerof; and alle men þat goon forþ[661] bi
þe weie gaderen awei þe grapis þerof? [14] A boor of þe wode[662]
distriede it; and a synguler wielde beeste deuouride it. [15] God of
vertues, be þou turned; biholde þou fro heuene, and se, and visite þis
vyne. [16] And make þou it parfite, which þi riȝthond plauntide; and
biholde þou on þe sone of man, which þou hast confe[r]myd[a] to þee.
[17] Thingis brent wiþ fier, and vndurmyned; shulen perische for þe
blamynge of þi cheer. [18] Thyn hond be maad on þe man of þi
f. 44ʳ riȝthond; and on þe sone of man,[663] whom þou hast | confermed to
þee. [19] And we departiden not fro þee;[664] þou shalt quykene us, and
we shulen inwardli clepe þi name. [20] Lord God of vertues, turne
þou us; and schewe þi face, and we shulen be saaf.

[PSALM 80]

*Exultate Deo*

[1] þe title of lxxx salm. *To þe ouercomere in þe pressours of Asaph.*[665]

[2] Make ȝe fulli ioie to God, oure helpere; synge ȝe hertli to God of

Ps. 79    ᵃ confermyd] confemyd

[PSALM 79 GLOSSES]

656.[i] þat is, for Crist and his chirche. Austin, Cassiodore, and summe cristen doctours and eld Ebreis expownen þis salm of Crist, and þe lettre acordiþ wel herto. *Lire here.*

657. þat is, þe puple of Israel, and kepist it diligentli as an herde kepiþ his flok. *Lire here.*

658. þat is, on þe delyueraunce of þe puple, for which Y preiede f. 43ᵛ þee. *Lire here.*

659. þat is, þe puple of Israel. *Lire here.*

660. Of biheest. *Lire here.*

661. Manye kingis bifor Nabugodonosor and aftir killiden Iewis and rauyschiden her goodis. *Lire here.*

662. A boor of þe wode, þat is, Nabugodonosor;

and a synguler wielde beeste, þat is, Antiok, þat was so synguler in pride, as if he hadde þe lond to seile þerinne and þe see to go þeronne on foot in ij book of Machabeis v capitulo; he was ful ferse bi cruel turmentis and newe-founden, to brynge þe puple of Israel ʽtoʼ[ii] brekyng of þe lawe.

In Ebreu it is, and þe mouyng of þe feeld deuouride it; in Ierom it is, and alle þe beestis of þe feeld deuouriden it, and bi þis mai be vndurstondun þe multitude of dyuerse heþene men þat weren in þe oost of Antiok, eiþer of oþere kyngis þat distrieden Iudee. *Lire here.*

663. þat is, on Christ, man, which is clepid þe sone of man, þat is, of þe blessed virgyn. *Lire here.*

664. þat is, bi turnynge awei [fro][iii] feiþ. *Lire here.* f. 44ʳ

[PSALM 80 GLOSSES]

665.[i] þis lxxx salm was ordeyned to be sungun in þe feeste of trumpis, to do þankyngis to God for þe fruytis of þe ȝeer gaderid þanne.

Gostli, þis salm mai be expowned, þat it be þe doyng of þankyngis of hooli chirche, for benefices of God ȝouen to cristen puple; and þe chirche seeþ þe kyndnesse of good men toward God, and þerfor he is reisid firste in þis salm into God bi ful out ioiynge and hertli song; þe

**Ps. 79 glosses**   [i] *the first part of this spiritual gloss also in* K   [ii] to] bi, *canc. and corrected by the scribe above the line of writing*   [iii] fro] bi *by dittography*
**Ps. 80 glosses**   [i] *in the bottom margin; this gloss also in margin of* K

Iacob. [3] Take 3e a salm,⁶⁶⁶ and 3yue 3e a tympan; a myrie sawtree
wiþ an harpe. [4] Blowe 3e wiþ a trumpe in neome;⁶⁶⁷ in þe noble dai
of 3oure solempnyte.⁶⁶⁸ [5] Forwhi comaundement is in Israel; and
doom is to God of Iacob. [6] He settide þat witnessyng in Ioseph;
whanne he 3ede out of þe lond⁶⁶⁹ of Egipt, he alargide a langage,
which he knew not. [7] He turnyde awei his bak fro birþuns;⁶⁷⁰ hise
hondis seruyden in a coffyn. [8] In tribulacioun þou inwardli clepidist
me, and Y delyuyride þee; I herde þee in þe hid place of tempest, I
prouyde þee at þe watris of a3enseiynge. [9] Mi puple, here þou, and I
shal be witnesse a3enes þee; Israel, if þou herist me, [10] a freisch
God⁶⁷¹ shal not be in þee, and þou shalt not worschipe an alien God.
[11] For I am þi Lord God, þat ledde þee out of þe lond of Egipt;
make large þi mouþ, and I shal filleᵃ it. [12] And my puple herde not
my vois; and Israel 3af not tent to me. [13] And I lefte hem⁶⁷² aftir
desiris of her herte; þei shulen go in her fyndyngis. [14] If my puple
hadden herd me; if Israel hadde go in my weies. [15] For nou3t in hap
f. 44ᵛ  I had maad low her enemyes; and I hadde sent myn hond on | men
doynge tribulacioun to hem. [16] The enemyes of þe Lord lieden to
hym;⁶⁷³ and her tyme⁶⁷⁴ shal be into worldis. [17] And he fedde hem
of þe fatnesse of wheete; and he fillide hem wiþ hony of þe stoon.⁶⁷⁵

[PSALM 81]

*Deus stetit in synagoga*

[1] þe title of lxxxj salm. þe salm of Asaph.⁶⁷⁶

God stood in þe synagoge of goddis;⁶⁷⁷ forsoþe he demeþ goddis in
þe myddil. [2] Hou longe demen 3e wickidnesse; and taken þe faces of
synneris? [3] Deme 3e to þe nedi man and to þe modirles child;

---

secounde, þe chirche seeþ þe vnkyndnesse of yuele men in þe chirche,
and in þe persoone of God it wlatiþ hem. *Lire here.*

666. Take 3e a salm, et cetera, þat is, take 3e gostli þingis and 3yue
3e temporal þingis;

a myrie sawtree wiþ an harpe, þat is, answere 3e bi goode werkis of
þe bodi to þe prechyng of Goddis word. *Austin here.*

667. þat is, in þe bigynnyng of þe newe moone;

668. of 3oure solempnyte: in Ebreu it is, in þe ende of þe dai of

---

Ps. 80    ᵃ fille] *corrected by the scribe on an erasure*

ȝoure feeste; in Ierom it is, <u>in þe myddil moneþe of ȝoure solempnyte</u>. *Lire here.*

669. þat is, þe puple of Israel <u>of þe lond of Egipt</u>: in Ebreu it is, <u>on þe lond of Egipt</u>. *Lire here.*

670. In `Ierom´ [ii] it is, <u>Y remouyde his shuldre fro birþuns</u>; <u>hise hondis seruyden in a coffyn</u>, þat is, in an instrument to bere out filþis; in Ierom it is, <u>hise hondis ȝeden awei fro a coffyn</u>. *Lire here.*

671. <u>A freisch god</u>: He is a freisch god þat is not euerlastinge God, as ben stoonys and þe goddis of heþene men. He þat bileueþ not Goddis sone euene wiþ þe fadir makiþ a freisch god to him. Eretikis maken alien goddis to hemsilf and setten symylacris in her herte, which is worse þan in þe temple; and eretikis ben maad templis and symylacris of false þingis and worþi to be scorned. *Austin here.*

672. In wiþdrawinge fro hem my grace þat kepiþ fro synnes. *Lire here.*

673. Whanne þei worschipiden a ȝotun calf;                    f. 44ᵛ

674. <u>and her tyme</u>, þat is, of punysching of þis synne, for it is kept into tyme to comynge. *Lire here.*

675. <u>Fatnesse of wheete</u>, þat is, wiþ breed maad of cleene flour of whete; <u>hony of þe stoon</u>, for bees maken hony in þe rochis of lond of biheest, where [h]on[y][iii] is gaderid plenteuousli; wherfor þat lond is seid fletyng wiþ hony. *Lire here.*

<u>Whete</u>, þat is, sacramentis; <u>hony of þe stoon</u>, þat is, þe wisdom of Crist. *Austyn here.*

## [PSALM 81 GLOSSES]

676.[i] Ebreis seyn and cristen doctours seyn þat Asaph made þis lxxxj salm aȝenes weiward iugis and repreueþ her wickidnesse, and axiþ on siche Goddis riȝtfulnesse, þat redusiþ siche þingis to equyte.

Gostli, þis salm mai be expowned aȝenes þe prestis and doctours of lawe of þe Iewis, þat condempneden þe deþ of Crist meke and pore. Wherfor bi Goddis doom þei weren slayn temporali of þe Romayns and weren takun prisoneris; and in þe laste doom, þei shulen be condempned euerelastyngli. *Lire here.*

677. þat is, in þe congr`e´gacioun[ii] of iust men. *Lire here.*

Eþer þus: God[iii] stood, þat is, Crist stood in þe myddis of Iewis and he was not knowun God. *Austin here.*

[ii] Ierom] Ebreu, *canc. and corrected by the scribe above the line of writing*      [iii] hony] lond
**Ps. 81 glosses**      [i] *in the bottom margin, linked to the title with a tie-mark*      [ii] congregacioun]
congragacioun, *first -a- canc. and corrected by the scribe above the line of writing*      [iii] God] Good

justefie ʒe þe meke man and pore. [4] Rauische⁶⁷⁸ ʒe out a pore
man; and delyuere ʒe þe nedi man fro þe hond of þe synnere. [5]
Thei knowen not, neiþer vndurstoden, þei goon in derknessis; alle
þe foundementis of erþe shulen be mouyd. [6] I seide, ʒe ben
goddis;⁶⁷⁹ and alle ʒe ben þe sones of hiʒ God. [7] But ʒe shulen die
as men; and ʒe shulen falle doun as oon of þe prynces.⁶⁸⁰ [8] Rise,
þou God, deme þou þe erþe; for þou shalt haue eritage in alle
folkis.

## [PSALM 82]

*Deus quis similis*

[1] *þe title of lxxxij salm. þe song of þe salm of Asaph.*⁶⁸¹

[2] God, who shal be lijk þee? God, be þou not stille, neþer be
þou peesid.⁶⁸² [3] For lo! þyn enemyes sowneden; and þei þat
hatiden þee reisiden þe heed. [4] Thei maden a wickid councel on
þi puple; [and]ᵃ þei þouʒten aʒenes þi seyntis. [5] Thei seiden,
Come ʒe, and leese we hem fro [þe]ᵇ folk; and þe name of Israel be
no more had in mynde. [6] For þei þouʒten wiþ oon acoord; [7] þe
tabernaclis of Ydumeis, and men of Ismael disposiden a testa-

f. 45ʳ   ment⁶⁸³ togidere aʒenes þee. | Moab and Agarenes, [8] Iebal and
Amon and Amalech; aliens⁶⁸⁴ wiþ hem þat dwellen in Tire. [9] For
Assur comeþ wiþ hem; þei ben maad into help to þe sones of Loþ.
[10] Make þou to hem as to Madian, and Sisara; as to Iabyn in þe
stronde of Cison. [11] Thei perischiden in Endor; þei weren maad
as a toord of erþe. [12] Putte þou þe prynces of hem as Oreb and
Ʒeb; and Ʒebee and Salmana. Alle þe prynces of hem [13] þat
seiden; Holde we bi eritage þe seyntuarie of God. [14] Mi God,
putte þou hem as a wheel;⁶⁸⁵ and as stobil bifor þe face of þe wynd.
[15] As fier þat brenneþ a wode; and as flawme brennynge hillis.
[16] So þou shalt pursue hem in þi tempest; and þou shalt disturble
hem in þyn ire.⁶⁸⁶ [17] Lord, fille þou þe faces of hem wiþ
schenschipe; and þei shulen seke þi name.⁶⁸⁷ [18] Be þei
ashamed,⁶⁸⁸ and be þei disturblid into þe world of world; and be
þei schent and perische þei. [19] And knowe þei þat þe Lord is
name to þee; þou aloone art þe hiʒest in ech lond.

Ps. 82    ᵃ and] *om.*    ᵇ þe] *om.*

678. þe puple of Iewis was not giltles of Cristis deþ, for þei suffriden Crist to be slayn of wickid men, whanne þei weren so manye þat þe prynces hadden dredde hem as þei dredden þe puple bifore. *Austin here.*

679. Not in kynde, but bi grace and office; for iugis ben bi office þe perfourmeris of Goddis riȝtfulnesse. *Lire here and þe glos here in partie.*

680. þat is, as proude feendis ȝe shulen falle doun into helle bi equyte of Goddis sentence. *Lire here.*

### [PSALM 82 GLOSSES]

681.[i] Asaph made þis lxxxij salm aȝenes Sen[n]acherib[ii] and his oost. þe seuene and seuenti salm spekiþ principali aȝenes Sennacherib, and expressiþ not puplis ioyned to him for þe hatrede of Iewis; but in þis salm þe puplis dwellinge in þe cumpas of Iewis ben expressid principali, þat excitiden Sennacherib to come into þe lond of Iuda in þe tyme of Eȝechie þe king.

Gostli, þis salm mai be þe preier of hooli chirche aȝenes þe enemyes of cristen men, þat telliþ mekeli bifor God þe wickidnesse of hem and axiþ deuoutli Goddis veniaunce on þis, bi ensaumple of elde wickid men punyschid of God. [*Lire here.*][iii]

682. þat is, wiþholde more fro bryngynge in of veniaunce. *Lire here.*

683. þat is, a stidfast couenaunt. *Lire here.*

684. In Ebreu it is, <u>Filisteis</u>. *Lire here.*                    f. 45[r]

685. þat is, make hem vnstidfast. *Lire here.*

686. þe ire of God is iust resoun of veniaunce. *Lire here.*

687. Not Sennacherib þat was obstynat in idolatrie and pride souȝte God, but sum men in his oost þat fledden wiþ him diden reuerence to God, and manye men whose frendis weren deed for þe pride of Sen[na]cherib,[iv] þouȝten to sle hym;

688. <u>Be þei ashamed</u>: þis is seid of Sen[n]acherib[v] and oþere men obstynat in yuel. *Lire here.*

---

**Ps. 82 glosses**    [i] *next to the title in the left margin; the second spiritual part of this gloss also in margin of* K    [ii] Sennacherib] Senacherib    [iii] Lire here] *om.*    [iv] Sennacherib] Sencherib    [v] Sennacherib] Senacherib

## [PSALM 83]

*Quam dilecta*

[1] þe title of lxxxiij salm. *To victorie on þe pressouris; þe salm of þe sones of Chore.*[689]

[2] Lord of vertues, þi tabernaclis[690] ben gretli loued; [3] my soule coueitiþ and failiþ into þe porchis of þe Lord. Myn herte and my fleisch; ful out ioieden into quyk God. [4] Forwhi a sparowe[691] fyndiþ an hous to itsilf; and a turtle <u>fyndiþ</u> a nest to itsilf, where it shal kepe hise briddis. Lord of vertues, þyn auteris;[692] my kyng, and my God. [5] Lord, blessid ben þei þat dwellen in þyn hous; þei shulen preise

f. 45ᵛ þee into þe worldis[693] of worldis. [6] Blessid | is þe man, whos helpe is of þee; he haþ disposid stiyngis in his herte, [7] in þe valei of teeris, in þe place which he haþ set.[694] [8] For þe 3yuere of þe lawe shal 3yue blessyng, þei shulen go fro vertu into vertu; God of goddis[695] shal be seyn in Sion. [9] Lord God of vertues, here þou my preier; God of Iacob, perseyue þou wiþ eeris. [10] God, oure defendere, biholde þou; and biholde into þe face of þi crist. [11] Forwhi o dai in þyn hallis is betere; þan a þousynde.[696] I chees to be abiect,[697] <u>eþer an outcaste</u>, in þe hous of my God; more þan to dwelle in þe tabernaclis of synneris.[698] [12] For God loueþ merci and treuþe; þe Lord shal 3yue grace and glorie. [13] He shal not bireue hem fro goodis þat goen in innocence; Lord of vertues, blessid is þe man þat hopiþ in þee.

## [PSALM 84]

*Benedixisti Domine*

[1] þe title of lxxxiiij salm. *To þe ouercomere;*[699] *þe song of þe sones of Chore.*[700]

[2] Lord, þou hast blessid þi lond; þou hast turned awei þe caitifte of Iacob. [3] Thou hast for3oue þe wickidnesse of þi puple; þou hast hilid alle þe synnes of hem. [4] Thou hast aswagid al þin ire; þou hast turned awei fro þe ire of þyn indignacioun. [5] God, oure helpe,[701] conuerte þou us; and turne awei þyn ire fro us. [6] Wher þou shalt be wrooþ to vs wiþouten ende; eþer shalt þou holde forþ þyn ire fro generacioun into generacioun? [7] God, þou conuertid[702] shalt quykene us; and þi puple shal be glad in þee. [8] Lord, shewe þi

f. 46ʳ merci to us; and 3yue þin helþe to us. | [9] I shal hereᵃ what þe Lord

Ps. 84        ᵃ here] here here

[PSALM 83 GLOSSES]

689.[i] þis salm declariþ þe desir of hooli men lyuynge in þis wrecchid world to come to heuenli blis. *Lire here.*

690. þe profete seiþ <u>þi tabernaclis</u> in plurel noumbre, for þe dyuerse statis of hem þat ben in blis bi dyuerse meritis of hem. *Lire here.*

691. þat is, an herte bi feiþ, hope, and charite fyndiþ God to itsilf; <u>and a turtil</u>, þat is, þe fleisch, <u>fyndiþ a neest</u>, þat is, þe vnyte of hooli chirche, where it shal kepe hise good werkis. *Austin here.*

692. Ben þo in whiche mannis desir is quyetid. *Lire here.*

693. þe Ebreu word here signefieþ wiþouten ende; in Ierom it is, <u>euere</u>. *Lire here.*

694. þat is, God himsilf haþ set place in þe staat of present   f. 45[v] wrecchidnesse to disserue blisful liyf, bi morenyng and wepyng. *Lire here.*

695. þat is, Crist of cristen men. *Austin here.*

696. Of good daies þat moun be had in present liyf. *Lire here.*

697. þat is, to lyue in mekenesse. *Lire here.*

698. þat is, excellencis of proude men. *Lire here.*

[PSALM 84 GLOSSES]

699. In Ebreu it is, <u>To þe ouercomyng; þe salm of þe sones of Chore</u>. *Lire here.*

700.[i] þis salm is þe doynge of þankyngis for þe turnynge aȝen of Iewis fro þe caitifte of Babiloyne; but principali it is profecie of þe perfite delyueraunce to be maad bi Crist in his incarnacioun and passioun. *Lire here.*

701. Here is set bise[ch]yng[ii] for gostli delyueraunce þat shal be maad bi Crist. *Lire here.*

702. þat is, to us bi þi blessid incarnacioun. *Lire here.*

703. þat is, verili, and of herte ben turned to Crist. In Ebreu and in   f. 46[r] Ierom it is, <u>And þei shulen not be turned to folie</u>, þat is, to idolatrie, which is þe moost folie. *Lire here.*

---

God shal speke in me; for he shal speke pees on his puple. And on hise hooli men; and on hem þat ben turned to herte.[703] [10] Neþeles his helþe is nyȝ men dredynge hym; þat glorie dwelle in oure lond.

Ps. 83 glosses     [i] *next to the first verse in the right margin; this gloss also in margin of* K
Ps. 84 glosses     [i] *this gloss also in margin of* K     [ii] bisechyng] bisegyng

[11] Merci and treuþe metten[704] hemsilf; riȝtfulnesse and pees weren kissid. [12] Treuþe cam forþ of erþe;[705] and riȝtfulnesse bihelde fro heuene. [13] For þe Lord schal ȝyue benygnete; and oure erþe shal ȝyue his fruyt. [14] Riȝtfulnesse[706] shal go bifore hym; and shal sette hise steppis in þe weie.

## [PSALM 85]

*Inclina Domine aurem tuam*

[1] *þe title of lxxxv salm. þe preier of Dauid.*[707]

Lord, bowe doun þyn eere and here me; for I am nedi and pore. [2] Kepe þou my lijf, for I am hooli;[708] my God, make þou saaf þi seruaunt hopynge in þee. [3] Lord, haue þou merci on me, for I criede al dai to þee; [4] make þou glad þe soule of þi seruaunt, forwhi, Lord, I haue reisid my soule to þee. [5] For þou, Lord, art swete and mylde; and of myche merci to alle men inwardli clepynge þee. [6] Lord, perseyue þou my preier wiþ eeris;[a] and ȝyue þou tent to þe vois of my bisechyng. [7] In þe dai of my tribulacioun I criede to þee; for þou herdist me. [8] Lord, noon among goddis is lijk þee; and noon is euene to þi werkis.[709] [9] Lord, alle folkis whiche euere þou madist, shulen come and worschipe bifor þee; and þei shulen glorifie þi name. [10] For þou art ful greet and makynge meruels; þou art God aloone. [11] Lord, lede þou me forþ in þi weie, and I shal entre in þi treuþe; myn herte be glad þat it drede | þi name. [12] Mi Lord God, I shal knoulech to þee in al myn herte; and I shal glorifie þi name wiþouten ende. [13] For þi merci is greet on me; and þou delyueridist my soule fro þe lowere helle.[710] [14] God, wickid men han rise up on me; and þe

f. 46ᵛ

---

704. þat is, camen togidere in þe persoone of Crist. [*Lire here.*]ⁱⁱⁱ

705. þat is, Crist was borun of þe blessid virgyn marie; ȝyue benygnyte, þat is, þe fulnesse of his grace; and þe blessid shal bere hir sone Crist, God and man. *Lire here.*

706.ⁱᵛ Riȝtfulnesse shal go bifor him, þat is, Ioon Baptist shal go bifor Crist, and shal sette steppis in þe weie of penaunce, for he lyuyde in penaunce and tauȝte it, bi which veri riȝtfulnesse is maad for synnes doon. *Lire here.*

Ps. 85    ᵃ perseyue þou my preier wiþ eeris] wiþ eeris perseyue þou my preier

---

ⁱⁱⁱ Lire here] *om.*    ⁱᵛ *the first part of this gloss, through* Baptist, *interlinear and underlined in* K; *also in margin of* V

[PSALM 85 GLOSSES]

707.[i] God my3te 3yue no grettir good to men, þan þat he made his kyndli sone heed to hem and shapide hem as membris of hym, þat he shulde be þe sone of God and þe sone of man, o God wiþ þe fadir and o man wiþ men. Ihesu Crist is oure prest and preieþ for us, and he as oure heed preieþ in us, and he as oure God is preied of us. *Austin on þe title of lxxxv salm.*

Comynli Ebreis and Latyn doctouris seien þat Dauiþ, beynge in þe persecucioun of Saul, made þis lxxxv salm for his delyueraunce and preiede God ful deuoutli.

Gostli, þis salm mai be expowned of ech cristen man set in tribulacioun bodili excitid of men eþer in gostli turment maad of fendis, which man preieþ God deuoutli for his delyueraunce and aleggiþ, firste, þe worþynesse of Goddis heryng. And on his part he aleggiþ his nedynesse, innocence, and contynuaunce of preier; and on Goddis part he aleggiþ merci, power, greet doynge, and onour. And ferþer, he formeþ his axinge þere, <u>Lord lede me forþ</u>, þat he be kept in good werk, and be bifor kept fro þe yuel of synne and of peyne, and so þat he be corounned at þe laste, in þe rewme of glorie. *Lire here.*

708. þat is, innocent anentis Saul. *Lire here.*

<u>Y am hooli</u>: Cristis bodi, þat is, cristen puple, seiþ verili Y am hooli, for it haþ take grace of hoolynesse, grace of baptym and remyssioun of synnes, siþen 'Alle cristen men cristenyd[ii] in Crist ben cloþid in Crist' [Gal 3: 27]. If þei seyn þat þei ben not hooli, þei doon wrong to þe heed. þe heed aloone is hooli and halewiþ, and nediþ noon halewyng. *Austin here.*

709. þat is, so my3ti as þou in werkis. *Lire here.*

710. Dauiþ disseruyde to go doun to þe lowere helle for þe sleyng of þe prestis of Nobe, for he was cause of her deþ and gilti for alle her lyues, as he knoulechide hymsilf to Abiaþar. And it was schewid to Dauiþ þat God hadde releessid þis synne. *Lire here.* f. 46ᵛ

þis world in which we ben dedli is seid þe hi3ere helle; þe lowere helle is whidur deed men goon, fro whennes God wolde delyuere oure soulis. þou delyuerist <u>my soule fro þe lowere helle</u> into which it hadde go doun if þou haddist not 3oue remedie, as a man kept fro siyknesse bi þe councel of a leche seiþ to hym, þou hast delyuerid me fro siyknesse. *Austyn here.*

---

**Ps. 85 glosses**    [i] *in the bottom margin; the final spiritual part of this gloss also in margin of* K
[ii] cristenyd] cloþid cristenyd, *by eyeskip*

synagoge[711] of myȝti men han souȝt my lijf; and þei han not set forþ
þee in her siȝt. [15] And þou, Lord God, doynge merci and merciful;
pacient and of myche merci, and soþfast. [16] Biholde on me and haue
merci on me, ȝyue þou þe empire to þi child; and make þou saaf þe
sone[b] of þyn handmaide. [17] Make þou wiþ me a signe in good, þat
þei see,[c] þat haten me, and be aschamed; for þou, Lord, hast helpid
me and hast comfortid me.

### [PSALM 86]

*Fundamenta*

[1] *þe title of lxxxvj salm. þe salm of þe song of þe sones of Chore.*[712]

The foundementis þerof[713] ben in hooli hillis; [2] þe Lord loueþ þe
ȝatis of Syon, more þan alle þe tabernaclis of Iacob. [3] Thou citee of
God, wiþouten ende;[714] gloriouse þingis ben seid [of][a] þee. [4] I shal
be myndeful of Raab and Babiloyne;[715] knowynge me. Lo! aliens[716]
and Tire and þe puple of Ethiopiens; þei weren þere. [5] Wher a man
shal seie to Sion,[717] and a man is borun þerinne; and þat man
alþerhiȝeste foundide it? [6] The Lord shal telle in þe scripturis of
puplis;[718] and of þese prynces þat weren þerinne. [7] As þe dwellynge
of alle þat ben glad; is in þee.[719]

### [PSALM 87]

*Domine Deus salutis mee*[a]

[1] *þe title of lxxxvij salm. In Ebreu þus: þe song of salm, to þe sones of
Chore to victorie on mahalat,*[720] *for to answere, þe lernyng of Heman
Eȝraite.*[721]

f. 47ʳ   [2] Lord God of myn helþe; I criede in dai and nyȝt bifore þee. [3]
Mi preier entre bifor þi siȝt; bowe doun þyn eere to my preier.
[4] For my soule is fillid wiþ yuelis;[722] and my lijf neiȝide to

---

711. þat is, congregacioun. *Lire here.*

### [PSALM 86 GLOSSES]

712.[i] As seynt Ierom, Austyn, and Cassiodore witnessen, þis salm

[b] sone] sones    [c] see] seen, -n *canc.*
**Ps. 86**    [a] of] to
**Ps. 87**    [a] Domine Deus salutis mee] *on f. 47ʳ, following the psalm title*

**Ps. 86 glosses**    [i] *next to the first verse in the right margin*

to þe lettre spekiþ of þe mysterie of Crist and of hooli chirche, which
mysterie þe sones of Chore knewen bi þe spirit of profesie. *Lire here.*

713. þe foundementis þerof, þat is, of hooli chirche, ben in hooli
hillis, þat is, in Crist, in apostlis and profetis;

714. þou citee of God, wiþouten ende: þus it is in Ebreu and Ierom
haþ here euere, þouȝ þis is left out in þe comyn Sauter;

715. Raab and Babiloyne: as Ebreis and Ierom seyn, þis word raab is
not here þe propir name of þat womman þat resseyuede þe
messangeris of Iosue in þe secounde chapitre of Iosue, but raab
signefieþ here pride, and þe puple of Egipt þat [bi pride][ii] was rebel to
God in þe tyme of Moises; but aftir þe deþ of Crist it resseyuede
mekeli þe feiþ of Crist bi þe prechyng of seynt Mark, as Ethiopiens
diden bi þe prechyng of seynt Maþeu;

716. Lo! aliens: in Ebreu and in Ierom it is, Lo! Palestyn; þei weren
þere: in Ebreu and in Ierom it is, þis is borun þere, þat is, ech of þe
puplis biforseid is borun þer`e´[iii] aȝen bi baptym;

717. Wher a man shal seie to Syon: in Ierom and in Ebreu it is, It
shal be seid to Syon;

718. in þe scripturis of puplis, þat is, in þe gospels and in þe
scripturis of apostlis, þat ben princes of þe chirche aftir Crist; in
Ebreu and in Ierom it is þus: þe Lord shal telle euere in þe scripturis
of puplis, þis man is borun þerinne, þat is, Crist himsilf is borun of þe
virgyn and hooli chirche;

719. is in þee, þat is, in þe staat of þe chirche regnynge in blis. *Lire
here.*

[PSALM 87 GLOSSES]

720. In Ierom it is, on þe queer; mahalat is an instrument of musike,
and it signefieþ also 'a queer' and 'siyknesse'. *Lire here.*

721.[i] As Ebreis seien, þis salm spekiþ of þe turment of Iewis, moost    f. 47ʳ
in þe caitifte of Babiloyne. But in treuþe, as Ierom, and Austyn, and
þe comyn glos witnessen, þis salm spekiþ of Cristis passioun, which
þe salmmakere biforsiȝ bi þe spirit of profesie and spak in þe persoone
of Crist. *Lire here.*

722. Of [bodili][ii] peyne. [*Lire here.*][iii]

---

[ii] þe puple of Egipt þat bi pride was rebel to God in þe tyme of Moises] Egipt þat was
rebel to God in þe tyme of Moises is signefiede here bi pride; *by dittography*    [iii] þere] þer,
*corrected in a gap between words by the scribe*
**Ps. 87 glosses**    [i] *next to the first verse on the next leaf, f. 47ʳ*    [ii] bodili] temporal, *perhaps due
to a misreading of* corporalis *in the translator's exemplar*    [iii] Lire here] *om.*

helle.⁷²³ [5] I am gessid wiþ hem þat goon doun into þe lake; I am maad as a man wiþout help, [6] and fre among deed men. As men woundid slepynge in sepulcris, of whiche men noon is myndeful aftir; and þei ben putte awei fro þyn hond.⁷²⁴ [7] Thei han putte me in þe lowere lake; in derk places and in þe schadewe of deþ. [8] Thi strong veniaunce is confermed on me; and þou hast brouȝte in alle þi wawis⁷²⁵ on me. [9] Thou hast maad fer fro me my knowun; þei han set me abhomynacioun to hemsilf. I am takun and I ȝede not out; [10] myn iȝen weren sijk for pouert. Lord, I criede to þee; al dai I spred abrood myn hondis to þee.⁷²⁶ [11] Wher þou shalt do meruelis to deed men;⁷²⁷ eiþer lechis shulen reise, and þei shulen knouleche to þee? [12] Wher ony man in sepulcre shal telle þi merci; and þi treuþe in perdicioun?⁷²⁸ [13] Wher þi meruelis shulen be knowun in derknessis; and þi riȝtfulnesse in þe lond of forȝetyng? [14] And, Lord, I criede to þee; and eerli my preier shal biforcomeᵇ to þee. [15] Lord, whi puttist þou awei my preier; turnest awei þi face fro me? [16] I am pore and in trauels fro myn ȝongþe; soþeli I am enhaunsid, and I am maad low, and disturblid. [17] Thi wraþþis passiden on me;⁷²⁹ and þi dredis distarbliden me. [18] Thei cumpassiden me as watir al dai; þei cum|passiden me togidere. [19] Thou madist fer fro me a frend and neiȝbore; and my knowun fro wrecchidnesse.⁷³⁰

f. 47ᵛ

[PSALM 88]

*Misericordias Domini*

[1] þe title of lxxx `viij´ ª salm. þe lernyng of Eþan Eȝraite.⁷³¹

[2] I schal synge wiþouten ende; þe mercies of þe Lord. In generacioun and into generacioun; I shal telle þi treuþe wiþ `my´ᵇ mouþ. [3] For þou seidist, wiþouten ende merci shal be bildid in heuenys;⁷³² þi treuþe shal be maad redi in þo. [4] I disposide a testament⁷³³ to my chosen men; I swor to Dauiþ, my seruaunt, [5] til into wiþouten ende I shal make redi þi seed. And I shal bilde þi seete;⁷³⁴ in generacioun and into generacioun. [6] Lord, heuenes shulen knouleche þi meruelis;⁷³⁵ and þi treuþe in þe chirche of seyntis. [7] For who in þe cloudis shal be maad euene to þe Lord;

---

ᵇ biforcome] come bifor
**Ps. 88** ª viij] *in margin in red, by the scribe* ᵇ my] þi, *canc. and corrected by the scribe above the line of writing*

723. <u>To helle</u>: þe Ebreu word here signefieþ boþe 'helle' and 'a[iv] sepulcre'. *Lire here.*

724. þat is, fro þe hond of þi proteccioun as to þe staat of present liyf. *Lire here.*

725. þat is, fersnesse of tribulacioun. *Lire here.*

726. þat is, my good werkis to þee. [*Austin*][v] here.

727. Crist ceesside neuere to do good werkis, but for hise good werkis profitiden to euerlastynge helþe to hem aloone þat ben chosun to blis. He seiþ[vi] suyngli, <u>wher þou shalt do meruelis to deed men</u>: bi þis he signefieþ þat sum men ben so deed in herte, þat so grete myraclis of Crist mouyden not hem to þe liyf of feiþ; eþer <u>lechis</u>, þat is, proude men bihetyng helþe of soulis bi þe crafte of her wisdom. *Austyn here.*

728. þat is, in þe helle of hem þat ben dampned, which is clepid perdicioun propirli. *Lire here.*

729. þat is, þe werkis of punyschyng camen on me. *Lire here.*

730. þat is, fro my wrecchidnesse, so þat it mai not be releuyd bi   f. 47[v] hem; in Ierom it is, <u>and þou hast takun awei my knowun</u>. *Lire here.*

## [PSALM 88 GLOSSES]

731.[i] þis lxxxviij salm spekiþ of þe abundaunce and euerelastyng- nesse of þe rewme of Dauiþ, which is fillid in Crist and in noon oþere; and Ebreis and Latyn doctouris seien þis acordyngli. *Lire here.*

732. For bi effect of Goddis merci aboute Cristis mysterie, þe fallyngis of aungelis is reparelid. *Lire here.*

733. þat is, lawe. *Lire here.*

734. If Crist sate not in vs, he shulde not gouerne vs. No man owiþ to preche þat þing wiþ tremblyng, wherof he mai not doute. Preche we þe treuþe of God, þe word of God, þe heestis of God, and þe sweryng of God. And in þese maneris be we maad stidfast on ech side, and in beringe God we ben heuenes;

735. <u>heuenys shulen knowe þi meruelis</u>: þou preisist þat deed men han rise aȝen; preise þou more þat lost men ben aȝenbouȝt. What grace, what merci of God! þou seest a man ȝistirdai þe swolowe of drunkennesse, todai an ournement of sobirnesse, ȝisterdai þe filþe of leccherie, todai[ii] þe fairnesse of temperaunce, ȝistirdai a blasfemere of

---

[iv] and a] and a and a, *the dittography not corrected*   [v] Austin] Lire   [vi] seiþ] seiþ seiþ, *the dittography not corrected*
**Ps. 88 glosses**   [i] *next to the title in the left margin; this gloss also in margin of* K   [ii] todai] todai an ournement of sobirnesse, an ournement of sobirnesse *canc.*

schal be lijk God among þe sones of God? [8] God, which is glorified
in þe councel of seyntis; is greet and dredeful[736] ouer alle þat ben in
his cumpas. [9] Lord God of vertues, who is lijk þee? Lord, þou art
my3ti, and þi treuþe is in þi cumpas. [10] Thou art Lord of þe power
of þe see; forsoþe þou aswagist þe stiryng of þe wawis þerof. [11]
Thou madist low þe proude as woundid; in þe arm of þi vertu þou
hast scaterid þyn enemyes. [12] Heuenes ben þyne, and þe erþe is
þyn; þou hast foundid þe world and þe fulnesse þerof; [13] þou
madist of nou3t þe norþ and þe see.[737] Thabor and Hermon shulen
make ful out ioie[738] in þi name; [14] þyn arm wiþ power. Thyn hond
f. 48ʳ  be maad stidefast, and | þi ri3thond be enhaunsid; [15] ri3tfulnesse
and doom is[c] þe makyng redi of þi seete. Merci and treuþe shulen go
bifor þi face; [16] blessid is þe puple þat kan hertli song. Lord, þei
shulen go in þe li3t[739] of þi cheer; [17] and in þi name þei shulen make
ful out ioie al dai; and þei shulen be enhaunsid in þi ri3tfulnesse. [18]
For þou art þe glorie of þe vertu of hem; and in þi good plesaunce
oure horn[740] shal be enhaunsid. [19] For oure taking up is of þe Lord;
and of þe hooli of Israel oure kyng. [20] Thanne þou spakist in
reuelacioun to þi seyntis and seidist, I haue set help in þe my3ti; and I
haue enhaunsid þe chosun m[a]n[d] of my puple. [21] I foond Dauiþ,
my seruaunt; I anoyntide hym wiþ myn hooli oile. [22] For myn hond
shal helpe hym; and myn arm shal conferme hym. [23] The enemy[741]
shal no þing profite in hym; and þe sone of wickidnesse[742] shal not leie
to, for to anoie hym. [24] And I shal sle hise enemyes fro his face; and
I shal turne into fli3t hem þat haten hym. [25] And my treuþe and
merci shal be wiþ hym; and his horn shal be enhaunsid in my name.
[26] And I shal set his hond in þe see; and his ri3thond in floodis. [27]
He shal inwardli clepe me, þou art my fadir; my God, and þe uptakere
of myn helþe. [28] And I shal sette hym þe firste gendrid sone; hi3ere
þan þe kyngis[743] of erþe. [29] Wiþouten ende I shal kepe my merci to
hym; and my testament feiþful to hym. [30] And I shal sette his seed
into þe world of world; and his troone as þe daies of heuene. [31]
f. 48ᵛ  Forsoþe | if hise sones forsaken my lawe; and goon not in my domes.
[32] If þei maken vnhooli my ri3tfulnessis; and kepen not my
comaundementis. [33] I shal visite in a 3erde þe wickidnessis of
hem; and in betyngis þe synnes of hem. [34] But I shal not scatere[744]
my merci fro hym; and in my treuþe I schal not anoie hym. [35]
Neiþer I shal make vnhooli my testament;[745] and I shal not make voide

---

[c] is] *corrected by the scribe on an erasure*     [d] man] men

God, todai a preisere of God. No doute, heuenys ben seid þe prechouris of Goddis word. *Austin here.*

736. In reuerence and onour. *Lire here.*

737. In Ierom it is, þe norþ and þe riȝt side, þat is, souþ. *Lire here.*

738. þat is, shulen be occasioun of ful out ioiyng for werkis of þi vertu shewid þere. *Lire here.*

739. þat is, in þe liȝt of kyndli resoun, which is a preente of Goddis   f. 48ʳ liȝt; and in þe liȝt of Goddis lawe. *Lire here.*

740. þat is, oure power. *Lire here.*

741. þat is, Saul wiþ hise knyȝtis. *Lire here.*

742. þat is, Absolon. *Lire here.*

743. þat is, of þat tyme; eþer hiȝere þan þe kyngis in þe cumpas of Iudee. *Lire here.*

744. þat is, Y shal not take al awei fro his eiris; not anoie hym, þat   f. 48ᵛ is, not bringe anoie þat mai not be rekenyd. *Lire here.*

745. þat is, my biheest maad to Dauiþ. *Lire here.*

746. þat is, þe rewme of Dauiþ in þe tyme of Sedechie. *Lire here.*

747. þat is, þe wallis<sup>iii</sup> of Ierusalem, and of oþere citees. *Lire here.*

748. þou hast turned awei, et cetera, til þidur, þou hast maad lesse þe daies, et cetera: al þis is seid of kyng Dauiþ bodili, þat we seke an oþere Dauiþ, þat is, Crist, þat myȝte not do synne. So Salomon þat for wisdom and prudence was gessid to be þe seed of Dauiþ, in which þe biheest of God maad to Dauiþ shulde be fillid, fel doun and ȝaf place for to set hope in Crist. *Austin here.*

---

þo þingis þat comen forþ of my lippis. [36] Onys I swor in myn hooli; I shal not lie to Dauiþ, [37] his seed<sup>e</sup> shal dwelle wiþouten ende. [38] And his troone as sunne in my siȝt, and as a parfite moone wiþouten ende; and a feiþful witnesse in heuene. [39] But þou hast putte awei and hast dispisid;<sup>746</sup> and hast dilaied þi crist. [40] Thou hast turned awei þe testament of þi seruaunt; þou madist vnhooli his seyntuarie in erþe. [41] Thou distriedist alle þe heggis<sup>747</sup> þerof; þou hast set þe stidfastnesse þer of drede. [42] Alle men passynge bi þe weie rauyschiden him; he is maad schenschipe to hise neiȝboris. [43] Thou hast enhaunside þe riȝthond of men oppressynge him; þou hast gladide alle hise enemyes. [44] Thou hast turned awei<sup>748</sup> þe help

<sup>iii</sup> wallis] wallis þer, þer *canc.*

<sup>e</sup> seed] seed sw-, sw- *canc.*

of his swerd; and þou helpidist not hym in batel. [45] Thou distriedist
him fro clensyng; and þou hast hurtlid doun his seete in erþe. [46]
Thou hast maad lesse þe daies of his tyme; þou hast bisched him wiþ
schenschipe. [47] Lord, hou longe turneste þou awei into þe ende;
schal þyn ire brenne out as fier?⁷⁴⁹ [48] Biþenke þou what is my

f. 49ʳ substaunce; for wher | þou hast ordeynede veynli alle þe sones of
men? [49] Who is a man þat shal lyue and shal not se deþ; shal
delyuere his soule fro þe hond of helle?⁷⁵⁰ [50] Lord, where ben þyn
elde mercies; as þou hast swore to Dauiþ in þi treuþe? [51] Lord, be
þou myndeful of þe schenschipe of þi seruauntis,⁷⁵¹ of manye heþene
men; which I helde togidere in my bosum. [52] Which þyn enemyes,
Lord, diden schenschipfuli; for þei dispisiden þe chaungyng⁷⁵² of þi
crist. [53] Blessid be þe Lord wiþouten ende;⁷⁵³ be it doon, be it doon.

[PSALM 89]

*Domine refugium*

[1] *þe title of lxxxix salm. þe preier of Moises, þe man of God.*⁷⁵⁴

Lord, þou art maad help to us; fro generacioun into generacioun.
[2] Bifor þat hillis weren maad,⁷⁵⁵ eþer þe erþe and [þe]ᵃ world was
formed; fro þe world and into þe world þou art God. [3] Turne þou⁷⁵⁶
not awei a man into lownesse; and þou seidist, ȝe sones of men be
conuertid. [4] For a þousynde ȝeer ben bifor þin iȝen; as ȝistirdai
which is passid, and as kepyng⁷⁵⁷ in þe nyȝt. [5] The ȝeeris of hem
shulen be;⁷⁵⁸ þat ben had for nouȝt. [6] Erli passe he as an eerbe, erli
florische he and passe; in þe euentid falle he doun, be he hard and

---

749. So þat it shal neuere be quenchid, as if he seie, Nay, siþen it is
propir to þee, to spare and to haue mercie. *Lire here.*

f. 49ʳ      750. þat is, noon, til Crist made raunsum in þe cros. *Lire here.*

751. þat is, of schenschipis doon to þi seruauntis; <u>which Y helde</u>,
þat is, Y dissymylide and suffride pacientli schenschip doon in me of
vnfeiþful men. *Lire here.*

752. <u>þe chaungyng of þi crist</u>: For þis, boþe Crist and cristen men
suffriden manye schenschipis, for þe liyf and techyng of scribis and
farisees is repreuyd bi þe techyng of Crist and of hise apostlis,
wherinne was summe chaungyng. In Ebreu and in Ierom it is, <u>for</u>

Ps. 89      ᵃ þe] *om.*

þei dispisiden þe steppis of þi crist.[iv] And þanne þe lettre is pleyn, for þe dedis and wordis of Crist þat ben hise steppis weren repreuyd of þe[v] prestis and of þe wise men of lawe, and cristen men aftirward suffriden manye schenschipes and turmentis of tirauntis, and for þei suffriden þis pacientli and ioiefuli, to sueþ in þe persoone of hem.

753. Blessid be þe Lord wiþouten ende, of alle þingis whiche he doiþ to us in prosperitees and aduersitees. *Lire here.*

## [PSALM 89 GLOSSES]

754.[i] þis lxxxix salm is þe preier of Moises to gete Goddis benefices to þe puple of Israel, whiche he ledde out of Egipt. To gete benefices in tyme to comyng, þe beste maner is, to shewe kyndnesse of benefices resseyued bifore.

þis salm mai be expowned gostli, þat it be þe preier of ech cristen man, which þat his preier be more able to be herd, þenkiþ firste on Goddis benefices ȝouun to mankynde, and so he axiþ ferþere to be liȝtned wiþ Goddis wisdom wiþinne[ii] his soule, and to be reulid bi Goddis vertu in his werkis wiþout forþ. *Lire here.*

755. þat is, bifor þat þe world was maad of nouȝt; fro þe world, et cetera, þat is, wiþout bigynnyng and wiþouten ende. *Lire here.*

756. Turne þou not awei a man into lownesse, þat is, lest a man be turned awei fro þin hiȝe þingis and euerelastynge, coueite temporal þingis and sauere erþeli þingis. *Austyn here.*

Eþer turne þou not, þat is, suffre þou not a man to be turned into lownesse, þat is, a man caste doun bi synne fro þe hiȝ staat in which he was lord of creturis to þe staat of present wrecchidnesse, in whiche he suffriþ disese, ȝhe of flies; ȝe sones of men be conuertid, in risinge aȝen to penaunce fro synne to grace. *Lire here.*

757. þat is, waking; in þe nyȝt: here endiþ þe vers in Ebreu and in Ierom;

758. shulen be in þe noumbre of þingis; þat ben had for nouȝt: in Ebreu þus, þou hast smyte hem wiþ wawis; þei shulen be sleepful; þat is, þei weren drenchid in þe greet flood, outakun viij persoones, and aftir þe greet flood mannis liyf was so short, þat is, semyde not but a short sleep; in Ierom þus: for þou hast smyte hem, þat is, wiþ watris of þe greet flood; þei shulen be a dreem, þat is, of no reputacioun. *Lire here.*

wexe drie. [7] For we han failid in þyn ire; and we ben disturblid in þi strong veniaunce. [8] Thou hast [set]^b oure wickidnessis in þi si3t;^759 oure world in þe li3tnyng of þi cheer. [9] For alle oure daies han failid; and we han failid in þyn ire. Oure 3eeris^760 shulen biþenke, as an ireyne; [10] þe daies of oure 3eeris ben in þo seuenti 3eeris;^761

f. 49^v  Forsoþe, if ei3ti 3eer ben | in my3ti men;^762 and þe more tyme of hem is trauel and sorewe. For myldnesse cam aboue; and we shulen be chastisid.^763 [11] Who knew þe power of þin ire; [12] and durste noumbre þin ire for þi drede? Make þi ri3thond so knowun; and make men lerned in herte bi wisdom. [13] Lord, be þou conuertid sumdeel; and be þou able to be preied on þi seruauntis.^764 [14] We weren fillid eerli wiþ þi merci; we maden ful out ioie and we delitiden in alle oure daies. [15] We weren glad for þe daies in whiche þou madist us meke; for þe 3eeris in whiche we sien yuelis. [16] Lord, biholde þou into þi seruauntis, and into þi werkis; and dresse þou þe sones of hem. [17] And þe schyn[yn]g^c of oure Lord God be on us; and dresse þou þe werkis of oure hondis on us, and dresse þou þe werk of oure hondis.

## [PSALM 90]

*Qui habitat*

[1] *þe nyntiþe salm haþ no title neþer in Ebreu neiþer in Ierom.*^765

He þat dwelliþ in þe help^766 of þe hi3este God; shal dwelle in þe proteccioun of God of heuene. [2] He shal seie to þe Lord, þou art myn uptakere and my refuyt; my God, I shal hope in hym. [3] For he delyuyride me fro þe snare of hunteris; and fro a sharp word.^767 [4] Wiþ hise shuldris he shal make schadewe to þee; and þou shalt haue hope vndur hise feþeris. [5] His treuþe shal cumpasse þee wiþ a sheeld; þou schalt not drede of ny3tis drede.^768 [6] Of an arowe fleynge in þe dai,^769 of a gobelyn goynge in derknessis;^770 of a sailyng and a

f. 50^r  myddai fend. [7] A þousynde shulen falle doun | fro þi side, and ten

---

759. In þi si3t, þat is, to punysche þo; oure world, þat is, þe cours of oure tymes; of þi cheer, þat is,^iii openli bifor þee;

760. Oure 3eeris, þat is, men lyuynge in oure [3]eeris;^iv shulen biþenke, as an ireyne, þat is, men studien and biþenken to gete onouris eþer richessis þat ben lost swiftli;

^b set] *om.*   ^c schynyng] schyng

^iii is] is men lyuynge in oure 3eeris, men lyuynge in oure 3eeris *canc.*   ^iv 3eeris] eeris

761. þe daies of oure ʒeeris ben in þo lxx ʒeeris, in Ebreu and in Ierom þus, ʿwe han wastid oure ʒeeris as a wordʹ;ᵛ

762. for if lxxx ʒeer ben in myʒti men, þat is, of strong complexioun. *Lire here.*

763. In Ebreu and in Ierom þus, For we passiden soone; and we han    f. 49ᵛ
flowen awei, þat is, fro present world, as a brid fro his neest. *Lire here.*

764. þat is, in heryng her preieris. *Lire here.*

[PSALM 90 GLOSSES]

765.ⁱ Ebreis seien þat þis nyntiþe salm was maad of Moyses, as þe salm biforgoynge. And as Moyses in þe salm biforgoynge axide benefices of God to þe puple goynge out of Egipt, so in þis salm he denounsiþ þe manyefold benefice[s]ⁱⁱ of God on þe puple.

Gostli, þis salm mai be expowned of ech cristen man hopynge in God, bi hope formed wiþ charite, bifor whom þe oost of fendis ouercomun wiþ Goddis help falliþ doun. And so he is enhaunsid fynali, and is corowned in heuene. *Lire here.*

766. þat is, hopiþ tristeli in his help. *Lire here.*

767. As briddes in an hegge dreden þe castyng of a stoon and fallen into nettis, so men þat dreden þe veyn wordis of rebuykeris and ben ashamed of veynⁱⁱⁱ dispisingis, fallen into þe snaris of hunteris, þat is, of fendis, and ben maad prisoneris of þe deuel. *Austyn here.*

768. Of nyʒtis drede: Whanne a man synneþ bi vnkunnyng, he synneþ as in þe nyʒt; whanne he synneþ wityngli, he synneþ as in þe dai;

769. an esi temptacioun in vnkunnynge men is nyʒtis drede; an esi temptacioun in kunnynge men, is an arowe biⁱᵛ dai;

770. but greuouse persecucioun—makyng siyk men in feiþ afeerd, þat knowen not ʒit þat þei ben cristen men, to dispise present þingis and for to hope heuenli þingis to comynge—is a gobelyn goynge in derknessis, and takiþ hem. But he þat woot þat he is a cristen man, for to hope heuenli goodis not temporal goodis and ʒyueþ stide for greuouse persecucioun, falliþ as in þe dai. *Austyn here.*

In Ebreu it is, of deber goinge in derknessis; and of quoteb wastynge in myddai. Rabi Salomon seiþ þat ʻdeberʼ and ʻquotebʼ ben names of fendis. *Lire here.*

---

ᵛ we han wastid oure ʒeeris as a word] *added by the scribe below the line of writing*
**Ps. 90 glosses**    ⁱ *in the top margin*    ⁱⁱ benefices] benefice    ⁱⁱⁱ veyn] veyn wordis of rebuykeris, wordis of rebuykeris *canc.*    ⁱᵛ bi] bi þe, þe *canc.*

þousynde fro þi riȝtside; forsoþe it shal not neiȝe[771] to þee. [8] Neþeles þou shalt biholde wiþ þyn iȝen; and þou shalt se þe ȝeldyng of synneris. [9] For þou, Lord, art myn hope; þou hast set þyn help alþerhiȝeste. [10] Yuel shal not come to þee; and a scourge shal not neiȝe to þi tabernacle. [11] For God haþ comaundide to hise aungelis of þee;[772] þat þei kepe þee in alle þi weies. [12] Thei schulen bere þee in þe hondis; lest perauenture þou hirt þi foot at a stoon. [13] Thou shalt go on a snake and a cocatrice; and þou shalt defoule a lioun and a dragoun. [14] For he hopide in me, I shal delyuere hym; I shal defende hym, for he knew my name. [15] He criede to me, and I shal here him, I am wiþ hym in tribulacioun; I shal delyuere him, and I shal glorifie hym. [16] I shal fille hym wiþ þe lengþe of daies; and I shal shewe myn helþe to hym.

## [PSALM 91]

*Bonum est confiteri*

[1] *þe title of lxxxxj salm. þe salm of song; in þe dai of sabat.*[773]

[2] It is good to knouleche to þe Lord; and to synge to þi name, þou hieste. [3] To schewe eerli[774] þi merci; and þi treuþe[775] bi nyȝt. [4] In a sautre of ten coordis;[776] wiþ song in harpe.[777] [5] For þou, Lord, hast delitid me in þi makyng; and I shal make ful out ioie in þe werkis of þyn hondis. [6] Lord, þi werkis be magnefied gretli; þi þouȝtis ben maad ful depe. [7] An vnwise man shal not knowe; and a fool shal not vndurstonde þese þingis. [8] Whanne synneris comen forþ, as hey; and | alle þei[a] apperen, þat worchen wickidnesse. That þei perische into þe world of world; [9] forsoþe þou, Lord, art þe hiȝeste, wiþouten ende. [10] For lo! Lord, þyn enemyes, for lo! þyn enemyes shulen perische; and alle shulen be scaterid þat worchen wickidnesse. [11] And myn horn shal be reisid as an vnycorn; and myn elde[778] in plenteuouse merci. [12] And myn iȝe dispiside myn enemyes; and whanne wickid men risen aȝenes me, myn eere shal here. [13] A iust man shal floure as a palm tree; he schal be multeplied as a cedre of Liban. [14] Men plauntid in þe hous of þe Lord; shulen floure in þe porchis of þe hous of oure God. [15] Ȝit þei shulen[779] be multeplied in plenteuouse eelde; [16] and þei shulen be suffryng wel. `[T]hat þei telle,[780] þat oure Lord God is riȝtful; and no wickidnesse is in him.´[b]

f. 50ᵛ

**Ps. 91**    [a] þei] þat, *canc. and* þei *added by the scribe above the line of writing*    [b] That þei telle . . . is in him] *added by the scribe in margin, the initial capital om.*

771. þat is, þe swerd of aduersaries shal not neiȝe to anoie þee. *Lire* f. 50ʳ
*here.*

772. þe deuel aleggide þis scripture seid of Crist, but as Ierom seiþ, he aleggide it falsli. *Lire here.*

[PSALM 91 GLOSSES]

773.ⁱ Ebreis seyn þat Moises made þis lxxxxj salm to be sungen in þe dai of sabat, þat was solempne anentis Iewis, for þe mynde of benefice of makyng of þe world. Firste, þis salm indusiþ men to do þankyngis for þe benefice of creacioun; þe secounde tyme, it shewiþ þe punyschyng of vnkynde men; and þe þridde tyme it shewiþ þe avaunsyng of kynde men þat louen wel God. *Lire here.*
God techiþ vs noon oþere song no but of feiþ, of hope, and of charite, þat oure feiþ be stidfast in hym, and þat we bileue into hym whom we seen not, þat we haue ioie whanne we seen. Sclaundris ben plenteuouse. No man feeliþ þo, no but he þat goþ in þe weie of God. It is seid to him in alle þe bookis of God, þat he suffre present þingis and hope þingis to comynge, and þat he loue God whom he seeþ not, þat he haue ioie whanne he shal se hym. *Austyn on þe title of lxxxxj salm.*

774. þat is, in þe tyme of prosperite;

775. and þi treuþe, þat is, þi riȝtfulnesse, bi niȝt, þat is, þe tyme of tribulacioun. *Lire here.*

776. þat is, in þe kepyng of ten heestis wiþ gladnesse;

777. wiþ song in harpe, þat is, in word and werk. *Austyn here.*

778. In Ebreu it is, and myn anoyntyng in abundaunce of oile; in f. 50ᵛ
Ierom it is, and myn eelde in plenteuouse oile. *Lire here.*

779. Ȝit þei shulen: in Ierom þus, ȝit þei shulen make fruyt in eelde; þei shulen be fat and bryngynge forþ bowis, þat is, bi þe fatnesse of grace þei shulen brynge forþ good werkis;

780. þat þei telle : here bigynneþ þe laste vers in Ebreu and in Ierom. *Lire here.*

Ps. 91 glosses    ⁱ *near the title in the right margin*

## [PSALM 92]

*Dominus regnauit*

*þe lxxxxij salm haþ no title, neþer in Ebreu neiþer in Ierom.*[781]

[1] The Lord[782] haþ regned, he is cloþid wiþ fairnesse; þe Lord is cloþid wiþ strengþe, and haþ gird hymsilf. For he made stidfast þe world;[783] þat shal not be mouyd. [2] God, þi seete was maad redi fro þat tyme; þou art fro þe world.[784] [3] Lord, þe floodis han reisid; þe floodis han reisid her vois.[785] Floodis reisiden her wawis;[786] [4] of þe vois of manye watris. The reisyngis of þe see[787] ben wondurful; þe Lord is wondurful[788] in hiȝe þingis. [5] Thi witnessyngis ben maad able to be bileuyd gretli; Lord, hoolynesse bicomeþ þyn hous, into þe lengþe of daies.

## [PSALM 93]

*Deus ulcionum*

*þe lxxxxiij salm haþ no title neþer in Ebreu neþer in Ierom.*[789]

f. 51ʳ    [1] God is Lord of veniaunces; | God of veniaunces dide freli. [2] Be þou enhaunsid þat demest þe erþe; ȝelde þou ȝeldyng to proude men. [3] Lord, hou longe synneris; Lord, hou longe shulen synneris haue glorie? [4] Thei shulen telle out, and shulen speke wickidnesse; alle men schulen speke [þat worchen]ᵃ vnriȝtfulnesse. [5] Lord, þei han maad low þi puple; and þei han disesid þyn eritage. [6] Thei killiden a widewe and a comeling; and þei han slayn fadirles children and modirles. [7] And þei seiden, þe Lord shal not se; and God of Iacob shal not vndurstonde. [8] Ȝe vnwise men in þe puple, vndurstonde; and, ȝe foolis, lerne sum tyme. [9] Schal not he here þat plauntide þe eere; eþer biholdiþ not he þat made þe iȝe? [10] Schal not he repreue þat chastisiþ folkis; which techiþ man kunnyng? [11] The Lord knowiþ þe þouȝtis of men; þat þo ben veyn. [12] Blessid is þe man whom þou, Lord, hast lerned; and hast tauȝte hym of þi lawe. [13] That þou aswage him fro yuele daies; til a

Ps. 93    ᵃ þat worchen] *om.*

## [PSALM 92 GLOSSES]

781.[i] Ebreis seyn þat Moises made þis lxxxxij salm. þe lettre of þis salm is fillid in þe rewme of Crist, and þe rewmes of þe world ben soget to it bi feiþ. *Lire here.*

782. þat is, þe Lord Ihesu Crist, veri God and veri man, <u>haþ regned</u>, for in his risyng aȝen he took power on ech creature. *Lire here.*

783. <u>He made stidfast þe world</u>: Crist was cloþid wiþ fairenesse to hem whiche he pleside; he was cloþide wiþ strengþe to hem in whiche he displeside. þerfor sue þou þi Lord, þat þou maist be his clooþ; come þou wiþ fairnesse to hem to whiche þi good werkis plesen; be þou strong aȝenes bacbiteris. Crist was gird wiþ mekenesse, forwhi strengþe is in mekenesse. Meke men ben as stoon; proude men vanyschen awei as smoke. *Austyn here.*

784. þat is, fro wiþout bigynnyng. *Austin here.*

785. þat is, emperours of Rome and oþere tirauntis comaundiden wiþ open vois þat cristen men shulden be distried eeuerywhere;

786. þat is, cruel persecuciouns aȝenes cristen men;[ii]

787. <u>þe reisyngis of þe see</u>, þat is, þe persecuciouns of seculer poweris aȝenes cristen feiþ;

788. þat made þe chirche encreesse most in persecuciouns. *Lire here.*

## [PSALM 93 GLOSSES]

789.[i] In þis salm Moises aȝenclepiþ þe puple fro errour aboute Goddis puruyaunce, and schewiþ þat Goddis puruyaunce strecchiþ forþ to alle þingis, and punyschiþ iustli synneris. *Lire here.*

Al þe lxxxxiij salm techiþ pacience in þe trauels of iust men, aȝenes þe prosperites of wickid men. Hooli men owen for to shyne among wickid men, as þe liȝtis of heuene doon; þat is to do her office, to haue þe herte in heuenys and to recke not of þe peynes of þe world, as þe sterris of heuene recken not. To seie þat þilke sterre is Mercurius [sterre],[ii] þat sterre is Saturnus sterre, þat sterre is[iii] Iouys sterre, is dispisyng of sterris. If þe sunne mai haue indignacioun, it haþ sharpliere indignacioun aȝenes þat man þat onouriþ it falsli þan aȝenes hym þat dispisiþ it, for þe wrong of þe Lord is more dispit to a good seruaunt. *Austyn here.*

**Ps. 92 glosses**    [i] *next to the opening verses in the left margin; also in* IK    [ii] cristen men] *corrected by the scribe on an erasure*
**Ps. 93 glosses**    [i] *in the bottom margin; the first historical part of this gloss also in* IK    [ii] sterre] *om.*    [iii] is] is is, *second* is *canc.*

diche⁷⁹⁰ be diggid to þe synnere. [14] For þe Lord shal not putte awei his puple; and he shal not forsake his eritage. [15] Til riȝtfulnesse be turned into doom; and who ben nyȝ it, alle þat ben of riȝtful herte. [16] Who shal rise wiþ me aȝenes my`s´doeris;ᵇ eþer who shal stonde wiþ me aȝenes hem þat worchen wickidnesse? [17] No but for þe Lord helpide me; almest my soule⁷⁹¹ hadde dwellide in helle. [18] If I seide, My foot was stirid; Lord, þi merci helpide me. [19] Aftir þe multitude of my sorewis in myn herte; þi comfortyngis maden glad my | soule. [20] Wher þe seete of wickidnesse cleueþ to þee; þat makist trauel⁷⁹² in comaundement? [21] Thei shulen take aȝenes þe soule of a iust man; and þei shulen condempne innocent blood.⁷⁹³ [22] And þe Lord was maad to me into refuyt; and my God was maad into þe help of myn hope. [23] And he schal ȝelde to hem þe wickidnesse of hem; and in þe malice of hem he shal leese hem, [oure Lord God schal lese hem].ᶜ

f. 51ᵛ

[PSALM 94]

*Venite exultemus Domino*

þe lxxxxiiij salm haþ no title in Ebreu neþer in Ierom.⁷⁹⁴

[1] Come ȝe,⁷⁹⁵ make we ful out ioie to þe Lord; hertli synge we to God, oure helþe. [2] Biforeocupie we his face in knoulechyng; and hertli synge we to him in salmes. [3] For God is a greet Lord and a greet kyng aboue alle goddis;⁷⁹⁶ for þe Lord shal not putte awei his puple. [4] For alle þe endis of erþe ben in his hond; and þe hiȝnesses of hillis ben hise. [5] For þe see is his and he made it; and hise hondis formeden þe drie lond. [6] Come ȝe,ᵃ herie we, and falle we doun bifor God, wepe we bifor þe Lord þat made us; [7] for he is oure Lord God. And we ben þe puple of his leseweᵇ and þe scheep of his hond. [8] If ȝe han herd his vois todai; nyle ȝe make hard ȝoure hertis. [9] As in þe terrynge to wraþþe; bi þe dai of temptacioun in desert. Where ȝoure fadris temptiden me; þei preuyden and sien my werkis. [10] Fourti ȝeer I was offendid

---

ᵇ mysdoeris] mydoeris, *corrected by the scribe above the line of writing*     ᶜ oure Lord God schal lese hem] *om.*

**Ps. 94**     ᵃ Come ȝe] Come we ȝe, we *canc.*     ᵇ þe puple of his lesewe] þe lesewe of his puple

790. þat is, bodili deþ, bi which þe bodi is putte in a diche of erþe;   f. 51ʳ
and euerelastinge deþ, bi which þe soule is put into þe diche of helle;
and at domesdai boþe bodi and soule shulen be put in helle. *Lire here.*

791. þat is, Y hadde be deed and biried; in Ebreu it is, <u>my soule
hadde dwellid in stilnesse</u>, forwhi vois is takun awei bi deþ. *Lire here.*

792. þat is, þat seist falsli, þat þou maist not fille þe comaundement   f. 51ᵛ
of God of þe entryng into þe lond of biheest. *Lire here.*

793. þat is, þei wolden haue slayn Moises and Aaron, Caleph and
Iosue; but þese iust men weren defendid bi Goddis proteccioun. *Lire
here.*

[PSALM 94 GLOSSES]

794.ⁱ Poul seiþ to Ebreis þe iij and iiij capitulo þat þis salm was
maad of Dauiþ, and it spekiþ not of þe entryng into þe lond of biheest
vndur Iosue, but of þe entryng into þe lond of lyuynge men þat shulde
be openyd bi Crist in þe tyme of grace, for bi his blessid passioun, he
remouyde þe lettyng. *Lire here.*

795. Bi feiþ and deuocioun. *Lire here.*

796. þat is, hooli aungelis and profetis and hooli men, þat ben
goddis bi grace. *Lire here.*

797. þat is, myn heestis, in whiche þei ouȝten go; and þis bi her
malice blyndynge hem. *Lire here.*

798. þat is, Y determyned wiþout reuokyng in þe werk of my
veniaunce. *Lire here.*

to þis generacioun; and I seide, Euere þei erren in herte. [11] And
þese men knewen not my weies;⁷⁹⁷ to whiche I swore in myn
ire,⁷⁹⁸ þei shulen not entre into | my reste.                    f. 52ʳ

---

**Ps. 94 glosses**   ⁱ *next to the title in the left margin; the first historical part of this gloss also
in* IK

## [PSALM 95]

*Cantate Domino*

þe lxxxxv salm haþ no title neiþer in Ebreu neiþer in Ierom.[799]

[1] Synge ȝe a newe[800] song to þe Lord; al erþe,[801] synge ȝe to þe Lord. [2] Synge ȝe to þe Lord and blesse ȝe his name; tel[l]e[a] ȝe his helþe fro dai into dai. [3] Telle ȝe his glorie amonge heþene men; his meruelis among alle puplis. [4] For þe Lord is greet and worþi to be preisid ful myche; he is ferdful aboue alle goddis. [5] For alle þe goddis of heþene men ben fendis; but þe Lord made heuenys. [6] Knoulechyng[802] and fairenesse is in his siȝt; hoolynesse and worþi doyng is in his halewyng. [7] Ȝe cuntreis of heþene men[803] brynge to þe Lord, brynge ȝe glorie and onour to þe Lord; [8] brynge ȝe to þe Lord, glorie to his name. Take ȝe sacrifices,[804] and entre ȝe into þe hallis of hym; [9] herie ȝe þe Lord in his hooli halle. Al erþe be mouyd of his face; [10] seie ȝe among heþene men, þat þe Lord haþ regnyd.[805] And he haþ amendid þe world, þat shal not be mouyd;[806] he shal deme puplis in equyte. [11] Heuenys be glad, and þe erþe make ful out ioie, þe see and þe fulnesse þerof be mouyd togidere; [12] feeldis shulen make ioie, and alle þingis þat ben in þo. Thanne alle þe trees of wodis shulen make ful out ioie [13] for þe face of þe Lord, for he comeþ; for he comeþ to deme þe erþe. He shal deme þe world in equyte; and puplis in his treuþe.

## [PSALM 96]

*Dominus regnauit exultet.*[a]

[1] þe lxxxxvj [salm][b] haþ no title, neiþer in Ebreu neþer in Ierom.[807]

---

f. 52ʳ            ## [PSALM 95 GLOSSES]

799.[i] þis lxxxxv salm spekiþ of þe tyme of Crist, þat bigan propirli at þe bigynnyng of prechyng of þe gospel.

Goostli, þis salm mai be expowned of ech cristen man, which is Goddis sone bi grace, as Crist is Goddis sone bi kynde. And þerfor as

Ps. 95        [a] telle] telþe
Ps. 96        [a] Dominus regnauit exultet] *on f. 52ᵛ, following the title*        [b] salm] *om.*

Ps. 95 glosses        [i] *in the bottom margin; the first historical part of this gloss also in* IK

doom of discrecioun on oþere men perteyneþ to Crist, so to ech cristen man is set eþer assigned doom of discrecioun on hise owne þouȝtis, spechis, and dedis: þat we consente not in herte to ony vniust þing, neþer brynge forþ bi mouþ ony vniust þing, neþer vse in dede ony vniust þing. *Lire here.*

800. Coueitise of fleisch syngiþ þe elde song; þe charite of God syngiþ a newe song. Veri loue is vois to God, and is a newe song. *Austin here.*

801. þat is, alle þat dwellen in erþe. *Lire here.*

802. We louen fairnesse; chese we firste knoulechyng, þat fairnesse sue. So greet power is in aungelis, þat if þei doon al þat þei moun, it mai not be suffrid; and ech man desiriþ þe power of aungelis, but he loueþ not þe riȝtfulnesse of aungelis. Firste loue þou riȝtfulnesse, and power shal su þee. *Austin here.*

803. þat is, conuertid to þe feiþ of Crist. *Lire here.*

804. Take ȝe sacrifices: not bolis, not sheep, but a contrite herte and maad meke. *Austin here.*

Eþer: Take ȝe sacrifices, þat is, enhaunse ȝe wiþ good[ii] preisyngis Cristis fleisch and blood vndur þe spice of breed and wyn, þat ben sacrid in dyuerse tymes. *Lire here.*

Eþer: Sacrifices moost acceptable to God ben merci, mekenesse, knoulechyng, pees, and charite. Bere we þe sacrifices, and we shulen abide sikirli þe comynge of þe iuge. *Austyn on þe laste vers of þis salm.*

805. Austin and Cassiodore adden þus, þe Lord haþ regned fro þe tree; but þis word fro þe tre is not in Ebreu neþer in Ierom neþer in Greek;

806. þat shal not be mouyd, þat is, fro þe treuþe of cristen feiþ þat shal stonde til to þe ende of þe world. *Lire here.*

## [PSALM 96 GLOSSES]

f. 52ᵛ

807.[i] þis lxxxxvj salm spekiþ of þe comyng of Crist to þe dom of discussioun, þat is, to reise good men to blis, and to caste doun wickid men to helle, as þe salm biforgoinge spekiþ of 'his'[ii] comynge to þe doom of discrecioun, þat is, to clepe sum men to feiþ bi grace, and to forsake oþere men in synne.

Gostli, þis salm mai be expowned of ech feiþful man, which is

f. 52ᵛ  The Lord haþ regnyd, þe erþe make ful out ioie; manye ilis be glad. [2] Cloude and derknesse in his cumpas; riȝtfulnesse and doom is amendyng⁸⁰⁸ of his seete. [3] Fier shal go bifor hym; and shal enflawme, eþer set afier, hise enemyes in cumpas. [4] Hise leitis shyneden to þe world; þe erþe siȝ and was mouyd. [5] Hillis as wex fletiden doun fro þe face of þe Lord; al erþe fro þe face of þe Lord. [6] Heuenys telden his riȝtfulnesse; and alle puplis sien his glorie. [7] Alle þat worschipen sculptils be schent,⁸⁰⁹ and þei þat han glorie in her symylacris; alle ȝe aungelis of þe Lord, worschipe hym. [8] Sion herde⁸¹⁰ and was glad, and þe douȝtris of Iuda maden ful out ioie; for þi domes, Lord. [9] For þou, Lord, art þe hiȝeste on al erþe; þou art greetli enhaunsid ouer alle goddis.⁸¹¹ [10] Ȝe þat louen þe Lord, hate yuel; þe Lord kepiþ þe soulis of hise seyntis; he shal delyuere hem fro þe hond of synnere.⁸¹² [11] Liȝt is risun to þe riȝtful man; and gladnesse to riȝtful men of herte. [12] Iust men, be ȝe glad in þe Lord; and knouleche ȝe to þe mynde of his halewyng.

[PSALM 97]

*Cantate Domino*

[1] *þe title of lxxxxvij salm: A salm.*⁸¹³

Synge ȝe a newe song to þe Lord; for he haþ do meruelis. His riȝthond⁸¹⁴ and his hooli arm; haþ maad helþe to hym. [2] The Lord haþ maad knowun his heelþe; in þe siȝt of heþene men he haþ
f. 53ʳ schewid his riȝtfulnesse.⁸¹⁵ [3] He biþouȝte on his merci; and on | hisᵃ treuþe to þe hous of Israel. Alle þe endis of erþe; sien þe helþe of oure God. [4] Al erþe make hertli ioie to God; synge ȝe, and make ȝe ful out ioie, and seie ȝe salm. [5] Synge ȝe to þe Lord in an harpe, in an harpe and vois of salm; [6] in trumpis betun out⁸¹⁶ wiþ hamer, and in vois of a trumpe of horn. Hertli synge ȝe in þe siȝt of þe Lord,⁸¹⁷ þe kyng; [7] þe see and þe fulnesse þerof be mouyd; þe world, and þei þat dwellen þerinne. [8] Floodis shulen make ioie wiþ hond, togidere hillis shulen make ful out ioie, [9] for siȝt of þe Lord; for he comeþ to deme þe erþe. He shal deme þe world in riȝtfulnesse; and puplis in equyte.

---

**Ps. 97**    ᵃ his] ois, *corrected by the scribe with overwriting*

Goddis sone bi grace[iii] as Crist[iv] is Goddis sone bi kynde; and þerfor
as general doom of discussyng perteyneþ to Crist, so synguler doom
of discussyng perteyneþ to ech feiþful man, in discussyng his owne
conscience, þat he punysche so bi penaunce al þat he fyndiþ þere of
yuel dedis, spechis, and þouȝtis, þat he ascape þe peyne of doom to
comynge, bi þis þat Poul seiþ in þe firste pistle to Corynthis xj
capitulo, 'If we demyden ussilf, we shulden not be demed of þe Lord'
[1 Cor 11: 31]. *Lire here.*

808. þat is, amending of þe world þat comeþ forþ of his iudicial
power, signefiede bi <u>seete</u>, shal be riȝtful and shal neuere be reuokid.
*Lire here.*

809. þat is, shulen flete doun, for he spekiþ of þing to comynge bi
þe maner of þing passid, for þe certeynte of profesie; <u>worshipen
sculptils</u>,[v] þat is, idols maad wiþ hondis. *Lire here.*

810. <u>Sion herde</u>: here bigynneþ þe vers in Ebreu and in Ierom;
<u>douȝtris of Iuda</u>, þat is, cristen soulis chosun to blis. *Lire here.*

811. þat is, hooli aungelis. *Lire here.*

812. þat is, of þe deuel, which is obstynat in synne, and euere
enforsiþ for to drawe oþere men to synne. *Lire here.*

### [PSALM 97 GLOSSES]

813.[i] þer is no more in Ebreu neiþer in Ierom. *Lire here.*

þouȝ manye cristen doctouris expownen þis salm of þe double
comyng of Crist, þat is, into þe world and to þe laste doom, it mai
couenabli be expowned of Cristis comynge into þe world and of þe
doom of discrecioun, bi which chosun men be clepid to feiþ; and þis
doom began at þe tyme of prechyng of Crist and of apostlis. *Lire here.*

814. þat is, Crist haþ maad helþe to þe honour of þe fadir. *Lire here.*

815. þat is, cristen feiþ þat iustefieþ. *Lire here.*

816. þei þat profiten in tribulacioun, as Iob dide, ben vndurston-  f. 53ʳ
dun bi trumpis betun out wiþ hameris; a trumpe of horn is a man
ouercomynge fleischli affecciouns and fleischli lustis. *Austin here.*

817. þat is, of Ihesu Crist, Lord of lordis and Kyng of kyngis. *Lire
here.*

---

ᶦᶦᶦ grace] grace and to forsake oþere men in synne   ᶦᵛ as Crist] *corrected by the scribe on an
erasure*   ᵛ *a dot above* sculptils *for an undrawn tie-mark; the second half of this gloss also in* K,
*erroneously attributed to* Augustine
**Ps. 97 glosses**   ᶦ *the first sentence continuous with the rubricated title and interlinear; the rest
next to the first verses in the left margin*

## [PSALM 98]

*Dominus regnauit irascantur*

[1] þe lxxxxviij salm haþ no title, neiþer in Ebreu neiþer in Ierom.[818]

The Lord haþ regned,[819] pupli[s][a] be wrooþ; þou þat sittist on cherubyn,[820] þe erþe be mouyd.[821] [2] The Lord is greet in Sion; and hiȝ aboue alle puplis. [3] Knouleche þei to þi grete name, for it is ferdful[822] and hooli; [4] and þe onour[823] of þe king loueþ doom. Thou hast maad redi dressyngis; þou hast maad dom and riȝtfulnesse in Iacob. [5] Enhaunce ȝe oure[b] Lord God; and worschipe ȝe þe stool of hise feet,[824] for it is hooli. [6] Moises and Aaron weren among hise prestis; and Samuel was among hem þat inwardli clepen his name. Thei inwardli clepiden þe Lord, and he herde hem; [7] in a piler of cloude he spak to hem. Thei kepten hise witnessyngis; and þe comaundement[825] which he ȝaf to hem. [8] Oure Lord God, þou | herdist hem; God, þou were merciful to hem, and þou tokist veniaunce on al her fyndyngis.[826] [9] Enhaunse ȝe oure Lord God, and worschipe ȝe in his hooli hil; for oure Lord God is hooli.

f. 53ᵛ

## [PSALM 99]

*Iubilate Deo omnis terra*

[1] þe titil of lxxxxix salm. A salm to knouleche. In Ierom þus: A salm for knouleching.[827]

---

## [PSALM 98 GLOSSES]

818.[i] Oure doctouris seyn comynli, þat Dauiþ made þis lxxxxviij salm of þe rewme of Crist. But þis exposicioun is more gostli þan literal. þerfor, Dauiþ made þis salm to induce þe puple to Goddis worschiping, and þis was aftir þat he hadde ouercome Filisteis and oþere aduersaries risyng aȝenes his rewme and aftir þat he hadde brouȝte þe arke of þe Lord into þe hil of Syon, wiþinne þe tabernacle whiche he hadde araied þerfor. And þere he ordeyned prestis and dekenes, for to herie God.

Gostli, þis salm mai be expowned of þe rewme of Crist, which he

---

Ps. 98    [a] puplis] pupliþ    [b] oure] ȝoure

Ps. 98 glosses    [i] *in the right margin and across the bottom margin; the first part of this gloss, through* þe rewme of Crist, *also in* I, *the entire first half of the gloss, through* for to herie God, *in* K

took in his risyng aȝen and assencioun, which rewme þe princes of Iewis
þat weren wrooþ enforsiden to distrie. And aftirward þe princes of
Romayns wolden do þe same, but at þe laste þe prynces of Romayns in
þe tyme of Constantyne weren soget to cristen feiþ bi her fre wille, and
Iewis weren brouȝte into þe seruage of cristen prynces. þerfore, in þis
salm Dauiþ telliþ þis rewme and indusiþ cristen puple to herie Crist, bi
ensaumple[ii] of elde fadris þat hadden þis knowing. þis exposicioun is
tauȝte wel in þe glos here and in oþere doctouris. *Lire here.*
    819. þat is, made Dauiþ to regne. *Lire here.*
    820. Cherubyn is interpretid þe fuylnesse of kunnyng. For God
passiþ al kunnyng, he is seid to sitte on þe fulnesse of kunnyng. If
charite is in þin herte, þere is þe fulnesse of lawe and þanne þou art þe
seete of God. In hauynge charite and fulnesse of kunnyng, þou art
maad þe seete of God and þou art maad heuene. *Austyn here.*
    821. In Ierom it is, be schakun. *Lire here.*
    822. þat is, worschipful. *Lire here.*
    823. In Ebreu and in Ierom it is, and þe empire of þe king loueþ
dom; redi dressyngis, þat is, moral comaundementis þat dressen into
þe laste ende;
    824. þe stool of hise feet, þat is, bifor þe arke of testament. *Lire here.*
Eþer þe stool of hise feet, þat is, þe manheed of Crist. *Austin here.*
    825. þat is, moral heestis. *Lire here.*
    826. þat is, defautis þat camen not forþ of þi stiryng, but of her fre   f. 53ᵛ
wille. *Lire here.*

[PSALM 99 GLOSSES]

    827.[i] þis salm was[ii] maad to be sungen in þe offryng of pesible
sacrifice, þat was offrid to God for summe benefice to be getun of him,
to which þe plesing of God is requyrid bifore; eþer for benefice now
getun, to whiche þe doyng of þankingis owen to sue.
    Gostli, þis salm mai be expowned þat it be aȝenclepyng of þe
comyn puple and of þe mynystris of þe chirche to þe heriyng of God
in þe offryng of þe sacramentis of þe auter, which owiþ to be offrid to
God þe fadir wiþ þe heriyngis of God. For þis is verili a pesible
sacrifice, bi whos offryng þe hiȝeste prest, Ihesu Crist, peside alle
þingis þat ben in heuene and in erþe, as Poul seiþ in þe firste chapitre
to Colosences. *Lire here.*

  [ii] bi ensaumple] bi ensaumple bi ensaumple, *the dittography not corrected*
  **Ps. 99 glosses**   [i] *next to the title in the left margin, a red paraph to begin the spiritual gloss;
the historical part of this gloss also in margin of* K    [ii] was] was was, *the dittography not canc.*

[2] Al erþe, synge ȝe hertli to God; serue ȝe þe Lord in gladnesse.
Entre ȝe in his siȝt; in ful out ioiynge. [3] Wite ȝe þat þe Lord hymsilf
is God; he made us, and not we maden us. His puple and þe scheep of
his lesewe, [4] entre ȝe into hise ȝatis in knoulechyng;⁸²⁸ entre ȝe into
hise porchis, knouleche ȝe to hym in ympnes. Herie ȝe his name, [5]
for þe Lord is swete, his merci is wiþouten ende; and his treuþe is in
generacioun and into generacioun.

[PSALM 100]

*Misericordiam et iudicium*

[1] *þe title of þe hundrid salm. þe salm of Dauiþ.*⁸²⁹

Lord, I shal synge to þee; merci and doom. I shal synge, [2] and I
shal vndurstonde in a weie wiþout wem; whanne þou shalt come to
me. I ȝede perfitli in þe innocence of myn herte; in þe myddil of myn
hous. [3] I settide not forþ bifor myn iȝen an vniust þing;⁸³⁰ I hatide
hem þat maden trespassyngis.⁸³¹ [4] A schrewide herte cleuyde not to
me; I knew not⁸³² a wickid man bowynge awei fro me. [5] I pursuyde
hym; þat bacbitide priuyli his neiȝbore. Wiþ þe proude iȝe and an
herte vnable to be fillid; I eet not wiþ þis. [6] Myn iȝen weren to þe
feiþful men of erþe, þat þei sitte wiþ me; he þat ȝede in a weie wiþout
f. 54ʳ  wem,⁸³³ mynystride | to me. [7] He þat doiþ pride, shal not dwelle in
þe myddil of myn hous; he þat spekiþ wickid þingis, seruyde not in þe
siȝt of myn iȝen. [8] In þe morewtid I killide alle þe synneris⁸³⁴ of
erþe; þat I shulde leese fro þe citee of þe Lord, alle men worchynge
wickidnesse.

[PSALM 101]

*Domine exaudi orationem meam*

[1] *þe title of þe hundrid and o salm. The preier of a pore man, whanne he
was angwischid, and sched out his speche bifor þe Lord.*⁸³⁵

[2] Lord, here þou my preier; and my cri come to þee. [3] Turne
þou not awei þi face fro me; in what euere dai I am troblid, bowe doun
þin eere to me. In what euere dai I shal inwardli clepe þee; here þou
me swiftli. [4] For my daies han failid as smoke; and my boonys han
dried up as critouns.⁸³⁶ [5] I am smytun as hei, and myn herte driede
up; for I haue forȝete to ete my breed. [6] Of þe vois of my weilyng;
my boon cleuyde to my fleisch.⁸³⁷ [7] I am maad lijk a pellican of
wildirnesse; I am maad as a nyȝt crowe in an hous. [8] I wakide; and I

828. Of Goddis heriynge. *Lire here.*

[PSALM 100 GLOSSES]

829.[i] Dauiþ made þis hundrid salm whanne he knew þat God hadde stablischid and confermyd him in þe rewme of Israel, and þerfore he purposide þanne stidfastli to vse wel þe power of þe kyng, þou3 he felde fro þis purpos bi his freelte and stiryng of þe deuel, in doynge avoutrie and manquellynge of Vrie, and in noumbryng of þe puple eþer summe oþere synnes, for whiche he dide veri penaunce.

þe moralte of þis salm is, þat ech prynce haue himsilf bi þe forme tau3te here of Dauiþ, deuoutli anentis God, cleneli and honestli to himsilf, and iustli to þe puple soget. *Lire here.*

830. þat is, to coueite eny vniust þing. *Lire here.*

831. Trespassingis, þat is, trespassouris of Goddis lawe. *Lire here.*

832. Y knew not, þat is, Y appreuyde not. *Austin here.*

833. þat is, in hoolynesse and honeste of liyf. *Lire here.*

834. þat is, þat weren worþi þe deþ for her synnes. *Lire here.*    f. 54r

[PSALM 101 GLOSSES]

835.[i] þis hundrid and o salm spekiþ of þe tyme of Crist, for in þe firste chapitre to Ebreis, Poul aleggiþ þe lettre of þis salm seid of Crist to þe lettre. þis salm spekiþ of þe angwisch of þe puple of Israel, preiynge wiþ desire for þe comynge of Crist. þis angwisch bifeld moost in þe tyme of Antiok þe noble.

Gostli, þis salm mai be expowned of ech man repentynge verili, which is turmentid for hise synnes bi penaunce, and bisechiþ God þat he come to him bi grace, and stablische him bi pacience in aduersitees, þat so in þe terme eþer ende of present liyf, he come to glorie. *Lire here.*

836.[ii] þat is, þat þat dwelliþ in þe panne of þe friyng. *Lire here.*

837. þat is, to my skyn, as Ierom and Ebreis seyn. *Lire here.*

Ps. 100 glosses    [i] *in the right margin; the first historical part of this gloss also in margin of* K
Ps. 101 glosses    [i] *next to the title in the right margin; this gloss also in margin of* K    [ii] *this gloss also in* bCGQSX

am maad as a solitarie sparowe in þe roof. [9] Al dai myn enemyes dispisiden me; and þei þat preisiden me[838] sworen aȝenes me.[839] [10] For I eet aischis as breed; and I medlide my drynke wiþ wepyng. [11] Fro þe face of þe ire of þyn indignacioun; for þou reisynge me hast hurtlid me doun. [12] Mi daies bowiden awei as [a][a] schadewe; and I wexide drie as hei. [13] But, Lord, þou dwellist wiþouten ende; and þi memorial in generacioun and into generacioun. [14] Lord, þou

f. 54ᵛ    risynge up | schalt haue merci on Sion;[840] for þe tyme to haue merci þerof comeþ, for þe tyme comeþ. [15] For þe stoones[841] þerof plesiden þi seruauntis; and þei shulen haue merci on þe lond þerof. [16] And, Lord, heþene men shulen drede þi name; and alle kyngis of erþe shulen drede þi glori. [17] For þe Lord haþ bildid Sion;[842] and he shal be seen in his glorie. [18] He bihelde on þe preier of meke men; and he dispiside not þe preier of hem. [19] Be þese þingis writun in an oþere generacioun; and þe puple[843] þat shal be maad shal preise þe Lord. [20] For he bihelde fro his [hiȝe][b] hooli place; þe Lord lokide fro heuene into erþe. [21] For to here þe weilyngis of feterid men; and for to vnbynde[844] þe sones of slayn men. [22] That þei telle in Sion[845] þe name of þe Lord; and his preisyng in Ierusalem. [23] In gaderyng togidere puplis into oon;[846] and kyngis, þat þei serue þe Lord. [24] It answeride to hym in þe weie of his vertu;[847] telle þou to me þe fewnesse of my daies.[848] [25] Aȝenclepe þou not me in þe myddil of my daies; þi ȝeeris ben in generacioun and into generacioun. [26] Lord, þou foundidist þe erþe in þe bigynnyng; and heuenes ben þe werkis of þyn hondis. [27] Tho shulen perische,[849] but þou dwellist perfitli; and alle shulen wexe eld as a clooþ. And þou shalt chaunge hem as an hilyng, and þo shulen be chaungid; [28] but þou art þe same þisilf,[850] and þi ȝeeris shulen not faile. [29] The sones of þi seruauntis schulen dwelle; and þe seed of hem shal be dressid into þe world.

## [PSALM 102]

*Benedic anima mea Domino*

[1] þe title of þe hundrid and ij salm. A salm to Dauiþ.[851]

f. 55ʳ    Mi soule, blesse | þou[852] þe Lord; and alle þingis þat ben wiþinne me, blesse his hooli name. [2] Mi soule, blesse þou þe Lord; and nyle þou forȝete alle þe ȝeldyngis of hym. [3] Which doiþ merci to alle þi

Ps. 101      ᵃ a] *om.*      ᵇ hiȝe] *om.*

838. In scorn. *Lire here.*

839. In Ierom þus: þei makinge ful out ioie of me, sworen bi me, þat is, bi an ooþ cursyng, settynge my wrecchidnesse for ensaumple and seiynge if Y do not þis, bifalle it yuele to me as to Iewis. *Lire here.*

840. þat is, on þe puple worschipyng God in Sion. *Lire here.*    f. 54ᵛ

841. þat is, feiþful men of Iewis conuertiden, plesiden þe postlis. *Lire here.*

842. þat is, hooli chirche þat bigan þere. *Lire here.*

843. þat is, cristen puple þat shal be maad in grace bi baptym. *Lire here.*

844. þat is, fro boondis of ign[o]raunce.ⁱⁱⁱ *Lire here.*

845. Bi Sion and Ierusalem is vndurstondun hooli chirche. *Lire here.*

846. þat is, into vnyte of feiþ formed wiþ charite. *Lire here.*

847. þat is, þe chirche answeride to Crist and it spekiþ of þing to comyng bi þe maner of þing passid, for þe certeynte of profesie; in þe weie of his vertu, þat is, pacience, þat shal be moost nedeful in þe persecucioun of Auntecrist;

848. Of my daies, þat is, of þe daies of my turment, þat Y mai be comfortid sumdeel bi þe shortnesse; in Ebreu and in Ierom þus: He turmentide my strengþe in þe weie; he made schort my daies;

my strengþe, for stronge men in feiþ shulen be turmentid þanne ouer mesure; in þe weie, of present liyf; my daies, þat is, of my turment for chosun men. *Lire here.*

849. Not as to substaunce but as to sum disposicioun. For bodies of heuene shulen moue fro ceessyng of place and bodies of elementis fro chaungyng and dyuersyng, while her substaunces shulen abide;

850. art þe same þisilf, þat is, vnchaungeable in al maner. *Lire here.*

## [PSALM 102 GLOSSES]

851.ⁱ Dauiþ made þis salm for to herie God, and he excitiþ men and aungelis and ech creature for to herie God. *Lire here.*

852. Mi soule blesse þou: bi soule ben vndurstondun alle þe    f. 55ʳ outward myȝtis of þe soule; bi þingis wiþ inne me ben vndurstondun þe innere myȝtis of þe soule, as vndurstondyng and wille and alle oþere. Blessyng is takun here for blessyng of knoulechyng, þat is, of Goddis heriyng, bi which þe lesse blessiþ þe more, and not for blessyng of halewyng, bi which þe more blessiþ þe lasse. *Lire here.*

þi soule sowne Goddis preisyngis, 'Whanne þou doist werk eiþer

---

ⁱⁱⁱ ignoraunce] ignaraunce
**Ps. 102 glosses**    ⁱ *next to the title in the left margin; this gloss also in margin of* K

wickidnessis; which heeliþ alle þi sijknessis. [4] Which aȝenbieþ þi lijf fro deþ; which corowneþ þee in merci and merciful doyngis. [5] Which filliþ þi desir in goodis; þi ȝongþe shal be renulid⁸⁵³ as þe ȝongþe of an egle. [6] The Lord doynge mercies; and doom to alle men suffrynge wrong. [7] [He]ᵃ made hise weies⁸⁵⁴ knowun to Moises; hise willis⁸⁵⁵ to þe sones of Israel. [8] The Lord is a merciful doere, and merciful in wille; longe abidinge and myche merciful. [9] He shal not be wrooþ wiþouten ende; and he shal not þretene wiþouten ende. [10] He dide not to us aftir oure synnes; neþer he ȝeldide to us aftir oure wickidnessis. [11] For bi þe hiȝnesse of heuene fro erþe; he made strong his merci on men dredynge hym. [12] As myche as þe eest is fer fro þe west; he made fer oure wickidnessis fro us. [13] As a fadir haþ merci on sones, þe Lord hadde merci on men dredynge him; [14] for he knew oure makyng.⁸⁵⁶ He biþouȝte þat we ben dust.⁸⁵⁷ [15] A man is as hei;⁸⁵⁸ his dai⁸⁵⁹ shal floure out so as a flour of þe feeld.⁸⁶⁰ [16] For þe spirit shal passe in hym, and shal not abide; and shal no more knowe his place.⁸⁶¹ [17] But þe merci of þe Lord is fro wiþout bigynnyng, and til into wiþouten ende; on men dredynge hym. And his riȝtfulnesse is into þe sones of sones; [18] to hem þat kepen [his]ᵇ testament.⁸⁶² And ben myndeful of hise comaundementis; to do þo. [19] The Lord haþ f. 55ᵛ maad redi his | seete in heuene; and his rewme shal be lord of alle. [20] Aungelis of þe Lord, blesse ȝe þe Lord; ȝe myȝti in vertu, doynge his word,⁸⁶³ to here þe vois of hise wordis. [21] Alle vertues of þe Lord, blesse ȝe þe Lord; ȝe mynystris of hym þat doon his wille. [22] Alle werkis of þe Lord, blesse ȝe þe Lord, in ech place of his lordschipe; my soule, blesse þou þe Lord.


[PSALM 103]

*Benedic anima mea Domino*

[1] *þe hundrid and iij salm haþ no title.*⁸⁶⁴

Mi soule, blesse þou þe Lord; my Lord God, þou art magnefied greetli.⁸⁶⁵ Thou hast cloþid knouleching⁸⁶⁶ and fairenesse; [2] and þou art cloþid wiþ liȝt, as wiþ a cloþ. And þou strecchist forþ heuene as a skyn; [3] and þou hilist wiþ watris þe hiȝere partis þerof. Which

Ps. 102     ᵃ He] *om.*     ᵇ his] my

etist, wher ȝe eten eiþer drynken eþer doon ony oþere þing, do ȝe alle þingis into þe glorie of God' [1 Cor 10: 31]. þe innocence of þi sleep is þe vois of þi soule, and blessiþ God. *Austin here.*

853. In þe risinge aȝen to comynge, in whiche þei shulen rise aȝen in mannis age. *Lire here.*

854. þat is, heestis of þe lawe;

855. Willis, þat is, hise bihestis þat schewen his wille. *Lire here.*

856. þat is, freelte enclynynge us to synne. *Lire here.*

857. As to þe bodi, which is resoluyd into dust;

858. as hey, greene at a litil tyme;

859. his dai, þat is, his liyf;

860. as a flour, which is dried at þe heete of þe sunne; so a mannis liyf is endid anoon, at þe heete of a feuer eþer of an oþere siyknesse. *Lire here.*

861. In Ierom it is, his place shal no more knowe hym. *Lire here.*

862. þat is, holden [it][ii] in herte and fillen it in werk. *Lire here.*

863. Doynge his word: 'ȝe'[iii] þat[iv] doon þe wille of þe Lord, blesse f. 55ᵛ hym, for alle men þat lyuen yuele, þouȝ þei ben stille wiþ tunge, cursen þe Lord bi her liyf. What profitiþ it þat þi tunge syngiþ heriyng, if þi lijf breþiþ out sacrilegie? In lyuynge yuele, þou hast sent manye tungis into blasfemye. þi tunge ȝyue tent to heriyng, and oþere tungis of hem þat biholden þee ȝyuen tent to blasfemyes. þerfor, if þou wolt blesse þe Lord, do þou his word, do his wille. If þou fyndist what yuel þou hast do, weile þou and knouleche. þi knoulechyng mai blesse þe Lord, if þi chaungyng dwelliþ stidfastli in blessyng. *Austyn here.*

[PSALM 103 GLOSSES]

864.[i] þer is no more in Ebreu neþer in Ierom. þis salm[m]akere[ii] indusiþ himsilf to herie God and bryngiþ resouns þerto; and efte he rehersiþ þe forseid heriyng. *Lire here.*

865. þat is, þou art of so greet excellence, þat þou maist not be heried of a creature, so myche as þou art worþi to be heried;

866. cloþid knoulechyng: bi knoulechyng is vndurstondun þe congregacioun of hooli aungelis knoulechyng to God bi þe knoule-chyng of Goddis heriyng; bi fairnesse is vndurstondun briȝte heuene. God is cloþid wiþ þese tweyne, for his glorie schyneþ pryncipali in þese creaturis. *Lire here.*

ⁱⁱ it] *om.*   ⁱⁱⁱ ȝe] *by the scribe above the line of writing*   ⁱᵛ þat] þat is, is *canc.*
**Ps. 103 glosses**   ⁱ *next to the title in the right margin; this gloss also in* I; *a variant gloss in* K: þe same glos þat þe salme bifore haþ   ⁱⁱ salm-makere] salmakere

settist a cloude þi stiyng;[867] which goist on þe feþeris of wyndis.[868]
[4] Which makist spiritis þyn aungelis;[869] and þi mynystris brennynge fier. [5] Which hast foundid þe erþe on his stabilnesse; it shal
not be bowid into þe world of world. [6] The depþe of watris[870] as a
clooþ is þe cloþyng þerof; watris shulen stonde[871] on hillis. [7] Tho
shulen fle fro þi blamyng; men shulen be aferd of þe vois of þi
þundur. [8] Hillis stien up and feeldis goen doun; into þe place
which þou hast foundid to þo. [9] Thou hast set a terme[872] which þei
shulen not passe; neþer þo shulen be turned for to hile þe erþe. [10]
And þou sendist out wellis in grete valeis; watris shulen passe
bitwixe þe myddis of hillis. [11] Alle þe beestis of þe feeld shulen
drynke; wielde assis shulen abide in her þirste.[873] [12] Briddis of þe
f. 56ʳ    eir shulen dwelle | on þo; fro þe myddis[874] of stoones þei shulen
ȝyue voices. [13] And þou moistist hillis[875] of her hiȝere þingis; þe
erþe shal be fillid of þe fruyt of þi werkis. [14] And þou bryngist forþ
hei to beestis; and eerbe to þe seruyce of men. That þou brynge forþ
breed of ʽþeʼ[a] erþe; [15] and þat wyn make glad þe herte of man.
That he make glad þe face wiþ oile; and þat breed make stidfast þe
herte of man. [16] The trees of þe feeld[876] shulen be fillid, and þe
cedris of þe Liban whiche he plauntide; [17] sparewis shulen make
nest þere. The hous of [þe][b] gerfaukun[877] is þe ledere of þo; [18] hiȝ
hillis ben refuytis to hertis; a stoon is refuyte to irchouns. [19] He
made þe moone into tymes; þe sunne knew his goynge doun. [20]
Thou hast set derknessis, and nyȝt is maad; alle beestis of þe wode
shulen go þerinne. [21] Liouns whelpis rorynge for to rauysche; and
to seke of God mete to hemsilf. [22] The sunne is risun, and þo ben
gaderid togidere; and þo shulen be set in her couchis. [23] A man
shal go out to his werk; and to his worchyng til to [þe][c] euentid. [24]
Lord, þi werkis ben magnefied ful[d] myche, þou hast maad alle þingis
in wisdom; þe erþe is fillid wiþ þi possessioun.[878] [25] The see is
greet and large to hondis;[879] þere ben crepynge beestis[880] of which is
no noumbre. Litle beestis wiþ grete; [26] schippis shulen passe þere.
This dragoun[881] which þou hast formed; for to scorne hym.[882]

---

867. In Ebreu and in Ierom it is, þi chaar. *Lire here.*
868. Of wyndis: þat is, þi swiftnesse passiþ þe swiftnesse of wyndis.
*Austyn here.*

**Ps. 103**    [a] þe] *added by the scribe in margin*    [b] þe] *om.*    [c] þe] *om.*    [d] ful] ful greetli,
greetli *canc.*

869. Which makist spiritis þin aungelis, þat is, messangeris. He seiþ brennynge in fier for aungelis brennen bi charite and ben spedeful to perfourme Goddis wille. *Lire here.*

870. þe depþe of watris, þat is, þe grete occian;

871. watris shulen stonde, þat is, watris of reyn þat ben gendrid in cloudis, shulen stonde on hillis. *Lire here.*

Eþer watris, þat is, persecuciouns of puplis shulen stonde on þe postlis and stidfast cristen men. *Austin here.*

872. To þe watris of occian. *Lire here.*

873. þat is, to be fillid wiþ þo watris in her þirst; þerfor Ierom haþ þus, and wilde assis shulen fille her þirste. *Lire here.*

874. In Ebreu it is, fro þe myddis of braunchis; and in Ierom it is, f. 56ʳ fro þe myddis of wodis. *Lire here.*

875. þat is, of cloudis ful of reyn gendrid on hillis. *Lire here.*

876. In Ebreu and in Ierom it is, þe trees of þe Lord, et cetera, briddis shulen make nest þere, for briddis of oþere kynde maken nest more in cedris, þan sparewen þat breden in þe roof of housis. *Lire here.*

877. þat is, in þe nest of gerfawcun which is in cedris. *Lire here.*

878. þat is, wiþ men and beestis, þat ben Goddis creaturis;

879. and large to hondis, þat is, in places, for þe [E]breuⁱⁱⁱ word here signefieþ boþe 'hondis' and 'places';

880. crepinge beestis, þat is, fischis. *Lire here.*

881. þis dragoun: In Ebreu and in Ierom þus, þou hast formed þis leuyatan, to pleie wiþ hym; þis dragoun eiþer leuyatan is a greet whal;

882. To scorne him eþer to pleie wiþ him: þat is, þat þe fischeris take him nyȝ þe lond where he mai not stire hymsilf, whidur he comeþ to deuoure oþere fischis. But [bi]ⁱᵛ þis dragoun eiþer leuyatan is vndurstondun principali þe deuel þat passiþ al bodili power in erþe, if he be suffrid to do al his power. Bi þe scornyng of þe whal is vndurstondun þe scornyng of þe deuel, for þe deuel bileuyng to deuoure Crist in his passioun and in hise membris in temporal persecucioun, which he stiriþ aȝenes hem, is defraudid of his purpos and aftir þe doom shal dwelle bounden in helle, for he shal no more be in þis derk eir, to þe excercise eþer trauelyng of hooli men. *Lire here.*

For to scorne him, þat is, þat he be scorned of Goddis aungelis; [*Austin here.*]ᵛ

[27] Alle þingis abiden of þee;<sup>883</sup> þat þou ȝyue to hem mete in tyme.
[28] Whanne þou shalt [ȝyue to hem, þei schulen gadere; whanne þou shalt]<sup>e</sup> opene þyn hond, alle þingis shulen be fillid wiþ good-
nesse.<sup>884</sup> [29] But | whanne þou shalt turne awei þe face, þei shulen
be disturblid; þou shalt take awei þe spirit of hem, and þei shulen
faile; and þei shulen turne aȝen into her dust. [30] Sende out<sup>885</sup> þi
spirit, and þei shulen be formed of þe newe; and þou shalt renule þe
face of [þe]<sup>f</sup> erþe. [31] The glorie of þe Lord be into þe world;<sup>886</sup> þe
Lord shal be glad in hise werkis. [32] Which biholdiþ þe erþe and
makiþ it to tremble; which touchiþ hillis, and þo smoken. [33] I shal
synge to þe Lord in my lijf;<sup>887</sup> I shal seie salm to my God, as longe as
I am. [34] Mi speche be myrie to him;<sup>888</sup> forsoþe I shal delite in þe
Lord. [35] Synneris<sup>889</sup> faile fro þe erþe, and wickid men <u>faile</u>, so þat
þei be not; my soule blesse þou þe Lord.

[PSALM 104]

*Confitemini Domino et inuocate*

[1] *þe title of þe hundrid and iiij salm. Alleluya.*<sup>890</sup>

Knoulech<sup>891</sup> ȝe to þe Lord, and inwardli clepe ȝe his name; telle ȝe
hise werkis among heþene men. [2] Synge ȝe to hym, and seie ȝe salm
to him, and telle ȝe alle hise meruelis; [3] be ȝe preisid<sup>892</sup> in his hooli
name. The herte of men sekynge þe Lord be glad; [4] seke ȝe þe Lord
and be ȝe confermyd; seke ȝe euere his face.<sup>893</sup> [5] Haue ȝe mynde on
hise meruelis, whiche he dide; on his grete wondris and domes of his
mouþ. [6] The seed of Abraham<sup>894</sup> his seruaunt; þe sones of Iacob his
chosen man. [7] He is oure Lord God; hise domes ben in al [þe]<sup>a</sup> erþe.
[8] He was myndeful of 'his'<sup>b</sup> testament into þe world;<sup>895</sup> of þe word
which he comaundide into a þousynde generaciouns.<sup>896</sup> [9] Which he
disposide to Abraham; and of his ooþ to Ysaac. [10] And he ordeynede
'it'<sup>c</sup> to Iacob into a comaundement; and [to]<sup>d</sup> Israel into euerlastinge |
testament. [11] And he seide, I shal ȝiue to þee þe lond of Chanaan; þe
cord of ȝoure eritage. [12] Whanne þei weren in a litil noumbre; and
þe comelyngis of h[e]m<sup>e</sup> weren ful fewe. [13] And þei passiden fro folk
into folk; and fro a rewme into anoþer puple. [14] He lefte not a man
to anoie hem; and he chastiside kyngis for hem. [15] Nile ȝe touche
my cristis;<sup>897</sup> and nyle ȝe do wickidli among my profetis. [16] And

<sup>e</sup> ȝue to hem . . . whanne þou schalt] *om.*    <sup>f</sup> þe] *om.*
**Ps. 104**    <sup>a</sup> þe] *om.*    <sup>b</sup> his] oure, *canc. and corrected by the scribe above the line of writing*
<sup>c</sup> it] *added by the scribe above the line of writing*    <sup>d</sup> to] *om.*    <sup>e</sup> hem] him

883. Alle þingis abiden of þee: If þou lyuest wel þou shalt haue
Crist þi mete; soþeli, if þou goist awei fro Crist, þou schalt be þe mete
of þe dragoun. If þou sauerist not erþeli þingis, þou art not erþe; if
þou art not erþe, þou art not etun of þe serpent. God ȝyueþ to þe
serpent his mete, whanne God wole and whom God wole. He demeþ
wel. He mai not be disseyued: he [ne]^vi ȝyueþ to þe serpent gold for
erþe. *Austyn here.*

884. þat is, wiþ good acording to her kynde. *Lire here.*

885. þat is, þou shalt sende out, for so it is in Ebreu and in Ierom.   f. 56^v
*Lire here.*

886. þat is, wiþouten ende. *Lire here.*

887. þat is, as longe as Y lyue. *Lire here.*

888. þat is, plesaunt bifor him. *Lire here.*

889. He spekiþ here of synneris and wickid men obstynat in her
malice. *Lire here.*

### [PSALM 104 GLOSSES]

890.^i þis hundrid and iiij salm is a stiryng to Goddis heriyng. And
firste þe profete^ii excitiþ þe puple for to herie God. And þat þis be
doon more spedili, he rehersiþ þe mynde of Goddis benefices. *Lire
here.*

891. þat is, bi knoulechyng of heriyng. *Lire here.*

892. þat is, do ȝe good werkis of kynde and for good entent of
Goddis glorie, þat so of þese werkis ȝe be preisid in þe name of þe
Lord. *Lire here.*

And þat men seinge ȝoure good werkis glorifie God. *Austyn here.*

893. þat is, presence. *Austin here.*

Eþer to plese in his siȝt. *Lire here.*

894. Ȝe þat ben þe seed of Abraham and ȝe þat ben þe sones of
Iacob, owen to haue mynde on þese þingis. *Lire here.*

895. þat is, wiþouten ende. *Austin here.*

896. þat is, to alle feiþful generaciouns. *Lire and Austin here.*

897. þat is, Abraham, Ysaac, and Iacob, þat weren cristis and   f. 57^r
profetis in bileuynge Cristis incarnacioun to comynge; wiþout which
feiþ, neuere man was recouncelid to God, neþer bifore neþer aftir þe
incarnacioun. *Austyn here.*

God clepide hungur on erþe; and he waastide al þe stidfastnesse of breed. [17] He sente a man bifore hem; Joseph was seeld into a seruaunt. [18] Thei maden lowe hise feet in stockis, irun passide by his soule;[898] [19] til þe word of hym cam. The speche of þe Lord enflawmyde hym,[899] [20] þe kyng sente and vnboond hym; þe prynce of puplis sente and delyueride hym. [21] He ordeynede him [þe][f] lord of his hous; and þe prynce of al his possessioun. [22] That he shulde lerne hise pryncis as hymsilf; and þat he shulde teche hise elde men prudence. [23] And Israel entride into Egipt; and Iacob was a comelyng in þe lond of Cham. [24] And God encreeside his puple greetli; and made hym stidfast on hise enemyes. [25] He turnyde[900] þe herte of hem, þat þei hatiden his puple; and diden gile aȝenes his seruauntis. [26] He sente Moises his seruaunt; þilke Aaron whom he chees. [27] He puttide in hem þe wordis of hise myraclis, and of hise grete wondris; in þe lond of Cham.[901] [28] He sente derknessis and made derk; and he made not bittir[902] hise wordis. [29] He turnyde þe watris of hem into blood; and he killide þe fischis of hem. [30] And þe lond of hem ȝaf pad|dockis; in þe pryuy places of þe kyngis of hem. [31] God seide and a fleisch flie[903] cam and gnattis; in alle þe coostis of hem. [32] He settide her reynes hail; fier brennynge in þe lond of hem. [33] And he smoot þe vynes of hem, and þe fige trees of hem; and al tobrak þe tree of þe coostis of hem. [34] He seide and a locuste[904] cam; and a bruke of which was no noumbre. [35] And it eet al þe hei in þe lond of hem; and it eet al þe fruyt of þe lond of hem. [36] And he killide ech þe firste gendrid þing in þe lond of hem; þe firste fruytis of[g] al þe trauel of hem. [37] And he ledde out hem wiþ siluer and gold; and noon was sijk in þe lynagis of hem. [38] Egipt was glad in þe goyng forþ of hem; for þe drede of hem lai on Egipcians. [39] He spredde abrood a cloude, into þe hilyng of hem; and fier þat it shynyde to hem bi nyȝt. [40] Thei axiden and a curlew[905] cam; and he fillide hem wiþ þe breed of heuene. [41] He brak a stoon and watris flowiden; floodis ȝeden forþ in þe drie place. [42] For he was myndeful of his hooli word; whiche he hadde to Abraham his child. [43] And he ledde out his puple in ful out ioiynge; and hise chosen men in gladnesse. [44] And he ȝaf to hem þe cuntreis of heþene men; and þei hadden in possessioun þe trauels of puplis. [45] That þei kepe hise iustefiyngis; and seke his lawe.

[f] þe] *om.*    [g] of] of þe lond of hem, þe lond of hem *canc.*

898. For of þe irone feteris he was turmentid not oneli in bodi but also in soule, þou3 he felde not fro þe vertu of pacience. *Lire here.*
899. In Ierom it is, <u>preuyde him</u>. *Lire here.*
900. God turnyde so þe herte of hem, þat bi enuye þei hatiden his puple. Not in makynge þe herte of hem yuele, but in doynge wel to his puple, he co[n]uertide<sup>iii</sup> her hertis yuel of fre wille to hatrede. *Austin here.*
901. þat is, in þe lond of Egipt. *Lire here.*
902. For whanne Farao bihi3te penaunce, God took awei þe veniaunce and so he made swete his word. *Lire here.*
903. þat is, þe multitude of fleish flies. *Lire here.* f. 57ᵛ
904. þat is, a multitude of locustis. *Lire here.*
905. þat is, þe multitude of curlewis. *Lire here.*

[PSALM 105 GLOSSES]

906.<sup>i</sup> <u>Alleluya</u> is set onys, for Goddis heriyng in present tyme; and efte, for his heriyng in heuene. For þe profete excitiþ men for to herie God; þe secounde tyme he axiþ Goddis grace. *Lire here.*
907. As if he seie, Noon, siþen he is of power wiþouten ende, and grettir þan ony preisyng. *Lire here.*
908. In demynge ri3tfuli, as to iugis; f. 58ʳ
909. <u>and doon ri3tfulnesse</u>, in lyuynge ri3tfuli wiþ þ[i]<sup>ii</sup> nei3bore, as to alle men; <u>in al tyme</u>, for he þat contynueþ þe good werk til into þe ende, shal be saaf. *Lire here.*
He kepiþ doom, þat demeþ ri3tfuli; he doiþ ri3tfulnesse, þat doiþ ri3tfuli. Eþer: kepiþ doom in feiþ and doiþ ri3tfulnesse in werk. *Austin here.*

[PSALM 105]

*Confitemini Domino*

[1] þe hundrid and fyueþe salm. *Alleluya, alleluya.*⁹⁰⁶

Knouleche 3e to þe Lord, for he is good; for his merci is wiþouten ende. [2] Who⁹⁰⁷ shal speke þe poweris of | þe Lord; shal make f. 58ʳ knowun alle hise preisyngis? [3] Blessid ben þei þat kepen doom;⁹⁰⁸ and doen ri3tfulnesse⁹⁰⁹ in al tyme. [4] Lord, haue þou mynde on us in

iii conuertide] couertide
Ps. 105 glosses  i next to the title in the left margin; this gloss also in I  ii þi] þe

þe good plesaunce of þi puple; visite þou us in þyn heelþe. [5] To se
in þe goodnesse of þi chosun men, to be glad in þe gladnesse of þi
folk; þat þou be heried wiþ þin eritage. [6] We han synned wiþ oure
fadris;⁹¹⁰ we han do vniustli, we han do wickidnesse. [7] Oure fadris in
Egipt vndurstoden not þi meruelis; þei weren not myndeful of þe
multitude of þi merci. And þei stiynge into þe see, into þe reed see,
terriden to wraþþe; [8] and he sauyde hem for his name, þat he shulde
make knowun his power. [9] And he departide þe reed see, and it was
dried; and he ledde forþ hem in þe depþis of watris as in desert. [10]
And he sauyde hem fro þe hond of hateris; and he aȝenbouȝte hem fro
þe hond of þe enemy. [11] And þe watir hilide men troblynge hem;
oon of hem abood not. [12] And þei bileuyden to hise wordis; and þei
preisiden þe heriynge of hym. [13] Thei hadden soone do,⁹¹¹ þei
forȝaten hise werkis; and þei abididen not⁹¹² his councel. [14] And þei
coueitiden coueitise in desert; and temptiden God in a place wiþout
watir. [15] And he ȝaf to hem þe axyng of hem; and he sente
fulnesse⁹¹³ into þe soulis of hem. [16] And þei wraþþiden Moyses
in þe castels; Aaron, þe hooli of þe Lord. [17] The erþe was openyd,
and swolewide Datan; and hilide on þe congregacioun^a of Abiron. [18]
And fier brente an hiȝ in þe synagoge of hem; flawme brente
f. 58ᵛ  synneris.⁹¹⁴ [19] And þei maden a calf in Oreb; | and worschipiden
a ȝotun⁹¹⁵ ymage. [20] And þei chaungiden her glorie;⁹¹⁶ into þe
licnesse of a calf etynge hei. [21] Thei forȝaten God þat sauyde hem,
þat dide grete werkis in Egipt, [22] meruelis in þe lond of Cham;
feerdful þingis in þe reed see. [23] And God seide þat he wolde leese
hem; if Moises, ʻhisʼ^b chosun man, hadde not stonde in þe brekyng⁹¹⁷
of his siȝt. That he shulde turne awei his ire; lest he loste hem. [24]
And þei hadden⁹¹⁸ þe desirable lond for nouȝt, þei bileuyden not to
his word, [25] and þei grucchiden in her tabernaclis; þei herden not þe
vois of þe Lord. [26] And he reiside his hond on hem; to caste doun
hem in desert. [27] And to caste awei her seed in naciouns; and for to
leese hem in cuntreis. [28] And þei maden sacrifice to Beelfegor; and
þei eeten þe sacrifices of deed beestis.⁹¹⁹ [29] And þei wraþþiden God
in her fyndyngis; and fallyng, eþer deþ, was multeplied in hem. [30]
And Fynees stood and pleside God; and þe veniaunce ceesside. [31]
And it was arrettid to hym to riȝtfulnesse; in generacioun and into
generacioun, til into wiþouten ende. [32] And þei wraþþiden God at

**Ps. 105**    ^a þe congregacioun] *corrected by a 3rd, more formal hand on an erasure*    ^b his]
þe, *canc. and corrected by the scribe above the line of writing*

910. þat is, as oure fadris, suynge þe synnes of hem. *Lire here.*

911. þat is, þei stoden litil tyme in þe heriyng of God;

912. <u>abididen not, et cetera</u>: þat is, þei abididen not pacientli þe tyme wherinne God disposide to helpe hem bi þe councel of his wille, but þei camen bifor it in grucching wiþout resoun. *Lire here.*

913. In Ebreu and in Ierom it is, <u>and he sente þynnesse into þe soulis of hem</u>, þat is, defaute of lyuyng and of quykenyng of bodies, for he killide manye of hem. *Lire here.*

914. Scripture is wont to clepe synneris ful wickid men and greuyd wiþ heuy birþun of synnes. *Austin here.*

915. þe Latyn word here signefieþ here propirli a grauun ymage, but þis word is set here for a ʒotun ymage, for þat calf was not maad bi grauyng but bi ʒetyng, as it is seid in xxxij capitulo of Exodi; wherfor in Ebreu and in Ierom it is, <u>and þei worschipiden a ʒotun ymage</u>. *Lire here.*

916. þat is, veri God, in whom þei ouʒten to haue glorie. *Lire here.*

917. Not þat he brak þe ire of God, but <u>in þe brekyng</u>, þat is, in þe veniaunce bi which þei shulden be slayn. *Austin here.*

For Moises bi hise preieris lettide þe affect of Goddis veniaunce. *Lire here.*

918. Here bigynneþ þe vers in Ebreu and in Ierom;

<u>for nouʒt</u>, þat is, þei settiden no priys þerbi, whanne þei wolden turne aʒen into Egipt. *Lire here.*

919. þat is, of fleisch of beestis offrid to idols. *Lire here.*

920. þat is, d[i]sturblid[iii] in soule, in so myche he doutide lest God wolde denye watir to hem for her malice, and so he bileuyde not fulli to Goddis word;

921. <u>and he departide in hise lippis</u>, þat is, shewide openli in þe maner of spekyng þe doutyng of his herte; for which þing anoon he was repreuyd of þe Lord and was excludid fro þe entryng of þe lond of biheest. *Lire here.*

922. Here bigynneþ þe vers in Ebreu and in Ierom. *Lire here.*

f. 58ᵛ

---

þe watris of aʒenseiynge; and Moises was trauelid[920] for hem, [33] for þei maden bittir his spirit, and he departide in hise lippis.[921] [34] Thei losten[922] not heþene men; whiche þe Lord seide to hem. [35] And þei

---

weren medlid among heþene men, and lernyden þe werkis of hem, [36] and seruyden þe grauun ymagis of hem; and it was maad to þem into sclaundir. [37] And þei offriden her sones; and her douȝtris to fendis. [38] And þei schedden out innocent blood, þe blood of her sones and of her douȝtris; whiche þei sacrifisiden to þe grauun ymagis of Chanaan. | And þe erþe was slayn⁹²³ in bloodis, [39] and was defoulid in þe werkis of hem; and þei diden fornycacioun⁹²⁴ in her fyndyngis. [40] And þe Lord was wrooþ bi stronge veniaunce aȝenes his puple; and hadde abhomynacioun of his eritage. [41] And he bitook hem into þe hondis of heþene men; and þei þat hatiden hem weren lordis of hem. [42] And her enemyes diden tribulacioun to hem, and þei weren mekid vndur þe hondis of enemyes; [43] ofte he delyueride hem. But þei wraþþiden hym in her councel; and þei weren maad low in her wickidnessis. [44] And he siȝ whanne þei weren set in tribulacioun; and he herde þe preier of hem. [45] And he was myndeful of his testament; and it repentide⁹²⁵ hym bi þe multitude of his merci. [46] And he ȝaf hem into mercies; in þe siȝt of alle men þat hadden take hem. [47] Oure Lord God, make þou us saaf; and gadere togidere us fro naciouns. That we knouleche to þyn hooli name; and haue glorie in þi preisyng. [48] Blessid be þe Lord God of Israel fro þe world and til into þe world;⁹²⁶ [and al þe puple shal seie],ᶜ Be it don,⁹²⁷ be it don.

f. 59ʳ

### [PSALM 106]

*Confitemini Domino*

[1] *þe title of þe hundrid and sixte salm. Alleluya.*⁹²⁸

Knoulech ȝe to þe Lord, for he is good; for his merci is into þe world.⁹²⁹ [2] Seie þei þat ben aȝenbouȝte of þe Lord; whiche he aȝenbouȝte fro þe hond of þe enemye; fro cuntreis he gaderide hem togidere. [3] Fro þe risyng of þe sunne and fro þe goynge doun; fro þe norþ and fro þe see. [4] Thei erriden in wildirnesse in a place wiþout watir; þei founden not weie of þe citee of dwellynge place. [5] Thei weren | hungri and þirsti; her soule failide in hem. [6] And þei crieden to þe Lord whanne þei weren set in tribulacioun; and he delyueride hem fro her nedynessis. [7] And he ledde forþ hemᵃ in[to]ᵇ þe riȝt weie; þat þei shulden go into þe citee of dwelling. [8] The

f. 59ᵛ

ᶜ and al þe puple schal seye] *om.*
**Ps. 106** ᵃ hem] hem forþ ᵇ into] to *om.*

923. þat is, pollutid. *Lire here.*

924. þat is, idolatrie in her synnes doon wiþ studie and greet diligence. *Lire here.*

925. þat is, hadde himsilf at þe manere of a repentere, whanne he brouȝte aȝen fro caitifte hem whiche he hadde maad prisoneris. *Lire here.*

926. þat is, fro wiþout bigynnynge til `in´toⁱᵛ wiþouten ende. *Austyn here.*

927. In Ebre[u]ᵛ it is onys, <u>Amen</u>. *Lire here.*

## [PSALM 106 GLOSSES]

928.ⁱ þis salm is a stiryng to doynge of þankyngis of what euere men delyuerid bi God fro perelis and angwischis.

Austyn seiþ þat þis salm is doyng of þankyngis for þe general redempcioun maad bi Crist, which redempcioun þe salmmakere biforsiȝ in spirit; and herto he bryngiþ þis lettre: <u>Seie þei now þat ben aȝenbouȝte of þe Lord</u>, et cetera, and fro whennes þis redempcioun is maad it sueþ, <u>fro þe risyng of þe sunne</u>, et cetera; but þe lettre suynge acordiþ not, which semeþ not of þe redempcioun maad bi Crist but more of delyueraunce fro summe bodili perelis. þe exposicioun of Austin semeþ more goostli þan literal vndurstonding. *Lire here.*

929. þat is, into wiþouten ende. *Austyn here.*

930. þat is, brynge hem to knouleche to which[e]ⁱⁱ þo ben doon. *Lire here.*

931. þat is, maad feble bi goynge of þe weie. *Lire here.*

932. þat is, God spekinge bi þe lawe and profetis. *Lire here.*

---

mercies of þe Lord knouleche⁹³⁰ to hym; and hise meruelis `knou-leche´ᶜ to þe sones of men. [9] For he fillide a voide man;⁹³¹ and he fillide wiþ goodis an hungri man. [10] <u>God delyueride</u> men sittynge in derknessis and in þe schadewe of deþ; and men prisoned in beggerie and in irun. [11] For þei maden bittir þe spechis⁹³² of God; and wraþþiden þe councel of þe hiȝeste. [12] And þe herte of hem was

ⁱᵛ into] *corrected by the scribe above the line of writing* ᵛ Ebreu] Ebre
**Ps. 106 glosses** ⁱ *next to the title in the right margin; this gloss also in margin of* K
ⁱⁱ whiche] whicho

ᶜ knouleche] *added in margin by the scribe*

maad meke in trauelis; and þei weren sijk, and noon was þat helpide. [13] And þei crieden to þe Lord, whanne þei weren set in tribulacioun; and he delyuyride hem fro her nedynessis. [14] And he ledde hem out of derknessis and schadewe of deþ; and brak þe boondis of hem. [15] The mercies⁹³³ of þe Lord knouleche to hym; and hise meruelis <u>knoulech</u> to þe sones of men. [16] For he al tobrak brasun ȝatis; and he brak irone barris. [17] He uptook hem fro þe weie of her wickidnesse; for þei weren maad low for her vnriȝtfulnessis. [18] The soule of hem wlatide al mete; and þei neiȝiden til to þe ȝatis of deþ. [19] And þei crieden to þe Lord whanne þei weren set in tribulacioun; and he delyuyride hem fro her nedynessis. [20] He sente his word and heelide hem; and delyueride hem fro þe perischyngis of hem. [21] The mercies of þe Lord knouleche to him; and hise meruelis to þe sones of men. [22] And offre þei þe sacrifice of heriyng; and telle þei hise wer|kis in ful out ioiyng.⁹³⁴ [23] Thei þat goon doun into þe see in schippis; and maken worchyng in manye watris. [24] Thei sien þe werkis of þe Lord; and hise meruelis in þe depþe. [25] He seide and þe spirit of tempest stood;⁹³⁵ and þe wawis þerof weren arerid. [26] Thei stien til to heuenys, and goen doun til to þe depþis; þe soule of hem failide in yuelis. [27] Thei weren troblid and þei weren mouyd as a drunken man; and al þe wisdom of hem was deuourid. [28] And þei crieden to þe Lord whanne þei weren set in tribulacioun; and he led out hem fro her nedynessis. [29] And he ordeynede þe tempest þerof into [a]ᵈ softe wynd, <u>eþer pesiblete</u>; and þe wawis þerof weren stille. [30] And þei weren glad for þo weren stille; and he ledde hem forþ into þe hauene of her wille. [31] The mercies of þe Lord knouleche to hym; and hise meruelis to þe sones of men. [32] And enhaunce þei hym in þe chirche of þe puple; and preise þei hym in þe chaier of eldere men. [33] He haþ set floodis⁹³⁶ into desert; and þe outgoyngis of watris⁹³⁷ into þirst. [34] <u>He haþ set</u> fruytful lond into saltnesse;⁹³⁸ for þe malice of men dwellyng þerinne. [35] He haþ set desert into poondis of watris; and erþe wiþout watir into ‘out‘goyngisᵉ of watris. [36] And he settide þere hungri men; and þei maden a citee of dwellinge. [37] And þei sowiden feeldis, and plauntiden vynes; and maden fruyt of birþe.⁹³⁹ [38] And he blesside hem, and þei weren multeplied gretli; and he made not lesse her werk-beestis.⁹⁴⁰ [39] And þei weren maad fewe; and þei weren trauelid of tribulacioun of yuelis and of sorewe. [40] Strijf was sched out on prynces; | and he made

f. 60ʳ

f. 60ᵛ

---

ᵈ a] *om.*    ᵉ outgoyngis] out- *added by the scribe above the line of writing*

933. þis vers is rehersid foure siþis in þis salm, for foure temptaciouns. þat ben: þe errour of treuþe and þe hungur of Goddis word, þe hardnesse to lyue wel, þe anoie of Goddis word, and temp[estes]<sup>iii</sup> of perels to gouerne þe chirche. Bi hou myche we ben onourid more, bi so myche we ben in more perel. He mai not knouleche to God þat wolde not taaste his swetnesse. For wherof shal he seie þat a þing is swete, which he knowiþ not? *Austin here.*

934. Of deuocioun, not of dissolucioun. *Lire here.*                    f. 60<sup>r</sup>

935. þis signefieþ not þe restyng of þe wynd, but more þe strengþe þerof; and þerfor in Ierom it is, <u>He seide and þe wynd of tempest roos</u>. *Lire here.*

936. In makyng þo drie, at þe maner of desert;

937. <u>and þe outgoyngis, et cetera</u>, þat is, wellis into drienesse. *Lire here.*

938. þat is, into bareynnesse. *Lire here.*

939. þat is, kyndli fruyt and good. *Lire here.*

940. þat is, he multeplied þo. *Lire here.*

941. þat is, suffride hem bi his iust doom to erre in goynge out of þe    f. 60<sup>v</sup> weie, fro þe<sup>iv</sup> doom of riȝt resoun. *Lire here.*

942. <u>Helpide þe pore man of beggerie</u>:<sup>v</sup> þis beggere is he þat arettiþ no þing to himsilf and abidiþ al of Goddis merci. Ech dai he crieþ bifor þe lordis ȝate, and knockiþ þat it be openyd to him, nakid and quakyng þat he be cloþid, and castiþ doun þe iȝen into þe erþe, and smytiþ þe breste. This pore man is manye meynees, manye puplis, manye chirchis, o chirche, o puple, o meynee, o scheep. God helpide ful myche þis begger, þis meke man, ȝhe, bi departyng of eretikis. *Austin here.*

943. <u>Forþ lambren</u>, þat is, multeplied hem in temporal goodis and children; <u>and al wickidnesse</u>, þat is, ech wickid man. *Lire here.*

---

hem<sup>941</sup> for to erre wiþout `þe´<sup>f</sup> weie, and not in þe weie. [41] And he helpide þe pore man fro pouert;<sup>942</sup> and settide [meynees]<sup>g</sup> as [a] scheep<sup>h</sup> bryngynge forþ lambren. [42] Riȝtful men shulen se and schulen be glad; and al wickidnesse<sup>943</sup> shal stoppe his mouþ. [43] Who

---

<sup>iii</sup> tempestes] temptacioun    <sup>iv</sup> fro þe] þe þe    <sup>v</sup> of beggerie] *the lemma in the psalm text reads* fro pouert\*

<sup>f</sup> þe] *added by the scribe above the line of writing*    <sup>g</sup> meynees] *om.*    <sup>h</sup> as a scheep] as scheep as scheep, a *om. and dittography canc.*

is wijs and shal kepe þese þingis; and shal vndurstonde þe mercies of
þe Lord?

*Paratum cor meum Deus*

[1] *þe title of þe hundrid and vij salm. The song of þe salm of Dauiþ.*⁹⁴⁴

[2] Myn herte is redi, God, myn herte is redi; I shal synge and I shal
seie salm in my glorie.⁹⁴⁵ [3] My glorie, rise þou up, sautre and harpe,
rise þou up; I shal rise up eerli. [4] Lord, I shal knouleche to þee
among puplis; and I shal seie salm to þee among naciouns. [5] Forwhi,
God, þi merci is greet on heuenys;⁹⁴⁶ and þi treuþe is til to þe cloudis.
[6] God, be þou enhaunsid aboue heuenes; and þi glorie ouer al erþe.
[7] That⁹⁴⁷ þi derlyngis be delyuerid, make þou saaf wiþ þi riȝthond
and here me; [8] God spak in his hooli. I shal make ful out ioie, and I
schal departe Siccyman; and I shal mete þe grete valei of tabernaclis.
[9] Galaad is myn, and Manasses is myn; and Effraym is þe uptakyng
of myn heed. Iuda is my king; [10] Moab is þe cawdrun of myn hope.
Into Ydumee I shal strecche forþ my schoo; aliens ben maad freendis
to me. [11] Who schal lede me forþ into a strong citee; who shal lede
me forþ til into Ydume? [12] Wher not þou, God, þat hast putte us
awei; and, God, shalt not þou go out in oure vertues? [13] Ȝyue þou
f. 61ʳ help to us of tribulacioun; for þe helþe of man is veyn. | [14] We
schulen make vertu in God; and he shal brynge oure enemyes to
nouȝt.

*Deus laudem meam*

[1] *þe title of þe hundrid and viij salm. In Ebreu þus: To victorie, þe salm
of Dauiþ. In Ierom þus: For victorie, þe song of Dauiþ.*⁹⁴⁸

[2] God, holde þou not stille my preisyng;⁹⁴⁹ for þe mouþ of þe
synnere⁹⁵⁰ and þe mouþ of þe gileful man is openyd on me. [3] Thei
spaken aȝenes me wiþ a gileful tunge, and þei cumpassiden me wiþ
wordis of hatrede; and fouȝten aȝenes me wiþout cause. [4] For þat
þing þat þei shulden loue me, þei bacbitiden me;⁹⁵¹ but I preiede. [5]
And þei settiden aȝenes me yuelis for goodis; and hatrede for my
loue. [6] Ordeyne þou⁹⁵² a synnere on him; and þe deuel stonde on
his riȝthalf. [7] Whanne he is demed, go he out condempned; and his

[PSALM 107 GLOSSES]

944. þis salm is þe doynge of þankingis for þe restoring of þe rewme of Israel into good staat in þe tyme of Dauiþ, whanne God hadde grauntid to him victorie of hise enemyes and moost of Ydumeis, whiche he brouȝte vndur tribute. *Lire here.*

945. þat is, my profesie, forwhi glorie is cleer knowing wiþ preisyng, and Dauiþ hadde ful cleer knowing among oþere profetis, and brouȝte his profesie bi þe maner of Goddis heriynge. *Lire here.*

946. þat is, cam forþ of Goddis merci þat whanne summe aungelis felden doun fro heuene, oþere abidyng weren confermyd. *Lire here.*

947. Here bigynneþ þe vers in Ebreu and in Ierom. *Lire here.*

[PSALM 108 GLOSSES]                                                    f. 61ʳ

948.[i] Seynt Petre seiþ in ij capitulo of Dedis þat þe lettre of þis hundrid salm and viij is vndurstondun of Cristis passioun; and Iudas bitraiede him for auarise and þe Iewis bitraied him for enuye. þe firste [part][ii] of þe salm declariþ þe peyne of Iewis for Cristis deþ, þat weren conquerid of Romayns and her lond was distried. þe secounde part declariþ þe[iii] ordenaunce of Mathie into þe office of apostle. *Lire here.*

949. þat is, dilaie þou not to here my preier, wherinne God is preisid;

950. mouþ of þe synnere, þat is, þe cumpenye of prestis þat firste knewen Crist þat he was sent of God, but þei hadden so greet enuye and hatrede aȝenes him, for he repreuyde her synnes, þat þis knowing of Crist was maad derk; of þe gileful, þat is, of Iudas þe traitour. *Lire here.*

951. Bacbitiden me: Herfor þei killiden Crist, for þei bacbitiden, denyinge him þe sone of God and seiynge þat, 'In þe prince of fendis he castiþ out fendis' [Luke 11: 15]. 'He haþ a fend and is wood. What heren ȝe him?' [John 10: 20]. Bi which bacbityng þei turnyden awei fro him þo men whose conuersacioun he souȝte. And herfor Crist seide raþere þis, to shewen þat þei anoien more þat bacbiten Crist and sleen soulis bi þis, þan þei þat bi cruelte killiden þe dedli fleisch of Crist. But Goddis spechis techen us, bi ensaumple of Crist, þat whanne we fynden vnkynde men ȝeldyng yuel for good, we preie for hem. *Austyn here.*

952. þat is, þou shalt ordeyne Caifas. *Lire here.*

---

**Ps. 108 glosses**    [i] *next to the title in the right margin*    [ii] part] *om.*    [iii] þe] þe office, office *canc.; a variant gloss in margin of* K: A glos: þis salm is seid of Crist to þe lettre, for Crist in þe xxij chapitre of Matthew and Poul in j chapitre and vj chapitre to Ebreis, aleggeþ þe lettre of þis salm seid of Crist, and so doon oolde doctours of Ebreis, and it mai be applied to Iudas. Li[re] he[re].

preier[953] be maad into synne. [8] Hise daies be maad fewe; and an
oþere take his bischopriche.[954] [9] Hise sones be maad fadirles; and
his wijf a widewe. [10] Hise sones[955] tremblyng be borun ouer and
begge; and be caste out of her abitaciouns. [11] An vsurer seke al his
catel;[956] and aliens rauysche hise trauelis. [12] [N]oon[a] helpere be to
hym; neþer ony be þat haue merci on hise modirles children. [13]
Hise sones be maad into perischyng; þe name of hym be doon awei
in o generacioun.[957] [14] The wickidnesse of hise fadris come aȝen
into mynde in þe siȝt of þe Lord; and þe synne of his modir be not
doon awei. [15] Be þei maad euere aȝenes þe Lord; and þe mynde of
hem perische fro erþe. [16] For þat[958] þing þat he þouȝte not to do
merci, [17] and he pursuyde a pore man and beggere;[959] [and][b] to sle
a man compunct in herte. | [18][c] And he louyde cursyng, and it shal
come to hym; and he nolde blessyng, and it shal be maad fer fro him.
And he cloþid cursyng as a clooþ, and it entride as watir into hise
innere þingis; and as oile in hise boonys. [19] Be it maad to him as a
clooþ wiþ which he is hilid; and as a girdil, wiþ which he is euere
gird. [20] This is þe werk[960] of hem þat bacbiten me anentis þe Lord;
and þat speken yuelis aȝenes my lijf. [21] And þou, Lord, Lord, do
wiþ me for þi name;[961] for þi merci is swete. Delyuere þou me, [22]
for I am nedi and pore; and myn herte is disturblid wiþinne me. [23]
I am takun awei as [a][d] schadewe, whanne it bowiþ awei; and I am
schakun awei as locustis.[962] [24] Mi knees[963] ben maad feble of
fastyng; and my fleisch was chaungid for oile.[964] [25] And I am maad
schenschipe to hem; þei sien me, and mouyden her heedis. [26] Mi
Lord God, helpe þou me; and make þou me saaf bi þi merci. [27]
And þei shulen wite þat þis is þyn hond; and þou, Lord, hast do it.
[28] Thei shulen curse and þou schalt blesse, þei þat risen aȝenes me
be schent; but þi seruaunt shal be glad. [29] Thei þat bacbiten me be
cloþid wiþ schame; and be þei hilid wiþ her shenschipe as wiþ a
double-clooþ.[965] [30] I shal knouleche to þe Lord greetli wiþ my
mouþ; and I shal herie hym in þe myddil of manye men. [31] Which
stood nyȝ on þe riȝthalf of a pore man;[966] to make saaf my soule fro
pursueris.

953. [Whanne he is demed]:[iv] þis is seid of Iudas; his preier, þat is, þe resoun of his mouþ, þat was maad to þe prynces of prestis þat þei shulden bitake to him a cumpenye of armed men;

954. an oþere take his bischopriche, þat is, apostleheed; wherfor bischopis in þe chirche ben successours of apostlis, as Decrees witnessen in xxj distinccioun capitulo, in nouo testamento. *Lire here.*

955. þat is, of þe puple of Iewis þat weren takun prisoneris and distried of þe Romayns;

956. An vserere: in Ierom it is, a[v] maistirful axere. *Lire here.*

957. þat is, wiþinne þe tyme of o generacioun; for þei þat leften of þe Iewis weren scaterid bi dyuerse partis of þe world and ben soiet to oþere folkis, so þat þei make not o puple bi hemsilf, hauynge ony lond eþer lordschipe. *Lire here.*

958. Here bigynneþ þe vers in Ebreu and in Ierom. *Lire here.*

959. þat is, Crist in hise membris, of whiche it is seid, 'As longe as ȝe diden to oon of myn leeste, ȝe diden to me' [Matt 25: 40]. What is to begge? No but to lyue at þe merci of men, as Iewis lyuen vndur þe kinges of þo heþene men into whiche þei ben translatid. *Austyn here.*

960. þat is, þe peyne þat is biforseid is ȝoldun for yuel werk. *Lire*   f. 61ᵛ *here.*

961. þat is, do þou merci in reisinge me aȝen and glorifiynge me, þat þi name be glorified bi myn enhaunsyng. *Lire here.*

962. þat is, passinge fro place to place in fleynge persecucioun. *Lire here.*

Eiþer þis is vndurstondun more couenabli in þe membris of Crist. [*Austin here.*][vi]

963. And My knees, et cetera: þis is also vndurstondun in þe membris of Crist. *Austin here.*

964. þat is, chaungid into leene for defaute of oile, wherinne is signefied þe scarsnesse of his mete, wantynge souful. þerfor in Ierom it is, and my fleisch was maad leene wiþouten oile; and in Ebreu it is, and my fleisch was maad leene of fatnesse. *Lire here.*

965. In Ierom it is, as wiþ a mentil. *Lire here.*

966. þat is, of Crist, pore in himsilf and in hise membris. *Lire here.*

---

[PSALM 109]

*Dixit Dominus Domino meo*[a]

[1] þe title of þe hundrid and ix salm. The salm of Dauiþ.[967]

f. 62[r]    The Lord[968] seide to my Lord: Sitte þou on my riȝt side. Til I putte þin enemyes; a stool of þi feet. [2] The Lord shal sende out fro Syon þe ȝerde of þi vertu;[969] be þou lord in þe myddis of þyn enemyes. [3] The bigynnyng[970] is wiþ þee in þe dai of þi vertu, in þe briȝtnessis of seyntis; I gendride þee of þe wombe bifor þe dai-sterre. [4] The Lord swoor,[971] and it shal not repente hym; þou art a preest wiþouten ende, bi þe ordre of Melchisedech. [5] The Lord on þi riȝt side; haþ broke kyngis in þe dai of his veniaunce. [6] He shal deme among naciouns, he shal fille fallyngis;[972] he shal shake heedis in þe lond of manye men.[973] [7] He drank of þe stronde in þe weie;[974] þerfor he enhaunsid þe heed.

[PSALM 110]

*Confitebor tibi domine*

[1] þe title of þe hundrid and tenþe salm. Alleluya.

Lord, I shal knouleche to þee in al myn herte; in þe councel and congregacioun of iust men. [2] The werkis of þe Lord ben grete; souȝt[a] out into alle hise willis. [3] His werk is knoulechyng and grete doyng; and his riȝtfulnesse dwelliþ into þe world of world. [4] The Lord merciful in wille and a merciful doere, haþ maad a mynde of hise meruelis; [5] he haþ ȝoue mete to men dredynge hym. He shal be myndeful of his testament into þe world; [6] he shal telle to his puple

[PSALM 109 GLOSSES]

967.[i] þis hundrid and ix salm is seid of Crist to þe lettre, for Crist in xxij capitulo of Matheu and Poul in j capitulo and vij capitulo to Ebreis aleggen þe lettre of þis salm seid of Crist, and so doon old doctours of Ebreis. *Lire here.*

f. 62[r]    968. þe Lord, þat is, God þe fadir, seide to my Lord, þat is, to Ihesu Crist, whom Dauiþ clepiþ his lord for resoun of his godheed, sitte þou on my riȝt side: þis was fillid in his assencioun;

Ps. 109    [a] Dixit Dominus Domino meo] *on f. 62[r], following the title*
Ps. 110    [a] souȝt] sout, *corrected by the scribe above the line of writing*

Ps. 109 glosses    [i] *next to the title in the left margin*

969. þe ȝerde of þi vertu, þat is, power to teche in alle langagis, to do myraclis to þe confermyng of teching. [*Lire here.*][ii]

þe ȝerde of þi vertu, þat is, þe rewme of þi power, for 'þou shalt gouerne hem in an ȝerde of irun' [Apoc. 2: 27]. The profete spekiþ not here of Cristis rewme, bi whiche he regneþ euere bi þe godheed, but of þe rewme bi which he bigan to regne in cristen men. *Austin here.*

970. þe bigynnyng, þat is, þe fadir, is wiþ þee, for þou art euene wiþ þe fadir and art departid fro hym bi persoone; in þe dai of þi vertu, þat is, in þe clerenesse of heuenli blisse, where Cristis vertu boþe of godhed and of manheed is seyn clereli of seyntis; and þe fadir seiþ to þe sone, Y gendride þee of þe wombe, þat is, of my substaunce, bifor þe dai-sterre, þat is, bifor þe makynge of sterris and of tyme, and so wiþout bigynnyng. [*Lire here.*][iii]

þe bigynnynge, et cetera: in Ebreu þus, þi puplis ben prynces in þe dai of þi vertu in hooli fairnesse; fro þe wombe of þe morewtid þe deew of þi ȝonge wexinge age is to þee:

þi puplis, þat is, apostlis and oþere disciplis, ben maad prynces on al erþe to teche þe gospel, in þe dai of þi vertu, þat is, in Witsundai, in whiche þi vertu was declarid bi þe sendyng of þe hooli goost in open signe; in hooli fairnesse, for þe grace of þe hooli goost halewiþ and makiþ fair; fro þe wombe of þe morewtid, þat is, of þe virgyn; þe deew, þat is, þe bodi formed bi þe vertu of þe hooli goost of þe clenneste blood of þe blessid virgyn, as deew is gendrid bi heuenli vertu in mater of moisture; of þi ȝonge[iv] wexynge age, for Goddis sone, vnchaungeable and euerelastynge, was maad a ȝong child and a ȝonge wexinge man and at þe laste a perfite man, in þe bodi takun of þe virgyn. *Lire here.*

971. þe Lord swoor, þat is, ordeynede stidfastli and wiþout chaunginge. *Lire here.*

972. Fallyngis: in Ebreu it is, deed bodies, for þe bodies of deed men shulen be reisid and fillid wiþ soulis bi Goddis vertu;

973. manye men: þat is, he shal dampne greuousli þe tirauntis of þis world, þat weren prynces and capteyns on oþere men, for in manye londis tirauntrie is more usid þan regnyng;

974. in þe weie, þat is, of þe fersnesse of tribulacioun and passioun in þis liyf. *Lire here.*

---

[ii] Lire here] *om.*    [iii] Lire here] *om.*    [iv] ȝonge] ȝonge ȝonge ȝonge, *only the third* ȝonge canc.*

þe vertu of hise werkis. [7] That he ȝyue to hem þe eritage of folkis; þe werkis of hise hondis ben treuþe and doom. [8] Alle hise comaundementis ben feiþful, confermed into þe world of world; maad in treuþe and | equyte. [9] The Lord sente redempcioun to hys puple; he comaundide his testament wiþouten ende. His name is hooli and dredeful; [10] þe bigynnyng of wisdom is þe drede of þe Lord. Good vndurstondyng^975 is to alle þat doen it; his preisyng dwelliþ into þe world of world.

### [PSALM 111]

*Beatus uir qui timet Dominum*

[1] *þe title of þe hundrid and xj salm.*^976 *Alleluya.*

Blessid is þe man þat drediþ þe Lord; he shal wilne ful myche in hise comaundementis. [2] His seed shal be myȝti in erþe; þe generacioun of riȝtful men shal be blessid. [3] Glorie and richessis ben in his hous; and his riȝtfulnesse^977 dwelliþ into þe world of world. [4] Liȝt is risun up in derknessis to riȝtful men; þe Lord^978 is merciful in wille, and a merciful doere and riȝtful. [5] The man is myrie þat doiþ merci and leeneþ, he disposiþ hise wordis in doom; for he shal not be moued wiþouten ende. [7] A iust man shal be in euerelastynge mynde; he shal not drede of an yuel hering.^979 His herte is redi for to hope in þe Lord; [8] his herte is confermyd, he shal not be moued, til he dispise hise enemyes.^980 [9] He spredde abrood,^981 he ȝafᶜ^982 to pore men; his riȝtfulnesse dwelliþ into þe world of world; his horn^983 shal be reisid in glorie. [10] A synnere shal se and shal be wrooþ; he schal gnaste wiþ hise teeþ and shal faile, eþer waxe rotun; þe desir of synneris shal perische.

### [PSALM 112]

*Laudate pueri Dominum*

[1] *þe title of þe hundrid and xij salm. Alleluya.*^984

Children,^985 preise ȝe þe Lord; preise ȝe þe name of þe Lord. [2] The name of þe Lord be blessid; fro þis tyme now and til into þe

---

975. þat is, þe vndurstondyng of Goddis heest is good to hem, þat fillen þe heest in dede bi verri vndurstondyng þerof. To hem þat doon it not, it is more harmful. *Lire here.*

[PSALM 111 GLOSSES]

976.[i] In summe bookis is addid, of þe turnyng aȝen of Aggey and of ȝacharie, but þis is neþer in Ebreu neþer in Ierom.

þis salm shewiþ þat blis shal be ȝoldun for þe werkis of merci and peyne to hem þat ben vnmerciful. *Lire here.*

977. þat is, þe merit of his riȝtfulnesse. *Lire here.*

978. In þe translacioun of lxx translatours is addid þis word, Lord, to shewe þat þis is referrid to God. *Lire here.*

979. þat is, of þis word seid of Crist to vnmerciful men, 'Go ȝe cursid into euerlastinge fier' [Matt 25: 41]. *Lire here.*

980. þat is, he shal not be mouyd fro stidfastnesse of vertu, for God shal defende him, til he haue fynal victorie of feendis whanne he dieþ in charite;

981. He spred abrood, for Goddis loue, wiþout ony takyng of persoones;

982. he ȝaf freli, wiþouten hope of erþeli ȝeldyng; to pore men, representyng Crist in xxv capitulo of Matheu, and not to flatereris neiþer to mynstrals, to whiche manye men ȝyuen largeli and no þing to pore men;

983. his horn, þat is, temporal myȝt eiþer power, which he vside to þe good of vertu, shal be reisid in glorie of heuene, where his power shal be encreessid. *Lire here.*

[PSALM 112 GLOSSES]

984.[i] þis hundrid and xij salm stiriþ men to herie God for his grete excellence. And he reisiþ hem þat ben oppressid vniustli, to grete onour sum tyme in þis world and to blisse of heuene, if þei suffren pacientli.

Bi allegorie, þis salm is expowned of þe castynge awei of þe puple of Iewis for vnbileue and of þe reisyng of heþene puple in þe goodis of grace, for þei resseyueden deuoutli cristen feiþ. And so þe synagoge is maad bareyn and abiect eiþer caste out, and hooli chirche is maad fruytful and ioieful in þe feiþ of heþene men conuertid to cristendoom. *Lire here.*

985. þat is, meke men and good seruauntis. *Lire here.*

Oure eeld be childische and oure childheed be eldische, þat is þat

world. [3] Fro þe risyng of þe sunne til to þe goyng doun; þe name of
f. 63ʳ  þe Lord is worþi to | be preisid. [4]ᵃ The Lord is hiȝ aboue alle folkis;
and his glorie is aboue heuenys. [5] Who is as oure Lord God, þat
dwelliþ in hiȝe þingis; [6] and biholdiþ meke þingis in heuene and in
erþe? [7] Reisynge a nedi man fro [þe]ᵇ erþe; and enhaunsyng a pore
man fro drit.⁹⁸⁶ [8] That he sette him wiþ prynces; wiþ þe prynces of
his puple. [9] Which makiþ a bareyn womman dwelle in þe hous; a
glad modir of sones.

[PSALM 113]

*In exitu Israel*

[1] *þe titil of þe hundrid and xiij salm. Alleluya.*⁹⁸⁷

In þe goynge out of Israel fro Egipt; of þe hous of Iacob fro þe
heþene puple. [2] Iudee⁹⁸⁸ was maad þe halewyng of hym; Israel þe
power of hym. [3] The see siȝ and fledde;⁹⁸⁹ Iordan was turned abak.
[4] Mounteynes ful out ioieden⁹⁹⁰ as rammes; and litle hillis as þe
lambren of scheep. [5] Thou see what was to þee, for þou fleddist; and
þou, Iordan, for þou were turned abak? [6] Mounteynes, ȝe maden ful
outioie as rammes; and litle hillis as þe lambren of scheep. [7] The
erþe was mouyd for þe face of þe Lord; for þe face of God of Iacob.
[8] Which turnyde a stoon into poondis of watris; and an hard roche
into wellis of watris. [9] Lord not to us, not to us;⁹⁹¹ but ȝyue þou
glorie to þi name. [10] On þi merci and þi treuþe; lest ony tyme
heþene men seyn, Where is þe God of hem? [11] Forsoþe oure God is
in heuene; dide alle þingis, what euere he wolde. [12] The symylacris
of heþene men ben siluer and gold; þe werkis of mennes hondis. [13]
Tho han mouþ and shulen not speke; þo han iȝen and shulen not se.
[14] Tho han eeris and shulen not here; þo han noseþirlis and shulen
f. 63ᵛ  not smelle. [15] Tho han | hondis and shulen not grope; þo han feet
and shulen not go; þo shulen not crie in her þrote. [16] Thei þat
maken þoo be maad lijk þo; and alle þat tristen in þo. [17] The hous of
Israel hopide in þe Lord; he is þe helpere ʻof hemʼᵃ and þe defendere
of hem. [18] The hous of Aaron hopide in þe Lord; he is þe helpere of
hem and þe defendere of hem. [19] Theiᵇ þat dredenᶜ þe Lord,

---

Ps. 112    ᵃ *a unique gloss here in margin of* K: þat is, þe lynage of Iuda was maad þe
halowing of him. Li[re] he[re]    ᵇ þe] *om.*
Ps. 113    ᵃ of hem] *added by the scribe in margin*    ᵇ Thei] The Lord was myndeful of us, *by
eyeskip to the next verse,* The *corrected to* Thei *in a gap between words by the scribe,* Lord was
myndeful of us *canc.*    ᶜ dreden] dreden in, in *canc.*

oure wisdom be not wiþ pride and oure mekenesse be not wiþ wisdom. *Austin here.*

986. þat is, fro a vile place and stynkyng. *Lire here.*        f. 63ʳ

[PSALM II3 GLOSSES]

987.ⁱ þe hundrid and xiij salm indusiþ men to herie God bi þe biholdyng of benefice ȝouun to þe puple of Israel in þe goyng out of Egipt.

Gostli, in þis salm ech synnere þat haþ gete merci is excitid to herie God for þe benefice of goyng out of synne vndurstondun bi Egipt, þat is interpretid derknesse; and Iudee, þat is knoulechyng, is maad his halewyng. þanne þe see, þat is þe bittirnesse of synne, fleeþ; Iordan, þat is þe streem of doom, is turned abak, þat is, fro þe doom of dampnacioun to þe doom of saluacioun. þe erþe is mouyd for þe face of þe Lord, for a man is mouyd bi þe mouyng of good worching, out of þe stoon—þat is, out of þe hard herte bifore rennen þe watris of deuocioun. Idolatrie is caste awei, for auarice is caste awei bi largenesse of almesdede, and God is worschipid bi feiþ, hope, and charite, and so God is blessid of a man quykened bi grace. *Lire here.*

988. In Ebreu and Ierom it is, Iudas, þat is, þe lynage of Iuda, was maad þe halewing of hym; Israel þe power of him, þat is, Israel was maad þe oost of God, for bi þe sones of Israel he castide out Cananeis fro þe lond of biheest. *Lire here.*

989. þat is, departide itsilf in wiþdrawyng itsilf fro þe myddil at Goddis heest, as if it hadde wit and vndurstonding; þe see siȝ and fledde bi figuratif speche, for at þe maner of a man vndurstonding, it ȝaf drie weie to þe sones of Israel;

990. Mounteynes ful out ioieden, þat is, mounteynes and litil hillis ȝauen cause of ioie to þe sones of Israel, for in þe passage of þe flood Arnon, grete brokun stoones on o side were[n]ⁱⁱ bowid doun til to þe toþer brynke of þe flood, and so ȝa[u]enⁱⁱⁱ passage to þe sones of Israel. In liyk maner, hillis bowid fro o side of þe flood til to þe toþer, semyden make ioie to þe comynge and passage of þe sones of Israel.ⁱᵛ *Lire here.*

991. þat is, þe glorie of þe forseid myracle be not arettid to us. *Lire here.*

**Ps. 113 glosses**    ⁱ *in the bottom margin*    ⁱⁱ weren] -n *rubbed away*    ⁱⁱⁱ ȝauen] -u- *rubbed away*    ⁱᵛ In liyk maner . . . sones of Israel] *the scribe inadvertently copies the second part of the gloss from LY first, before the first lemma in verse 4:* Mounteynes, *etc.*

hopiden in þe Lord; he is þe helpere of hem and þe defendere of hem.
[20] The Lord was myndeful of us; and blesside us. He blesside þe
hous of Israel; he blesside þe hous of Aaron. [21] He blesside alle men
þat dreden þe Lord; he blesside þe litle men wiþ þe grettere. [22] The
Lord adde, eiþer encreesse, [on]$^d$ ȝou; on ȝou and [on]$^e$ ȝoure sones.
[23] Blessid be ȝe of þe Lord; þat made heuene and erþe. [24]
Heuene$^{992}$ of heuene is to þe Lord; but he ȝaf erþe$^{993}$ to þe sones of
men. [25] Lord, not deed men shulen herie þee; neþer alle men þat
goon doun into helle. [26] But we þat lyuen, blessen þe Lord; fro þis
tyme now and til into þe world.

## [PSALM 114]

*Dilexi*

[1] *þe title of þe hundrid and xiiij salm. Alleluya.*$^{994}$

I louyde þe Lord; for þe Lord shal here þe vois of my preier. [2] For
he bowide doun his eere to me; and I shal inwardli clepe in my daies.
[3] The sorewis of deþ cumpassiden me; and þe perels of helle
founden me. I foond tribulacioun and sorewe; [4] and I clepide
inwardli þe name of þe Lord. Thou, Lord, delyuere my soule; [5]
þe Lord is merciful and iust; and oure God doiþ merci. [6] And þe
Lord kepiþ litle children; I was mekid and he delyueride me. [7] Mi
soule, turne þou into þi reste; | for þe Lord haþ do wel to þee. [8] For
he haþ delyueride my soule fro deþ, myn iȝen fro wepingis, my feet fro
fallyng doun. [9] I shal plese þe Lord; in þe cuntrei of hem þat lyuen.

f. 64$^r$

## [PSALM 115]

*Credidi propter*

*þe hundrid and fiftene salm haþ no title outirli.*$^{995}$

[1] I bileuyde,$^{996}$ for which þing I spak; forsoþe I was maad low ful
myche.$^{997}$ [2] I seide in my passyng;$^{998}$ Ech man is a liere.$^{999}$ [3] What
shal I ȝelde to þe Lord; for alle þingis whiche he ȝeldide to me? [4] I

---

f. 63$^v$    992. For his glorie schyneþ more þere in hooli aungelis. *Lire here.*
993. þat is, to her dwelling for present liyf, in which if þei lyuen
iustli and worshipen God duli, þei shulen be takun to heuenli
dwellynge wiþ hooli aungelis. *Lire here.*

$^d$ on] *om.*    $^e$ on] *om.*

## [PSALM 114 GLOSSES]

994.[i] Dauiþ made þis salm for his delyueraunce fro perelis in persecucioun of[ii] Saul.

Gostli, þis salm mai be expowned of ech cristen man delyuerid bi God fro turment bodili eþer gostli, which man[iii] knoulechiþ his delyueryng and doiþ þankyngis to God. *Lire here.*

## [PSALM 115 GLOSSES]

f. 64[r]

995.[i] þe hundrid and xv salm spekiþ of Dauiþ set in persecucioun of Absolon, in which persecucioun he synnyde bi disseite of Siba sclaundryng falsli his lord Myphibosech. And Dauiþ suffride pacientli þat persecucioun and bihiȝte doynge of þankingis to be delyuerid þerfro.

Gostli, þis salm mai be expowned of ech feiþful man, which þouȝ he falliþ sumtyme bi disseit of an oþere man, knoulechiþ his vnkunnyng mekeli and suffriþ pacientli tribulacioun risynge on him, and whanne he is delyuerid þerof, he þankiþ God deuoutli. *Lire here.*

Also, þis salm mai be expowned in þe persoone of martris, of which ech seiþ þus, <u>Y bileuyde, et cetera</u>, þat is, Y bileuyde perfitli, for þei bileuen not perfitli þat nylen speke þat þing þat þei bileuen. [*Austin here.*][ii]

996. þat is, ouerliȝtli to þe wordis of Siba; <u>Y spak</u>, ouerhedeli in grauntyng to him þe eritage of his lord;

997. <u>maad low ful myche</u>: in Ebreu it is, <u>Y was turmentide ful myche</u>;

998. <u>Y seide in my passyng</u>, þat is, disturbling, and þerfor in Ebreu it is, <u>Y seide in myn hastynesse eþer in myn sudeynnesse.</u> *Lire here.*

999. <u>Maad low ful myche</u>: he signefieþ þat he suffride manye tribulaciouns for Goddis word, which he helde and spak feiþfuli; <u>in my passyng</u>, þat is, drede which he suffride of pursueris manaassyng his deþ; <u>Ech man is a liere</u>: as myche as perteyneþ to man himsilf he is a liere, but bi Goddis grace he is maad soþfast, þat he ȝue not stide to þe tribulaciouns of enemyes but speke and denye not þat þat he bileueþ. In so myche, men shulen[iii] not be lieris as þei shulen not be men, for þei shulen be goddis and sones of þe hiȝeste. *Austin here.*

---

shal [take]ᵃ þe cuppe¹⁰⁰⁰ of helþe; and I shal inwardli clepe þe name of
þe Lord. [5] I shal ȝelde my vowis to þe Lord bifor al his puple; [6] þe
deþ of seyntis of þe Lord is precious in his siȝt. [7] A! Lord, for I am
þi seruant; I am þi seruaunt, and þe sone of þyn handmaide. Thou
hast broke my boondis, [8] to þee I shal [offre]ᵇ a sacrifice of heriyng;
and I shal inwardli clepe þe name of þe Lord. [9] I shal ȝelde my vowis
to þe Lord, in þe siȝt of al his puple; [10] in þe forȝerdisᶜ of þe hous of
þe Lord, in þe [myd] of þee,ᵈ Ierusalem.

<h3 style="text-align:center">[PSALM 116]</h3>

*Laudate Dominum omnes gentes*
[1] *þe title of þe hundrid and xvj salm. Alleluya.*¹⁰⁰¹

Alle heþene men,¹⁰⁰² herie ȝe þe Lord; alle puplis, herie ȝe hym. [2]
For his merci is confermyd on us; and þe treuþe of þe Lord dwelliþ
wiþouten ende.

<h3 style="text-align:center">[PSALM 117]</h3>

*Confitemini Domino*
[1] *þe title of þe hundrid and xvij salm. Alleluya.*¹⁰⁰³

Knouleche ȝe¹⁰⁰⁴ to þe Lord, for he is good; for his merci is
wiþouten ende. [2] Israel seie now, for he is good; [for]ᵃ his merci is
wiþouten ende. [3] The hous of Aaron seie now; for his merci is
wiþouten ende. [4] The[i]ᵇ þat dreden | þe Lord, seie now; for his
merci is wiþouten ende. [5] Of tribulacioun I inwardli clepide þe
Lord; and þe Lord [herde]ᶜ me in largenesse. [6] The Lord is an
helpere to me; I shal not drede¹⁰⁰⁵ what a man shal do to me. [7] The
Lord is an helpere to me; and I shal dispise myn enemyes. [8] It is
betere for to triste in þe Lord; þan for to triste in man. It is betere for
to hope in þe Lord; þan for to hope in prynces. [10] Alle folkis
cumpassiden me; and in þe name of þe Lord it bifelde, for I am
avengid on hem. [11] Thei cumpassynge cumpassiden me; and in þe
name of þe Lord, for I am auengide on hem. [12] Thei cumpassiden
[me]ᵈ as bees,¹⁰⁰⁶ and þei brenten out as fierᵉ doiþ amonge þornes; and

f. 64ᵛ

**Ps. 115**    ᵃ take] ȝelde    ᵇ offre] sacrifice    ᶜ forȝerdis] *other LV copies,* porchis (EV
porche)    ᵈ in þe myd of þee] in þe myddil of þee; *the scribe has conflated here the readings of
EV and LV:* cf. in þe myddil of þi Ierusalem *(EV, from the incorrect Latin* in medio tuo
Hierusalem*) and* in þe myd of þee Hierusalem *(LV, from Gall.* in medio tui Hierusalem*)*
**Ps. 117**    ᵃ for] *om.*    ᵇ Thei] The    ᶜ herde] *om.*    ᵈ me] *om.*    ᵉ fier] *corrected by the scribe
on an erasure*

1000. þe cuppe of helþe, þat is, þe fersnesse of persecucioun; þe name of þe Lord, for my delyueraunce fro þat persecucioun. *Lire here.*

## [PSALM 116 GLOSSES]

1001.[i] þis hundrid and xvj salm indusiþ alle puplis boþe heþene and Iewis for to herie God for þe comyng of Crist, þat made o chirche of Iewis and heþene men to þe glorie and onour of God. And to þis vndurstondyng, Poul aleggiþ þis salm in xv capitulo to Romayns. *Lire here.*

1002. þat is, þat shulen be clepid to Cristis feiþ. *Lire here.*

## [PSALM 117 GLOSSES]

1003.[i] þis salm indusiþ men to herie God and bryngiþ resoun þerto. *Lire here.*

1004. Bi knouleching of heriyng. *Austin here.*

1005. þat is, bi drede castynge doun fro vertu. *Lire here.*    f. 64[v]

1006. Cumpassynge an honycoomb; so pursueris cumpassiden Crist. [*Austin*][ii] *here.*

1007. Bi al þe cours of kyndli lijf, seide Dauiþ. *Lire here.*

1008. þat is, nei3ynge to feiþ and sacramentis of þe chirche, bi whiche entryng is 3ouun to glorie; þis 3ate, þat is, Crist hymsilf. *Lire here.*

---

in þe name of þe Lord, for I am avengid on hem. [13] I was hurlid and turned vpsodoun, þat I shulde falle doun; and þe Lord took me up. [14] The Lord is my strengþe and my heriyng; and he is maad to me into helþe. [15] The vois of ful out ioiyng and of helþe; be in þe tabernaclis of iust men. [16] The ri3thond of þe Lord haþ do vertu, þe ri3thond of þe Lord enhaunside me; þe ri3thond of þe Lord haþ do vertu. [17] I schal not die,[1007] but I shal lyue; and I shal telle þe werkis of þe Lord. [18] The Lord chastisyng haþ chastisid me; and he 3af not me to deþ. [19] Open 3e to me þe 3atis[1008] of ri3tfulnesse, and I shal entre bi þo, and I shal knoulech to þe Lord; [20] þis 3ate is of þe Lord, and iust men shulen entre bi it. [21] I shal knoulech to þee, for þou herdist me; and art maad to me into helþe. [22] The

---

Ps. 116 glosses     [i] *next to the title in the right margin*
Ps. 117 glosses     [i] *next to the first verse in the right margin*     [ii] Austin] Lire

f. 65<sup>r</sup> stoon<sup>1009</sup> which þe bilderis repreueden; þis is maad into þe heed | of
þe corner. [23] This þing is maad of þe Lord; and it is wondurful bifor
oure i3en. [24] This is þe dai<sup>1010</sup> which þe Lord made; make we ful out
ioie and be we glad þerinne. [25] A! Lord, make þou me saaf, A! Lord,
make þou wel prosperite; [26] blessid is he þat comeþ in þe name<sup>1011</sup>
of þe Lord. We blessen 3ou<sup>1012</sup> of þe hous of þe Lord; [27] God is
Lord, and haþ 3oue li3t to us. Ordeyne 3e a solempne dai in þicke
puplis; til to þe horn of þe auter. [28] Thou art my God, and I shal
knouleche to þee; þou art my God, and I shal enhaunse þee. I shal
knoulech to þee, for þou herdist me; and þou art maad to me into
helþe. [29] Knouleche 3e to þe Lord, for he is good; for his merci is
wiþouten ende.

# [PSALM 118]

*Beati immaculati in uia*

[1] *þe title of þe hundrid and xviij salm. Alleluya.*<sup>1013</sup>

Blessid ben men wiþout wem<sup>1014</sup> in þe weie; þat goon in þe lawe of
þe Lord.<sup>1015</sup> [2] Blessid ben þei þat seken hise witnessyngis; seken
hym in al þe herte.<sup>1016</sup> [3] For þei þat worchen wickidnesse;<sup>1017</sup> 3eden
not in hise weies. [4] Thou hast comau[n]did;<sup>a</sup> þat þyn heestis be kept
gretli. [5] I wolde þat my weies be dressid; to kepe þi iustefiyngis.<sup>1018</sup>
[6] Thanne I shal not be schent; whanne I shal biholde parfitli in alle
þyn heestis. [7] I shal knouleche to þee in þe dressyng of herte; in þat
þat I lernyde þe domes of þi ri3tfulnesse. [8] I shal kepe þi
iustefiyngis; forsake þou not me on ech side.

*In quo corrigit*

[9] In what þing amendiþ a 3onge wexynge man his weie? in
f. 65<sup>v</sup> kepinge | þi wordis. [10] In al myn herte I sou3te þee; putte þou me
not awei<sup>1019</sup> fro þyn heestis. [11] In myn herte I hidde þi spechis; þat I
do not synne a3enes þee. [12] Lord, þou art blessid; teche þou me þi
[iusti]fiyngis.<sup>b</sup> [13] In my lippis<sup>1020</sup> I haue pronounside; alle þe domes
of þi mouþ. [14] I delitide in þe weie of þi witnessyngis; as in alle
richessis. [15] I schal be excercisid, eþer bisili ocupied, in þyn heestis;
and I shal biholde þi weies. [16] I shal biþenke in þi iustefiyngis; I shal
not for3ete þi wordis.

Ps. 118     <sup>a</sup> comaundid] comaudid     <sup>b</sup> iustifiyngis] magnefiyngis

1009. þat is, Crist himsilf, which þe bilderis, þat is, þe prestis and techeris of Iewis, to whose office it bifelde to bilde þe puple in feiþ and vertues; þis is maad into þe heed of þe corner, makynge o chirche of Iewis and of heþene men, of which chirche he is heed and shepparde.

This vers must nedis be vndurstondun of Crist to þe lettre, forwhi Crist in xxj capitulo of Matheu and xx capitulo of Luyk and Petre in iiij capitulo of Dedis aleggen þis vers seid of Crist to þe lettre; and so doiþ Rabi Salomon on þe v capitulo of Mychee, þere: 'And þou Bethleem art litil, et cetera' [Mic 5: 2]. *Lire here.*

1010. þat is, þe tyme of þe newe testament, wherinne treuþe is f. 65ʳ shewid þat was hid in þe elde testament. *Lire here.*

1011. þat is, Crist, þat cam in þe name of þe fadir for þe helþe of þe world. *Lire here.*

þerfor he is cursid, þat comeþ in his owene name, þat is, sekiþ his owne glorie. As Crist seid of Antecrist to þe Iewis, 'If an oþere shal come in his owne name, ȝe shulen take him' [John 5: 43]. *Austin here.*

1012. þis is þe word of apostlis þat weren þe firste in hooli chirche, and blessiden puplis in tellinge þe treuþe of þe gospel and in mynystringe sacramentis. *Lire here.*

## [PSALM 118 GLOSSES]

1013.ⁱ þe hundrid salm and xviij spekiþ of blis. Blis is in treuþe and in dede, and þus it is had oneli in heuene. Blis is also in hope, and þus it is had in present liyf bi excercise of good werkis. þerfor þis salm spekiþ of blis as it is had in present liyf. *Lire here.*

1014. þat is, þat han no wem of dedlyⁱⁱ synne;

1015. in þe lawe of þeⁱⁱⁱ Lord, in fillinge hise heestis in werk. *Lire here.*

1016. þat is, vndurstondinge and loue. *Lire here.*

1017. þat is, of vnfeiþfulnesse eiþer þei þat obeien to desiris of synne. *Lire here.*

1018. þat is, þin heestis, þat perteynen [to]ⁱᵛ perfit riȝtfulnesse. *Lire here.*

1019. þat is, resseyue þou me to þe knowing and fillyng of þyn f. 65ᵛ heestis. *Lire here.*

1020. þat is, Y holde not stille ony of þi domes, whiche þou woldist make knowun to me bi þi spechis. *Austyn here.*

---

Ps. 118 glosses ⁱ *next to the title in the right margin; this gloss also in margin of* K ⁱⁱ dedly] *corrected by the scribe on an erasure* ⁱⁱⁱ þe] þe le-, le- *canc.* ⁱᵛ to] *om.*

*Retribue seruo tuo*

[17] Зelde to þi seruaunt; quykene þou me, and I shal kepe þi wordis. [18] Liзtne þou myn iзen; and I shal biholde [þe]ᶜ meruelis of þi lawe. [19] I am a comelynge in erþe; hide þou not¹⁰²¹ þyn heestis fro me. [20] Mi soule couetide; to desire þi iustefiyngis in al tyme. [21] Thou blamedist þe proude; þei ben cursid þat bowen awei¹⁰²² fro þyn heestis. [22] Do þou awei fro me schenschipe¹⁰²³ and dispisyng; for I souзte þi witnessyngis. [23] Forwhi prynces¹⁰²⁴ saten and spaken aзenes me; but þi seruaunt was excercisid in þi iustifiyngis. [24] Forwhi and þi witnessyngis is my þenkyng; and my councel is þi iustefiyngis.

*Adhesit pauimento*

[25] Mi soule cleuyde to þe pawment;¹⁰²⁵ quykene þou me bi þi word. [26] I telde out my weies, and þou herdist me; teche þou me þi iustefiyngis. [27] Lerne þou me þe weie of þi iustefiyngis;¹⁰²⁶ and I f. 66ʳ shal be excercisid in þi meruelis. [28] Mi soule nappide for a|noie; conferme þou me in þi wordis. [29] Remoue þou fro me þe weie of wickidnesse; and in þi lawe haue þou merci on me. [30] I chees þe weie of treuþe; I forзat not þi domes. [31] Lord, I cleuyde to þi witnessyngis; nyle þou schende me. [32] I ran¹⁰²⁷ þe weie of þi comaundementis; whanne þou alargidist myn herte.¹⁰²⁸

*Legem pone*

[33] Lord, sette þou [to]ᵈ me [a lawe],ᵉ þe weie of þi iustifiyngis; and I shal seke it euere. [34] Зyue þou vndurstondinge to me, and I shal seke þi lawe; and I shal kepe it in al myn herte. [35] Lede me forþ in þe paþ of þyn heestis; for I wolde it. [36] Bowe þou doun myn herte into þi witnessyngis; and not into auarice. [37] Turne þou awei [m]ynᶠ iзen, þat þo seen not vanyte;¹⁰²⁹ quykene þou me in þi weie. [38] Ordeyne þi speche to þi seruaunt; in þi drede. [39] Kitte awei my schenschipe,¹⁰³⁰ which I supposide;¹⁰³¹ for þi domes ben myrie. [40] Lo! I coueitide þi comaundementis; quykene þou me in þyn equyte.¹⁰³²

*Et ueniat super nos*

[41] And, Lord, þi merci come on me; þin helþe come bi þi speche. [42] And I shal answere a word to men seiynge schenschipe to me; for

---

ᶜ þe] *om.*     ᵈ to] *om.*     ᵉ a lawe] *om.*     ᶠ myn] þyn

1021. þat is, schewe þo to me. *Lire here.*

1022. Oþere þing is, to fille not bi freelte eþer bi ignoraunce Goddis heestis; oþere þing is, to bowe awei fro þo bi pride, as þei diden þat gendriden us dedlich into þese yuelis. *Austin here.*

God castide doun fro heuene þe aungelis þat weren proude, and þe<sup>v</sup> former fadir and modir, [for]<sup>vi</sup> dispisynge Goddis heest, fro erþeli paradiys; and for breking of Goddis heest þei weren cursid. *Lire here.*

1023. Of curse; and dispisyng, of brekinge of þe lawe;

1024. prynces, þat is, fendis þat treten ofte togidere to caste doun hooli men and lettrid, in dispit of Goddis heestis. *Lire here.*

1025. þat is, my soule is ioyned to an erþeli bodi and corruptible, þat greueþ þe soule; quykene þou me, þat is, make stronge in me þe liyf of grace, to bere liȝtli þe birþun of bodi. *Lire here.*

þis cleuynge signefieþ here fleischli desir of þe soule, bi which 'þe fleisch coueitiþ aȝenes þe spirit' [Gal 5: 17]. Cleuyde to þe pawment, þat is, I am deed; quykene þou me: to cleue to erþeli þingis is þe deþ of soule. þerfor, þis man wole be delyuerid fro erþeli þingis and seie wiþ Poul, 'Oure lyuynge is in heuene' [Phil 3: 20]. *Austin here.*

1026. In Greek it is seid openliere: Make þou me to vndurstonde þi iustefiyngis. *Austin here.*

1027. Goynge esili in þe weie of vertu;                                    f. 66<sup>r</sup>

1028. alargidist bi þe ȝifte of charite, þat makis Goddis heestis esy. *Lire here.*

1029. þat is, in spectaclis indusynge to þe yuele of leccherie. *Lire here.*

1030. þat is, occasioun to falle into schentful synne;

1031. which Y supposide, þat is, dredde, and þerfor in Ierom it is which Y dredde. *Lire here.*

1032. þat is, þi grace, þat iustefieþ a wickid man. *Lire here.*

1033. þat is, Y encreesside hope bi þi chastisyngis. [*Austin*]<sup>vii</sup> here.

---

I hopide in þi wordis. [43] And take þou not awei fro my mouþ þe word of treuþe outirli; for I hopide aboue<sup>1033</sup> in þi domes. [44] And I shal kepe þi lawe euere; into þe world and into þe world of<sup>g</sup> world.

<sup>v</sup> þe] for þe, *due to eyeskip*     <sup>vi</sup> for] *om.*     <sup>vii</sup> Austin] Lire

<sup>g</sup> of] of 'the', *erroneously corrected by the scribe above the line of writing*

[45] And I 3ede in largenesse;[1034] for I sou3te þi comaundementis. [46] And I spak of þi witnessyngis in þe si3t of kyngis; and I was not f. 66ᵛ schent. | [47] And I biþou3te in þyn heestis; whiche I louyde. [48] And I reiside myn hondis to þi comaundementis, whiche I louyde; and I shal be exercisid in þi iustefiyngis.[1035]

*Memor esto*

[49] Lord, haue þou mynde on þi word[1036] to þi seruaunt; in which word þou hast 3oue hope to me. [50] This comfortide me in my lownesse;[1037] for þi word quykenyde me. [51] Proude men diden wickidli bi alle þingis; but I bowide not awei fro þi lawe. [52] Lord, I was myndeful on þi domes fro þe world; and I was comfortide. [53] Failyng[1038] helde me; for synneris forsakynge þi lawe. [54] Thi iustefiyngis weren delitable to me to be sungen; in þe place of my pilgrymage. [55] Lord, I hadde mynde of þi name bi ny3t; and I kepte þi lawe. [56] This þing[1039] was maad to me; for I sou3te þi iustefiyngis.

*Porcio mea Domine*

[57] Lord, my part; I seide to kepe þi lawe. [58] I bisou3te þi face in al myn herte; haue þou merci on me bi þi speche. [59] I biþou3te my weies;[1040] and I turnyde my feet into þi witnessyngis. [60] I am redi and I am not disturblid; to kepe þi comaundementis. [61] The coordis of synneris[1041] han biclippid me; and I haue not for3ete þi lawe. [62] At mydny3t[1042] I roos to knouleche to þee;[1043] on þe domes of þi iustefiyngis. [63] I am parcener of alle þat dreden þee; and kepen þyn heestis. [64] Lord, þe erþe is ful of þi merci; teche þou me þi iustefiyngis.

f. 67ʳ *Bonitatem fecisti*

[65] Lord, þou hast do goodnesse[1044] wiþ þi seruaunt; bi þi word. [66] Teche þou me goodnesse, and lore,[1045] eþer chastisyng, and kunnyng;[1046] for I bileuyde to þyn heestis. [67] Bifor þat I was maad meke, I trespasside; þerfor I kepte þi speche. [68] Thou art good; and in þi goodnesse teche þou me þi iustefiyngis. [69] The wickidnesse of hem þat ben proude[1047] is multeplied on me; but in al myn herte I shal seke þyn heestis. [70] The herte of hem is cruddid, eþer maad hard, as mylke;[1048] but I biþou3te þi lawe. [71] It is good to me, þat þou hast maad me meke; þat I lerne þi iustefiyngis. [72] The lawe of þi mouþ is betere to me; þan þousyndis[1049] of gold and of siluer.

1034. þat is, of charite þat loueþ also enemyes. *Lire here.*

1035. þat is, in þe werkis of þin heestis þat iustefien, whanne þei f. 66ᵛ
ben fillid in du maner. *Lire here.*

1036. þis word is biheest of blis, þat was maad to Abraham and hise
sueris. *Lire here.*

1037.ᵛⁱⁱⁱ Bi which a man is maad low bi tribulacioun. *Austin
here.*

In Ebreu it is, <u>on my turment</u>. *Lire here.*

1038. þat is, grete drede; and þerfor in Ierom it is, <u>Hidouste helde
me</u>. *Lire here.*

1039. þat is, þis þing þat Y kepte þi lawe, Y dide not bi mysilf, but
bi þi grace ӡouun to me. *Austin and Lire here.*

1040. þat is, goyngis forþ in goodnesse þat ben slow bi mannis
freelte, but hasti bi Goddis grace. *Lire here.*

1041. þat is, þe temptaciouns of fendis. *Lire here.*

1042. þat is, in þe greuouse part of tribulacioun. *Austin here.*

1043. <u>To knoulech to þee</u>, þat is, to knoulech to þee bi knoulechyng
of heriyng, for bi þin hooli doomⁱˣ þou woldist kepe me in
riӡtfulnesse. *Lire here.*

1044. þat is, þou hast maad þat goodnesse delitide me. *Austyn here.* f. 67ʳ

<u>Do goodnesse</u>: in ӡyuynge to him a soule maad to þin ymage, and in
abidyng aboue þis þe goodis of grace þat makenˣ a soule liyk to God.
And þese goodis of grace weren ӡouun to man in þe staat of
innocence; and aftir fallyng into synne, þese ben ӡouen in baptym
and weren ӡouun in circumcisioun in þe elde lawe. [*Lire here.*]ˣⁱ

1045. þat is, of þingis þat perteynen to vertues;

1046. <u>and kunnyng</u>, þat is, of kyndli þingis. *Lire here.*

<u>Lore eþer chastising</u>, þat signefieþ tribulacioun amending, is lerned
not bi heryng neþer bi redyng neþer bi þenkyng, but bi felyng in
dede. *Austyn here.*

1047. <u>þat ben proude</u>: þat is, of fendis enforsynge to hurle men to
synne. *Lire here.*

1048. þat is, þristide togidere in malice, for wickid spiritis ben
hardid in malice. *Lire here.*

1049. þat charite loue[þ]ˣⁱⁱ more þe lawe of God, þan coueitise
loueþ þousyndis of gold and of siluer. *Austin here.*

---

ᵛⁱⁱⁱ *this gloss also in margin of* V *(damaged)*      ⁱˣ doom] doi, *corrected by the scribe with
overwriting*      ˣ þat maken] þat maken þat maken, *second* þat maken *canc.*      ˣⁱ Lire here] *om.*
ˣⁱⁱ loueþ] loue

*Manus tue*

[73] Thyn hondis[1050] maden me and formeden me; ȝyue þou vndurstonding[1051] to me, þat I lerne þyn heestis. [74] Thei þat dreden þee shulen se me, and shulen be glad; for I hopide more on þi wordis. [75] Lord, I knewe þat þi domes ben equyte; and in þi treuþe þou hast maad me meke. [76] Thi merci[1052] be maad, þat it comforte me; bi þi speche to þi seruaunt. [77] Thi merciful doyngis come to me, and I shal lyue;[1053] for þi lawe is my þenkyng. [78] Thei þat ben proude be schent, for vniustli þei diden wickidnesse aȝenes me; but I shal be excercisid in þin heestis. [79] Thei þat dreden þee be turned to me;[1054] and þei þat knowen þi witnessyngis.[1055] [80] Myn herte be maad vnwemmed in þi iustefiyngis; þat I be not schent.

*Defecit in salutare*

f. 67ᵛ    [81] Mi soule failide[1056] in|to þyn heelþe; and I hopide more on þi word. [82] Myn iȝen[1057] failiden into þi speche; seiynge, Whanne shalt þou comforte me?[1058] [83] For I am maad as a bowge[1059] in forst;ʰ I haue not forȝete þi iustefiyngis. [84] Hou manye ben þe daies of þi seruaunt; whanne þou shalt make doom of hem þat pursuen me? [85] Wickid men telden to me ianglyngis;[1060] but not as þi lawe. [86] Alle þi comaundementis ben treuþe; wickid men han pursued[1061] me, helpe þou me. [87] Almest þei endiden me in erþe; but I forsook not þi comaundementis. [88] Bi þi merci quykene þou me; and I shal kepe þe witnessyngis of þi mouþ.[1062]

*In eternum Domine*

[89] Lord, þi word[1063] dwelliþ in heuene; wiþouten ende. [90] Thi treuþe dwelliþ in generacioun and into generacioun; þou hast foundide þe erþe, and it dwelliþ. [91] The dai lastiþ contynueli bi þyn ordenaunce; for alle þingis serue[1064] to þee. [92] No but [þat]ⁱ þi lawe was `my´ʲ þenkyng; þanne perauenture I hadde perischid in my lownesse.[1065] [93] Wiþouten ende I shal not forȝete þi iustefiyngis; for in þo þou hast quykened me. [94] I am þyn, make þou me saaf; for I haue souȝte þi iustefiyngis. [95] Synneris aboden me[1066] for to leese

---

1050. þat is, power and wisdom; eþer þe sone and þe holi goost. *Austin here.*

ʰ forst] *corrected by the scribe on an erasure*    ⁱ þat] *om.*    ʲ my] þi, *canc. and corrected by the scribe above the line of writing*

1051. þat is, to knowe and loue þee. *Lire here.*

1052. In doynge awei of myn offencis. *Lire here.*

1053. Now bi liyf of grace and of glorie in heuene. *Lire here.*

1054. þat is, to helpe me;

1055. þi witnessyngis, in vndurstonding and worchyng. *Lire here.*

1056. þat is a good failyng and schewiþ desir of good not getun 3it, but coueitid moost gredili and moost strongli. *Austyn here.*

As myche as a soule is reisid in contemplacioun, þat is in þou3t and loue of God and heuenli blis, so myche it is wiþdrawun fro occupacioun of outtirmere wittis. And a soule failiþ in a maner, in as myche as it ceessiþ fro outward dede, and is sopun up in contemplacioun of hi3este good and in delitynge suynge; and sich failyng is ful heelful. *Lire here.*

1057. þat is, myn innere i3en. þis failyng comeþ not of siyknesse of f. 67ᵛ soule, but of þe strengþe of desire. *Austin here.*

1058. In perfit blis. *Lire here.*

1059. As a bowge: Whanne gostli desiris brennen, fleishli desiris wexen coold. Y am maad as a bowge: þe brennyng of coueitise was slow, þat þe mynde of char[i]teˣⁱⁱⁱ shulde be hoot. *Austin here.*

A bowge in forst semeþ forsakun and no more profitable to mennis vsis. So men 3ouun to contemplacioun ben arettid foolis in worldli þingis, and of worldli men þei ben holdun foolis and woode; and neþeles in treuþe þei ben wisest men, for wisdom stondiþ propirli in contemplacioun of þe firste cause, þat is, God. *Lire here.*

1060. þat is, delitable excersisyngis in wordis. *Austin here.*

1061. Vnfeiþful men and eretikes pursuen trewe men, and sekynge to sle hem, whiche þei moun not bi wordis turne awei fro treuþe. *Lire here.*

1062.ˣⁱᵛ þat is, þe ten hestis and þe wordis of þe gospel. *Lire here.*

1063. þat is, reuelacioun maad to aungelis. *Lire here.*

1064. As if he seide, Myche strongliere þe reuelacioun of þi treuþe, nedeful to þe reulyng of mannis helþe, shal dwelle stabili;

1065. Y hadde perischide in my lownesse, þat is, bi þe hurling of corrupcioun of my fleisch, which bi his vilete is þe resoun of my mekenesse;

1066. Synneris aboden me, þat is, wickid spiritis obstynat in synne;

ˣⁱⁱⁱ charite] charte   ˣⁱᵛ *gloss interlinear, the phrase* þe gospel *distinguished with a red paraph from the tie-mark at the next lemma*

me;[1067] I vndurstood þi witnessyngis. [96] I siȝ þe ende of al ende;[1068] þi comaundement is ful large.[1069]

*Quomodo dilexi*

[97] Lord, hou louyde[1070] I þi lawe; al dai it is my þenking. [98] Aboue myn enemyes þou madist me prudent bi þi comaundement;[1071] for it is to me wiþouten ende. [99] I vndurstood aboue alle men techynge me; | for þi witness[yng]is[k] is my þenkyng. [100] I vndurstood aboue elde men; for I souȝte þi comaundementis. [101] I forbeed my feet fro al euel weie; þat I kepe þi wordis. [102] I bowide not fro þi domes; for þou hast set lawe to me. [103] Thi spechis ben ful swete to my chekis;[1072] aboue hony to my mouþ. [104] I vndurstood of þyn heestis; þerfor I hatide al þe weie of wickidnesse.

f. 68ʳ

*Lucerna pedibus meis*

[105] Thi word is a lanterne to my feet; and liȝt to my paþis. [106] I swor and purposide stidfastli; to kepe þe domes of þi riȝtfulnesse. [107] I am maad low[1073] bi alle þingis; Lord, quykene þou me be þi word. [108] Lord, make þou wel plesynge þe wilful þingis of my mouþ; and teche þou me þi domes. [109] Mi soule is euere in myn hondis;[1074] and I forȝat not þi lawe. [110] Synneris settiden a snare to me; and I erride not fro þi comaundementis. [111] I purchaside þi witnessyngis bi eritage[1075] wiþouten ende; for þo ben [þe][l] ful ioiyng of myn herte. [112] I bowide myn herte to do þi iustefiyngis wiþouten ende; for ȝeldyng.[1076]

*Iniquos odio*

[113] I hatide wickid men;[1077] and I louyde þi lawe. [114] Thou art myn helpere and myn takere-up; and I hopide more on þi word. [115] Ȝe wickide men, bowe awei fro me; and I shal seke þe comaundementis[1078] of my God. [116] Uptake þou me bi þi word, and I shal lyue; and schende þou not me fro myn abidyng.[1079] [117] Helpe þou me and I shal be saaf; and I shal þenke euere in þi iustefiyngis. [118] Thou | hast forsake[1080] alle men goynge awei fro þi domes; for þe þouȝt of hem is vniust. [119] I arettide alle þe synneris of erþe brekeris of [þe][m] lawe;[1081] þerfor I louyde þi witnessyngis. [120] Naile þou my fleischis wiþ þi drede;[1082] for I dredde of þi domes.[1083]

f. 68ᵛ

---

k witnessingis] witnessis    l þe] *om.*    m þe] *om.*

1067. <u>leese me</u>, bi fallynge into synne. *Lire here.*
Eþer þat Y shulde consente to hem to yuel, þanne þei shulen leese me. *Austyn here.*

1068. <u>Y siȝ þe ende of al ende</u>, þat is, of mannis perfeccioun;

1069. <u>þi comaundement is ful large</u>, þat is, charite,<sup>xv</sup> þat loueþ frendis and enemyes. *Lire here.*
Eþer al ende eþer perfeccioun is to stryue for treuþe til to þe deþ, and to suffre pacientli alle yuelis, for þe souereyn good. *Austin here.*

1070. þat is, Y louyde gretli, and he spekiþ þis in þe persoone of feiþful puple. *Lire here.*

1071. þat is, verili vndurstondun of me bi þi liȝtnyng. *Lire here.*

1072. þat is, þilke swetnesse which þe Lord ȝyueþ þat oure erþe    f. 68ʳ
ȝyue his fruyt, þat is, þat we do good verili wel, not for drede of fleischli yuel, but for delityng of goostli good. *Austin*<sup>xvi</sup> here.

<u>To my chekis</u>, þat is, to þe hiȝere myȝtis of my soule, bi whiche þe swetnesse of heuenli þingis is feelid and taastid in sum maner. *Lire here.*

1073. þat is, Y suffride ful greet persecucioun, for I purposide stidfastli to kepe þe domes of Goddis riȝtfulnesse. *Austyn here.*

<u>Maad lowe</u>, þat is, myche bowid doun and greued of þe corruptible fleisch þat greueþ þe soule. *Lire here.*

1074. þat is, in perels. *Lire here.*

1075. þat is, vnmouabli, as myche as is of my desire. *Lire here.*

1076.<sup>xvii</sup> þat is, for euerlastinge helþe. *Lire here.*

1077. Not her kynde, but her wickidnesse. *Austin here.*

1078. þat is, cleneli wiþout medling of ȝoure errour, for vnfeiþful men shulen be fled, for perel lest symple men be corrupt of hem. *Lire here.*

1079. þat is, suffre þou not me to be putte awei fro blis, which Y hope. *Lire here.*

1080. þat is, <u>brouȝt to nouȝt</u>, as it is in Greek. *Austin here.*    f. 68ᵛ

1081. Eþer writun, eþer of kynde, eþer ȝouun in paradijs. *Austin here.*

1082. þat is, sle þou fleischli stiringes. *Lire here.*

In Greek it is, <u>Naile þou bi nailis</u>, þat is, ȝyue þou to me chast drede, to which to be axid þe drede of lawe brouȝte me. My fleischli desiris be refreyned bi þi chast drede. Charite drediþ bi chast drede to do synne, ȝhe, þouȝ no peyne sueþ. It demeþ þat peyne sueþ, whanne for þe loue of riȝtfulnesse, it arettiþ synne peyne. *Austin here.*

1083. <u>Y dredde of þi domes</u>, bi which þou drenchidist al þe world for þe synne of leccherie in þe greet flood of Noe, and brentist Sodom

---

<sup>xv</sup> þat is charite] þat is charite þat is charite, *second* þat is charite *canc.*    <sup>xvi</sup> Austin] *corrected by the scribe on an erasure*    <sup>xvii</sup> *gloss interlinear*

*Feci iudicium*

[121] I dide doom and riȝtfulnesse;[n] bitake þou not me to hem[1084] þat falsli calengen me. [122] Take up þi seruaunt into goodnes; þei þat ben proude calengen not me. [123] Myn iȝen failiden into þin[1085] helþe; and into þe speche of þi riȝtfulnesse. [124] Do þou wiþ þi seruaunt bi þi merci; and teche þou me þi iustefiyngis.[1086] [125] I am þi seruaunt, ȝyue þou vndurstonding to me; þat I kunne þi witnessyngis. [126] Lord, it is tyme to do; þei han distried þi lawe.[1087] [127] Therfor I louyde þi comaundementis; more þan gold and topaȝion.[1088] [128] Therfor I was dressid to alle þyn heestis; I hatide al wickid weie.

*Mirabilia*

[129] Lord, þi witnessyngis[1089] ben wondurful;[1090] þerfor my soule souȝte þo. [130] Declaryng of þi wordis liȝtneþ; and ȝyueþ vndurstondyng to meke men. [131] I openyde my mouþ and drow þe spirit;[1091] for I desiride þi comaundementis. [132] Biholde þou on me and haue merci on me; bi þe doom of hem[1092] þat louen þi name. [133] Dresse þou my goyngis bi þi speche; þat al vnriȝtfulnesse haue not lordschipe of me. [134] Aȝenbie þou me fro þe false calengis of men; þat I kepe þyn heestis. [135] Liȝtne þi face[1093] on þi seruaunt; and teche þou me þi iustefiyngis. [136] Myn iȝen ledden forþ þe out| goyngis of watris; for þei kepten not þi lawe.

f. 69ʳ

*Iustus es Domine*

[137] Lord, þou art iust; and þi doom[1094] is riȝtful. [138] Thou hast comaundid riȝtfulnesse,[1095] þi witnessyngis;[1096] and þi treuþe gretli to be kept. [139] Mi feruent loue made me to be meltid; for myn enemys forȝaten þi wordis. [140] Thi speche is gretli set afire;[1097] and þi seruaunt louyde it. [141] I am ȝong and dispisid; I forȝat not þi iustefiyngis. [142] Lord, þi riȝtfulnesse[1098] is riȝtfulnesse wiþouten ende; and þi lawe is treuþe. [143] Tribulacioun and angwisch founden

---

and oþere foure citees wiþ þe fier of brymstoon, for þe vilete of leccherie. þe biholdyng of þese domes nailiþ þe fleisch bi drede, in beringe doun vnleueful stiryngis þerof. *Lire here.*

1084. þat is, to fendis sekinge euere to anoie me. *Lire here.*

[n] riȝtfulnesse] *cf. note to 4:2 above*

1085. As if he seide, Y mai not gete it bi myn owne vertu, for it passiþ þe kyndli power and wit of man. *Lire here.*

1086. þat^{xviii} Y mai take þo bi vndurstondyng and fille þo in werk. *Lire here.*

1087. þat is, eretikis and weiward techeris han peruertid þe veri^{xix} vndurstonding of þi lawe; þerfor it is nedeful þat þou ʒyue and kepe veri vndurstonding þerof to þi seruauntis. *Lire here.*

1088. Is a ful preciouse stoon. *Lire here.*

1089. Heuene and erþe ʒyuen witnessyng of þe goodnesse and greetnesse of God. *Austin here.*

1090. þat is, hooli scripturis confermyd bi þi witnessingis. *Lire here.*

1091. þat is, I ʼheldʼ^{xx} abrood vndurstondyng bi enforsyng to take Goddis word and I drow þe spirit of vndurstonding, which is ʒouen to hem þat desiren it. *Lire here.*

1092. þat is, as þou hast disposid iustli to hem þat louen þee. *Lire here.*

1093. Liʒtne þi face, þat is, make knowun þi presence in helpynge me; and teche þou me þi iustefiyngis, þat is, þat Y do in werk. þouʒ men heren and holden in mynde þat þat þei heren, þei shulen not be demed to haue lerned if þei doon not. For Crist seiþ, ʻEch þat herde of þe fadir and lernyde, comeþ to meʼ [John 6: 45]. þerfor he þat doiþ not Goddis word, þat is, comeþ not to Crist, lernyde not. *Austin here.*

1094. þat is, þi lawe, bi which þe doom of oþere men owiþ to be  f.69^r ʒouun;

1095. þou hast comaundide riʒtfulnesse, þat is, þi conteynynge riʒtfulnesse; and is set here for þat is; in Ierom þus: þou hast comaundide þe riʒtfulnesse of þi witnessyngis. *Lire here.*

1096. þi witnessingis: Riʒtfulnesse in tribulacioun and nede ben þe martirdomes of God, þat is, witnessingis for whiche þe martris be corowned. *Austin here.*

1097. Set afire, for it enflawmeþ to Goddis loue. *Lire here.*

1098. For þe riʒtfulnesse which is bi feiþ, lediþ to euerelastynge blis; and þi lawe is treuþe, for it mai not conteyne ony falsnesse. Wherfor it is seid not oneli trewe, but treuþe outirli eþer treuþe itsilf, to signefie þe clennesse of treuþe. *Lire here.*

^{xviii} þat] þat is   ^{xix} veri] veri vnst-, vnst- *canc.*   ^{xx} held] knew, *canc. and corrected by the scribe above the line of writing*

me; þyn heestis is my þenking. [144] Thi witnessyngis is equyte wiþouten ende; зyue þou vndurstondyng to me, and I shal lyue.[1099]

*Clamaui in toto corde*

[145] I criede[1100] in al myn herte,[1101] Lord, here þou me; [and]° I shal s`e´eke[P] þi iustefiyngis. [146] I criede to þee, make þou me saaf; þat I kepe þi comaundementis. [147] I biforcam in ripenesse[1102] and I criede; I hopide aboue on þi wordis.[1103] [148] Myn iзen biforcamen to þee ful eerli; þat I shulde biþenke þi speches. [149] Lord, here þou my[q] vois bi þi merci;[r] and quykene þou me bi þi doom. [150] Thei þat pursuen me[1104] neiзiden to wickidnesse; forsoþe þei ben maad fer fro þi lawe. [151] Lord, þou art nyз; and alle þi weies ben treuþe. [152] In þe bigynnyng I knew of þi witnessyngis; for þou hast foundide þo wiþouten ende.[1105]

*Vide humilitatem*

f. 69ᵛ    [153] Se þou my me|kenesse, and delyuere þou me; for I forзat not þi lawe. [154] Deme þou my doom,[1106] and aзenbie þou me; quykene þou me for þi speche. [155] Helþe is fer fro synneris; for þei souзten not þi iustefiyngis. [156] Lord, þi mercies ben manye; quykene þou me bi þi dom.[s] [157] Thei ben manye þat pursuen me and doon tribulacioun to me; I bowide not awei fro þi witnessyngis. [158] I siз brekeris of þe lawe, and I was meltid;[1107] for þei kepten not þi[t] spechis. [159] Lord, se þou, for I louede þi comaundementis; quykene þou me in þi merci. [160] The bigynnyng of þi wordis is treuþe; alle þe domes of þi riзt[wis]nesse[u] ben wiþouten ende.

*Principes*

[161] Prynces pursuyden me wiþout cause; and myn herte dredde of þi wordis. [162] I shal be glad on þi spechis; as he þat fyndiþ manye spuylis. [163] I hatide and wlatide wickidnesse; forsoþe I louyde þi lawe. [164] I seide heriyngis to þee seuene siþis[1108] in þe dai; on þe domes of þi riзtfulnesse. [165] Miche pees is to hem þat louen þi lawe; and no sclaundir is to hem. [166] Lord, I bood þyn helþe; and I louyde þyn heestis. [167] Mi soule kepte þi witnessyngis; and louyde þo

---

° and] om.    [P] seke] speke, -p- *canc. and corrected by the scribe aboue the line of writing*
[q] Lord, here þou my] [H]ere þou me Lord here þou my, *initial capital om.*, [H]ere þou me *canc.*    [r] þi merci] þi preier merci, preier *canc.*    [s] dom] wisdom, wis- *canc.*    [t] þi] þi iustefiyngis, iustefiyngis *canc.*    [u] riзtwisnesse] riзtfulnesse; *only one other manuscript reads with* B 554 *riзtfulnesse here, hence my emendation; cf. FM ii. 867*

1099. þat is, ʒyue þou vndurstondyng to me to knowe þo and fille þo in werk, and I shal lyue bi liyf of grace in present tyme and of glorie in tyme of comynge. *Lire here.*

1100. I criede in al myn herte: No doute þat þe<sup>xxi</sup> cry to þe Lord is maad in veyn, which is maad of hem þat preien wiþ sown of bodili vois, not wiþ ententif<sup>xxii</sup> herte to þe Lord. þe cry of herte is greet entent eþer desir of þouʒte. Whanne þis cri is in þe preier, it declariþ grete loue of þe desirere and axere þat he dispeir not of effect. þanne me crieþ in al þe herte, whanne me þenkiþ not on oþere þing. He þat syngiþ þis salm remembriþ þat his preier is sich. *Austyn here.*

1101. þat is, vndurstonding and loue, feruentli and deuoutli. *Lire here.*

1102. In mydnyʒt whanne ʻit isʼ <sup>xxiii</sup> tyme<sup>xxiv</sup> for to rest and vnripeli, þat is, vncouenable to do ony þing bi wakyng; and bi Grekis it shal be seid in vnripenesse. *Austin here.*

1103. þat is, more þan in þe wordis of alle oþere men, for þi wordis moun conteyne no falsnesse. *Lire here.*

1104. þat is, þei þat pursuyden me wickidli, neiʒiden to me. *Lire here.*

1105. þat is, þat þing þat God bihiʒte bi þo is euerelastinge. [*Austin*]<sup>xxv</sup> here.

1106. þat is, ʒyue þe sentence for me aʒenes þe deuel, þat holdiþ    f. 69<sup>v</sup> me prisoner. *Lire here.*

1107. þat is, Y flowide out wiþ teeris, and þerfor in Ierom it is, and I morenyde. *Lire here.*

1108. þat is, euere. *Austin here.*

---

gretli. [168] I kepte þi comaundementis and þi witnessyngis; for alle my weies ben in þi siʒt.

*Appropinquet*

[169] Lord, my bisechyng come nyʒ in þi siʒt; bi þi speche ʒyue þou vndurstondynge to me. [170] Myn axyng entre in þi siʒt; bi þi speche delyuere þou me. [171] [M]i<sup>v</sup> | lippis<sup>w</sup> shulen telle out an    f. 70<sup>r</sup> ympne; whanne þou hast tauʒte me þi iustefiyngis. [172] Mi tunge shal pronounce þi speche; forwhi alle þi comaundementis ben equyte.

<sup>xxi</sup> þat þe] þat ne þe    <sup>xxii</sup> ententif] ententif Lord, Lord *canc.*    <sup>xxiii</sup> it is] *added by the scribe above the line of writing*    <sup>xxiv</sup> tyme] tyme is, is *canc.*    <sup>xxv</sup> Austin] Lire

<sup>v</sup> Mi] *initial capital om.*    <sup>w</sup> lippis] lippis lippis, *second* lippis *canc.*

[173] Thyn hond be maad, þat it saue me; for I haue chose þyn heestis. [174] Lord, I coueitide þyn helþe;<sup>1109</sup> and þi lawe is my þenkyng. [175] Mi soule<sup>x</sup> shal lyue and shal herie þee; and þi domes shulen helpe me. [176] I erride as a scheep þat perischide;<sup>1110</sup> Lord, seke þi seruaunt, for I forʒat not þi comaundementis.

[PSALM 119]

*Ad Dominum cum tribularer*

[1] *þe title of þe hundrid and xix salm. þe song of greces eiþer steieris.*<sup>1111</sup>

Whanne I was set in tribulacioun, I criede to þe Lord; and he herde me. [2] Lord, delyuere þou my soule fro wickid lippis; and fro a gileful tunge. [3] What shal be ʒouun to þee;<sup>a 1112</sup> eþer what shal be leid to þee; to a gileful tunge? [4] Scharpe arowis of þe myʒti;<sup>1113</sup> wiþ coolis þat maken desolat.<sup>1114</sup> [5] Allas to me! for my dwelling<sup>b 1115</sup> in an alien lond is maad long, I dwellide wiþ men dwellynge in Cedar; [6] my soule was myche a comelyng. [7] I was pesible wiþ hem þat hatiden pees; whanne I spak to hem, þei inpyngneden, eiþer aʒenseiden, me wiþoute cause.

1109. þat is, euerelastynge heelþe, which is in þee. *Lire here.*
1110. As to reputacioun of worldli men. *Lire here.*

## [PSALM 119 GLOSSES]

1111.[i] þis hundrid and xix salm is þe preier of sum hooli man for delyueraunce of þe puple of Israel fro þe caitifte of Babiloyne.

Gostli, þis salm mai be expowned of ech feiþful man set in tribulaciouns bodili eþer gostli bi temptacioun of fendis, of which he axiþ deuoutli to be delyuerid, and þat þe fendis be dryuun awei fro inpungnyng of feiþful men and be closid doun in helle; and þis man siȝhiþ for dilaie of his remedie. *Lire here.*

1112. What shal be ȝouun to þee: þe profete turneþ his word to þe puple of Babiloyne, and axiþ what peyne shal be ȝouun to punysche þe synnes of her tunge;

1113. Scharpe arowis of þe myȝti, þat is, of Perseis and Medeis stirid of God to sle men of Babiloyne wiþ sharpe arowis;

1114. wiþ coolis þat maken desolat: in Ebreu and in Ierom it is, wiþ þe coolis of iunepere trees, whiche kepen fier a ȝeer whanne þo ben hilid wiþ aischis; and bi þis is vndurstodun þe fier of helle vnquench-able, for þe men of Babiloyne weren þe worste ydolatrours;

1115. for my dwelling: in Ebreu and in Ierom it is, my pilgrymage. *Lire here.*